THE ROVER

AND OTHER PLAYS

APHRA BEHN (1640?–1689), playwright, poet, and novelist, was born in Kent. In her youth she travelled to Surinam, then an English colony, which was later made the setting for her novel *Oroonoko*. In the 1660s she went to Antwerp as a spy in the service of Charles II; she returned to England in debt. Her first play, *The Forced Marriage*, was performed by the Duke's Company at Lincoln's Inn Fields in 1670. After this her plays were regularly performed by the Duke's Company and its successor the United Company; clever plotting, fast pacing, and innovative stage-craft made her work very popular. Her fame was made with the great success of *The Rover* (1677). Her dramatic work included tragedy and tragicomedy, but her strongest work was in comedy. As a supporter of James, Duke of York, Behn wrote political satire at the time of the Exclusion crisis. In the 1680s she turned to writing poetry, translations, and fiction, inspired by her Tory political convictions and her intellectual interests in science and materialistic philosophy. She returned to the theatre with *The Lucky Chance* (1686) and the popular farce *The Emperor of the Moon* (1687). She died in April 1689.

JANE SPENCER is a Lecturer in English Literature in the School of English and American Studies, University of Exeter. Her publications include *The Rise of the Woman Novelist: From Aphra Behn to Jane Austen* (1986) and *Elizabeth Gaskell* (1993).

MICHAEL CORDNER is Reader in the Department of English and Related Literature at the University of York. He has edited editions of George Farquhar's *The Beaux' Stratagem*, the *Complete Plays* of Sir George Etherege, and *Four Comedies* of Sir John Vanbrugh. His editions include *Four Restoration Marriage Comedies* and he is completing a book on *The Comedy of Marriage 1660–1737*.

PETER HOLLAND is Professor of Shakespeare Studies and Director of the Shakespeare Institute, University of Birmingham.

MARTIN WIGGINS is a Fellow of the Shakespeare Institute and Lecturer in English at the University of Birmingham.

OXFORD DRAMA LIBRARY

J. M. Barrie
Peter Pan and Other Plays

Aphra Behn
The Rover and Other Plays

George Farquhar
The Recruiting Officer and Other Plays

John Ford
'Tis Pity She's a Whore and Other Plays

Ben Jonson
The Alchemist and Other Plays

Christopher Marlowe
Doctor Faustus and Other Plays

Thomas Middleton
A Mad World, My Masters and Other Plays

Arthur Wing Pinero
Trelawny of the 'Wells' and Other Plays

J. M. Synge
The Playboy of the Western World and Other Plays

Oscar Wilde
The Importance of Being Earnest and Other Plays

Campion, Carew, Chapman, Daniel, Davenant, Jonson, Townshend
Court Masques

Chapman, Kyd, Middleton, Tourneur
Four Revenge Tragedies

Coyne, Fitzball, Jones, Lewes, Sims
The Lights o' London and Other Plays

Dryden, Lee, Otway, Southerne
Four Restoration Marriage Comedies

OXFORD WORLD'S CLASSICS

APHRA BEHN

The Rover
The Feigned Courtesans
The Lucky Chance
The Emperor of the Moon

Edited with an Introduction by
JANE SPENCER

OXFORD
UNIVERSITY PRESS

OXFORD
UNIVERSITY PRESS

Great Clarendon Street, Oxford OX2 6DP

Oxford University Press is a department of the University of Oxford.
It furthers the University's objective of excellence in research, scholarship,
and education by publishing worldwide in

Oxford New York

Athens Auckland Bangkok Bogotá Buenos Aires Calcutta
Cape Town Chennai Dar es Salaam Delhi Florence Hong Kong Istanbul
Karachi Kuala Lumpur Madrid Melbourne Mexico City Mumbai
Nairobi Paris São Paulo Shanghai Singapore Taipei Tokyo Toronto Warsaw

with associated companies in Berlin Ibadan

Oxford is a registered trade mark of Oxford University Press
in the UK and in certain other countries

Published in the United States
by Oxford University Press Inc., New York

British Library Cataloguing in Publication Data

Data available

Library of Congress Cataloging in Publication Data
Behn, Aphra, 1640–1689
The rover / Aphra Behn; edited with an introduction by Jane
Spencer; general editor, Michael Cordner.
I. Spencer, Jane. II. Cordner, Michael. III. Title. IV. Series.
PR3317.A6 1995   822'.4—dc20   95–5205

ISBN 0-19-283451-7

5 7 9 10 8 6 4

Printed in Great Britain by
Cox & Wyman Ltd.
Reading, Berkshire

CONTENTS

ACKNOWLEDGEMENTS

I am grateful to the British Academy and to the University of Exeter Research Committee for grants in support of work on this edition. Staff at the British Library, the Bodleian Library, the University of Exeter Library, the National Library of Scotland, the University of London Library, and the Librarian of Worcester College, Oxford, have been very helpful. Michael Cordner, as General Editor, has given patient and generous guidance. I am grateful to all those who have given of their time and expertise to help me, including Jonathan Barry, Rosalind Boxall, Susan Carlson, Peter Corbin, Steven Dykes, Karen Edwards, Colin Jones, Nesta Jones, Douglas Sedge, and Eva Simmons. Special thanks go to M. J. Kidnie for her careful and helpful collation work; to Dawn Lewcock for discussing the staging of Behn's plays with me; to Mary Ann O'Donnell for advice on questions of bibliography and copy-text; to Sergio Mazzarelli, Luisa Quartermaine, and Martin Wiggins for their help with Behn's Italian; and to Gareth Roberts for sharing his alchemical and magical knowledge. I am grateful to all the Exeter University students taking the special option on Aphra Behn in 1993–4 for stimulating discussions that have helped my work. I thank my husband, Hugh Glover, for all his support. As parents we both depend on a network of friends, relatives, and childcare workers to keep our professional lives going: I'd like to record thanks here to Sue Cloke, Jill Courtney, Pat Donald, Joyce Ebdon, Pauline Roycroft, Margaret Spencer, Philip Spencer, and the staff of Puffins nursery.

INTRODUCTION

Behn's Life and Career

Aphra Behn's colourful and mysterious life has swallowed up attention at the expense of her writing. Her biographers have traced their disparate ways through contemporary records, remarks from her acquaintances, apparently autobiographical remarks within her fiction, and three versions of a memoir published soon after her death.[1] She was born in Kent, and her first surname is generally believed to have been Johnson, but her family origins are still disputed. Perhaps she was Eaffry, the child of Bartholomew Johnson and Elizabeth Denham christened in 1640—the daughter of a barber and a wetnurse, who transcended her class origins to become an educated writer; perhaps she was of more genteel origin, an Aphra whose mother, an illegitimate daughter of Lady Mary Sidney Wroth, provided her with an appropriately scandalous relationship to a feminine literary tradition; or perhaps she was someone else again.[2] In her youth she travelled to Surinam, later claiming that her father was appointed the colony's lieutenant-general. She returned to England in 1664, and at some point became known as Mrs Behn. Her husband, who according to the memoirs was a merchant of Dutch extraction, has never been definitively traced; he is usually conveniently supposed to have died in the plague of 1665. Perhaps he was the seaman Johan Behn, whom she could possibly have met on the return journey from Surinam; and perhaps her life without him indicates separation rather than his death.[3] It is even possible that she made him up. A widow's status

[1] The first memoir appeared with her posthumously published *Younger Brother* in 1696; a fuller version, by 'A Gentlewoman of her Acquaintance' in her *Histories and Novels* later the same year; and an expanded account by 'One of the Fair Sex' in the third edition of *All the Histories and Novels* in 1698.

[2] The case for Behn as the daughter of Bartholomew Johnson and Elizabeth Denham is presented in Maureen Duffy, *The Passionate Shepherdess* (London: Jonathan Cape, 1977). The alternative theory, which would connect Behn with Lady Mary Wroth and the Countess of Pembroke, is put forward by Sharon Valiant. See Mary Ann O'Donnell, 'Tory Wit and Unconventional Woman: Aphra Behn', in K. M. Wilson and F. J. Warnke (eds.), *Women Writers of the Seventeenth Century* (Athens, Ga.: University of Georgia Press, 1989), 342.

[3] See Jane Jones, 'New Light on the Background and Early Life of Aphra Behn', *Notes and Queries*, NS 37: 3 (Sept. 1990), 288–93.

gave the best chance of an independent life for a woman, and might have been especially useful for one who, like Behn, accepted a commission to visit the Netherlands as a spy for Charles II. Her brief was to obtain information from William Scott, whom she had known in Surinam. He provided her with a warning of the Dutch fleet's invasion of the Thames, but her superiors took no notice, and refused to pay her expenses. She returned to London in debt at the end of 1666, and at one point was threatened with debtors' prison, though we do not know if she was actually imprisoned. From 1667 to 1670 there is very little record of her life, and then in 1670 she suddenly appears as the author of *The Forc'd Marriage*, produced by the Duke's Company at Lincoln's Inn Fields.

At this time there were two theatre companies in London, licensed by Charles II after the Restoration, and presenting a mixture of revived plays from the sixteenth and early seventeenth centuries, and new plays by court wits like Wycherley and Etherege and professional writers like Dryden and Shadwell. Actresses, for the first time, were regularly performing in London's public theatres, and women were beginning to appear as playwrights, too: plays by Katherine Philips and Frances Boothby were performed in the 1660s. How Behn found her way into this theatrical world we do not know. One possibility is that she became the mistress of someone connected with the theatre, but there is no positive evidence. It may be that she had some contact with the pre-Restoration theatre when spending time in Lord Willoughby's house, next to the house where Davenant put on operas in the late 1650s.[4] Another suggestion is that she was introduced to the theatre through Sir Thomas Killigrew. Killigrew was the proprietor of one of the theatre companies, the King's Company, to which she gave feathers from Surinam used in a production of *The Indian Queen*. She certainly knew Killigrew, who had recommended her as a spy to Lord Arlington. She may have worked as a hack adapter of old plays for a while;[5] at any rate, her first play showed a knowledge of stagecraft indicative of some sort of theatrical experience.

Killigrew's King's Company did not bring out Behn's play, though; the rival company, the Duke's Company, did. Possibly the fact that a woman—Lady Davenant, taking over from her deceased husband—

---

[4] See Henry A. Hargreaves, 'The Life and Plays of Mrs. Aphra Behn', Diss. (Duke University, 1960), 70.

[5] See O'Donnell, 'Tory Wit', 344.

was at this time running the Duke's Company was an encouraging factor. Anyway, Behn was a success with the Duke's Company, and continued to write for it, and for its successor the United Company, during her long stage career. She tailored her roles to suit its leading actors and actresses, and exploited the resources of its successive theatres.

Behn produced at least eighteen plays (others are of doubtful attribution). Her early efforts, *The Forced Marriage* and *The Amorous Prince*, were in tragicomedy; in *Abdelazar* (1676) she wrote a tragedy of revenge. Mostly, though, she wrote comedies, and it was as a writer of comedy that she demanded recognition. *The Dutch Lover* failed in 1673, but *The Rover*, first performed in the spring of 1677, made her reputation. It seems to have been first presented as a man's work: the prologue calls the author 'he' and the earliest quartos were anonymous. But by the third issue of the first edition Behn's name was on the title-page, and it is as the author of *The Rover* that she has been best known ever since. Other comedies followed, including *Sir Patient Fancy* in 1678 and *The Rover, Part II* in 1681.

When *The Feigned Courtesans* was performed in 1679, its prologue complained that the fuss over the Popish Plot was keeping audiences away from the plots presented on stage; and during the next few years politics dominated Behn's stage career, as the country was dominated by conflict over the succession to Charles II. Once it had become known that his brother and heir James, Duke of York, was Catholic, political opposition focused on the Whig attempt to debar James from succession and find a Protestant king. The king's role was at stake as well as his religion, with the choice to be made between Stuart absolutism and a crown brought under Parliamentary control. Behn's plays are strongly anti-Whig and anti-Puritan. *The Roundheads* (1681) suggests that the Whigs of the 1680s threaten a return to the Commonwealth of the 1640s, and *The City Heiress* (1682) has a satirical portrait of the Whig statesman Shaftesbury. These allegiances are not surprising in plays written for a theatre whose patron was the Duke of York himself, but Behn's commitment to Toryism and the Stuart monarchy was genuine and lifelong. Like other Tories she satirized the commercialism of Whigs and the hypocrisy of prudish Puritans; and like some other women of her time she considered a royalist court, with its tradition of educated ladies, its atmosphere of sexual openness, and the political power it afforded the wives and mistresses of nobility and royalty, a more hospitable place than a mercantile city where women were part of the merchandise.[6]

Behn, supporter of the Catholic James, may have been Catholic herself, either by upbringing or conversion. Some of her dedications are to prominent Catholic noblemen, and some plays express sympathy with Catholicism. She made no public profession of her religion, though, and some of her work suggests rather a sceptical and anti-religious viewpoint. Like her lover John Hoyle, she was an admirer of Lucretius, who argued against the existence of an afterlife. She wrote that reason was a better guide than faith, and she liked to imagine a Golden Age before religion and law had controlled a natural and joyous human sexuality. Her dislike of Puritan reformers centred on her belief in their sexual hypocrisy and repression; and when she did write religious verse it was to gloss the Lord's Prayer with the claim that her own trespasses were of the kind a loving God must forgive, for they were sins of love.

If Behn's imagination delighted in the thought of a world before kingly authority, in Restoration reality she opposed any rebellion against the Stuarts. In 1682 she wrote an epilogue for the play *Romulus and Hersilia*, attacking the Duke of Monmouth, the king's illegitimate son and focus of the hopes for a Protestant succession, for rebelling against his father. This piece of loyalty went too far for Charles's taste, and Behn was arrested. It has been suggested that this episode contributed to her silence as a playwright over the next few years, but probably the strongest factor was general lack of opportunity in the theatres. The King's Company collapsed in 1682 and the Duke's Company took it over to become the United Company. Fewer new plays were put on in the following years, and Behn was forced into other areas. She continued to write poetry, publishing a collection in 1684; she translated poetry, scientific writing, and fiction from French, and she began to write her own innovative fiction. *Love-Letters Between a Nobleman and his Sister* appeared from 1684 to 1687, and a number of shorter novels, including her most famous, *Oroonoko*, based on her Surinam experiences, appeared shortly before her death.

Behn returned to the stage later in the 1680s, and *The Lucky Chance* (1686) is one of her best comedies, with an underlying bitterness not characteristic of her earlier work. It was followed in 1687 by *The*

---

[6] The attractiveness of royalism and absolutism to Tory feminists in the 17th cent. is argued in Catherine Gallagher, 'Embracing the Absolute: The Politics of the Female Subject in Seventeenth-Century England', *Genders*, 1: 1 (1988), 24–39.

Emperor of the Moon, a dazzling farce combining the techniques of *commedia dell'arte* with the spectacular displays found in the new operas.

By this time Behn was ill, and her last years were ones of poverty, sickness, and political defeat. She lived to see James II deposed and William of Orange on the English throne; and she pointedly addressed her poem of welcome not to him but to his wife Mary, James's daughter. She died in 1689 and was buried in Westminster Abbey—the traditional burial of a poet, and one that would have gratified a writer who, as the years passed, aspired to unite professional writing with the pursuit of literary immortality. 'I am not content to write for a third day only', she wrote in *The Lucky Chance*, 'I value fame as much as if I had been born a hero.'

Restoration Theatres and Behn's Stagecraft

The theatre where Behn made most of her claims to third days' profits and heroic fame was the Dorset Garden theatre, built for the Duke's Company and in operation by the end of 1671. Of the four plays in this volume, three were first produced at Dorset Garden. *The Lucky Chance*, written when the United Company had the use of the former King's Company venue as well as its own, was first put on at Drury Lane. Both theatres had the long platform stage, reaching out into the pit and close to boxes and galleries, that fostered the Restoration intimacy between players and audience; and they also had the scenic area behind the proscenium arch, increasingly used in the later Restoration period for spectacular scenery and other effects. A notable feature of the stage was the proscenium doors (two each side, with balconies above) used for exits and entrances. Less is known about the layout of Dorset Gardens than of Drury Lane, and there is a flourishing controversy over its exact dimensions and function, some seeing it as a theatre with an exceptionally long scenic area, specializing in operatic spectacle, others considering it a general theatre not very different in design and use from Drury Lane.[7] Whatever the truth of this, Behn was working for a company that was concerned to find out about the latest in scenic design and to incorporate

---

[7] For opposing views on the theatre's function, and summaries of the debate over its dimensions, see John R. Spring, 'The Dorset Garden Theatre: Playhouse or Opera House?', *Theatre Notebook*, 34 (1980) 60–9, and Robert D. Hume, 'The Nature of the Dorset Garden Theatre', *Theatre Notebook*, 36 (1982), 99–109.

spectacular effects into its dramas. She was a great asset to the Duke's Company, developing into a theatrical innovator who used the whole stage area, with forestage scenes increasingly interspersed with acting in the scenic area behind the arch. Her characters weave in and out of the scenery, move around between scenic area and forestage, and carry on more than one action simultaneously, using different areas of the stage. Sometimes they operate in a fictional darkness, when the audience can see them and they can't see each other.[8]

One of Behn's hallmarks is the frequent use of the 'discovery' scene, when one set of scenery, painted on shutters, is drawn back to reveal actors in place behind. The successive revelation of a number of scenes, painted in perspective, was itself a visual novelty that delighted Restoration audiences; and Behn incorporated such visual effects into dramatic action, revealing the foolish Blunt, gulled by the jilting wench Lucetta, crawling out of a sewer (in *The Rover*), or (in *The Lucky Chance*) Lady Fulbank, 'supposed in bed', stoically waiting for the unattractive husband who will turn out to be her desirable young lover. Exactly how these effects were achieved is another subject of debate for theatre historians, who disagree on how many shutter positions would be available behind the proscenium arch to carry the different sets of scenery.[9] For the purposes of commentary I have assumed two shutter positions behind the proscenium arch, with more than one set of grooves at each shutter position for carrying the scenes. This gives two discovery spaces, allowing for two successive discoveries: one when a scene at the first position is drawn back to reveal a scene at the second shutter, another when this second shutter is drawn back to reveal a scene on a backcloth.[10]

All the plays here show Behn's dexterity with stagecraft. *The Rover* makes clever use of trapdoors and discoveries, and gives Angellica a balcony for her territory; *The Feigned Courtesans* makes complicated comic use of the proscenium doors; *The Lucky Chance* has a complicated sequence of discovery scenes; and *The Emperor of the Moon* is a triumphant spectacle, with its successive discoveries of

[8] For my discussion of Behn's stagecraft I am indebted to the very full account in Dawn Lewcock, 'Aphra Behn on the Restoration Stage', Ph.D. thesis (Cambridgeshire College of Art and Technology, 1987).

[9] For a discussion of theories about the number of shutters and shutter positions see Jocelyn Powell, *Restoration Theatre Production* (London: RKP, 1984), 56.

[10] Another discovery space, further forward, could be created by using a drop curtain (perhaps the proscenium curtain, perhaps a curtain just behind the proscenium arch) in front of the first pair of shutters. Behn uses this in *The Emperor of the Moon*, 2.3.

Parnassus and a temple, its large flying machine and smaller swooping chariots, its actors pretending to be a tapestry, its twenty-foot telescope, and its talking head.

The Rover

The Rover, the earliest of the plays here, is based on Sir Thomas Killigrew's two-part, ten-act drama *Thomaso, or the Wanderer*, written during the Interregnum and centring on the amorous adventures of a cavalier in exile. Behn reacted angrily to charges of plagiarism, and certainly she was only following common practice in drawing on a source in earlier drama; but she does take far more from *Thomaso* than she acknowledges in her defensive postscript, and many of her lines are close echoes of Killigrew's. Her reshaping of his work, though, makes *The Rover* very much her own play. It is not just that *The Rover*, with its tight organization, swift pace, and clever use of the stage provides the theatrical flair lacking in *Thomaso*, a play of interesting but long-drawn-out ideas. Behn's manipulation of the characters and situations set up by Killigrew shows her engaging in a thoughtful dialogue with the earlier play, revising its notion of heroic male and female roles, and in the process producing distinctive versions of such stock Restoration characters as the rakish hero, the abandoned mistress, and the witty heroine.

Killigrew's Thomaso is a recognizable precursor of the Restoration rake hero, very much in charge of events as he wanders at his ease in a world full of whores. He has affairs with Angellica Bianca and Saretta in the course of the action, while Paulina remembers him fondly as her first lover. Yet Thomaso decisively reforms, pledging to leave his wandering life for marriage to the rich and virginal Serulina, whom he saves from the threat of rape by the fool Edwardo. Behn makes her Willmore far less dignified, giving Thomaso's heroic exploits in the siege of Pamplona and his romantic devotion to a chaste lady to Belvile, while transferring some of the fool's actions, like the drunken attempt on the lady's chastity, to Willmore. Her rake-hero is more of a bemused bungler than a clever plotter. Compared to heroes like Wycherley's Horner and Etherege's Dorimant, he is both more indulgently and less admiringly treated. From Killigrew's Angellica Bianca Behn takes the idea of treating a courtesan and cast-off mistress (often a figure of fun in Restoration comedy) with sympathy and a sense of the seriousness of her position. Killigrew's Angellica sharply rebukes Thomaso with her attack on the double standard. But she is presented as a victim and her attitude to Thomaso is humble to the point of self-abnegation. At the end Paulina reports that Angellica is leaving the country, leaving behind her plea for forgiveness for having tried to prevent the marriage to Serulina. Behn's Angellica, much stronger, threatens Willmore with a pistol in a scene where he is left looking foolish.

However, Hellena is the character Behn changes most. In a way she is a completely new character: a witty heroine, rather like a warmer version of Etherege's Harriet, who substitutes for the paler Serulina as the hero's match. Behn makes her outspoken and demanding, transferring to her some smutty lines Killigrew had given to a male character, and giving her gipsy and boy disguises that allow her more scope for action than Killigrew's heroine. The name is taken from Killigrew: in *Thomaso*, Helena is 'an old decayed blind, out of Fashion whore', who begs the mountebank to make her young, beautiful, and lovable again.[11] Tricked by the mountebank's wife, she takes the wrong restorative bath and her body is transformed to that of the rogue Scarramucha. The last we hear of her she is reported to be horrified to find herself with beard and breeches. Behn performs another act of transformation to create her Hellena, who is given youth and beauty and, for a while, the breeches, too—and unlike Killigrew's Helena, she is able to use them to her advantage.

The empowerment of the main female characters and the gentle fun poked at the rake's dignity distinguish Behn's version of the carnival world of comedy. It is masculine authority which is turned upside down in the Neapolitan carnival. Lucetta tricks Blunt and tips him in the sewer; Florinda, Hellena, and Valeria slip away from Don Pedro's care and pursue the men they desire. While Angellica Bianca, advertising herself through her pictures, presents herself to male characters and audience alike as an object of desire, the male characters too are objectified by Behn's theatrical vision, and they are given less control over their representations. Behn's frequent use of discoveries has been taken as evidence that, more than other Restoration playwrights, she presents female bodies as fetish objects to the male spectator;[12] but in *The Rover* it is not only women who are discovered. Not the courtesan, but a courtesan's gull, Blunt, is

[11] Thomas Killigrew, *Thomaso, or, The Wanderer: A Comedy* (London: Printed by J.M. for Henry Herringman, 1663), Part I, Act 4, scene 2, p. 363.

[12] Elin Diamond, '*Gestus* and Signature in Aphra Behn's *The Rover*', *ELH* 56 (1989), 535.

revealed to the audience semi-naked and helpless. He is an object only of scorn and laughter; Belvile, who is discovered—heroic and vulnerable—at the beginning of the fourth act, is presented as an object of desire. Close enough to contemporary portrayals of the rake-hero to be popular with men in the audiences and with leading actors, *The Rover* nevertheless manages to subject masculine figures to a female gaze.

The gaze is sometimes an angry one. Carnival comedy is sometimes threatened by a resurgence of male power misused, as when Blunt threatens to rape and beat Florinda, or by a vision of female helplessness, as when Angellica realizes she loves Willmore and can never keep him. The comic ending, with its incorporation of male and female characters into prevailing patriarchal structures, is ruffled by these disturbances. Behn constructed a delicate balance between Hellena and Angellica, between the lighter and darker sides of women's attempts to win a game where men have stacked the cards. The defeat of Angellica perhaps left her unsatisfied. In the second part of *The Rover* she killed Hellena off and re-ran the contest between rich virgin and lovelorn courtesan for Willmore's love. This time she gave the hero to the courtesan, La Nuche, gesturing towards a utopian future of unwedded bliss. For the contemporary audience this reversal was a repetition with variation, for William Smith and Elizabeth Barry, who had played Willmore and Hellena in 1677, played Willmore and La Nuche in 1681.

The Feigned Courtesans

The Feigned Courtesans, or a Night's Intrigue was performed and printed in 1679, two years after *The Rover*. The play, or a version of it, may possibly be the one performed in 1677 as *A Midnight's Intrigue*, but the earlier play is lost.[13] *The Feigned Courtesans* is not based on any identified source, though the general framework of swift and complicated intrigue is familiar enough in Spanish-influenced comedy of the time. Like *The Rover* it employs cross-dressing and other disguises to gain freedom of action for the heroines. Cornelia, Marcella, and Laura Lucretia all pretend to be boys and to be courtesans. Play is made with the different standards of honour applied to men and women, as Marcella and Cornelia violate the masculine honour of truth to be true to the feminine honour of

[13] See William Van Lennep *et al.*, *The London Stage*, pt. I, *1660–1700* (Carbondale: Southern Illinois University Press, 1960), 249.

chastity, tricking their would-be customers into paying for services never rendered. Mistaken identities and mistaken doors lead to confusion on confusion. Female identity is slippery: the courtesan Silvianetta doesn't exist at all, but two women pretend to be her and several men are convinced they are about to make love to her. The play celebrates what attacks on the theatre condemned, the deceitfulness of women and of acting.

Women who disguise and deceive are usurping the role of the comic trickster servant, a parallel made explicit in this play by the heroines' dependence on their own male servant, Petro, to do their dirty work for them. He is the most versatile at disguise, and the women only pull off their trick of being virginal courtesans by virtue of his splendid inventiveness in tricking money from the play's two gulls, the comic squire Sir Signal Buffoon and his Puritan tutor Tickletext. Women and servants share the subordination that carnival comedy momentarily overturns, and they share, too, a fluidity of identity that makes them dominate the comic action, and that places in perspective the single-minded devotion to honour exhibited by men like Fillamour and Octavio.

Though less overtly political than Behn's anti-Whig satires of the early 1680s, *The Feigned Courtesans* made its author's Catholic sympathies abundantly clear at a time when anti-Catholic feeling in London was approaching hysterical levels. Set in Rome, near the famous Vatican church of St Peter's, the play marries its English heroes to Italian Catholic women, and has the sympathetic Fillamour defend the beauty of Roman art against the iconoclastic fervour of a ridiculous Puritan divine. Tickletext's hypocrisy is revealed with comic gusto as he avoids criticism of his whoring by declaring his intention to convert all the courtesans of Rome. His ranting equation of Popish idolatry with prostitution is typical of the Protestant attitude to the 'Whore of Babylon', comically invoked in the prologue. Cleverly putting the enemy's labels to use, Behn defends Catholicism, and, implicitly, the courtesan—or rather the freedom of action that the courtesan is made to represent here.

The Lucky Chance

While the intrigue form and foreign setting of *The Feigned Courtesans* allows for a wish-fulfilling emphasis on female agency, *The Lucky Chance*, set in contemporary London, contains a more sombre analysis of women's relation to courtship and marriage. Again this is a play without a major source, though some plot elements are taken from earlier plays—Lady Fulbank's having Gayman led to her house by 'devils' from Shirley's *The Lady of Pleasure* (1635), and her sending him anonymous donations of money from Dryden's *The Wild Gallant* (1663).[14] Low-life scenes, like the one in Alsatia with the debt-ridden Gayman parleying with his landlady, and contemporary references to plots, riots, and the City authorities' clash with royal prerogative, establish a much more realistic setting for the old comic plot of the younger generation outwitting the old. The enemy to be outwitted is embodied in the City merchants Sir Feeble Fainwould and Sir Cautious Fulbank, who have used their commercial power to buy brides. There is a new seriousness about the examination of unhappy marriage bonds, anticipating the themes taken up by Vanbrugh and Southerne in the 1690s.

Both main plots turn on dodging unwanted marriages. Belmour and Leticia do so without challenging the institution itself: their story, involving their own verbal contract of marriage, violated by Leticia because she has been tricked into believing Belmour dead, and the non-consummation of the subsequent marriage to Sir Feeble, gives the young lovers' wishes the sanction of law. Gayman and Julia are not so lucky. Julia's marriage to Sir Cautious, apparently entered into in a conscious decision to take his full bank rather than pleasure with Gayman, cannot be so easily set aside, and she takes her own virtue and self-control too seriously for cuckolding to provide a simple solution. The interlocking actions of the play concern Gayman's attempts to consummate his love for Julia and Leticia's attempts to avoid consummating her marriage to Sir Feeble. While Belmour and Leticia bring off their project with comic tricks, Gayman and Lady Fulbank find their successes turning sour. Lady Fulbank, taking her husband's money to bribe her lover to a bedroom encounter that he supposes to be with an ugly old hag, and Gayman, dicing with Sir Cautious to win a night with Julia, enter into the world of commercial values that has separated them in the first place. Possibly in the first encounter, planned by Julia, and certainly by the second, orchestrated by Gayman, they become lovers; but the comic bed-trick is not allowed to resolve matters completely. Lady Fulbank is furious at having been made an object of exchange between husband and lover. Divorce and remarriage are not an option. Julia is left with the uneasy

---

[14] See the discussion in Eva Simmons, ' "Virtue Intire": Aphra Behn's Contribution, in her Comedies, to the Marriage Debates of the Seventeenth Century', Ph.D. thesis (London, 1990), 364.

solution of being bequeathed to Gayman if Sir Cautious dies, and in the meantime an adulterous affair may or may not continue.

The Emperor of the Moon

The Emperor of the Moon blends *commedia dell'arte*, farce, and spectacle to produce a dazzling entertainment. Behn would have had the chance to see Italian troupes in London in the 1670s,[15] but her main source, *Arlequin, empereur dans la lune*, was played by Italian artists in Paris in 1684. It seems to me likely that Behn visited Paris and saw this work performed, though I have no documentary evidence; or perhaps she had details of it from a friend. Summers suggests she read an edition published in 1684, but the extant printed sources date from the 1690s.[16] Only the French scenes by Nolant de Fatouville, developed for the sake of the Parisian audience, were published. The players improvised a good deal and it is likely that many of the *commedia*'s effects have gone unrecorded. Behn takes her characters and many of the *lazzi* (comic turns) from *Arlequin empereur*, but incorporates them into a tightly structured plot most uncharacteristic of *commedia dell'arte*.

Behn's plot involves the usual pairs of young lovers, who employ the zanies Scaramouch and Harlequin to trick Doctor Baliardo into sanctioning the weddings of his daughter and niece in the belief that their suitors are the emperor of the moon and the prince of Thunderland. For the doctor's delusions, Behn draws on a wide range of current intellectual trends. The new science of astronomy, alluded to by the huge telescope, is obviously a main theme, and Behn, like Fatouville, uses recent books of fantastic voyages for the idea of an inhabited moon-world which can communicate with the earth. The new ideas opened up by astronomy fascinated Behn, who translated Fontanelle's *Entretiens sur la pluralité des mondes* as *A Discovery of New*

---

[15] Italian troupes visited London in 1673 and 1678–9. See K. Richards and L. Richards, *The Commedia dell'Arte: A Documentary History* (Oxford: Blackwell, 1990), 265–6.

[16] See the introduction to *The Emperor of the Moon* in Hughes and Scouten, *Ten English Farces*, 40–1. Scenes from *Arlequin empereur* appear in Evariste Gheradi, *Le Théâtre italien* (Paris, 1695). Further editions, some containing more complete versions of the play, appeared in 1698, 1721, and 1741. *Arlequin empereur* may have been published earlier than this: an undated edition published at Troyes is mentioned, without any copies being located, in Henry Lancaster, *A History of French Dramatic Literature in the Seventeenth Century*, pt. IV, vol. 2 (Baltimore: Johns Hopkins Press, 1940), 615.

Worlds in 1688, together with an 'Essay on Translated Prose' containing her own remarks on Copernican theory. What we think of as early scientific discovery was not then clearly separated from studies now dismissed as magical, and the doctor's interests range promiscuously through astronomy, astrology, medicine, alchemy, cosmography, and the strange spiritualism of the Rosicrucian brotherhood. Behn unites these themes through a controlling metaphor of vision and blindness. The play teems with visual tricks, from the nymph placed in the glass of the telescope, and the cart that turns into a calash, to the tapestry made of real people, each effect contributing to the point that all the doctor's 'scopes' don't allow him to see what is going on around him. His misogyny, which leads to the Rosicrucian renunciation of mortal women and the attempted seclusion of Elaria and Bellemante, is lightly touched on, but is clearly a factor in his comic blindness. The doctor both watches a series of spectacular effects, and is made into a comic spectacle himself. His cure is effected through a deliberate and sustained illusion engineered by Charmante and Cinthio, which is then shattered, leaving him to come to terms with the truth.

The 'farce' put on by the young lovers for Doctor Baliardo is, of course, put on for the audience too. Curtains and shutters are used to create a complex succession of discovery scenes: three successive discoveries in the second act and two in the triumphant final scene, ending in a perspective leading right back to the wall of the theatre, showing a temple and featuring the voice of the 'emperor' speaking through a trumpet. A large flying machine for the zodiac and the moon-chariot, and the smaller chariots that zoom across the stage, add to the spectacle. If the foolish doctor is deceived by appearances, those same illusions are what delight the audience. In her use of stage illusion here Behn is at the very forefront of Restoration stage development, vying with the new operas; and she uses her stagecraft with a characteristic clever playfulness. From the joking use of the speaking head in the prologue, to the revelation that the knights of the sun are only Harlequin and Scaramouch, Behn teases her audience to see through the deceptions she sets up. The result is a play that, in the best Quixotic tradition, enchants even as it mocks the victims of enchantment.

Performances of Behn's Plays

Behn's comedies were very popular with her contemporaries, and for much of the eighteenth century. Seventeenth-century stage records are very incomplete, but it is known that *The Rover* was revived at least four times in the 1680s and several times in the 1690s.[17] In 1703 it was revived at Drury Lane and is recorded every year, except 1719, till 1743. Leading actors held on tenaciously to the role of Willmore—Robert Wilks played him for over twenty-five years and Lacy Ryan for over twenty. Rival theatre companies vied to attract audiences to the play: in 1730 three separate productions, at Drury Lane, Lincoln's Inn Fields, and Goodman's Fields, were put on in the same season. The play's gaiety and its freedom from the very specific political message that dated some of her other plays made it easily adaptable to later tastes. Some scenes, notably Blunt's undressing on stage, were early targets for stage reform, and the play was gradually bowdlerized to accommodate the more exacting standards of propriety that developed during the century. Angellica's role, with its hints of the themes developed in pathetic tragedy, seems to have been emphasized in the early years of the century, with the part being played by famous tragediennes like Elizabeth Barry and Mary Porter; in the middle years more prominence was given to Hellena's part, as played by Peg Woffington, famous for breeches roles. A Covent Garden production of the late 1750s returned to some of the bawdy elements that earlier productions had toned down. From its long run it must have attracted audiences, but it attracted strong criticism too, and after 1760 the play was only revived in altered form. John Philip Kemble's *Love in Many Masks*, performed at Drury Lane in 1790, is Behn's play with considerable cuts, sanitizing Willmore, softening Angellica, and quietening Hellena down. After this *The Rover* was dropped entirely until a spate of revivals, beginning in the 1970s, showed that the play can still entertain. The best-known of these, John Barton's Stratford and London production of 1986–7, altered the text considerably; others have stuck closer to Behn's original. The play's balance of comic and serious themes leaves scope for interpretation, and modern Willmores range from Jeremy Irons's merry roisterer, 'lovable even when he is throwing up into someone else's hat',[18] to Steven Dykes's 'bit of a bastard', who attacks honourable Spaniards from behind and marries money.[19]

[17] Records of 17th- and 18th-cent. performances of Behn's plays are taken from Van Lennep *et al.*, *The London Stage*, pts. I–V (Carbondale: Southern Illinois University Press, 1960–8).

[18] Lois Potter, 'Transforming a Super-Rake', review of *The Rover* at the Swan Theatre, *TLS* 25 July 1986, 817.

[19] Steven Dykes played Willmore in the New Cross Theatre production directed by Nesta Jones in 1991, and described his version of the character to me in an interview, 2 Oct. 1991.

The second most-performed Behn play is *The Emperor of the Moon*. Its use of spectacle heralded an eighteenth-century trend, and it was often revived at Lincoln's Inn Fields by John Rich, a manager who encouraged and developed English pantomime. Its reliance on visual rather than verbal effects made it a good choice to put on 'by desire' for the entertainment of foreign dignitaries, and it was often used as an afterpiece. It was made a showcase for presenting new singing and dancing talent, and from time to time new 'scenes and machines' were advertised, as well as special effects borrowed from eighteenth-century operas. Like *The Rover*, it was put on in the Dublin theatres as well as in London. After the 1750s it was almost forgotten, but in 1777 and 1778 a shortened version was performed by marionettes in the Patagonian Theatre, a puppet-theatre in Exeter Change on the Strand.[20] *The Emperor of the Moon* has been revived in recent years; there was a student production in 1975 and there have been revivals in the early 1990s.[21] New scenic effects have been developed to adapt the play to twentieth-century staging. In Carol MacVey's 1992 production in Iowa City, the final scene showed a high staircase reaching up to the moon, which a member of the audience was invited to climb with Harlequin.[22]

The Feigned Courtesans was much less successful. There were probably several performances in 1679 and 1680, and the play may have been revived in the 1690s, but the only eighteenth-century revivals recorded were in 1716 and 1717. Of the four plays here it has had the least attention in the twentieth century, though it has been revived.

The Lucky Chance was never as popular as *The Rover*, though it apparently brought in a good box office in 1686. As Behn's preface

[20] The altered text was published as *The Emperor of the Moon. A Dialogue Pantomime . . . As performed at the Patagonian Theatre* (London: T. Sherlock, 1777). Performances were advertised in *The Gazetteer and New Daily Advertiser*, Saturday, 22 Mar. 1777, and further issues up till 29 Apr. (12 performances mentioned in all); and *Morning Chronicle and London Advertiser*, 10 Apr. 1778. For a discussion of the Patagonian Theatre see George Speaight, *The History of the English Puppet Theatre* (London: Harrap and Co., 1955), 117–24.

[21] The first 20th-cent. performance I know of is the one mentioned by Beryl Russell as having been performed by Edge Hill College students in March 1975. See Beryl W. Russell, 'A Critical Introduction to Aphra Behn's *The Emperor of the Moon*', M.Litt. (University of Lancaster, 1987), 69.

[22] This production is discussed by Susan Carlson in an unpublished paper, 'Aphra Behn's *The Emperor of the Moon*: Staging Seventeenth-Century Farce for Twentieth-Century Tastes', delivered at the Mid-American Theater Conference, Minneapolis, 12 Mar. 1994.

indicates, it was immediately (and, considering the standards applied to male-authored plays, unfairly) criticized for indecency, with Sir Feeble's throwing open his gown to frighten the women singled out for comment. The greater sensitivity of its subject matter, with Gayman and Lady Fulbank's adultery, made it less adaptable to the eighteenth-century stage. It was revived at Lincoln's Inn Fields in 1718, but after that its only appearance on the eighteenth-century stage was as an adaptation: Hannah Cowley's *A School for Greybeards* (1786), based on Behn's play, cut out the adultery altogether and still caused such an uproar at the idea of a marriage, however unconsummated, being set aside, that it had to be altered before the second performance.[23] The very theme that made *The Lucky Chance* too risky for the eighteenth-century stage has made it especially appropriate for the twentieth, and Jules Wright's 1984 production at the Royal Court exploited the feminist potential of this play about the difficulties of marriage.

Aphra Behn protested several times that her works had been undervalued because of her sex, and made her own claim for them carefully. When, in the preface to *The Lucky Chance*, she claimed that a fair hearing would lead to the conclusion that 'that person had made as many good comedies, as any one man that has writ in our age', she was not making an empty boast. Her works have had to wait longer than many other Restoration comedies to be rediscovered, but now Behn is beginning to get her hearing, and theatre companies today have shown that her handling of intrigue, spectacle, farce, and satire make her still an entertaining and thought-provoking playwright.

[23] Hannah Cowley, *A School for Greybeards* (London: G. G. J. and J. Robinson, 1786), 'An Address', pp. iii–ix.

NOTE ON THE TEXTS

The Rover

The copytext is the first edition of 1677 (Q1), the only one printed in Behn's lifetime. The text has been collated with the second edition of 1697 (Q2), the third edition of 1709 (Q3), the first collected edition of Behn's plays in 1702 (C1), and the second of 1724 (C2); and with the modern editions of Summers, Link, Jeffares, and Todd.

The Feigned Courtesans

The copytext is the first edition of 1679 (Q), the only one printed in Behn's lifetime and the only edition of the play as a single work. The text has been collated with C1 and C2, and with the modern editions of Summers, Ludwig, and Lyons and Morgan.

The Lucky Chance

The copytext is the first edition of 1687 (Q), the only one printed in Behn's lifetime. The text has been collated with C1 and C2, and with the modern editions of Summers, Jeffares, Coakley, and Morgan.

The Emperor of the Moon

Two editions were published in Behn's lifetime, the first in 1687 (Q1) and the second in 1688 (Q2). Q2 shows evidence of careful editing, probably by Behn herself, who was ill, but still working at this time. It corrects numerous errors and introduces relatively few new ones. I have therefore used Q2 as the copytext, collated with Q1, C1, C2, and with the modern editions of Summers and Hughes and Scouten.

In all the texts, spelling and punctuation have been modernized; stage-directions have been standardized and expanded where necessary; and speech-prefixes have been regularized and printed in full. Where common expressions occur in a number of forms I have adopted one as standard; thus 'hark'ee' silently replaces a number of variants in the texts. In modernizing the punctuation I have tried to make the syntax clear without flattening out indications of pauses and emphasis which might be helpful to actors. Accents have been employed to indicate syllabic vowels in past participle and preterite:

thus *blessèd* is monosyllabic, *blessèd* is disyllabic. The few French words have also been modernized.

The extensive Italian in *The Feigned Courtesans* presents a particular problem. Q's use of the language is very erratic, and is often mixed with French, Spanish, and Latin forms. With some speakers, especially Tickletext and Sir Signal, Behn introduces errors for comic effect. It is difficult to distinguish between deliberate errors and Behn's own or the compositor's errors. Behn also at times uses a dialectal form of the language. Where Q's reading seems to be simply authorial or compositor's error I have changed to standard modern Italian; but I have tried to preserve usages which indicate deliberate error, or which reflect the influence of Spanish, French, and Latin on Behn's Italian. I have supplied accents, separated words wrongly elided, and stand-ardized *signor* and *signora*. I have recorded substantive departures from copytext in the notes and have offered translations and glosses.

The setting of verse and prose in early editions presents another problem. Behn writes a very loose blank verse, and her prose rhythms are often close to verse, so that a line or two that scans as regular blank verse sometimes appears in the middle of a prose passage. The practices of the early compositors do not always help. Sometimes passages of regular blank verse are printed as prose; more often, lines have been broken up to make space for stage-directions, and this lineation has been interpreted as verse lineation, and adopted in later editions. I have tried to interpret Behn's verse flexibly, not insisting that everything that is not regular blank verse must be prose, but not keeping as verse lines that I think have been broken up for other reasons. Occasionally I have offered new lineations where these seem to render the verse better. I have recorded departures from copytext in the notes. I do not see my solutions as definitive, and I recommend readers to judge the verse and prose with their own ears.

I am deeply indebted to the work of all previous editors of Behn. Like all her modern editors I have found Montague Summers's complete edition, for all its shortcomings, indispensable. He is often a helpful guide on verse-settings, where some later editors seem too willing to turn everything into prose. Link's edition of *The Rover* is one of the few to attempt thorough modernization of punctuation, and though I often differ from him I have found his work invaluable. The editions by Coakley, Hughes and Scouten, Ludwig, and Todd have been of particular help to me in preparing my explanatory notes. Finally, Mary Ann O'Donnell's *Aphra Behn: An Annotated Biblio-graphy* has put all Behn scholars in her debt.

Editions Collated, with Abbreviations Used in Notes

The Rover

Q1 = *The Rover. Or, The Banish't Cavaliers. As it is Acted At His Royal Highness the Duke's Theatre* (London: John Amery, 1677).

Q2 = *The Rover; or, The Banish't Cavaliers. As it was Acted by His Majesty's Servants, at the Theatre in Little-Lincoln's-Inn-Fields* (London: J. Orme for Richard Wellington, 1697).

Q3 = *The Rover: or, The Banish'd Cavaliers. As it is Acted at the Theatre-Royal in Drury-Lane* (London: Richard Wellington, 1709).

L = *The Rover*, edited by Frederick M. Link, Regents Restoration Drama Series (Lincoln: University of Nebraska Press, 1967).

J = *The Rover.* In vol. 2 of *Restoration Comedy*, ed. A. Norman Jeffares (London: Folio Press, 1974).

T = *The Rover*, in *Oroonoko, The Rover and Other Works*, ed. Janet Todd (Harmondsworth: Penguin, 1992).

The Feigned Courtesans

Q = *The Feign'd Curtizans, or, A Night's Intrigue. A Comedy. As it is Acted at the Duke's Theatre* (London: Jacob Tonson, 1679).

Lud = 'A Critical Edition of Aphra Behn's Comedy *The Feigned Courtesans* (1679), with Introduction and Notes', by Judith Karyn Ludwig, Ph.D. thesis (Yale University, 1976).

LM = *The Feigned Courtesans*, in *Female Playwrights of the Restoration: Five Comedies*, ed. Paddy Lyons and Fidelis Morgan (London: J.M. Dent, 1991).

The Lucky Chance

Q = *The Luckey Chance, or an Alderman's Bargain. A Comedy. As it is Acted by their Majesty's Servants* (London: R.H. for W. Canning, 1687).

Co = *Aphra Behn's The Luckey Chance (1687): A Critical Edition*, ed. Jean A. Coakley (New York and London: Garland, 1987).

M = *The Lucky Chance*, in *The Female Wits: Women Playwrights on the London Stage 1660–1720*, ed. Fidelis Morgan (London: Virago, 1981).

The Emperor of the Moon

Q1 = *The Emperor of the Moon: A Farce. As it is Acted by Their Majesties Servants, at the Queens Theatre* (London: R. Holt, 1687).

Q2 = *The Emperor of the Moon: A Farce. As it is Acted by Their Majesties Servants, at the Queens Theatre* (London: R. Holt, 1688).

HS = *The Emperor of the Moon*, in *Ten English Farces*, ed. Leo Hughes and A.H. Scouten (Austin: University of Texas, 1948).

Collections

C1 = *Plays Written by the late Ingenious Mrs. Behn, Entire in Two Volumes* (London: Jacob Tonson and R. Wellington, 1702).

C2 = *Plays Written by the Late Ingenious Mrs. Behn. In Four Volumes* (London: Mary Poulson, 1724).

S = *The Works of Aphra Behn*, ed. Montague Summers, 6 vols. (London: William Heinemann, 1915).

SELECT BIBLIOGRAPHY

Bibliographical

Mary Ann O'Donnell's *Aphra Behn: An Annotated Bibliography of Primary and Secondary Sources* (New York and London: Garland, 1986) is the standard primary bibliography and the best guide to secondary sources up to and including 1985. Also useful is J. M. Armistead's *Four Restoration Playwrights: A Reference Guide to Thomas Shadwell, Aphra Behn, Nathaniel Lee, and Thomas Otway* (Boston: G. K. Hall, 1984).

Biographical

Though current research is offering alternatives to her account of Behn, Maureen Duffy's *The Passionate Shepherdess: Aphra Behn 1640–89* (London: Jonathan Cape, 1977) remains the most thorough biography so far. Angeline Goreau's *Reconstructing Aphra: A Social Biography of Aphra Behn* (Oxford: Oxford University Press, 1980) is interesting for its discussion of Behn's position as a woman writer. There is an account of Behn in Sara Heller Mendelson, *The Mental World of Stuart Women* (Brighton: Harvester, 1987), ch. 3. For overviews of recent biographical work see Mary Ann O'Donnell, 'Tory Wit and Unconventional Woman: Aphra Behn', in K. M. Wilson and F. J. Warnke (eds.), *Women Writers of the Seventeenth Century* (Athens, Ga., and London: University of Georgia Press, 1989), 341–54, and Janet Todd, 'General Introduction', *The Works of Aphra Behn*, vol. 1, *Poetry* (London: William Pickering, 1992), pp. ix–xxxv.

Critical

Until the revival of interest in Behn in the late 1970s there was little critical discussion of her plays. George Woodcock's *The Incomparable Aphra* (London: Boardman, 1948) is still of interest. Frederick M. Link's *Aphra Behn* (New York: Twayne, 1968) offers useful discussions of all of her plays. Behn's work is interestingly treated in some general studies of seventeenth-century drama, including Robert D. Hume, *The Development of English Drama in the Late Seventeenth Century* (Oxford: Clarendon Press, 1976), Laura Brown, *English Dramatic Form 1660–1760: An Essay in Generic History* (New Haven, Conn.: Yale University Press, 1981), and Edward Burns, *Restoration Comedy: Crises of Desire and Identity* (London: Macmillan, 1987). Jacqueline Pearson's *The Prostituted Muse: Images of Women and Women Dramatists 1642–1737* (London: Harvester Press, 1988) is the most detailed study to date of Behn in relation to women dramatists of the seventeenth and eighteenth centuries. Susan Carlson's *Women and Comedy: Rewriting the British Theatrical Tradition* (Ann

Arbor, Mich.: University of Michigan Press, 1991) has an interesting chapter on Behn's use of comedy. A number of recent theses have been devoted to Behn: important among these are Eva I. Simmons, ' "Virtue Intire": Aphra Behn's Contribution, in her Comedies, to the Marriage Debates of the Seventeenth Century' (Ph.D. University of London, 1990), and Dawn Lewcock, 'Aphra Behn on the Restoration Stage' (Ph.D. Cambridgeshire College of Arts and Technology, 1987), which gives detailed attention to Behn's stagecraft. Articles on Behn's plays have appeared in recent journals: particularly provocative are Catherine Gallagher, 'Who was that Masked Woman? The Prostitute and the Playwright in the Comedies of Aphra Behn', in *Women's Studies: An Interdisciplinary Journal*, 15: 1 (1988), 23–42, and Elin Diamond, '*Gestus* and Signature in Aphra Behn's *The Rover*', *ELH* 56 (1989), 519–41. Gallagher's article is reprinted in a recent collection devoted to Behn criticism: Heidi Hutner (ed.), *Rereading Aphra Behn: History, Theory and Criticism* (Charlottesville, Va., and London: University Press of Virginia, 1993). This collection contains three other chapters on the plays: Jane Spencer, ' "Deceit, Dissembling, all that's Woman": Comic Plot and Female Action in *The Feigned Courtesans*', Heidi Hutner, 'Revisioning the Female Body: Aphra Behn's *The Rover*, Parts I and II', and Susan Green, 'Semiotic Modalities of the Female Body in Aphra Behn's *The Dutch Lover*'.

Recent feminist historicist work has focused on Behn, as well as other seventeenth-century and eighteenth-century women writers, in relation to questions of female subjectivity. Ros Ballaster's *Seductive Forms: Women's Amatory Fiction 1684–1740* (Oxford: Clarendon Press, 1991) discusses Behn along with Delarivier Manley and Eliza Haywood. There is some discussion of Behn in two important recent collections on early women's writing: Clare Brant and Diane Purkiss (eds.), *Women, Texts and Histories 1575–1760* (London: Routledge, 1992), and Isobel Grundy and Susan Wiseman (eds.), *Women, Writing, History 1640–1740* (London: Batsford, 1992).

General background studies

Historical

K. H. D. Haley, *The First Earl of Shaftesbury* (Oxford: Clarendon Press, 1968); Tim Harris, Paul Seaward, and Mark Goldie (eds.), *The Politics of Religion in Restoration England* (Oxford: Blackwell, 1990); J. R. James (ed.), *The Restored Monarchy 1660–1688* (London: Macmillan, 1969); John Kenyon, *The Popish Plot* (Harmondsworth: Penguin, 1974); Jennifer Levin, *The Charter Controversy in the City of London, 1660–1688, and Its Consequences* (London: Athlone Press, 1969).

Theatrical

Arthur Gewirtz, *Restoration Adaptations of Early Seventeenth-Century Comedies* (Washington: University Press of America, 1982); Peter Holland, *The*

Ornament of Action: Text and Performance in Restoration Comedy (Cambridge: Cambridge University Press, 1979); Leo Hughes, *A Century of English Farce* (Princeton, NJ: Princeton University Press, 1956); John Loftis, *The Spanish Plays of Neoclassical England* (New Haven, Conn.: Yale University Press, 1973); Curtis A. Price, *Music in the Restoration Theatre* (UMI Research Press, 1979); David Thomas, *Theatre in Europe: A Documentary History. Restoration and Georgian England, 1660–1788* (Cambridge: Cambridge University Press, 1989).

A CHRONOLOGY OF APHRA BEHN

1640?   Aphra Johnson born in Kent.

1663   Travels to Surinam.

1664   Returns to England; probably marries Mr Behn.

1665   Probable death of or separation from husband.

1666   Travels to Holland as spy for English government; returns home, threatened with debtors' prison.

1670   *The Forced Marriage*, Lincoln's Inn Fields.

1671   *The Amorous Prince*, Lincoln's Inn Fields.

1673   *The Dutch Lover*, Dorset Garden.

1676   *Abdelazer or The Moor's Revenge*, Dorset Garden.
       The Town Fop or Sir Timothy Tawdry, Dorset Garden.

1677   *The Rover*, Dorset Garden.

1678   *Sir Patient Fancy*, Dorset Garden.

1679   *The Feigned Courtesans*, Dorset Garden.
       Probable performance of *The Young King*, Dorset Garden.

1681   *The Rover, Part II*, Dorset Garden.
       The Roundheads, or the Good Old Cause, Dorset Garden.
       The False Count, Dorset Garden.

1682   Duke's Company takes over King's Company; United Company formed.
       Like Father, Like Son, Dorset Garden.
       The City Heiress, Dorset Garden.
       Warrant for Behn's arrest after attack on Monmouth in epilogue to *Romulus and Hersilia*. Behn possibly leaves England until late 1683.

1683–5   Works on poetry, translations, and novels.

1684   *Love-Letters Between a Nobleman and His Sister*, Part I.
       Poems Upon Several Occasions, with A Voyage to the Isle of Love.

1685   *Love-Letters*, Part II.

1686   *The Lucky Chance*, Drury Lane.

1687   *The Emperor of the Moon*, Dorset Garden.
       Love-Letters, Part III.

1688   *The Fair Jilt*.
       Oroonoko, or the Royal Slave.

1689   16 April, Behn dies. Buried in Westminster Abbey.
       The Widow Ranter, Drury Lane.

1696   *The Younger Brother*, Drury Lane.

THE ROVER,
or
The Banished Cavaliers

The earliest recorded performance of the play was at the Dorset Garden Theatre on 24 March 1677, with the following cast:

MEN

Don Antonio (the viceroy's son)	*Mr Jevon*
Don Pedro (a noble Spaniard, his friend)	*Mr Medbourne*
Belvile (an English colonel in love with Florinda)	*Mr Betterton*
Willmore (the rover)	*Mr Smith*
Frederick (an English gentleman, and friend to Belvile and Blunt)	*Mr Crosby*
Blunt (an English country gentleman)	*Mr Underhill*
Stephano (servant to Don Pedro)	*Mr Richards*
Philippo (Lucetta's gallant)	*Mr Percival*
Sancho (pimp to Lucetta)	*Mr John Lee*
Biskey, and Sebastian (two bravos to Angellica)	
Officers and Soldiers	
[Diego,] Page (to Don Antonio)	

WOMEN

Florinda (sister to Don Pedro)	*Mrs Betterton*
Hellena (a gay young woman designed for a nun, and sister to Florinda)	*Mrs Barry*
Valeria (a kinswoman to Florinda)	*Mrs Hughes*
Angellica Bianca (a famous courtesan)	*Mrs Quin*°
Moretta (her woman)	*Mrs Leigh*
Callis (governess to Florinda and Hellena)	*Mrs Norris*
Lucetta (a jilting wench)	*Mrs Gillow*
Servants, other Masqueraders (men and women)	

THE SCENE

Naples, in Carnival time

Prologue

Written by a person of quality

Wits, like physicians, never can agree,
When of a different society:°
And Rabel's drops were never more cried down°
By all the learned doctors of the town,
Than a new play whose author is unknown;   5
Nor can those doctors with more malice sue
(And powerful purses) the dissenting few,
Than those with an insulting pride, do rail
At all who are not of their own cabal.°
   If a young poet hit your humour right,°   10
You judge him then out of revenge and spite:
So amongst men there are ridiculous elves,
Who monkeys hate for being too like themselves.
So that the reason of the grand debate,
Why wit so oft is damned when good plays take,°   15
Is that you censure as you love or hate.°
   Thus, like a learned conclave, poets sit,
Catholic judges both of sense and wit,
And damn or save as they themselves think fit.
Yet those who to others' faults are so severe,   20
Are not so perfect but themselves may err.
Some write correct, indeed, but then the whole
(Bating their own dull stuff i'th' play) is stole:
As bees do suck from flowers their honeydew,
So they rob others, striving to please you.   25
   Some write their characters genteel and fine,
But then they do so toil for every line,
That what to you does easy seem, and plain,
Is the hard issue of their labouring brain.
And some th'effects of all their pains we see,   30
Is but to mimic good extempore.°
Others, by long converse about the town,
Have wit enough to write a lewd lampoon,
But their chief skill lies in a bawdy song.
In short, the only wit that's now in fashion,   35

Is but the gleanings of good conversation.
As for the author of this coming play,
I asked him what he thought fit I should say°
In thanks for your good company today:
He called me fool, and said it was well known,   40
You came not here for our sakes, but your own.
New plays are stuffed with wits, and with debauches,
That crowd and sweat like cits in May-day coaches.°

1.1

A chamber

Enter Florinda and Hellena

FLORINDA What an impertinent thing is a young girl bred in a
nunnery! How full of questions! Prithee, no more, Hellena, I have
told thee more than thou understand'st already.

HELLENA The more's my grief; I would fain know as much as you,
which makes me so inquisitive; nor is't enough I know you're a   5
lover, unless you tell me too who 'tis you sigh for.

FLORINDA When you're a lover, I'll think you fit for a secret of that
nature.

HELLENA 'Tis true, I never was a lover yet; but I begin to have a
shrewd guess what 'tis to be so, and fancy it very pretty to sigh,   10
and sing, and blush, and wish, and dream and wish, and long and
wish to see the man, and when I do, look pale and tremble, just as
you did when my brother brought home the fine English colonel
to see you—what do you call him? Don Belvile.

FLORINDA Fie, Hellena.   15

HELLENA That blush betrays you. I am sure 'tis so; or is it Don
Antonio, the viceroy's son? Or perhaps the rich old Don Vincentio,
whom my father designs you for a husband? Why do you blush
again?

FLORINDA With indignation; and how near soever my father thinks   20
I am to marrying that hated object, I shall let him see I understand
better what's due to my beauty, birth and fortune, and more to my
soul, than to obey those unjust commands.

HELLENA Now hang me, if I don't love thee for that dear disobe-
dience. I love mischief strangely, as most of our sex do, who are   25
come to love nothing else. But tell me, dear Florinda, don't you
love that fine *Inglese*?° For I vow, next to loving him myself, 'twill
please me most that you do so, for he is so gay and so handsome.

FLORINDA Hellena, a maid designed for a nun ought not to be so
curious in a discourse of love.   30

HELLENA And dost thou think that ever I'll be a nun? Or at least till
I'm so old, I'm fit for nothing else: faith, no, sister; and that which
makes me long to know whether you love Belvile, is because I hope
he has some mad companion or other that will spoil my devotion.
Nay, I'm resolved to provide myself this Carnival,° if there be e'er   35

a handsome proper° fellow of my humour above ground, though I
ask first.

FLORINDA Prithee be not so wild.

HELLENA Now you have provided yourself of a man, you take no
care for poor me. Prithee tell me, what dost thou see about me that   40
is unfit for love? Have I not a world of youth? A humour gay? A
beauty passable? A vigour desirable? Well-shaped? Clean-limbed?
Sweet-breathed? And sense enough to know how all these ought
to be employed to the best advantage? Yes, I do, and will; therefore
lay aside your hopes of my fortune by my being a devotee,° and   45
tell me how you came acquainted with this Belvile; for I perceive
you knew him before he came to Naples.

FLORINDA Yes, I knew him at the siege of Pamplona:° he was then
a colonel of French horse, who, when the town was ransacked,
nobly treated my brother and myself, preserving us from all   50
insolences; and I must own, besides great obligations, I have I
know not what that pleads kindly for him about my heart, and will
suffer no other to enter. But see, my brother.

        Enter Don Pedro, Stephano with a masking habit,° and Callis

PEDRO Good morrow, sister. Pray when saw you your lover Don
Vincentio?   55

FLORINDA I know not, sir—Callis, when was he here?—for I consider it so little, I know not when it was.

PEDRO I have a command from my father here to tell you you ought
not to despise him, a man of so vast a fortune, and such a passion
for you.—Stephano, my things.   60

        [Don Pedro] puts on his masking habit

FLORINDA A passion for me? 'Tis more than e'er I saw, or he had a
desire should be known. I hate Vincentio, sir, and I would not have
a man so dear to me as my brother follow the ill customs of our
country, and make a slave of his sister;° and, sir, my father's will
I'm sure you may divert.   65

PEDRO I know not how dear I am to you, but I wish only to be
ranked in your esteem equal with the English colonel Belvile. Why
do you frown and blush? Is there any guilt belongs to the name of
that cavalier?

FLORINDA I'll not deny I value Belvile. When I was exposed to such   70
dangers as the licensed lust of common soldiers threatened, when
rage and conquest flew through the city, then Belvile, this criminal
for my sake,° threw himself into all dangers to save my honour:
and will you not allow him my esteem?

6

PEDRO Yes, pay him what you will in honour; but you must consider   75
Don Vincentio's fortune, and the jointure he'll make you.

FLORINDA Let him consider my youth, beauty and fortune, which
ought not to be thrown away on his age and jointure.

PEDRO 'Tis true, he's not so young and fine a gentleman as that
Belvile; but what jewels will that cavalier present you with? Those   80
of his eyes and heart?°

HELLENA And are not those better than any Don Vincentio has
brought from the Indies?°

PEDRO Why how now! has your nunnery breeding taught you to
understand the value of hearts and eyes?   85

HELLENA Better than to believe Vincentio's deserve value from any
woman: he may perhaps increase her bags, but not her family.°

PEDRO This is fine! Go, up to your devotion: you are not designed
for the conversation of lovers.

HELLENA (*aside*) Nor saints, yet awhile, I hope.—Is't not enough you   90
make a nun of me, but you must cast my sister away too, exposing
her to a worse confinement than a religious life?

PEDRO The girl's mad! It is a confinement to be carried into the
country, to an ancient villa belonging to the family of the
Vincentios these five hundred years, and have no other prospect   95
than that pleasing one of seeing all her own that meets her eyes: a
fine air, large fields and gardens, where she may walk and gather
flowers!

HELLENA When, by moonlight? For I am sure she dares not
encounter with the heat of the sun; that were a task only for Don   100
Vincentio and his Indian breeding,° who loves it in the dog
days.° And if these be her daily divertisements, what are those of
the night? To lie in a wide moth-eaten bedchamber, with furniture
in fashion in the reign of King Sancho the First;° the bed, that
which his forefathers lived and died in.   105

PEDRO Very well.

HELLENA This apartment, new furbished° and fitted out for the
young wife, he (out of freedom) makes his dressing room, and
being a frugal and a jealous coxcomb, instead of a valet to uncase
his feeble carcass, he desires you to do that office: signs of favour,   110
I'll assure you, and such as you must not hope for, unless your
woman be out of the way.

PEDRO Have you done yet?

HELLENA That honour being past, the giant stretches itself, yawns
and sighs a belch or two, loud as a musket, throws himself into   115

bed, and expects you in his foul sheets;° and ere you can get
yourself undressed, calls you with a snore or two: and are not these
fine blessings to a young lady?

PEDRO Have you done yet?

HELLENA And this man you must kiss: nay, you must kiss none but   120
him, too—and nuzzle through his beard to find his lips. And this
you must submit to for threescore years, and all for a jointure.

PEDRO For all your character of Don Vincentio, she is as like to
marry him as she was before.

HELLENA Marry Don Vincentio! Hang me, such a wedlock would be   125
worse than adultery° with another man. I had rather see her in the
Hôtel de Dieu,° to waste her youth there in vows, and be a
handmaid to lazars and cripples, than to lose it in such a marriage.

PEDRO [*to Florinda*] You have considered, sister, that Belvile has no
fortune to bring you to; banished his country, despised at home,   130
and pitied abroad.

HELLENA What then? The viceroy's son is better than that old Sir
Fifty. Don Vincentio!° Don Indian! He thinks he's trading to
Gambo° still, and would barter himself (that bell and bauble)° for
your youth and fortune.   135

PEDRO Callis, take her hence, and lock her up all this Carnival, and
at Lent she shall begin her everlasting penance in a monastery.

HELLENA I care not; I had rather be a nun than be obliged to marry
as you would have me, if I were designed for't.

PEDRO Do not fear the blessing of that choice; you shall be a nun.   140

HELLENA Shall I so? You may chance to be mistaken in my way of
devotion. A nun! yes, I am like to make a fine nun! I have an
excellent humour for a grate. (*Aside*) No, I'll have a saint of my
own to pray to shortly, if I like any that dares venture on me.°

PEDRO Callis, make it your business to watch this wildcat.—As for   145
you, Florinda, I've only tried you all this while, and urged my
father's will; but mine is, that you would love Antonio: he is brave
and young, and all that can complete the happiness of a gallant
maid. This absence of my father will give us opportunity to free
you from Vincentio by marrying here, which you must do   150
tomorrow.

FLORINDA Tomorrow!

PEDRO Tomorrow, or 'twill be too late. 'Tis not my friendship to
Antonio which makes me urge this, but love to thee, and hatred to
Vincentio; therefore resolve upon tomorrow.   155

FLORINDA Sir, I shall strive to do as shall become your sister.

PEDRO I'll both believe and trust you. Adieu.
 Exeunt Pedro and Stephano

HELLENA As becomes his sister! That is, to be as resolved your way
 as he is his.
 Hellena goes to Callis

FLORINDA [*aside*] I ne'er till now perceived my ruin near;°   160
 I've no defence against Antonio's love,
 For he has all the advantages of nature,
 The moving arguments of youth and fortune.

HELLENA But hark you, Callis, you will not be so cruel to lock me
 up indeed, will you?   165

CALLIS I must obey the commands I have; besides, do you consider
 what a life you are going to lead?

HELLENA Yes, Callis, that of a nun: and till then I'll be indebted a
 world of prayers to you, if you'll let me now see, what I never did,
 the divertisements of a Carnival.   170

CALLIS What, go in masquerade? 'Twill be a fine farewell to the
 world, I take it; pray, what would you do there?

HELLENA That which all the world does, as I am told: be as mad as
 the rest, and take all innocent freedoms. Sister, you'll go too, will
 you not? Come, prithee be not sad. We'll outwit twenty brothers,   175
 if you'll be ruled by me. Come, put off this dull humour with your
 clothes, and assume one as gay, and as fantastic, as the dress my
 cousin Valeria and I have provided, and let's ramble.°

FLORINDA Callis, will you give us leave to go?

CALLIS (*aside*) I have a youthful itch of going myself.—Madam, if I   180
 thought your brother might not know it, and I might wait on you;
 for by my troth, I'll not trust young girls alone.

FLORINDA Thou seest my brother's gone already, and thou shalt
 attend and watch us.
 Enter Stephano

STEPHANO Madam, the habits are come, and your cousin Valeria is   185
 dressed and stays for you.

FLORINDA 'Tis well. I'll write a note, and if I chance to see Belvile,
 and want° an opportunity to speak to him, that shall let him know
 what I've resolved in favour of him.

HELLENA Come, let's in and dress us.   190
 Exeunt

1.2

A long street°

Enter Belvile melancholy, Blunt, and Frederick

FREDERICK Why, what the devil ails the colonel, in a time when all
the world is gay, to look like mere Lent° thus? Hadst thou been
long enough in Naples to have been in love, I should have sworn
some such judgement had befallen thee.

BELVILE No, I have made no new amours since I came to Naples.   5

FREDERICK You have left none behind you in Paris?

BELVILE Neither.

FREDERICK I cannot divine the cause then, unless the old cause, the
want of money.

BLUNT And another old cause, the want of a wench; would not that   10
revive you?

BELVILE You are mistaken, Ned.

BLUNT Nay, 'adsheartlikins, then thou'rt past cure.

FREDERICK I have found it out: thou hast renewed thy acquaintance
with the lady that cost thee so many sighs at the siege of Pamplona;   15
pox on't, what d'ye call her—her brother's a noble Spaniard,
nephew to the dead general—Florinda. Aye, Florinda: and will
nothing serve thy turn but that damned virtuous woman? Whom
on my conscience thou lovest in spite, too, because thou seest little
or no possibility of gaining her.   20

BELVILE Thou art mistaken, I have interest enough in that lovely
virgin's heart to make me proud and vain, were it not abated by
the severity of a brother, who perceiving my happiness—

FREDERICK Has civilly forbid thee the house?

BELVILE 'Tis so, to make way for a powerful rival, the viceroy's son,   25
who has the advantage of me in being a man of fortune, a Spaniard,
and her brother's friend; which gives him liberty to make his court,
whilst I have recourse only to letters, and distant looks from her
window, which are as soft and kind

As those which heaven sends down on penitents.   30

BLUNT Heyday! 'Adsheartlikins, simile! By this light the man is quite
spoiled.—Fred, what the devil are we made of, that we cannot be
thus concerned for a wench? 'Adsheartlikins, our cupids are like
the cooks of the camp: they can roast or boil a woman, but they
have none of the fine tricks to set 'em off, no hogoes to make the   35
sauce pleasant and the stomach sharp.

FREDERICK I dare swear I have had a hundred as young, kind and handsome as this Florinda; and dogs eat me if they were not as troublesome to me i'th' morning as they were welcome o'er night.

BLUNT And yet I warrant he would not touch another woman, if he 40 might have her for nothing.

BELVILE That's thy joy, a cheap whore.

BLUNT Why, 'adsheartlikins, I love a frank soul: when did you ever hear of an honest woman that took a man's money? I warrant 'em good ones. But, gentlemen, you may be free: you have been kept 45 so poor with parliaments and protectors° that the little stock you have is not worth preserving; but I thank my stars, I had more grace than to forfeit my estate by cavaliering.°

BELVILE Methinks only following the court should be sufficient to entitle 'em to that. 50

BLUNT 'Adsheartlikins, they know I follow it to do it no good, unless they pick a hole in my coat° for lending you money now and then, which is a greater crime to my conscience, gentlemen, than to the Commonwealth.°

Enter Willmore

WILLMORE Ha! Dear Belvile! Noble colonel! 55

BELVILE Willmore! Welcome ashore, my dear rover! What happy wind blew us this good fortune?

WILLMORE Let me salute my dear Fred, and then command me. [*To Frederick*] How is't, honest lad?

FREDERICK Faith, sir, the old compliment, infinitely the better to see 60 my dear mad Willmore again. Prithee, why cam'st thou ashore? And where's the prince?°

WILLMORE He's well, and reigns still lord of the watery element. I must aboard again within a day or two, and my business ashore was only to enjoy myself a little this Carnival. 65

BELVILE Pray know our new friend, sir; he's but bashful, a raw traveller, but honest,° stout, and one of us.

WILLMORE (*embraces Blunt*)° That you esteem him gives him an interest here.

BLUNT Your servant, sir. 70

WILLMORE But well, faith, I'm glad to meet you again in a warm climate, where the kind sun has its god-like power still over the wine and women. Love and mirth are my business in Naples, and if I mistake not the place, here's an excellent market for chapmen of my humour. 75

BELVILE See, here be those kind merchants of love you look for.

*Enter several men in masking habits, some playing on music,
others dancing after, women dressed like courtesans, with papers
pinned on their breasts, and baskets of flowers in their hands*

BLUNT 'Adsheartlikins, what have we here?

FREDERICK Now the game begins.

WILLMORE Fine pretty creatures! May a stranger have leave to look
and love? (*Reads the papers*) What's here: 'Roses for every month'?   80

BLUNT Roses for every month? What means that?

BELVILE They are, or would have you think they're courtesans, who
here in Naples are to be hired by the month.

WILLMORE Kind; and obliging to inform us. [*To a woman*] Pray,
where do these roses grow? I would fain plant some of 'em in a   85
bed of mine.

WOMAN Beware such roses, sir.

WILLMORE A pox of fear: I'll be baked with thee between a pair of
sheets (and that's thy proper still),° so I might but strew such roses
over me, and under me. Fair one, would you would give me leave   90
to gather at your bush this idle month; I would go near to make
somebody smell of it all the year after.

BELVILE And thou hast need of such a remedy, for thou stink'st of
tar and ropes' ends, like a dock or pest-house.

*The woman puts herself into the hands of a man, and [both
begin to leave]*

WILLMORE Nay, nay, you shall not leave me so.   95

BELVILE By all means use no violence here.

[*Exeunt man and woman*]

WILLMORE Death! Just as I was going to be damnably in love, to
have her led off! I could pluck that rose out of his hand, and even
kiss the bed the bush grew in.°

FREDERICK No friend to love like a long voyage at sea.   100

BLUNT Except a nunnery, Fred.

WILLMORE Death! But will they not be kind, quickly be kind? Thou
know'st I'm no tame sigher, but a rampant lion of the forest.

*Advances, from the farther end of the scenes,° two men dressed
all over with horns° of several sorts, making grimaces at one
another, with papers pinned on their backs*

BELVILE Oh the fantastical rogues, how they're dressed! 'Tis a satire
against the whole sex.   105

WILLMORE Is this a fruit that grows in this warm country?

BELVILE Yes: 'tis pretty to see these Italians start, swell and stab, at
the word cuckold, and yet stumble at horns on every threshold.

WILLMORE See what's on their back. (*Reads*) 'Flowers of every
night': ah, rogue, and more sweet than roses of every month! This   110
is a gardener of Adam's own breeding.°
     [*The two men dressed in horns*] *dance*

BELVILE What think you of those grave people? Is a wake in
Essex° half so mad or extravagant?

WILLMORE I like their sober grave way: 'tis a kind of legal authorized
fornication, where the men are not chid for't, nor the women   115
despised, as amongst our dull English; even the monsieurs want
that part of good manners.°

BELVILE But here in Italy, a monsieur is the humblest best-bred
gentleman: duels are so baffled by bravos,° that an age shows not
one but between a Frenchman and a hangman, who is as much too   120
hard for him on the Piazza, as they are for a Dutchman on the
New Bridge.° But see, another crew.
     Enter Florinda, Hellena, and Valeria, dressed like gipsies;
     Callis and Stephano, Lucetta, Philippo, and Sancho in masquerade

HELLENA Sister, there's your Englishman, and with him a handsome
proper fellow. I'll to him, and instead of telling him his fortune,
try my own.   125

WILLMORE Gipsies, on my life; sure these will prattle if a man cross
their hands.°
     [*Willmore*] *goes to Hellena*
Dear, pretty, and I hope young, devil, will you tell an amorous
stranger what luck he's like to have?

HELLENA Have a care how you venture with me, sir, lest I pick your   130
pocket, which will more vex your English humour, than an Italian
fortune will please you.

WILLMORE How the devil cam'st thou to know my country and
humour?

HELLENA The first I guess by a certain forward impudence, which   135
does not displease me at this time; and the loss of your money will
vex you, because I hope° you have but very little to lose.

WILLMORE Egad, child, thou'rt i'th' right; it is so little, I dare not
offer it thee for a kindness. But cannot you divine what other
things of more value I have about me, that I would more willingly   140
part with?

HELLENA Indeed no, that's the business of a witch, and I am but a
gipsy yet. Yet, without looking in your hand, I have a parlous°
guess 'tis some foolish heart you mean, an inconstant English
heart, as little worth stealing as your purse.   145

WILLMORE   Nay, then thou dost deal with the devil, that's certain:
thou hast guessed as right, as if thou hadst been one of that
number it has languished for. I find you'll be better acquainted
with it; nor can you take it in a better time, for I am come from
sea, child, and Venus not being propitious to me in her own   150
element,° I have a world of love in store. Would you would be
good-natured and take some on't off my hands.

HELLENA   Why, I could be inclined that way, but for a foolish vow I
am going to make—to die a maid.

WILLMORE   Then thou art damned without redemption, and as I am   155
a good Christian, I ought in charity to divert so wicked a design;
therefore prithee, dear creature, let me know quickly when and
where I shall begin to set a helping hand to so good a work.

HELLENA   If you should prevail with my tender heart, as I begin to
fear you will, for you have horrible loving eyes, there will be   160
difficulty in't that you'll hardly undergo for my sake.

WILLMORE   Faith, child, I have been bred in dangers, and wear a
sword that has been employed in a worse cause than for a handsome kind woman. Name the danger; let it be anything but a long
siege, and I'll undertake it.   165

HELLENA   Can you storm?

WILLMORE   Oh, most furiously.

HELLENA   What think you of a nunnery wall? For he that wins me,
must gain that first.

WILLMORE   A nun! Oh how I love thee for't! There's no sinner like   170
a young saint. Nay, now there's no denying me: the old law had
no curse, to a woman, like dying a maid; witness Jephtha's
daughter.°

HELLENA   A very good text this, if well handled; and I perceive,
Father Captain, you would impose no severe penance on her who   175
were inclined to console herself before she took orders.

WILLMORE   If she be young and handsome.

HELLENA   Aye, there's it: but if she be not—

WILLMORE   By this hand, child, I have an implicit faith,° and dare
venture on thee with all faults. Besides, 'tis more meritorious to   180
leave the world when thou hast tasted and proved the pleasure
on't. Then 'twill be a virtue in thee, which now will be pure
ignorance.

HELLENA   I perceive, good Father Captain, you design only to make
me fit for heaven. But if, on the contrary, you should quite divert 185
me from it, and bring me back to the world again, I should have

a new man to seek, I find; and what a grief that will be. For when
I begin, I fancy I shall love like anything; I never tried yet.

WILLMORE Egad, and that's kind. Prithee, dear creature, give me
credit for a heart, for faith I'm a very honest fellow. Oh, I long to   190
come first to the banquet of love, and such a swingeing appetite I
bring! Oh, I'm impatient. Thy lodging, sweetheart, thy lodging, or
I'm a dead man!

HELLENA Why must we be either guilty of fornication or murder if
we converse with you men? And is there no difference between   195
leave to love me, and leave to lie with me?

WILLMORE Faith, child, they were made to go together.

LUCETTA ([aside to Sancho,] pointing to Blunt) Are you sure this is
the man?

SANCHO When did I mistake your game?   200

LUCETTA This is a stranger, I know by his gazing; if he be brisk, he'll
venture to follow me, and then, if I understand my trade, he's
mine. He's English, too, and they say that's a sort of good-natured
loving people,° and have generally so kind an opinion of themselves, that a woman with any wit may flatter 'em into any sort of   205
fool she pleases.

> [Lucetta] often passes by Blunt, and gazes on him; he struts
> and cocks, and walks and gazes on her

BLUNT [aside] 'Tis so, she is taken: I have beauties which my false
glass at home did not discover.

FLORINDA [aside] This woman watches me so, I shall get no
opportunity to discover myself to him, and so miss the intent of   210
my coming. ([To Belvile,] looking in his hand) But as I was saying,
sir, by this line you should be a lover.

BELVILE I thought how right you guessed: all men are in love, or
pretend to be so. Come, let me go, I'm weary of this fooling.

> [Belvile] walks away. [Florinda] holds him, he strives to get
> from her

FLORINDA I will not, till you have confessed whether the passion   215
that you have vowed Florinda, be true or false.

BELVILE (turn[ing] quick towards her) Florinda!

FLORINDA Softly.

BELVILE Thou hast named one will fix me here for ever.

FLORINDA She'll be disappointed, then, who expects you this night   220
at the garden gate; and if you fail not, as—(looks on Callis, who
observes them) let me see the other hand—you will go near to do,
she vows to die or make you happy.

BELVILE What canst thou mean?

FLORINDA That which I say; farewell.   225

    [Florinda] offers to go

BELVILE Oh, charming sibyl,° stay; complete that joy, which as it is
    will turn into distraction! Where must I be? At the garden gate? I
    know it; at night, you say? I'll sooner forfeit heaven than disobey.

    Enter Don Pedro and other maskers, and pass over the stage

CALLIS Madam, your brother's here.

FLORINDA Take this to instruct you farther.   230

    [Florinda] gives [Belvile] a letter, and goes off

FREDERICK Have a care, sir, what you promise; this may be a trap
    laid by her brother to ruin you.

BELVILE Do not disturb my happiness with doubts.

    [Belvile] opens the letter

WILLMORE *[to Hellena]* My dear pretty creature, a thousand bless-
    ings on thee! Still in this habit, you say? And after dinner at this   235
    place.

HELLENA Yes, if you will swear to keep your heart, and not bestow
    it between this and that.

WILLMORE By all the little gods of love, I swear I'll leave it with you,
    and if you run away with it, those deities of justice will revenge me. 240

    Exeunt all the women [except Lucetta]

FREDERICK Do you know the hand?

BELVILE 'Tis Florinda's.

All blessings fall upon the virtuous maid.

FREDERICK Nay, no idolatry: a sober sacrifice I'll allow you.

BELVILE Oh, friends, the welcom'st news! The softest letter! Nay,   245
    you shall all see it; and could you now be serious, I might be made
    the happiest man the sun shines on!

WILLMORE The reason of this mighty joy?

BELVILE See how kindly she invites me to deliver her from the
    threatened violence of her brother: will you not assist me?   250

WILLMORE I know not what thou mean'st, but I'll make one at any
    mischief where a woman's concerned. But she'll be grateful to us
    for the favour, will she not?

BELVILE How mean you?

WILLMORE How should I mean? Thou know'st there's but one way   255
    for a woman to oblige me.

BELVILE Do not profane; the maid is nicely virtuous.

WILLMORE Ho,° pox, then she's fit for nothing but a husband: let
    her e'en go, colonel.

FREDERICK Peace, she's the colonel's mistress, sir.   260

WILLMORE Let her be the devil, if she be thy mistress, I'll serve her.
Name the way.

BELVILE Read here this postscript.

    [Belvile] gives [Willmore] a letter

WILLMORE (*reads*) 'At ten at night, at the garden gate, of which, if I
cannot get the key, I will contrive a way over the wall. Come   265
attended with a friend or two.'——Kind heart, if we three cannot
weave a string to let her down a garden wall, 'twere pity but the
hangman wove one for us all.

FREDERICK Let her alone for that.° Your woman's wit, your fair kind
woman, will out-trick a broker or a Jew, and contrive like a Jesuit in 270
chains.° But see, Ned Blunt is stolen out after the lure of a damsel.

    Exeunt Blunt and Lucetta

BELVILE So, he'll scarce find his way home again, unless we get him
cried by the bellman in the market-place, and 'twould sound
prettily: 'a lost English boy° of thirty'.

FREDERICK I hope 'tis some common crafty sinner, one that will fit   275
him. It may be she'll sell him for Peru;° the rogue's sturdy,° and
would work well in a mine. At least I hope she'll dress him for our
mirth: cheat him of all, then have him well-favouredly banged, and
turned out naked at midnight.

WILLMORE Prithee, what humour is he of, that you wish him so   280
well?

BELVILE Why, of an English elder brother's humour. Educated in a
nursery, with a maid to tend him till fifteen, and lies with his
grandmother till he's of age; one that knows no pleasure beyond
riding to the next fair, or going up to London with his right   285
worshipful father in parliament time, wearing gay clothes, or
making honourable love to his lady mother's laundry-maid; gets
drunk at a hunting match, and ten to one then gives some proofs
of his prowess. A pox upon him, he's our banker, and has all our
cash about him, and if he fail, we are all broke.°   290

FREDERICK Oh, let him alone for that matter: he's of a damned
stingy quality, that will secure our stock. I know not in what
danger it were indeed if the jilt should pretend she's in love with
him, for 'tis a kind believing coxcomb; otherwise, if he part with
more than a piece of eight, geld him—for which offer he may   295
chance to be beaten, if she be a whore of the first rank.

BELVILE Nay, the rogue will not be easily beaten, he's stout enough.
Perhaps, if they talk beyond his capacity, he may chance to exercise

his courage upon some of them; else I'm sure they'll find it as
difficult to beat·as to please him.   300

WILLMORE 'Tis a lucky devil to light upon so kind a wench!

FREDERICK Thou hadst a great deal of talk with thy little gipsy,
couldst thou do no good upon her? For mine was hard-hearted.

WILLMORE Hang her, she was some damned honest person of
quality, I'm sure, she was so very free and witty. If her face be but   305
answerable to her wit and humour, I would be bound to constancy
this month to gain her. In the meantime, have you made no kind
acquaintance since you came to town? You do not use to be honest
so long, gentlemen.

FREDERICK Faith, love has kept us honest: we have been all fired   310
with a beauty newly come to town, the famous Paduana,° Angellica
Bianca.

WILLMORE What, the mistress of the dead Spanish general?

BELVILE Yes, she's now the only adored beauty of all the youth in
Naples, who put on all their charms to appear lovely in her sight: 315
their coaches, liveries, and themselves, all gay as on a monarch's
birthday,° to attract the eyes of this fair charmer, while she has the
pleasure to behold all languish for her that see her.

FREDERICK 'Tis pretty to see with how much love the men regard
her, and how much envy the women.   320

WILLMORE What gallant has she?

BELVILE None: she's exposed to sale, and four days in the week she's
yours—for so much a month.

WILLMORE The very thought of it quenches all manner of fire in me;
yet prithee, let's see her.   325

BELVILE Let's first to dinner, and after that we'll pass the day as you
please; but at night ye must all be at my devotion.

WILLMORE I will not fail you.

    [*Exeunt*]

2.1

The long street

*Enter Belvile and Frederick in masking habits, and Willmore
in his own clothes, with a vizard in his hand*

WILLMORE But why thus disguised and muzzled?

BELVILE Because whatever extravagances we commit in these faces,
our own may not be obliged to answer 'em.

WILLMORE I should have changed my eternal buff too; but no
matter, my little gipsy would not have found me out then; for if   5
she should change hers, it is impossible I should know her, unless
I should hear her prattle. A pox on't, I cannot get her out of my
head. Pray heaven, if ever I do see her again, she prove damnably
ugly, that I may fortify myself against her tongue.

BELVILE Have a care of love, for o' my conscience she was not of a   10
quality to give thee any hopes.°

WILLMORE Pox on 'em, why do they draw a man in then? She has
played with my heart so, that 'twill never lie still, till I have met
with some kind wench that will play the game out with me. Oh
for my arms full of soft, white, kind—woman! such as I fancy   15
Angellica.

BELVILE This is her house, if you were but in stock to get admittance. They have not dined yet: I perceive the picture is not out.

Enter Blunt

WILLMORE I long to see the shadow of the fair substance; a man may
gaze on that for nothing.   20

BLUNT Colonel, thy hand—and thine, Fred. I have been an ass, a
deluded fool, a very coxcomb from my birth till this hour, and
heartily repent my little faith.

BELVILE What the devil's the matter with thee, Ned?

[BLUNT] Oh, such a mistress, Fred, such a girl!   25

WILLMORE Ha! Where?

FREDERICK Aye, where?

[BLUNT] So fond, so amorous, so toying and so fine; and all for sheer
love, ye rogue! Oh, how she looked and kissed, and soothed my
heart from my bosom; I cannot think I was awake, and yet   30
methinks I see and feel her charms still!—Fred, try if she have not
left the taste of her balmy kisses upon my lips.

[Blunt] kisses [Frederick]

BELVILE Ha, ha, ha!

WILLMORE Death, man, where is she?

[BLUNT] What a dog was I to stay in dull England so long! How have   35
I laughed at the colonel when he sighed for love! But now the little
archer has revenged him, and by this one dart, I can guess at all
his joys, which then I took for fancies, mere dreams and fables.
Well, I'm resolved to sell all in Essex, and plant here forever.

BELVILE What a blessing 'tis, thou hast a mistress thou dar'st boast   40
of; for I know thy humour is rather to have a proclaimed clap, than
a secret amour.

WILLMORE Dost know her name?

BLUNT Her name? No, 'adsheartlikins, what care I for names? She's
fair, young, brisk and kind, even to ravishment; and what a pox   45
care I for knowing her by any other title?

WILLMORE Didst give her anything?

BLUNT Give her! Ha, ha, ha! Why, she's a person of quality; that's
a good one, give her! 'Adsheartlikins, dost think such creatures are
to be bought? Or are we provided for such a purchase? Give her,   50
quoth ye? Why, she presented me with this bracelet, for the toy of
a diamond I used to wear. No, gentlemen, Ned Blunt is not
everybody.° She expects me again tonight.

WILLMORE Egad, that's well; we'll all go.

BLUNT Not a soul: no, gentlemen, you are wits; I am a dull country   55
rogue, I.

FREDERICK Well, sir, for all your person of quality, I shall be very glad
to understand your purse be secure: 'tis our whole estate at present,
which we are loth to hazard in one bottom.° Come, sir, unlade.

BLUNT Take the necessary trifle, useless now to me, that am beloved   60
by such a gentlewoman. 'Adsheartlikins, money! Here, take mine
too.

FREDERICK No, keep that to be cozened, that we may laugh.

WILLMORE Cozened! Death! Would I could meet with one that
would cozen me of all the love I could spare tonight.   65

FREDERICK Pox, 'tis some common whore, upon my life.

BLUNT A whore! Yes, with such clothes, such jewels, such a house,
such furniture, and so attended! A whore!

BELVILE Why yes,° sir, they are whores, though they'll neither
entertain you with drinking, swearing, or bawdry; are whores in all   70
those gay clothes, and right jewels; are whores with those great
houses richly furnished with velvet beds, store of plate, handsome
attendance, and fine coaches; are whores, and arrant ones.

WILLMORE Pox on't, where do these fine whores live?

BELVILE Where no rogues in office, ycleped constables, dare give 'em   75
laws, nor the wine-inspired bullies of the town break their
windows; yet they are whores, though this Essex calf° believe 'em
persons of quality.

BLUNT 'Adsheartlikins, y'are all fools; there are things about this
Essex calf, that shall take with the ladies, beyond all your wit and   80
parts. This shape and size, gentlemen, are not to be despised; my
waist too, tolerably long, with other inviting signs that shall be
nameless.

WILLMORE Egad, I believe he may have met with some person of
quality that may be kind to him.   85

BELVILE Dost thou perceive any such tempting things about him,
that should make a fine woman, and of quality, pick him out from
all mankind, to throw away her youth and beauty upon; nay, and
her dear heart too? No, no, Angellica has raised the price too high.

WILLMORE May she languish for mankind till she die, and be   90
damned for that one sin alone.

> *Enter two bravos [Biskey and Sebastian], and hang up a*
> *great picture of Angellica's against the balcony, and two little*
> *ones at each side of the door*

BELVILE See there the fair sign to the inn where a man may lodge
that's fool enough to give her price.

> *Willmore gazes on the picture*

BLUNT 'Adsheartlikins, gentlemen, what's this?

BELVILE A famous courtesan, that's to be sold.   95

BLUNT How, to be sold! Nay then, I have nothing to say to her. Sold!
What impudence is practised in this country! With what order and
decency whoring's established here by virtue of the Inquisition!
Come, let's begone, I'm sure we're no chapmen for this commodity.   100

FREDERICK Thou art none, I'm sure, unless thou couldst have her in
thy bed at a price of a coach in the street.

WILLMORE How wondrous fair she is. A thousand crowns a month?
By heaven, as many kingdoms were too little. A plague of this
poverty, of which I ne'er complain but when it hinders my   105
approach to beauty, which virtue ne'er could purchase.

> *[Willmore] turns from the picture*

BLUNT What's this?° (*Reads*) 'A thousand crowns a month'! 'Adsheartlikins, here's a sum! Sure 'tis a mistake. [*To bravo*] Hark you,
friend, does she take or give so much by the month?

FREDERICK A thousand crowns! Why, 'tis a portion for the Infanta.°   110
BLUNT Hark'ee, friends, won't she trust?°
BRAVO This is a trade, sir, that cannot live by credit.°
  Enter Don Pedro in masquerade, followed by Stephano
BELVILE See, here's more company; let's walk off awhile.
  Exeunt [Belvile, Willmore, Frederick, and Blunt]; Pedro reads
PEDRO Fetch me a thousand crowns, I never wished to buy this
  beauty at an easier rate.   115
  [Pedro] passes off [the stage]. Enter Angellica and Moretta in
  the balcony, and draw a silk curtain
ANGELLICA Prithee, what said those fellows to thee?
BRAVO Madam, the first were admirers of beauty only, but no
  purchasers; they were merry with your price and picture, laughed
  at the sum, and so passed off.
ANGELLICA No matter, I'm not displeased with their rallying;   120
  their wonder feeds my vanity, and he that wishes but to buy
  gives me more pride, than he that gives my price can make my
  pleasure.
BRAVO Madam, the last I knew through all his disguises to be Don
  Pedro, nephew to the general, and who was with him in Pamplona.   125
ANGELLICA Don Pedro, my old gallant's nephew! When his uncle
  died he left him a vast sum of money; it is he who was so in love
  with me at Padua, and who used to make the general so jealous.
MORETTA Is this he that used to prance before our window, and take
  such care to show himself an amorous ass? If I am not mistaken,   130
  he is the likeliest man to give your price.
ANGELLICA The man is brave and generous, but of an humour so
  uneasy and inconstant that the victory over his heart is as soon lost
  as won: a slave that can add little to the triumph of the conqueror;
  but inconstancy's the sin of all mankind, therefore I'm resolved   135
  that nothing but gold shall charm my heart.
MORETTA I'm glad on't: 'tis only interest that women of our
  profession ought to consider, though I wonder what has kept you
  from that general disease of our sex so long, I mean that of being
  in love.   140
ANGELLICA A kind, but sullen star under which I had the happiness
  to be born. Yet I have had no time for love: the bravest and noblest
  of mankind have purchased my favours at so dear a rate, as if no
  coin but gold were current with our trade. But here's Don Pedro
  again; fetch me my lute, for 'tis for him, or Don Antonio the   145
  viceroy's son, that I have spread my nets.

Enter at one door Don Pedro, Stephano; Don Antonio and Diego [his page] at the other door with people following him in masquerade, anticly attired, some with music. [Angellica closes the curtain. Pedro and Antonio] both go up to the picture

ANTONIO A thousand crowns! Had not the painter flattered her, I should not think it dear.

PEDRO Flattered her! By heaven, he cannot. I have seen the original, nor is there one charm here more than adorns her face and eyes; 150 all this soft and sweet, with a certain languishing air, that no artist can represent.

ANTONIO What I heard of her beauty before had fired my soul, but this confirmation of it has blown it to a flame.

PEDRO Ha! 155

PAGE [to Antonio] Sir, I have known you throw away a thousand crowns on a worse face, and though you're near your marriage, you may venture a little love here; Florinda will not miss it.

PEDRO (aside) Ha! Florinda! Sure 'tis Antonio.

ANTONIO Florinda! name not those distant joys; there's not one 160 thought of her will check my passion here.

PEDRO [aside] Florinda scorned! And all my hopes defeated, of the possession of Angellica!

A noise of a lute above. Antonio gazes up

Her injuries, by heaven, he shall not boast of.

SONG (*to a lute above*)°

 When Damon first began to love   165
 He languished in a soft desire,
 And knew not how the gods to move,
 To lessen or increase his fire:
 For Celia in her charming eyes
Wore all Love's sweets, and all his cruelties.   170

 But as beneath a shade he lay,
 Weaving of flowers for Celia's hair,
 She chanced to lead her flock that way,
 And saw the amorous shepherd there.
 She gazed around upon the place,   175
 And saw the grove (resembling night)
 To all the joys of love invite,
Whilst guilty smiles and blushes dressed her face.
At this the bashful youth all transport grew,

> *And with kind force he taught the virgin how*   180
> *To yield what all his sighs could never do.*

> *Angellica throws open the curtains, and bows to Antonio, who*
> *pulls off his vizard and bows and blows up kisses. Pedro,*
> *unseen, looks in his face. [The curtains close]*

ANTONIO By heaven, she's charming fair!

PEDRO 'Tis he, the false Antonio!

ANTONIO (*to the bravo*) Friend, where must I pay my offering of love?
My thousand crowns I mean.   185

PEDRO That offering I have designed to make,
And yours will come too late.

ANTONIO Prithee begone: I shall grow angry else,
And then thou art not safe.

PEDRO My anger may be fatal, sir, as yours,   190
And he that enters here may prove this truth.°

ANTONIO I know not who thou art, but I am sure thou'rt worth my
killing, for aiming at Angellica.

> *[Antonio and Pedro] draw and fight. Enter Willmore and Blunt*

BLUNT 'Adsheartlikins, here's fine doings.

WILLMORE Tilting° for the wench, I'm sure.—Nay gad, if that   195
would win her, I have as good a sword as the best of ye.

> *[Blunt and Willmore] draw and part [Antonio and Pedro]*

Put up, put up, and take another time and place, for this is
designed for lovers only.

> *They all put up [their swords]*

PEDRO We are prevented; dare you meet me tomorrow on the Molo?°
For I've a title to a better quarrel,   200
That of Florinda, in whose credulous heart,
Thou'st made an interest, and destroyed my hopes.

ANTONIO Dare!
I'll meet thee there as early as the day.

PEDRO We will come thus disguised, that whosoever chance to get   205
the better, he may escape unknown.

ANTONIO It shall be so.

> *Exeunt Pedro and Stephano*

Who should this rival be? unless the English colonel, of whom I've
often heard Don Pedro speak: it must be he, and time he were
removed, who lays a claim to all my happiness.   210

> *Willmore having gazed all this while on the picture, pulls*
> *down a little one*

WILLMORE This posture's loose and negligent,
The sight on't would beget a warm desire
In souls whom impotence and age had chilled.
This must along with me.

BRAVO What means this rudeness, sir? Restore the picture.   215

ANTONIO [*aside*] Ha! Rudeness committed to the fair Angellica!—
Restore the picture, sir.

WILLMORE Indeed I will not, sir.

ANTONIO By heaven, but you shall.

WILLMORE Nay, do not show your sword: if you do, by this dear   220
beauty, I will show mine too.

ANTONIO What right can you pretend to't?

WILLMORE That of possession, which I will maintain. You, perhaps,
have a thousand crowns to give for the original.

ANTONIO No matter, sir, you shall restore the picture—   225
[*The curtains open;*] *Angellica and Moretta* [*appear*] *above*

ANGELLICA Oh, Moretta! What's the matter?

ANTONIO —Or leave your life behind.

WILLMORE Death! you lie; I will do neither.
[*Willmore and Antonio*] *fight; the Spaniards join with*
Antonio, Blunt [*joins with Willmore,*] *laying on like mad*

ANGELLICA Hold, I command you, if for me you fight.
They leave off and bow

WILLMORE [*aside*] How heavenly fair she is! Ah, plague of her price.   230

ANGELLICA You, sir, in buff, you that appear a soldier, that first
began this insolence—

WILLMORE 'Tis true, I did so, if you call it insolence for a man to
preserve himself: I saw your charming picture and was wounded;
quite through my soul each pointed beauty ran; and wanting a   235
thousand crowns to procure my remedy, I laid this little picture to
my bosom, which, if you cannot allow me, I'll resign.

ANGELLICA No, you may keep the trifle.

ANTONIO You shall first ask me leave, and [*flourishing his sword*]
this.   240
[*They*] *fight again as before. Enter Belvile and Frederick,*
who join with the English

ANGELLICA Hold! Will you ruin me?—Biskey, Sebastian, part 'em.
The Spaniards are beaten off. [*Exeunt all the men*]

MORETTA Oh madam, we're undone! A pox upon that rude fellow,
he's set on to ruin us: we shall never see good days, till all these
fighting poor rogues are sent to the galleys.

Enter Belvile, Blunt, Frederick, and Willmore with his shirt bloody

BLUNT 'Adsheartlikins, beat me at this sport, and I'll ne'er wear 245 sword more.

BELVILE (*to Willmore*) The devil's in thee for a mad fellow, thou art always one at an unlucky adventure. Come, let's begone whilst we're safe, and remember these are Spaniards, a sort of people that know how to revenge an affront.° 250

FREDERICK [*to Willmore*] You bleed! I hope you are not wounded.

WILLMORE Not much: a plague on your dons, if they fight no better they'll ne'er recover Flanders.° What the devil was't to them that I took down the picture?

BLUNT Took it! 'Adsheartlikins, we'll have the great one too; 'tis 255 ours by conquest. Prithee, help me up, and I'll pull it down.

ANGELLICA [*to Willmore*] Stay, sir, and ere you affront me farther, let me know how you durst commit this outrage. To you I speak sir, for you appear a gentleman.

WILLMORE To me, madam? [*To his companions, taking leave of them*] 260 Gentlemen, your servant.

Belvile stays [Willmore]

BELVILE Is the devil in thee? Dost know the danger of entering the house of an incensed courtesan?

WILLMORE I thank you for your care, but there are other matters in hand, there are, though we have no great temptation. Death! let me go. · 265

FREDERICK Yes, to your lodging, if you will; but not in here. Damn these gay harlots; by this hand, I'll have as sound and handsome a whore for a patacoon. Death, man, she'll murder thee.

WILLMORE Oh! fear me not. Shall I not venture where a beauty calls, a lovely charming beauty? For fear of danger! when, by heaven, 270 there's none so great as to long for her, whilst I want money to purchase her.

FREDERICK° Therefore 'tis loss of time, unless you had the thousand crowns to pay.

WILLMORE It may be she may give a favour; at least I shall have the 275 pleasure of saluting° her when I enter and when I depart.

BELVILE Pox, she'll as soon lie with thee as kiss thee, and sooner stab than do either. You shall not go.

ANGELLICA Fear not, sir, all I have to wound with is my eyes.

BLUNT Let him go: 'adsheartlikins, I believe the gentlewoman means well. 280

BELVILE Well, take thy fortune; we'll expect you in the next street. Farewell, fool, farewell.

WILLMORE 'Bye, colonel.
　　[Willmore] goes in
FREDERICK The rogue's stark mad for a wench.
　　Exeunt

[2.2]

A fine chamber
Enter Willmore, Angellica, and Moretta°

ANGELLICA Insolent sir, how durst you pull down my picture?

WILLMORE Rather, how durst you set it up, to tempt poor amorous
　　mortals with so much excellence? which I find you have but too
　　well consulted by the unmerciful price you set upon't. Is all this
　　heaven of beauty shown to move despair in those that cannot buy?　　5
　　and can you think th'effects of that despair should be less
　　extravagant than I have shown?

ANGELLICA I sent for you to ask my pardon, sir, not to aggravate
　　your crime: I thought I should have seen you at my feet imploring
　　it.　　10

WILLMORE You are deceived; I came to rail at you,
　　And rail such truths too, as shall let you see
　　The vanity of that pride, which taught you how
　　To set such price on sin:°
　　For such it is whilst that which is love's due　　15
　　Is meanly bartered for.

ANGELLICA Ha, ha, ha! Alas, good captain, what pity 'tis your
　　edifying doctrine will do no good upon me.—Moretta! fetch the
　　gentleman a glass, and let him survey himself, to see what charms
　　he has—(*aside, in a soft tone*) and guess my business.　　20

MORETTA He knows himself of old: I believe those breeches and he
　　have been acquainted ever since he was beaten at Worcester.°

ANGELLICA Nay, do not abuse the poor creature.

MORETTA Good weather-beaten corporal,° will you march off? We
　　have no need of your doctrine, though you have of our charity: but　　25
　　at present we have no scraps, we can afford no kindness for God's
　　sake. In fine, sirrah, the price is too high i'th' mouth° for you;
　　therefore troop, I say.

WILLMORE [*offering money to Moretta*] Here, good forewoman of the
　　shop, serve me,° and I'll be gone.　　30

MORETTA Keep it to pay your laundress (your linen stinks of the gun room),° for here's no selling by retail.

WILLMORE Thou hast sold plenty of thy stale ware at a cheap rate.

MORETTA Aye, the more silly kind heart I, but this is an age wherein beauty is at higher rates. In fine, you know the price of this.   35

WILLMORE I grant you 'tis here set down, a thousand crowns a month: pray, how much may come to my share for a pistole? Bawd, take your black lead and sum it up, that I may have a pistole's worth of this vain gay thing, and I'll trouble you no more.

MORETTA [aside] Pox on him, he'll fret me to death.—Abominable   40
fellow, I tell thee, we only sell by the whole piece.

WILLMORE 'Tis very hard, the whole cargo or nothing. [To Angel-
lica] Faith, madam, my stock will not reach it, I cannot be your chapman. Yet I have countrymen in town, merchants of love like me: I'll see if they'll put in for a share; we cannot lose much by it,   45
and what we have no use for, we'll sell upon the Friday's mart, at 'Who gives more?' I am studying, madam, how to purchase you, though at present I am unprovided of money.

ANGELLICA [aside] Sure, this from any other man would anger me; nor shall he know the conquest he has made. [To Willmore] Poor   50
angry man, how I despise this railing.

WILLMORE Yes, I am poor; but I'm a gentleman,°
And one that scorns this baseness which you practise.
Poor as I am, I would not sell myself,
No, not to gain your charming high-prized person.   55
Though I admire you strangely for your beauty,
Yet I contemn your mind.
And yet I would at any rate enjoy you,
At your own rate, but cannot: see here
The only sum I can command on earth;   60
I know not where to eat when this is gone.
Yet such a slave I am to love and beauty,
This last reserve I'll sacrifice to enjoy you.
Nay, do not frown, I know you're to be bought,
And would be bought by me, by me,   65
For a mean trifling sum, if I could pay it down:
Which happy knowledge I will still repeat,
And lay it to my heart; it has a virtue in't,
And soon will cure those wounds your eyes have made.
And yet, there's something so divinely powerful there—   70
Nay, I will gaze, to let you see my strength.

Holds her, looks on her, and pauses and sighs
By heaven, bright creature, I would not for the world
Thy fame were half so fair as is thy face.
    Turns her away from him
ANGELLICA (*aside*) His words go through me to the very soul.
    [*To Willmore*] If you have nothing else to say to me—   75
WILLMORE Yes; you shall hear how infamous you are,
    For which I do not hate thee,
    But that secures my heart, and all the flames it feels
    Are but so many lusts;
    I know it by their sudden bold intrusion.   80
    The fire's impatient and betrays; 'tis false:
    For had it been the purer flame of love,
    I should have pined and languished at your feet,
    Ere found the impudence to have discovered it.
    I now dare stand your scorn, and your denial.   85
MORETTA [*aside*] Sure she's bewitched, that she can stand thus
    tamely and hear his saucy railing.—Sirrah, will you be gone?
ANGELLICA (*to Moretta*) How dare you take this liberty? With-
    draw.°—Pray tell me, sir, are not you guilty of the same mercenary
    crime? When a lady is proposed to you for a wife, you never   90
    ask how fair, discreet, or virtuous she is; but what's her fortune:
    which if but small, you cry 'she will not do my business', and
    basely leave her, though she languish for you. Say, is not this as
    poor?
WILLMORE It is a barbarous custom, which I will scorn to defend in   95
    our sex, and do despise in yours.
ANGELLICA Thou'rt a brave fellow! put up thy gold, and know
    That were thy fortune large as is thy soul,
    Thou shouldst not buy my love, couldst thou forget
    Those mean effects of vanity   100
    Which set me out to sale,
    And as a lover, prize my yielding joys.°
    Canst thou believe they'll be entirely thine,
    Without considering they were mercenary?
WILLMORE I cannot tell, I must bethink me first. (*Aside*) Ha, death,   105
    I'm going to believe her.
ANGELLICA Prithee, confirm that faith; or if thou canst not, flatter
    me a little, 'twill please me from thy mouth.
WILLMORE (*aside*) Curse on thy charming tongue! dost thou return
    My feigned contempt with so much subtlety?   110

[*To Angellica*] Thou'st found the easiest way into my heart,
Though I yet know, that all thou say'st is false.
    [*Willmore*] turn[*s*] *from her in rage*
ANGELLICA By all that's good, 'tis real;
    I never loved before, though oft a mistress.
    Shall my first vows be slighted?   115
WILLMORE (*aside*) What can she mean?
ANGELLICA (*in an angry tone*) I find you cannot credit me.
WILLMORE I know you take me for an arrant ass,
    An ass that may be soothed into belief,
    And then be used at pleasure;   120
    But, madam, I have been so often cheated
    By perjured, soft, deluding hypocrites,
    That I've no faith left for the cozening sex,
    Especially for women of your trade.
ANGELLICA The low esteem you have of me, perhaps   125
    May bring my heart again:
    For I have pride, that yet surmounts my love.
        She turns with pride; he holds her
WILLMORE Throw off this pride, this enemy to bliss,
    And show the power of love: 'tis with those arms
    I can be only vanquished, made a slave.   130
ANGELLICA Is all my mighty expectation vanished?
    No, I will not hear thee talk: thou hast a charm
    In every word that draws my heart away;
    And all the thousand trophies I designed,
    Thou hast undone. Why art thou soft?   135
    Thy looks are bravely rough, and meant for war.
    Couldst thou not storm on still?
    I then perhaps had been as free as thou.
WILLMORE (*aside*) Death, how she throws her fire about my soul!
    —Take heed, fair creature, how you raise my hopes,   140
    Which once assumed pretends to all dominion.°
    There's not a joy thou hast in store
    I shall not then command;
    For which I'll pay thee back my soul, my life!
    Come, let's begin th'account this happy minute!   145
ANGELLICA And will you pay me then the price I ask?
WILLMORE Oh, why dost thou draw me from an awful worship,
    By showing thou art no divinity?
    Conceal the fiend, and show me all the angel!

Keep me but ignorant, and I'll be devout   150
And pay my vows for ever at this shrine.
  Kneels and kisses her hand

ANGELLICA The pay I mean, is but thy love for mine.
Can you give that?

WILLMORE: Entirely; come, let's withdraw, where I'll renew my
vows, and breathe 'em with such ardour thou shalt not doubt my   155
zeal.

ANGELLICA Thou hast a power too strong to be resisted.
  Exeunt Willmore and Angellica

MORETTA Now, my curse go with you. Is all our project fallen to
this: to love the only enemy to our trade? Nay, to love such a
shameroon; a very beggar, nay, a pirate beggar, whose business is 160
to rifle, and be gone; a no-purchase, no-pay tatterdemalion, and
English picaroon; a rogue that fights for daily drink, and takes a
pride in being loyally lousy!° Oh, I could curse now, if I durst.
This is the fate of most whores.

   Trophies, which from believing fops we win,   165
   Are spoils to those who cozen us again.

  [*Exit*]

3.1

A street°

*Enter Florinda, Valeria, [and] Hellena, in antic, different
dresses, from what they were in before; [and] Callis, attending*

FLORINDA I wonder what should make my brother in so ill a
humour? I hope he has not found out our ramble this morning.

HELLENA No: if he had, we should have heard on't at both ears, and
have been mewed up this afternoon; which I would not for the
world should have happened. Hey ho, I'm as sad as a lover's lute. 5

VALERIA Well, methinks we have learnt this trade of gipsies as
readily as if we had been bred upon the road to Loretto;° and yet
I did so fumble, when I told the stranger his fortune, that I was
afraid I should have told my own and yours by mistake. But,
methinks, Hellena has been very serious ever since. 10

FLORINDA I would give my garters she were in love, to be revenged
upon her for abusing me.—How is't, Hellena?

HELLENA Ah, would I had never seen my mad monsieur! And yet,
for all your laughing, I am not in love; and yet this small
acquaintance, o' my conscience, will never out of my head. 15

VALERIA Ha, ha, ha; I laugh to think how thou art fitted with a lover,
a fellow that I warrant loves every new face he sees.

HELLENA Hum, he has not kept his word with me here, and may be
taken up: that thought is not very pleasant to me. What the deuce
should this be now, that I feel? 20

VALERIA What is't like?

HELLENA Nay, the lord knows; but if I should be hanged, I cannot
choose but be angry and afraid, when I think that mad fellow
should be in love with anybody but me. What to think of myself
I know not: would I could meet with some true damned gipsy, that 25
I might know my fortune.

VALERIA Know it! why there's nothing so easy: thou wilt love this
wandering inconstant, till thou find'st thyself hanged about his
neck, and then be as mad to get free again.

FLORINDA Yes, Valeria, we shall see her bestride his baggage horse, 30
and follow him to the campaign.

HELLENA So, so, now you are provided for, there's no care taken of
poor me. But since you have set my heart a-wishing, I am resolved
to know for what; I will not die of the pip,° so I will not.

FLORINDA Art thou mad to talk so? Who will like thee well enough   35
to have thee, that hears what a mad wench thou art?

HELLENA Like me! I don't intend every he that likes me shall have
me, but he that I like: I should have stayed in the nunnery still, if
I had liked my lady abbess as well as she liked me. No, I came
thence not, as my wise brother imagines, to take an eternal farewell   40
of the world, but to love, and to be beloved; and I will be beloved,
or I'll get one of your men, so I will.

VALERIA Am I put into the number of lovers?

HELLENA You? why, coz, I know thou'rt too good-natured to leave
us in any design: thou wouldst venture a cast,° though thou comest   45
off a loser, especially with such a gamester. I observed° your man,
and your willing ear incline that way; and if you are not a lover,
'tis an art soon learnt, that I find. (*Sighs*)

FLORINDA I wonder how you learned to love so easily. I had a
thousand charms to meet my eyes and ears, ere I could yield; and   50
'twas the knowledge of Belvile's merit, not the surprising person,
took my soul. Thou art too rash, to give a heart at first sight.

HELLENA Hang your considering lover; I never thought beyond the
fancy that 'twas a very pretty, idle, silly kind of pleasure to pass one's
time with: to write little soft nonsensical billets, and with great   55
difficulty and danger receive answers, in which I shall have my beauty
praised, my wit admired (though little or none), and have the vanity
and power to know I am desirable. Then I have the more inclination
that way, because I am to be a nun, and so shall not be suspected to
have any such earthly thoughts about me; but when I walk thus, and   60
sigh thus, they'll think my mind's upon my monastery, and cry, 'how
happy 'tis she's so resolved'; but not a word° of man.

FLORINDA What a mad creature's this!

HELLENA I'll warrant, if my brother hears either of you sigh, he cries
gravely, 'I fear you have the indiscretion to be in love, but take   65
heed of the honour of our house, and your own unspotted fame',
and so he conjures on till he has laid the soft-winged god in your
hearts, or broke the bird's nest.°

    Enter Belvile, Frederick, and Blunt

But see, here comes your lover; but where's my inconstant? Let's
step aside, and we may learn something.   70

    [*Hellena, Florinda, Valeria, and Callis*] *go aside*

BELVILE What means this? The picture's taken in.

BLUNT It may be the wench is good-natured, and will be kind gratis.
Your friend's a proper handsome fellow.

BELVILE I rather think she has cut his throat and is fled. I am mad
he should throw himself into dangers; pox on't, I shall want him,   75
too, at night. Let's knock and ask for him.

HELLENA My heart goes a pit-a-pat, for fear 'tis my man they talk
of.
    [The men] knock; Moretta [appears] above

MORETTA What would you have?

BELVILE Tell the stranger that entered here about two hours ago,   80
that his friends stay here for him.

MORETTA A curse upon him for Moretta: would he were at the devil;
but he's coming to you.
    [Enter Willmore, from Angellica's house]

HELLENA *[aside]* Aye, aye, 'tis he! Oh, how this vexes me.

BELVILE And how and how, dear lad, has fortune smiled? Are we to   85
break her windows, or raise up altars to her, ha?

WILLMORE Does not my fortune sit triumphant on my brow? Dost
not see the little wanton god there all gay and smiling? Have I not
an air about my face and eyes, that distinguish me from the crowd
of common lovers?° By heaven, Cupid's quiver has not half so   90
many darts as her eyes! Oh, such a bona roba! to sleep in her arms
in lying in fresco, all perfumed air about me.

HELLENA *(aside)* Here's fine encouragement for me to fool on.

WILLMORE Hark'ee, where didst thou purchase that rich canary we
drank today? Tell me, that I may adore the spigot, and sacrifice to   95
the butt! The juice was divine, into which I must dip my rosary,
and then bless all things that I would have bold or fortunate.

BELVILE Well, sir, let's go take a bottle, and hear the story of your
success.

FREDERICK Would not French wine do better?   100

WILLMORE Damn the hungry balderdash; cheerful sack has a generous virtue in't inspiring a successful confidence, gives eloquence to
the tongue, and vigour to the soul, and has in a few hours
completed all my hopes and wishes! There's nothing left to raise
a new desire in me. Come, let's be gay and wanton; and,   105
gentlemen, study, study what you want, for here are friends that
will supply gentlemen. *[Jingles gold]* Hark! what a charming° sound
they make: 'tis he and she gold° whilst here, and shall beget new
pleasures every moment.

BLUNT But hark'ee, sir, you are not married, are you?   110

WILLMORE All the honey of matrimony, but none of the sting,°
friend.

BLUNT 'Adsheartlikins, thou'rt a fortunate rogue!

WILLMORE I am so, sir, let these inform you! Ha, how sweetly they
   chime! Pox of poverty, it makes a man a slave, makes wit and   115
   honour sneak; my soul grew lean and rusty for want of credit.

BLUNT 'Adsheartlikins, this I like well, it looks like my lucky bargain!
   Oh, how I long for the approach of my squire, that is to conduct
   me to her house again. Why, here's two provided for.

FREDERICK By this light, y'are happy men.   120

BLUNT Fortune is pleased to smile on us, gentlemen, to smile on us.
       Enter Sancho and pulls down Blunt by the sleeve. They go aside

SANCHO Sir, my lady expects you. She has removed all that might
   oppose your will and pleasure, and is impatient till you come.

BLUNT Sir, I'll attend you. [*Aside*] Oh, the happiest rogue! I'll take
   no leave, lest they either dog me, or stay me.   125
       Exit [Blunt] with Sancho

BELVILE But then the little gipsy is forgot?

WILLMORE A mischief on thee for putting her into my thoughts, I
   had quite forgot her else, and this night's debauch had drunk her
   quite down.

HELLENA Had it so, good captain!   130
       [*Hellena*] *claps [Willmore] on the back*

WILLMORE (*aside*) Ha! I hope she did not hear me.

HELLENA What, afraid of such a champion?

WILLMORE Oh, you're a fine lady of your word, are you not? To
   make a man languish a whole day—

HELLENA In tedious search of me.   135

WILLMORE Egad, child, thou'rt in the right: hadst thou seen what a
   melancholy dog I have been ever since I was a lover, how I have
   walked the streets like a capuchin,° with my hands in my sleeves,
   faith, sweetheart, thou wouldst pity me.

HELLENA [*aside*] Now, if I should be hanged, I can't be angry with   140
   him, he dissembles so heartily. [*To Willmore*] Alas, good captain,
   what pains you have taken: now were I ungrateful not to reward
   so true a servant.

WILLMORE Poor soul, that's kindly said, I see thou bearest a
   conscience. Come then, for a beginning show me thy dear face.   145

HELLENA I'm afraid, my small acquaintance, you have been staying
   that swingeing stomach° you boasted of this morning: I then
   remember my little collation would have gone down with you,
   without the sauce of a handsome face; is your stomach so queasy
   now?   150

35

WILLMORE Faith, long fasting, child, spoils a man's appetite. Yet if
you durst treat, I could so lay about me still—

HELLENA And would you fall to, before a priest says grace?

WILLMORE Oh fie, fie, what an old out-of-fashioned thing hast thou
named? Thou couldst not dash me more out of countenance   155
shouldst thou show me an ugly face.

> *Whilst he is seemingly courting Hellena, enter Angellica,*
> *Moretta, Biskey, and Sebastian, all in masquerade. Angellica*
> *sees Willmore and stares*

ANGELLICA Heavens, 'tis he! and passionately fond to see another
woman.

MORETTA What could you less expect from such a swaggerer?

ANGELLICA Expect? As much as I paid him: a heart entire,   160
Which I had pride enough to think whene'er I gave,
It would have raised the man above the vulgar,
Made him all soul! and that all soft and constant.

HELLENA You see, captain, how willing I am to be friends with you
(till time and ill luck make us lovers), and ask you the question   165
first, rather than put your modesty to the blush, by asking me; for
alas, I know you captains are such strict men, and such severe
observers of your vows to chastity, that 'twill be hard to prevail
with your tender conscience to marry a young willing maid.

WILLMORE Do not abuse me, for fear I should take thee at thy word,   170
and marry thee indeed, which I'm sure will be revenge sufficient.

HELLENA O' my conscience, that will be our destiny, because we are
both of one humour: I am as inconstant as you, for I have
considered, captain, that a handsome woman has a great deal to do
whilst her face is good, for then is our harvest-time to gather   175
friends; and should I in these days of my youth, catch a fit of
foolish constancy, I were undone; 'tis loitering by daylight in our
great journey. Therefore, I declare, I'll allow but one year for love,
one year for indifference, and one year for hate; and then, go hang
yourself: for I profess myself the gay, the kind, and the inconstant.   180
The devil's in't if this won't please you.

WILLMORE Oh, most damnably. I have a heart with a hole quite
through it too, no prison mine to keep a mistress in.

ANGELLICA (*aside*) Perjured man! how I believe thee now.

HELLENA Well, I see our business as well as humours are alike: yours   185
to cozen as many maids as will trust you, and I as many men as
have faith. See if I have not as desperate a lying look, as you can
have for the heart of you.

[Hellena] pulls off her vizard: [Willmore] starts
How do you like it, captain?

WILLMORE Like it! by heaven, I never saw so much beauty! Oh, the   190
charms of those sprightly black eyes, that strangely fair face, full
of smiles and dimples, those soft round melting cherry lips, and
small even white teeth! Not to be expressed, but silently adored!
[Hellena replaces her vizard] Oh, one look more, and strike me
dumb, or I shall repeat nothing else till I'm mad.   195
He seems to court her to pull off her vizard: she refuses

ANGELLICA I can endure no more; nor is it fit to interrupt him, for
if I do, my jealousy has so destroyed my reason, I shall undo him;
therefore I'll retire—*(to one of her bravos)* and you, Sebastian,
follow that woman, and learn who 'tis—*(to the other bravo)* while
you tell the fugitive I would speak to him instantly.   200
*Exit [Angellica.] [During] this [time] Florinda is talking to
Belvile, who stands sullenly. Frederick [is] courting Valeria*

VALERIA Prithee, dear stranger, be not so sullen, for though you have
lost your love, you see my friend frankly offers you hers to play
with in the meantime.

BELVILE Faith, madam, I am sorry I can't play at her game.

FREDERICK *[to Valeria]* Pray leave your intercession and mind your   205
own affair, they'll better agree apart: he's a modest sigher in
company, but alone no woman 'scapes him.

FLORINDA *[aside]* Sure, he does but rally; yet if it should be
true—I'll tempt him farther. *[To Belvile]* Believe me, noble
stranger, I'm no common mistress, and for a little proof on't, wear   210
this jewel. Nay, take it, sir, 'tis right, and bills of exchange° may
sometimes miscarry.

BELVILE Madam, why am I chose out of all mankind to be the object
of your bounty?

VALERIA There's another civil question asked.   215

FREDERICK *[aside]* Pox of's modesty, it spoils his own markets and
hinders mine.

FLORINDA Sir, from my window I have often seen you, and women
of my quality have so few opportunities for love, that we ought to
lose none.   220

FREDERICK Aye, this is something! Here's a woman! *[To Valeria]*
When shall I be blessed with so much kindness from your fair
mouth? *(Aside to Belvile)* Take the jewel, fool.

BELVILE You tempt me strangely, madam, every way—

FLORINDA *(aside)* So, if I find him false, my whole repose is gone.   225

BELVILE —And but for a vow I've made to a very fair lady, this
goodness had subdued me.

FREDERICK [*aside to Belvile*] Pox on't, be kind, in pity to me be kind,
for I am to thrive here but as you treat her friend.

HELLENA Tell me what you did in yonder house, and I'll   230
unmask.

WILLMORE Yonder house? Oh—I went to—a—to—why, there's a
friend of mine lives there.

HELLENA What, a she or a he friend?

WILLMORE A man, upon honour! a man. A she friend? no, no,   235
madam, you have done my business, I thank you.

HELLENA And was't your man friend, that had more darts in's eyes,
than Cupid carries in's whole budget of arrows?

WILLMORE So—

HELLENA 'Ah, such a bona roba! to be in her arms is lying in fresco,   240
all perfumed air about me.' Was this your man friend too?

WILLMORE So—

HELLENA That gave you 'the he and the she gold, that begets young
pleasures'?

WILLMORE Well, well, madam, then you see there are ladies in the   245
world that will not be cruel; there are, madam, there are.

HELLENA And there be men too, as fine, wild, inconstant fellows as
yourself; there be, captain, there be, if you go to that now:
therefore I'm resolved—

WILLMORE Oh!   250

HELLENA —To see your face no more—

WILLMORE Oh!

HELLENA —Till tomorrow.

WILLMORE Egad, you frighted me.

HELLENA Nor then neither, unless you'll swear never to see that lady   255
more.

WILLMORE See her! Why, never to think of womankind again.

HELLENA Kneel, and swear.

[*Willmore*] *kneels;* [*Hellena*] *gives him her hand*

WILLMORE I do, never to think, to see, to love, nor lie—with any
but thyself.   260

HELLENA Kiss the book.

WILLMORE (*kisses her hand*) Oh, most religiously.

HELLENA [*aside*] Now, what a wicked creature am I, to damn a
proper fellow.

CALLIS (*to Florinda*) Madam, I'll stay no longer, 'tis e'en dark.   265

FLORINDA [*to Belvile*] However, sir, I'll leave this with you, that
  when I'm gone, you may repent the opportunity you have lost by
  your modesty.
      [*Florinda*] *gives* [*Belvile*] *the jewel, which is her picture, and*
      exit. He gazes after her

WILLMORE 'Twill be an age till tomorrow, and till then I will most
  impatiently expect you. Adieu, my dear pretty angel.   270
      Exeunt all the women

BELVILE Ha! Florinda's picture: 'twas she herself. What a dull dog
  was I! I would have given the world for one minute's discourse
  with her.

FREDERICK This comes of your modesty! Ah, pox o' your vow, 'twas
  ten to one but we had lost the jewel by't.   275

BELVILE Willmore! The blessed'st opportunity lost! Florinda,
  friends, Florinda!

WILLMORE Ah, rogue! Such black eyes, such a face, such a mouth,
  such teeth—and so much wit!

BELVILE All, all, and a thousand charms besides.   280

WILLMORE Why, dost thou know her?

BELVILE Know her? Aye, aye, and a pox take me with all my heart
  for being modest.

WILLMORE But hark'ee, friend of mine, are you my rival? and have
  I been only beating the bush° all this while?   285

BELVILE I understand thee not. I'm mad, see here—
      [*Belvile*] *shows the picture*

WILLMORE Ha! whose picture's this? 'Tis a fine wench!

FREDERICK The colonel's mistress, sir.

WILLMORE Oh, oh,—here. (*Gives the picture back*) I thought it had
  been another prize. Come, come, a bottle will set thee right again.   290

BELVILE I am content to try, and by that time 'twill be late enough
  for our design.

WILLMORE Agreed.
      Love does all day the soul's great empire keep,
      But wine at night lulls the soft god asleep.   295
      Exeunt

3.2

Lucetta's house°

Enter Blunt and Lucetta with a light

LUCETTA Now we are safe and free: no fears of the coming home of
my old jealous husband, which made me a little thoughtful when
you came in first, but now love is all the business of my soul.

BLUNT I am transported! (*Aside*) Pox on't, that I had but some fine
things to say to her, such as lovers use. I was a fool not to learn   5
of Fred a little by heart before I came. Something I must say. [*To
Lucetta*] 'Adsheartlikins, sweet soul! I am not used to compliment,
but I'm an honest gentleman, and thy humble servant.

LUCETTA I have nothing to pay for so great a favour, but such a love
as cannot but be great, since at first sight of that sweet face and   10
shape, it made me your absolute captive.

BLUNT (*aside*) Kind heart, how prettily she talks! Egad, I'll show her
husband a Spanish trick: send him out of the world, and marry
her; she's damnably in love with me, and will ne'er mind
settlements, and so there's that saved.   15

LUCETTA Well, sir, I'll go and undress me, and be with you instantly.

BLUNT Make haste then, for 'adsheartlikins, dear soul, thou canst not
guess at the pain of a longing lover, when his joys are drawn within
the compass of a few minutes.

LUCETTA You speak my sense, and I'll make haste to prove it.   20

Exit [Lucetta]

BLUNT 'Tis a rare girl, and this one night's enjoyment with her, will
be worth all the days I ever passed in Essex. Would she would go
with me into England; though to say truth, there's plenty of
whores already. But a pox on 'em, they are such mercenary
prodigal whores, that they want such a one as this, that's free and   25
generous, to give 'em good examples. Why, what a house she has,
how rich and fine!

Enter Sancho

SANCHO Sir, my lady has sent me to conduct you to her chamber.

BLUNT Sir, I shall be proud to follow.

Exit Sancho

Here's one of her servants too! 'Adsheartlikins, by this garb and   30
gravity, he might be a justice of peace in Essex, and is but a pimp
here.

Exit

[3.3]

The scene changes to a chamber with an alcove bed in it, a table, etc. Lucetta in bed°

Enter Sancho and Blunt, who takes the candle of Sancho at the door

SANCHO Sir, my commission reaches no farther.

BLUNT Sir, I'll excuse your compliment.

     Exit Sancho

—What, in bed, my sweet mistress?

LUCETTA You see, I still out-do you in kindness.

BLUNT And thou shalt see what haste I'll make to quit scores.° 5
    [*Aside*] Oh, the luckiest rogue!

      [*Blunt*] *undresses himself*°

LUCETTA Should you be false or cruel now!

BLUNT False! 'Adsheartlikins, what dost thou take me for? A Jew? An insensible heathen? A pox of thy old jealous husband; an he were dead, egad, sweet soul, it should be none of my fault, if I did 10
  not marry thee.

LUCETTA It never should be mine.

BLUNT Good soul! I'm the fortunatest dog!

LUCETTA Are you not undressed yet?

BLUNT As much as my impatience will permit. 15
    Goes towards the bed in his shirt, drawers, etc.

LUCETTA Hold, sir, put out the light, it may betray us else.

BLUNT Anything; I need no other light, but that of thine eyes!
    [*Aside*] 'Adsheartlikins, there I think I had it.

      [*Blunt*] *puts out the candle;° the bed descends° [by means of a*
      trap]; he gropes about to find it

Why—why—where am I got? What, not yet? Where are you, sweetest?—Ah, the rogue's silent now, a pretty love-trick this: how 20
she'll laugh at me anon!—You need not, my dear rogue, you need not! I'm all on fire already. Come, come, now call me in pity.— Sure I'm enchanted! I have been round the chamber, and can find neither woman, nor bed. I locked the door, I'm sure she cannot go that way; or if she could, the bed could not.—Enough, enough, my 25
pretty wanton, do not carry the jest too far.—Ha, betrayed! Dogs! Rogues! Pimps! Help! help!

      [*Blunt*] *lights on a trap, and is let down.° Enter Lucetta,*
      Philippo, and Sancho with a light

PHILIPPO Ha, ha, ha, he's dispatched finely.

LUCETTA Now, sir, had I been coy, we had missed of this booty.

PHILIPPO Nay, when I saw 'twas a substantial fool, I was mollified;   30
but when you dote upon a serenading coxcomb, upon a face, fine
clothes, and a lute, it makes me rage.

LUCETTA You know I was never guilty of that folly, my dear Philippo,
but with yourself. But come, let's see what we have got by this.

PHILIPPO A rich coat! Sword and hat; these breeches, too, are   35
well-lined! See here, a gold watch! a purse—ha! gold: at least two
hundred pistoles! A bunch of diamond rings, and one with the
family arms! A gold box, with a medal of his king,° and his lady
mother's picture! These were sacred relics, believe me! See, the
waistband of his breeches have a mine of gold: old Queen Bess's;   40
we have a quarrel to her ever since eighty-eight, and may therefore
justify the theft,° the Inquisition might have committed it.

LUCETTA See, a bracelet of bowed gold!° These his sisters tied about
his arm at parting. But well, for all this, I fear his being a stranger
may make a noise and hinder our trade with them hereafter.   45

PHILIPPO That's our security; he is not only a stranger to us, but to the
country too. The common shore into which he is descended, thou
know'st, conducts him into another street, which this light will hinder
him from ever finding again. He knows neither your name, nor that of
the street where your house is; nay, nor the way to his own lodgings.   50

LUCETTA And art not thou an unmerciful rogue, not to afford him
one night for all this? I should not have been such a Jew.

PHILIPPO Blame me not, Lucetta, to keep as much of thee as I can
to myself. Come, that thought makes me wanton: let's to bed!—
Sancho, lock up these.   55

> This is the fleece which fools do bear,
> Designed for witty men to shear.

Exeunt

[3.4]

*The scene changes, and discovers Blunt, creeping out of a
common-shore,° his face, etc., all dirty*

BLUNT (*climbing up*) Oh lord! I am got out at last, and, which is a
miracle, without a clue;° and now to damning and cursing! But if
that would ease me, where shall I begin? with my fortune, myself,

or the quean that cozened me? What a dog was I to believe in woman! Oh, coxcomb! Ignorant conceited coxcomb! to fancy she could be enamoured with my person, at first sight enamoured! Oh, I'm a cursed puppy! 'tis plain, fool was writ upon my forehead! She perceived it; saw the Essex calf there; for what allurements could there be in this countenance, which I can endure because I'm acquainted with it? Oh, dull silly dog, to be thus soothed into a cozening! Had I been drunk, I might fondly have credited the young quean, but as I was in my right wits, to be thus cheated confirms it: I am a dull believing English country fop.° But my comrades! Death and the devil, there's the worst of all; then a ballad° will be sung tomorrow on the Prado,° to a lousy tune, of the enchanted 'squire, and the annihilated° damsel; but Fred, that rogue, and the colonel, will abuse me beyond all Christian patience. Had she left me my clothes, I have a bill of exchange at home, would° have saved my credit, but now all hope is taken from me. Well, I'll home, if I can find the way, with this consolation, that I am not the first kind believing coxcomb; but there are, gallants, many such good natures amongst ye.

And though you've better arts to hide your follies,
'Adsheartlikins, y'are all as arrant cullies.

[*Exit*]

[3.5]

The garden in the night°

Enter Florinda in an undress,° *with a key and a little box*

FLORINDA Well, thus far I'm in my way to happiness: I have got myself free from Callis; my brother too, I find by yonder light, is got into his cabinet, and thinks not of me; I have by good fortune got the key of the garden back-door. I'll open it to prevent Belvile's knocking; a little noise will now alarm my brother. Now am I as fearful as a young thief. (*Unlocks the door*) Hark, what noise is that? Oh, 'twas the wind that played amongst the boughs. Belvile stays long, methinks; it's time. Stay, for fear of a surprise I'll hide these jewels in yonder jessamine.

[*Florinda*] *goes to lay down the box. Enter Willmore, drunk*

WILLMORE What the devil is become of these fellows, Belvile and Frederick? They promised to stay at the next corner for me, but who the devil knows the corner of a full moon? Now, whereabouts

am I? Ha, what have we here, a garden! A very convenient place
to sleep in. Ha, what has God sent us here? A female! By this light,
a woman! I'm a dog if it be not a very wench!°   15

FLORINDA [*aside*] He's come!—Ha, who's there?

WILLMORE Sweet soul! let me salute thy shoe-string.

FLORINDA [*aside*] 'Tis not my Belvile. Good heavens! I know him
not.—Who are you, and from whence come you?

WILLMORE Prithee, prithee, child, not so many hard questions. Let   20
it suffice I am here, child. Come, come kiss me.

FLORINDA Good gods! what luck is mine?

WILLMORE Only good luck child, parlous good luck. Come hither.
[*Aside*] 'Tis a delicate shining wench; by this hand, she's perfumed,
and smells like any nosegay.—Prithee, dear soul, let's not play the   25
fool, and lose time, precious time; for as Gad shall save me, I'm as
honest a fellow as breathes, though I'm a little disguised° at
present. Come, I say; why, thou mayst be free with me, I'll be very
secret. I'll not boast who 'twas obliged me, not I: for hang me if I
know thy name.   30

FLORINDA Heavens! what a filthy beast is this!

WILLMORE I am so, and thou ought'st the sooner to lie with me for
that reason: for look you, child, there will be no sin in't, because
'twas neither designed nor premeditated; 'tis pure accident on both
sides, that's a certain thing now. Indeed, should I make love to   35
you, and vow you° fidelity, and swear and lie till you believed and
yielded, that were to make it wilful fornication, the crying sin of
the nation. Thou art therefore, as thou art a good Christian,
obliged in conscience to deny me nothing. Now, come, be kind
without any more idle prating.   40

FLORINDA Oh, I am ruined!—Wicked man, unhand me.

WILLMORE Wicked! Egad, child, a judge, were he young and
vigorous, and saw those eyes of thine, would know 'twas they gave
the first blow, the first provocation. Come, prithee let's lose no
time, I say; this is a fine convenient place.   45

FLORINDA Sir, let me go, I conjure you, or I'll call out.

WILLMORE Aye, aye, you were best to call witness to see how finely
you treat me, do.

FLORINDA I'll cry murder, rape, or anything, if you do not instantly
let me go.   50

WILLMORE A rape! Come, come, you lie, you baggage, you lie: what,
I'll warrant you would fain have the world believe now that you
are not so forward as I. No, not you! Why, at this time of night,

was your cobweb door set open, dear spider, but to catch flies? Ha,
come, or I shall be damnably angry. Why, what a coil is here!   55
FLORINDA Sir, can you think—
WILLMORE —That you would do't for nothing? Oh, oh, I find what
    you would be at. Look here, here's a pistole for you. Here's a work
    indeed! Here, take it I say.
FLORINDA For heaven's sake, sir, as you're a gentleman—   60
WILLMORE So—now, now—she would be wheedling me for more.—
    What, you will not take it then, you are resolved you will not?
    Come, come, take it, or I'll put it up again, for look ye, I never
    give more. Why how now mistress, are you so high i'th' mouth a
    pistole won't down with you? Ha, why, what a work's here! In   65
    good time! Come, no struggling to be gone; but an y'are good at a
    dumb wrestle, I'm for ye, look ye, I'm for ye.
        [*Florinda*] *struggles with* [*Willmore*]. *Enter Belvile and Frederick*
BELVILE The door is open. A pox of this mad fellow, I'm angry that
    we've lost him; I durst have sworn he had followed us.
FREDERICK But you were so hasty, colonel, to be gone.   70
FLORINDA Help, help! Murder! Help! Oh, I am ruined.
BELVILE Ha, sure that's Florinda's voice!
        [*Belvile*] *comes up to* [*Florinda and Willmore*]
    A man!—Villain, let go that lady.
        A noise [*offstage*]. *Willmore turns and draws, Frederick*
        interposes
FLORINDA [*aside*] Belvile! Heavens, my brother too is coming, and
    'twill be impossible to escape.—Belvile, I conjure you to walk   75
    under my chamber window, from whence I'll give you some
    instructions what to do. This rude man has undone us.
        Exit [*Florinda*]
WILLMORE Belvile!
        Enter Pedro, Stephano, and other servants, with lights
PEDRO I'm betrayed! Run, Stephano, and see if Florinda be safe.
        Exit Stephano. [*The two groups of men*] *fight, and Pedro's*
        party beats [*Willmore's party*] *out*
    So, whoe'er they be, all is not well; I'll to Florinda's chamber.   80
        Going out, [*Pedro*] *meets Stephano* [*re-entering*]
STEPHANO You need not, sir; the poor lady's fast asleep and thinks
    no harm. I would not awake her, sir, for fear of frighting her with
    your danger.
PEDRO I'm glad she's there.—Rascals, how came the garden door
    open?   85

45

STEPHANO That question comes too late, sir. Some of my fellow
servants masquerading, I'll warrant.

PEDRO Masquerading! a lewd custom to debauch our youth. [*Aside*]
There's something more in this than I imagine.

Exeunt

[3.6]

The street

*Enter Belvile in rage, Frederick holding him, and Willmore
melancholy*

WILLMORE Why, how the devil should I know Florinda?

BELVILE Ah, plague of your ignorance! If it had not been Florinda,
must you be a beast, a brute, a senseless swine?

WILLMORE Well, sir, you see I am endued with patience; I can bear;
though egad, y'are very free with me, methinks. I was in good   5
hopes the quarrel would have been on my side, for so uncivilly
interrupting me.

BELVILE Peace, brute, whilst thou'rt safe. Oh, I'm distracted.

WILLMORE Nay, nay, I'm an unlucky dog, that's certain.

BELVILE Ah, curse upon the star that ruled my birth, or whatsoever   10
other influence that makes me still so wretched!

WILLMORE Thou break'st my heart with these complaints; there is
no star in fault, no influence but sack, the cursed sack I drunk.

FREDERICK Why, how the devil came you so drunk?

WILLMORE Why, how the devil came you so sober?   15

BELVILE A curse upon his thin skull, he was always beforehand that
way.

FREDERICK Prithee, dear colonel, forgive him, he's sorry for his fault.

BELVILE He's always so after he has done a mischief. A plague on all
such brutes!   20

WILLMORE By this light, I took her for an arrant harlot.

BELVILE Damn your debauched opinion! Tell me, sot, hadst thou so
much sense and light about thee to distinguish her woman,° and
couldst not see something about her face and person, to strike an
awful reverence into thy soul?   25

WILLMORE Faith no, I considered her as mere° a woman as I could
wish.

BELVILE 'Sdeath, I have no patience.—Draw, or I'll kill you.

WILLMORE Let that alone till tomorrow, and if I set not all right
  again, use your pleasure.   30
BELVILE Tomorrow! damn it,
  The spiteful light will lead me to no happiness.
  Tomorrow is Antonio's, and perhaps
  Guides him to my undoing; oh, that I could meet
  This rival, this powerful fortunate!   35
WILLMORE What then?
BELVILE Let thy own reason, or my rage, instruct thee.
WILLMORE I shall be finely informed then, no doubt. Hear me,
  colonel, hear me: show me the man and I'll do his business.
BELVILE I know him no more than thou, or if I did I should not need 40
  thy aid.
WILLMORE This you say is Angellica's house; I promised the kind
  baggage to lie with her tonight.
      [*Willmore*] *offers to go in.*° *Enter Antonio and his page.*
      Antonio knocks on [*Angellica's door with*] *the hilt of his sword*
ANTONIO You paid the thousand crowns I directed?
PAGE To the lady's old woman, sir, I did.   45
WILLMORE Who the devil have we here?
BELVILE I'll now plant myself under Florinda's window, and if I find
  no comfort there, I'll die.
      Exeunt Belvile and Frederick. Enter Moretta
MORETTA Page!
PAGE Here's my lord.   50
WILLMORE How is this? A picaroon going to board my frigate?—
  Here's one chase gun for you.
      Drawing his sword, [*Willmore*] *jostles Antonio, who turns and*
      draws. [*Willmore and Antonio*] *fight. Antonio falls*
MORETTA Oh bless us, we're all undone!
      [*Moretta*] *runs in and shuts the door*
PAGE Help! Murder!
      Belvile returns at the noise of fighting
BELVILE Ha, the mad rogue's engaged in some unlucky adventure again. 55
      Enter two or three masqueraders
MASQUERADER Ha, a man killed!
WILLMORE How, a man killed? Then I'll go home to sleep.
      [*Willmore*] *puts up* [*his sword*] *and reels out. Exeunt*
      masqueraders another way
BELVILE Who should it be? Pray heaven the rogue is safe, for all my
  quarrel to him.

As Belvile is groping about, enter an officer and six soldiers

SOLDIER Who's there?   60

OFFICER So, here's one dispatched. Secure the murderer.

BELVILE Do not mistake my charity for murder! I came to his
assistance.

Soldiers seize on Belvile

OFFICER That shall be tried, sir.—St Jago,° swords drawn in the
carnival time!   65

[Officer] goes to Antonio

ANTONIO Thy hand, prithee.

OFFICER Ha, Don Antonio! [*To soldiers*] Look well to the villain
there. [*To Antonio*] How is it, sir?

ANTONIO I'm hurt.

BELVILE Has my humanity made me a criminal?   70

OFFICER Away with him.

BELVILE What a cursed chance is this!

Exeunt soldiers with Belvile

ANTONIO [*aside*] This is the man that has set upon me twice. (*To the
officer*) Carry him to my apartment, till you have farther orders
from me.   75

Exit Antonio, led

4.1

A fine room

Discovers Belvile° as by dark, alone

BELVILE When shall I be weary of railing on fortune, who is resolved
never to turn with smiles upon me? Two such defeats in one night
none but the devil, and that mad rogue, could have contrived to
have plagued me with. I am here a prisoner, but where, heaven
knows; and if there be murder done, I can soon decide the fate of   5
a stranger in a nation without mercy; yet this is nothing to the
torture my soul bows with, when I think of losing my fair, my dear
Florinda. Hark, my door opens: a light; a man, and seems of
quality; armed, too! Now shall I die like a dog, without defence.

> *Enter Antonio in a night-gown, with a light; his arm in a scarf,*
> *and a sword under his arm. He sets the candle on the table*

ANTONIO Sir, I come to know what injuries I have done you, that   10
could provoke you to so mean an action as to attack me basely,
without allowing time for my defence.

BELVILE Sir, for a man in my circumstances to plead innocence,
would look like fear: but view me well, and you will find no marks
of coward on me, nor anything that betrays that brutality you   15
accuse me with.

ANTONIO In vain, sir, you impose upon my sense. You are not only
he who drew on me last night, but yesterday before the same
house, that of Angellica.°
Yet there is something in your face and mien   20
That makes me wish I were mistaken.

BELVILE I own I fought today, in the defence of a friend of mine, with
whom you (if you're the same) and your party were first engaged.
Perhaps you think this crime enough to kill me,
But if you do, I cannot fear you'll do it basely.   25

ANTONIO No, sir, I'll make you fit for a defence with this.

> *[Antonio] gives [Belvile] the sword*

BELVILE This gallantry surprises me; nor know I how to use this
present, sir, against a man so brave.

ANTONIO You shall not need; for know, I come to snatch you from
a danger that is decreed against you: perhaps your life, or long   30
imprisonment; and 'twas with so much courage you offended, I
cannot see you punished.°

BELVILE How shall I pay this generosity?°

ANTONIO It had been safer to have killed another, than have
    attempted me. To show your danger, sir, I'll let you know my   35
    quality: and 'tis the viceroy's son, whom you have wounded.°

BELVILE The viceroy's son!
    (*Aside*) Death and confusion! was this plague reserved
    To complete all the rest? Obliged by him!
    The man of all the world I would destroy.   40

ANTONIO You seem disordered, sir.

BELVILE Yes, trust me, sir, I am, and 'tis with pain
    That man receives such bounties,
    Who wants the power to pay 'em back again.

ANTONIO To gallant spirits 'tis indeed uneasy;   45
    But you may quickly overpay me, sir.

BELVILE Then I am well. (*Aside*) Kind heaven! but set us even,
    That I may fight with him and keep my honour safe.
    —Oh, I'm impatient, sir, to be discounting
    The mighty debt I owe you. Command me quickly.   50

ANTONIO I have a quarrel with a rival, sir,
    About the maid we love.

BELVILE (*aside*) Death, 'tis Florinda he means.
    That thought destroys my reason,
    And I shall kill him.   55

ANTONIO My rival, sir,
    Is one has all the virtues man can boast of—

BELVILE (*aside*) Death, who should this be?

[ANTONIO] He challenged me to meet him on the Molo
    As soon as day appeared, but last night's quarrel   60
    Has made my arm unfit to guide a sword.

BELVILE I apprehend you, sir; you'd have me kill the man that lays
    a claim to the maid you speak of. I'll do't; I'll fly to do't!

ANTONIO Sir, do you know her?

BELVILE No, sir, but 'tis enough she is admired by you.   65

ANTONIO Sir, I shall rob you of the glory on't,
    For you must fight under my name and dress.

BELVILE That opinion must be strangely obliging that makes you
    think I can personate the brave Antonio, whom I can but strive to
    imitate.°   70

ANTONIO You say too much to my advantage. Come, sir, the day
    appears that calls you forth. Within, sir, is the habit.°
        Exit Antonio

BELVILE   Fantastic fortune, thou deceitful light,
> That cheats the wearied traveller by night,
> Though on a precipice each step you tread,   75
> I am resolved to follow where you lead.

Exit

[4.2]

The Molo

Enter Florinda and Callis in masks, with Stephano

FLORINDA (*aside*) I'm dying with my fears; Belvile's not coming as I expected under my window, makes me believe that all those fears are true. [*To Stephano*] Canst thou not tell with whom my brother fights?°

STEPHANO No, madam, they were both in masquerade. I was by   5
when they challenged one another, and they had decided the quarrel then, but were prevented by some cavaliers, which made 'em put it off till now; but I am sure 'tis about you they fight.

FLORINDA (*aside*) Nay, then 'tis with Belvile, for what other lover have I that dares fight for me? (Except Antonio, and he is too much   10
in favour with my brother.) If it be he, for whom shall I direct my prayers to heaven?

STEPHANO Madam, I must leave you, for if my master see me, I shall be hanged for being your conductor. I escaped° narrowly for the excuse I made for you last night i'th' garden.   15

FLORINDA And I'll reward thee for't; prithee, no more.

> *Exit Stephano. Enter Don Pedro in his masking habit*

PEDRO Antonio's late today; the place will fill, and we may be prevented.

> [*Pedro*] *walks about*

FLORINDA (*aside*) Antonio? Sure I heard amiss.

PEDRO But who will not excuse a happy lover,
> When soft fair arms confine the yielding neck,   20
> And the kind whisper languishingly breathes,
> 'Must you be gone so soon?'
> Sure I had dwelt forever on her bosom.

> *Enter Belvile dressed in Antonio's clothes*

But stay, he's here.

FLORINDA [*aside*] 'Tis not Belvile, half my fears are vanished.   25

PEDRO Antonio!

BELVILE (*aside*) This must be he. [*To Pedro*] You're early, sir; I do
not use to be outdone this way.

PEDRO The wretched, sir, are watchful, and 'tis enough you've the
advantage of me in Angellica.   30

BELVILE (*aside*) Angellica! Or° I've mistook my man, or else Antonio.
Can he forget his interest in Florinda, and fight for common
prize?°

PEDRO Come, sir, you know our terms.

BELVILE (*aside*) By heaven, not I.—No talking, I am ready, sir.   35
          [*Belvile*] *offers to fight. Florinda runs in* [*between the two men*]

FLORINDA (*to Belvile*) Oh, hold! Whoe'er you be, I do conjure you
hold! If you strike here, I die.

PEDRO Florinda!

BELVILE Florinda imploring for my rival!

PEDRO Away, this kindness is unseasonable.   40
          [*Pedro*] *puts* [*Florinda*] *by.* [*Belvile and Pedro*] *fight;*
          [*Florinda*] *runs in just as Belvile disarms Pedro*

FLORINDA Who are you, sir, that dares° deny my prayers?

BELVILE Thy prayers destroy him: if thou wouldst preserve him,
Do that thou'rt unacquainted with, and curse him.
          [*Florinda*] *holds* [*Belvile*]

FLORINDA By all you hold most dear, by her you love,
I do conjure you, touch him not.   45

BELVILE By her I love!
See, I obey, and at your feet resign
The useless trophy of my victory.
          [*Belvile*] *lays his sword at* [*Florinda's*] *feet*

PEDRO Antonio, you've done enough to prove you love Florinda.

BELVILE Love Florinda! Does heaven love adoration, prayer, or   50
penitence? Love her! Here, sir, your sword again.
          [*Belvile*] *snatches up the sword and gives it* [*to Pedro*]
Upon this truth I'll fight my life away.

PEDRO No, you've redeemed my sister, and my friendship.
          [*Pedro*] *gives Florinda* [*to Belvile*]. [*Pedro*] *pulls off his*
          vizard to show his face, and puts it on again

BELVILE Don Pedro!

PEDRO Can you resign your claims to other women,   55
And give your heart entirely to Florinda?

BELVILE Entire! as dying saints' confessions are!
I can delay my happiness no longer:
This minute let me make Florinda mine!

PEDRO This minute let it be: no time so proper;   60
    This night my father will arrive from Rome,
    And possibly may hinder what we purpose.

FLORINDA Oh heavens! This minute!
    Enter masqueraders, and pass over

BELVILE [*to Florinda*] Oh, do not ruin me!

PEDRO The place begins to fill, and that we may not be observed, do   65
    you walk off to St Peter's church, where I will meet you, and
    conclude your happiness.

BELVILE I'll meet you there. (*Aside*) If there be no more saints'
    churches in Naples.

FLORINDA Oh stay, sir, and recall your hasty doom!   70
    Alas, I have not yet prepared my heart
    To entertain so strange a guest.

PEDRO Away, this silly modesty is assumed too late.

BELVILE Heaven, madam! what do you do?

FLORINDA Do? Despise the man that lays a tyrant's claim   75
    To what he ought to conquer by submission.

BELVILE You do not know me; move a little this way.
    [*Belvile*] *draws* [*Florinda*] *aside*

FLORINDA Yes, you may force me even to the altar,
    But not the holy man that offers there
    Shall force me to be thine.   80
    Pedro talks to Callis this while

BELVILE Oh, do not lose so blest an opportunity!
    See, 'tis your Belvile, not Antonio,
    Whom your mistaken scorn and anger ruins.
    [*Belvile*] *pulls off his vizard*

FLORINDA Belvile!
    Where was my soul it could not meet thy voice,   85
    And take this knowledge in?
    As they are talking, enter Willmore, finely dressed, and
    Frederick

WILLMORE No intelligence! No news of Belvile yet. Well, I am the
    most unlucky rascal in nature. Ha, am I deceived, or is it he? Look,
    Fred, 'tis he, my dear Belvile.
    [*Willmore*] *runs and embraces* [*Belvile*]. *Belvile's vizard falls*
    out [*of his*] *hand*

BELVILE Hell and confusion seize thee!   90

PEDRO Ha, Belvile! I beg your pardon, sir.
    [*Pedro*] *takes Florinda from* [*Belvile*]

BELVILE Nay, touch her not; she's mine by conquest, sir,
  I won her by my sword.

WILLMORE Didst thou so? and egad, child, we'll keep her by the sword.
    [*Willmore*] *draws on Pedro. Belvile goes between* [*Willmore*
    and Pedro]

BELVILE Stand off!   95
  Thou'rt so profanely lewd, so cursed by heaven,
  All quarrels thou espousest must be fatal.

WILLMORE Nay, an you be so hot, my valour's coy, and shall be
  courted when you want it next. (*Puts up his sword*)

BELVILE (*to Pedro*) You know I ought to claim a victor's right,   100
  But you're the brother to divine Florinda,
  To whom I'm such a slave: to purchase her
  I durst not hurt the man she holds so dear.

PEDRO 'Twas by Antonio's, not by Belvile's sword
  This question should have been decided, sir.   105
  I must confess much to your bravery's due,
  Both now, and when I met you last in arms:
  But I am nicely punctual in my word,°
  As men of honour ought, and beg your pardon.
  For this mistake another time shall clear.   110
  (*Aside to Florinda as they are going out*)
  This was some plot between you and Belvile,
  But I'll prevent you.
    [*Exeunt Pedro and Florinda.*] *Belvile looks after* [*Florinda*],
    and begins to walk up and down in rage

WILLMORE Do not be modest now and lose the woman, but if we
  shall fetch her back, so.

BELVILE Do not speak to me.   115

WILLMORE Not speak to you? Egad, I'll speak to you, and will be
  answered, too.

BELVILE Will you, sir?

WILLMORE I know I've done some mischief, but I'm so dull a puppy,
  that I'm the son of a whore if I know how, or where. Prithee   120
  inform my understanding.

BELVILE Leave me, I say, and leave me instantly.

WILLMORE I will not leave you in this humour, nor till I know my crime.

BELVILE Death, I'll tell you, sir!
    [*Belvile*] *draws and runs at Willmore. Frederick interposes.*
    [*Willmore begins to run*] *out, Belvile after him. Enter*
    Angellica, Moretta, and Sebastian

ANGELLICA Ha! Sebastian, is not that Willmore? Haste, haste and   125
    bring him back.
        [Exeunt Willmore and Belvile]
FREDERICK The colonel's mad: I never saw him thus before. I'll after
    'em lest he do some mischief, for I am sure Willmore will not draw
    on him.
        Exit [Frederick]
ANGELLICA I am all rage! my first desires defeated!   130
    For one, for aught he knows, that has
    No other merit than her quality,°
    Her being Don Pedro's sister: he loves her!
    I know 'tis so. Dull, dull, insensible;
    He will not see me now, though oft invited,   135
    And broke his word last night: false perjured man!
    He that but yesterday fought for my favours,
    And would have made his life a sacrifice
    To've gained one night with me,
    Must now be hired and courted to my arms.   140
MORETTA I told you what would come on't, but Moretta's an old
    doting fool. Why did you give him five hundred crowns, but to set
    himself out for other lovers? You should have kept him poor, if
    you had meant to have had any good from him.
ANGELLICA Oh, name not such mean trifles; had I given   145
    Him all my youth has earned from sin,°
    I had not lost a thought, nor sigh upon't.
    But I have given him my eternal rest,
    My whole repose, my future joys, my heart!
    My virgin heart, Moretta! Oh, 'tis gone!   150
        Enter Willmore and Sebastian
MORETTA Curse on him, here he comes. How fine she has made him
    too.
        Angellica turns and walks away
WILLMORE How now, turned shadow?
    Fly when I pursue, and follow when I fly? (*Sings*)

        Stay, gentle shadow of my dove,
          And tell me ere I go,   155
        Whether the substance may not prove
          A fleeting thing like you.

        As [Angellica] turns, she looks on [Willmore]
    There's a soft kind look remaining yet.

ANGELLICA Well, sir, you may be gay: all happiness, all joys pursue   160
you still; fortune's your slave, and gives you every hour choice of
new hearts and beauties, till you are cloyed with the repeated bliss,
which others vainly languish for.
But know, false man, that I shall be revenged.
      [*Angellica*] *turns away in rage*

WILLMORE So, gad, there are of those° faint-hearted lovers, whom   165
such a sharp lesson next their hearts, would make as impotent as
fourscore. Pox o' this whining! My business is to laugh and love;
a pox on't, I hate your sullen lover; a man shall lose as much time
to put you in humour now, as would serve to gain a new woman.

ANGELLICA I scorn to cool that fire I cannot raise,   170
Or do the drudgery of your virtuous mistress.

WILLMORE A virtuous mistress! Death, what a thing thou hast found
out for me! Why, what the devil should I do with a virtuous
woman? A sort of ill-natured creatures, that take a pride to torment
a lover. Virtue is but an infirmity in woman; a disease that renders   175
even the handsome ungrateful; whilst the ill-favoured, for want of
solicitations and address, only fancy themselves so. I have lain with
a woman of quality, who has all the while been railing at whores.

ANGELLICA I will not answer for your mistress's virtue,
Though she be young enough to know no guilt;   180
And I could wish you would persuade my heart
'Twas the two hundred thousand crowns you courted.

WILLMORE Two hundred thousand crowns! What story's this, what
trick? What woman? Ha!

ANGELLICA How strange you make it. Have you forgot the creature   185
you entertained on the Piazza last night?

WILLMORE (*aside*) Ha, my gipsy worth two hundred thousand
crowns? Oh, how I long to be with her. Pox, I knew she was of
quality.

ANGELLICA False man! I see my ruin in your face.   190
How many vows you breathed upon my bosom,
Never to be unjust: have you forgot so soon?

WILLMORE Faith no, I was just coming to repeat 'em. But here's a
humour, indeed, would make a man a saint. (*Aside*) Would she
would be angry enough to leave me, and command me not to wait   195
on her.

      Enter Hellena, dressed in man's clothes

HELLENA [*aside*] This must be Angellica, I know it by her mumping
matron here; aye, aye, 'tis she! My mad captain's with her too, for

all his swearing. How this unconstant humour makes me love him! [*To Moretta*] Pray, good grave gentlewoman, is not this Angellica? 200

MORETTA My too young sir, it is. [*Aside*] I hope 'tis one from Don Antonio.

    [*Moretta*] *goes to Angellica*

HELLENA (*aside*) Well, something I'll do to vex him for this.

ANGELLICA [*to Moretta*] I will not speak with him; am I in humour to receive a lover? 205

WILLMORE Not speak with him! Why, I'll begone, and wait your idler minutes. Can I show less obedience to the thing I love so fondly?

    [*Willmore*] *offers to go*

ANGELLICA A fine excuse, this! Stay.

WILLMORE And hinder your advantage? Should I repay your boun- 210
ties so ungratefully?

ANGELLICA [*to Hellena*] Come hither, boy—[*to Willmore*] that I may
    let you see
How much above the advantages you name
I prize one minute's joy with you.

WILLMORE Oh, you destroy me with this endearment. [*Aside,*] 215
impatient to be gone) Death! how shall I get away?—Madam, 'twill
not be fit I should be seen with you; besides, it will not be
convenient; and I've a friend—that's dangerously sick.

ANGELLICA I see you're impatient; yet you shall stay.

WILLMORE (*aside*) And miss my assignation with my gipsy. 220

    [*Willmore*] *walks about impatiently. Moretta brings Hellena,*
    who addresses herself to Angellica

HELLENA Madam,
You'll hardly pardon my intrusion
When you shall know my business,
And I'm too young to tell my tale with art;
But there must be a wondrous store of goodness, 225
Where so much beauty dwells.

ANGELLICA A pretty advocate, whoever sent thee.
Prithee proceed. (*To Willmore, who is stealing off*) Nay, sir, you
    shall not go.

WILLMORE (*aside*) Then I shall lose my dear gipsy forever. Pox on't,
she stays me out of spite. 230

[HELLENA] I am related to a lady, madam,
Young, rich, and nobly born, but has the fate
To be in love with a young English gentleman.

Strangely she loves him, at first sight she loved him,
But did adore him when she heard him speak;   235
For he, she said, had charms in every word,
That failed not to surprise, to wound and conquer.

WILLMORE (*aside*) Ha! Egad, I hope this concerns me.

ANGELLICA 'Tis my false man he means: would he were gone.
This praise will raise his pride, and ruin me. (*To Willmore*) Well,   240
Since you are so impatient to be gone,
I will release you, sir.

WILLMORE (*aside*) Nay, then I'm sure 'twas me he spoke of: this
cannot be the effects of kindness in her.
—No, madam, I've considered better on't,   245
And will not give you cause of jealousy.

ANGELLICA But, sir, I've—business, that—

WILLMORE This shall not do; I know 'tis but to try me.

ANGELLICA Well, to your story, boy—(*aside*) though 'twill undo me.

HELLENA With this addition to his other beauties,   250
He won her unresisting tender heart:
He vowed, and sighed, and swore he loved her dearly;
And she believed the cunning flatterer,
And thought herself the happiest maid alive.
Today was the appointed time by both   255
To consummate their bliss;
The virgin, altar, and the priest were dressed;
And whilst she languished for th'expected bridegroom,
She heard, he paid his broken vows to you.

WILLMORE [*aside*] So, this is some dear rogue that's in love with me,   260
and this way lets me know it; or if it be not me, she° means
someone whose place I may supply.

ANGELLICA Now I perceive
The cause of thy impatience to be gone,
And all the business of this glorious dress.   265

WILLMORE Damn the young prater, I know not what he means.

HELLENA Madam,
In your fair eyes I read too much concern,
To tell my farther business.

ANGELLICA Prithee, sweet youth, talk on: thou mayst perhaps   270
Raise here a storm that may undo my passion,
And then I'll grant thee anything.

HELLENA Madam, 'tis to entreat you (oh unreasonable)
You would not see this stranger;

For if you do, she vows you are undone,   275
  Though nature never made a man so excellent,
  And sure he'd been a god, but for inconstancy.

WILLMORE (*aside*) Ah, rogue, how finely he's instructed! 'Tis plain:
  some woman that has seen me *en passant*.

ANGELLICA Oh, I shall burst with jealousy! Do you know the man   280
  you speak of?

HELLENA Yes, madam, he used to be in buff and scarlet.

ANGELLICA (*to Willmore*) Thou, false as hell, what canst thou say to
  this?

WILLMORE By heaven—   285

ANGELLICA Hold, do not damn thyself—

HELLENA —Nor hope to be believed.

      [*Willmore*] *walks about*, [*Angellica and Hellena*] *follow*

ANGELLICA Oh, perjured man!
  Is't thus you pay my generous passion back?

HELLENA Why would you, sir, abuse my lady's faith?   290

ANGELLICA And use me so inhumanly?°

HELLENA A maid so young, so innocent—

WILLMORE Ah, young devil.

ANGELLICA Dost thou not know thy life is in my power?

HELLENA Or think my lady cannot be revenged?   295

WILLMORE (*aside*) So, so, the storm comes finely on.

ANGELLICA Now thou art silent; guilt has struck thee dumb.
  Oh, hadst thou still been so, I'd lived in safety.

      [*Angellica*] *turns away and weeps*

WILLMORE (*aside to Hellena*) Sweetheart, the lady's name and house,
  quickly: I'm impatient to be with her.   300

      [*Willmore*] *looks towards Angellica to watch her turning, and*
      as she comes towards them he meets her

HELLENA (*aside*) So, now is he for another woman.

WILLMORE The impudent'st young thing in nature; I cannot persuade him out of his error, madam.

ANGELLICA I know he's in the right, yet thou'st a tongue
  That would persuade him to deny his faith.   305

      In rage, [*Angellica*] *walks away*

WILLMORE (*said softly to Hellena*) Her name, her name, dear boy.

HELLENA Have you forgot it, sir?

WILLMORE (*aside*) Oh, I perceive he's not to know I am a stranger
  to his lady. [*To Hellena*] Yes, yes, I do know, but—I have forgot
  the—   310

Angellica turns. [Willmore addresses her]
By heaven, such early confidence I never saw.

ANGELLICA Did I not charge you with this mistress, sir?
Which you denied, though I beheld your perjury.
This little generosity of thine has rendered back my heart.
[Angellica] walks away

WILLMORE *[aside to Hellena]* So, you have made sweet work here, 315
my little mischief; look your lady be kind and good-natured now,
or I shall have but a cursed bargain on't.
Angellica turns towards them. [He addresses her]
The rogue's bred up to mischief; art thou so great a fool to credit
him?

ANGELLICA Yes, I do, and you in vain impose upon me. 320
—Come hither, boy, is not this he you spake of?

HELLENA I think it is; I cannot swear, but I vow he has just such
another lying lover's look.
Hellena looks in [Willmore's] face; he gazes on her

WILLMORE *[aside]* Ha, do not I know that face? By heaven, my little
gipsy. What a dull dog was I! Had I but looked that way I'd known 325
her. Are all my hopes of a new woman banished? *[To Hellena]*
Egad, if I do not fit thee for this, hang me. *[To Angellica]* Madam,
I have found out the plot.

HELLENA *[aside]* Oh lord, what does he say? Am I discovered now?

WILLMORE Do you see this young spark here? 330

HELLENA *[aside]* He'll tell her who I am.

WILLMORE Who do you think this is?

HELLENA *[aside]* Aye, aye, he does know me. *[To Willmore]* Nay,
dear captain! I am undone if you discover me.

WILLMORE *[aside to Hellena]* Nay, nay, no cogging; she shall know 335
what a precious mistress I have.

HELLENA *[aside to Willmore]* Will you be such a devil?

WILLMORE *[aside to Hellena]* Nay, nay, I'll teach you to spoil sport
you will not make. *[To Angellica]* This small ambassador comes not
from a person of quality, as you imagine, and he says; but from a 340
very arrant gipsy, the talking'st, prating'st, canting'st little animal
thou ever saw'st.

ANGELLICA What news you tell me: that's the thing I mean.

HELLENA *(aside)* Would I were well off the place! If ever I go
a-captain-hunting again— 345

WILLMORE Mean that thing, that gipsy thing? Thou mayst as well
be jealous of thy monkey or parrot as of her: a German motion°

were worth a dozen of her, and a dream were a better enjoyment;
a creature of a constitution fitter for heaven than man.

HELLENA (*aside*) Though I'm sure he lies, yet this vexes me.   350

ANGELLICA You are mistaken: she's a Spanish woman
Made up of no such dull materials.

WILLMORE Materials! Egad, an she be made of any that will either
dispense or admit of love, I'll be bound to continence.

HELLENA (*aside to [Willmore]*) Unreasonable man, do you think so?   355

[WILLMORE] You may return, my little brazen head, and tell your
lady, that till she be handsome enough to be beloved, or I dull
enough to be religious, there will be small hopes of me.

ANGELLICA Did you not promise, then, to marry her?

WILLMORE Not I, by heaven.   360

ANGELLICA You cannot undeceive my fears and torments,
Till you have vowed you will not marry her.°

HELLENA (*aside*) If he swears that, he'll be revenged on me indeed
for all my rogueries.

ANGELLICA I know what arguments you'll bring against me, fortune,   365
and honour.

WILLMORE Honour? I tell you, I hate it in your sex; and those that
fancy themselves possessed of that foppery,° are the most imper-
tinently troublesome of all womankind, and will transgress nine
commandments to keep one: and to satisfy your jealousy, I swear—   370

HELLENA (*aside to him*) Oh, no swearing, dear captain.

WILLMORE —If it were possible I should ever be inclined to marry,
it should be some kind young sinner; one that has generosity
enough to give a favour handsomely to one that can ask it
discreetly; one that has wit enough to manage an intrigue of love.   375
Oh, how civil such a wench is, to a man that does her the honour
to marry her!

ANGELLICA By heaven, there's no faith in anything he says.
     Enter Sebastian

SEBASTIAN Madam, Don Antonio—

ANGELLICA Come hither.   380

HELLENA [*aside*] Ha, Antonio! He may be coming hither, and he'll
certainly discover me. I'll therefore retire without a ceremony.
     Exit Hellena

ANGELLICA I'll see him; get my coach ready.

SEBASTIAN It waits you, madam.

WILLMORE [*aside*] This is lucky. [*To Angellica*] What, madam, now   385
I may be gone, and leave you to the enjoyment of my rival?

ANGELLICA Dull man, that canst not see how ill, how poor,
     That false dissimulation looks: begone,
     And never let me see thy cozening face again,
     Lest I relapse and kill thee.   390
WILLMORE Yes, you can spare me now. Farewell, till you're in better
     humour. [*Aside*] I'm glad of this release; now for my gipsy:
     For though to worse we change, yet still we find
     New joys, new charms, in a new miss that's kind.°
          Exit Willmore   395
ANGELLICA He's gone, and in this ague of my soul
     The shivering fit returns:
     Oh, with what willing haste he took his leave,
     As if the longed-for minute were arrived
     Of some blessed assignation.
     In vain I have consulted all my charms,   400
     In vain this beauty prized, in vain believed
     My eyes could kindle any lasting fires;
     I had forgot my name, my infamy,°
     And the reproach that honour lays on those
     That dare pretend a sober passion here.   405
     Nice reputation, though it leave behind
     More virtues than inhabit where that dwells,
     Yet that once gone, those virtues shine no more.
     Then since I am not fit to be beloved,
     I am resolved to think on a revenge   410
     On him that soothed me thus to my undoing.
          Exeunt

4.3

A street°

*Enter Florinda and Valeria, in habits different from what
they have been seen in*

FLORINDA We're happily escaped, and yet I tremble still.
VALERIA A lover and fear! Why, I am but half an one, and yet I have
     courage for any attempt. Would Hellena were here; I would fain have
     had her as deep in this mischief as we: she'll fare but ill else, I doubt.
FLORINDA She pretended a visit to the Augustine nuns, but I believe   5
     some other design carried her out; pray heaven we light on her.
     Prithee, what didst do with Callis?

VALERIA When I saw no reason would do good on her, I followed
her into the wardrobe, and as she was looking for something in a
great chest, I toppled her in by the heels, snatched the key of the   10
apartment where you were confined, locked her in, and left her
bawling for help.

FLORINDA 'Tis well you resolve to follow my fortunes, for thou
darest never appear at home again after such an action.

VALERIA That's according as the young stranger and I shall agree.   15
But to our business: I delivered your note to Belvile, when I got
out under pretence of going to mass. I found him at his lodging,
and believe me it came seasonably; for never was man in so
desperate a condition. I told him of your resolution of making your
escape today, if your brother would be absent long enough to   20
permit you; if not, to die rather than be Antonio's.

FLORINDA Thou shouldst have told him I was confined to my
chamber, upon my brother's suspicion that the business on the
Molo was a plot laid between him and I.

VALERIA I said all this, and told him your brother was now gone to   25
his devotion; and he resolves to visit every church till he find him,
and not only undeceive him in that, but caress him so as shall delay
his return home.

FLORINDA Oh heavens, he's here, and Belvile with him too.
   [*Florinda and Valeria*] *put on their vizards. Enter Don
   Pedro, Belvile,* [*and*] *Willmore; Belvile and Don Pedro
   seeming in serious discourse*

VALERIA Walk boldly by them, and I'll come at distance, lest he   30
suspect us.
   [*Florinda*] *walks by* [*Don Pedro, Belvile, and Willmore*], *and
   looks back on them*

WILLMORE Ha! A woman, and of an excellent mien.

PEDRO She throws a kind look back on you.

WILLMORE Death, 'tis a likely wench, and that kind look shall not
be cast away: I'll follow her.   35

BELVILE Prithee, do not.

WILLMORE Do not? By heavens, to the antipodes, with such an
invitation.
   [*Florinda*] *goes out, and Willmore follows her*

BELVILE 'Tis a mad fellow for a wench.
   [*Exit Valeria, following Willmore and Florinda.*] *Enter
   Frederick*

FREDERICK Oh colonel, such news!   40

63

BELVILE Prithee, what?

FREDERICK News that will make you laugh in spite of fortune.

BELVILE What, Blunt has had some damned trick put upon him: cheated, banged or clapped?

FREDERICK Cheated, sir; rarely cheated of all but his shirt and 45 drawers. The unconscionable whore, too, turned him out before consummation, so that, traversing the streets at midnight, the watch found him in this fresco,° and conducted him home. By heaven, 'tis such a sight, and yet I durst as well been hanged as laughed at him, or pity him; he beats all that do but ask him a 50 question, and is in such an humour!

PEDRO Who is't has met with this ill usage, sir?

BELVILE A friend of ours, whom you must see for mirth's sake. *(Aside)* I'll employ him to give Florinda time for an escape.

PEDRO What is he? 55

BELVILE A young countryman of ours, one that has been educated at so plentiful a rate, he yet ne'er knew the want of money, and 'twill be a great jest to see how simply° he'll look without it; for my part I'll lend him none, an the rogue know not how to put on a borrowing face, and ask first;° I'll let him see how good 'tis to 60 play our parts whilst I play his.—Prithee, Fred, do you go home and keep him in that posture till we come.

> *Exeunt [Frederick, Don Pedro, and Belvile]. Enter Florinda*
> *from the farther end of the scene, looking behind her*

FLORINDA I am followed still. Ha, my brother, too, advancing this way: good heavens defend me from being seen by him.

> *[Florinda] goes off. Enter Willmore, and after him Valeria, at*
> *a little distance*

WILLMORE Ah, there she sails! She looks back as she were willing to 65 be boarded; I'll warrant her prize.°

> *[Willmore] goes out, Valeria following. Enter Hellena, just as*
> *he goes out, with a page*

HELLENA Ha, is not that my captain that has a woman in chase? 'Tis not Angellica.—Boy, follow those people at a distance, and bring me an account where they go in.

> *Exit page*

—I'll find his haunts, and plague him everywhere. Ha, my brother. 70

> *Belvile, Willmore, [and] Pedro cross the stage. Hellena runs off*

[4.4]

Another street°

Enter Florinda

FLORINDA What shall I do? My brother now pursues me; will no kind power protect me from his tyranny? Ha, here's a door open; I'll venture in, since nothing can be worse than to fall into his hands; my life and honour are at stake, and my necessity has no choice.

[*Florinda*] *goes in. Enter Valeria, and Hellena's page peeping after Florinda*

PAGE Here she went in; I shall remember this house.   5

Exit page

VALERIA This is Belvile's lodging; she's gone in as readily as if she knew it. Ha, here's that mad fellow again. I dare not venture in; I'll watch my opportunity.

[*Exit Valeria.*] *Enter Willmore, gazing about him*

WILLMORE I have lost her hereabouts. Pox on't, she must not 'scape me so.   10

Goes out

[4.5]

Scene changes to Blunt's chamber;° discovers him sitting on a couch in his shirt and drawers, reading

BLUNT So, now my mind's a little at peace, since I have resolved revenge. A pox on this tailor, though, for not bringing home the clothes I bespoke; and a pox of all poor cavaliers: a man can never keep a spare suit for 'em; and I shall have these rogues come in and find me naked, and then I'm undone; but I'm resolved to arm myself; the rascals shall not insult over me too much.   5

Puts on an old rusty sword, and buff belt

Now, how like a morris dancer I am equipped! A fine ladylike whore to cheat me thus, without affording me a kindness for my money! A pox light on her, I shall never be reconciled to the sex more: she has made me as faithless as a physician,° as uncharitable   10 as a churchman, and as ill-natured as a poet. Oh, how I'll use all womankind hereafter! What would I give to have one of 'em within my reach now! Any mortal thing in petticoats, kind fortune, send me, and I'll forgive thy last night's malice! Here's a cursed book,

too, *A Warning to All Young Travellers*, that can instruct me how   15
to prevent such mischiefs now 'tis too late. Well, 'tis a rare
convenient thing to read a little now and then, as well as hawk and
hunt.

[Blunt] sits down again and reads. Enter to him Florinda

FLORINDA This house is haunted, sure; 'tis well furnished and no
living thing inhabits it. Ha, a man; heavens, how he's attired! Sure   20
'tis some rope-dancer, or fencing master. I tremble now for fear,
and yet I must venture now to speak to him.—Sir, if I may not
interrupt your meditations—

[Blunt] starts up and gazes

BLUNT Ha, what's here? Are my wishes granted? And is not that a
she creature? 'Adsheartlikins, 'tis!—What wretched thing art thou,   25
ha?

FLORINDA Charitable sir, you've told yourself already what I am: a
very wretched maid, forced by a strange unlucky accident, to seek
a safety here, and must be ruined, if you do not grant it.

BLUNT Ruined! Is there any ruin so inevitable as that which now   30
threatens thee? Dost thou know, miserable woman, into what den
of mischiefs thou art fallen, what abyss of confusion, ha? Dost not
see something in my looks that frights thy guilty soul, and makes
thee wish to change that shape of woman for any humble animal,
or devil? For those were safer for thee, and less mischievous.   35

FLORINDA Alas, what mean you, sir? I must confess, your looks have
something in 'em makes me fear, but I beseech you, as you seem
a gentleman, pity a harmless virgin, that takes your house for
sanctuary.

BLUNT Talk on, talk on, and weep too, till my faith return. Do,   40
flatter me out of my senses again. A harmless virgin with a pox!
As much one as t'other, 'adsheartlikins. Why, what the devil, can
I not be safe in my house for you; not in my chamber? Nay, even
being naked, too, cannot secure me: this is an impudence greater
than has invaded me yet. Come, no resistance.   45

[Blunt] pulls [Florinda] rudely

FLORINDA Dare you be so cruel?

BLUNT Cruel? 'Adsheartlikins, as a galley-slave, or a Spanish whore.
Cruel, yes: I will kiss and beat thee all over; kiss, and see thee all
over; thou shalt lie with me too, not that I care for the enjoyment,
but to let thee see I have ta'en deliberated malice to thee, and will   50
be revenged on one whore for the sins of another. I will smile and
deceive thee, flatter thee, and beat thee, kiss and swear, and lie to

thee, embrace thee and rob thee, as she did me; fawn on thee, and strip thee stark naked, then hang thee out at my window by the heels, with a paper of scurvy verses fastened to thy breast, in praise   55
of damnable women. Come, come along.

FLORINDA Alas, sir, must I be sacrificed for the crimes of the most
        infamous of my sex? I never understood the sins you name.

BLUNT Do, persuade the fool you love him, or that one of you can
        be just or honest; tell me I was not an easy coxcomb, or any strange   60
        impossible tale: it will be believed sooner than thy false showers or
        protestations. A generation of damned hypocrites! To flatter my
        very clothes from my back! Dissembling witches! Are these the
        returns you make an honest gentleman, that trusts, believes, and
        loves you? But if I be not even with you—come along, or I shall—   65
            Enter Frederick

FREDERICK Ha, what's here to do?

BLUNT 'Adsheartlikins, Fred, I am glad thou art come, to be a
        witness of my dire revenge.

FREDERICK What's this, a person of quality too, who is upon the
        ramble to supply the defects of some grave impotent husband?   70

BLUNT No, this has another pretence: some very unfortunate acci-
        dent brought her hither, to save a life pursued by I know not who,
        or why, and forced to take sanctuary here at fools' haven.
        'Adsheartlikins, to me, of all mankind, for protection? Is the ass to
        be cajoled again, think ye?—No, young one, no prayers or tears   75
        shall mitigate my rage; therefore prepare for both my pleasures of
        enjoyment and revenge, for I am resolved to make up my loss here
        on thy body: I'll take it out in kindness and in beating.

FREDERICK Now, mistress of mine, what do you think of this?

FLORINDA I think he will not, dares not be so barbarous.   80

FREDERICK Have a care, Blunt: she fetched a deep sigh; she is
        enamoured with thy shirt and drawers, she'll strip thee even of
        that. There are of her calling such unconscionable baggages, and
        such dexterous thieves, they'll flay a man and he shall ne'er miss
        his skin, till he feels the cold. There was a countryman of ours   85
        robbed of a row of teeth while he was a-sleeping, which the jilt
        made him buy again when he waked.—You see, lady, how little
        reason we have to trust you.

BLUNT 'Adsheartlikins, why this is most abominable.

FLORINDA Some such devils there may be, but by all that's holy, I   90
        am none such; I entered here to save a life in danger.

BLUNT For no goodness, I'll warrant her.

FREDERICK Faith, damsel, you had e'en confessed° the plain truth, for we are fellows not to be caught twice in the same trap: look on that wreck, a tight vessel when he set out of haven, well trimmed and laden; and see how a female picaroon of this island of rogues has shattered him; and canst thou hope for any mercy?   95

BLUNT No, no, gentlewoman, come along; 'adsheartlikins, we must be better acquainted.—We'll both lie with her, and then let me alone to bang her.   100

FREDERICK I'm ready to serve you in matters of revenge that has a double pleasure in't.

BLUNT Well said.—You hear, little one, how you are condemned by public vote to the bed within; there's no resisting your destiny, sweetheart.   105

[Blunt] pulls [Florinda]

FLORINDA Stay, sir; I have seen you with Belvile, an English cavalier: for his sake use me kindly; you know him, sir.

BLUNT Belvile, why yes, sweeting, we do know Belvile, and wish he were with us now; he's a cormorant at whore and bacon,° he'd have a limb or two of thee, my virgin pullet; but 'tis no matter, we'll   110
leave him the bones to pick.

FLORINDA Sir, if you have any esteem for that Belvile, I conjure you to treat me with more gentleness; he'll thank you for the justice.

FREDERICK Hark'ee, Blunt, I doubt we are mistaken in this matter.

FLORINDA Sir, if you find me not worth Belvile's care, use me as you   115
please; and that you may think I merit better treatment than you threaten, pray take this present.

[Florinda] gives [Blunt] a ring. He looks on it

BLUNT Hum, a diamond! Why, 'tis a wonderful virtue now that lies in this ring, a mollifying virtue; 'adsheartlikins, there's more persuasive rhetoric in't, than all her sex can utter.   120

FREDERICK I begin to suspect something; and 'twould anger us vilely to be trussed up for a rape upon a maid of quality, when we only believe we ruffle a harlot.

BLUNT Thou art a credulous fellow, but 'adsheartlikins, I have no faith yet: why, my saint prattled as parlously as this does; she   125
gave me a bracelet too, a devil on her, but I sent my man to sell it today for necessaries, and it proved as counterfeit as her vows of love.

FREDERICK However, let it reprieve her till we see Belvile.

BLUNT That's hard, yet I will grant it.   130

Enter a servant

SERVANT Oh, sir, the colonel is just come in with his new friend and
a Spaniard of quality, and talks of having you to dinner with 'em.
BLUNT 'Adsheartlikins, I'm undone; I would not see 'em for the
world. Hark'ee, Fred, lock up the wench in your chamber.
FREDERICK Fear nothing, madam; whate'er he threatens, you are safe   135
whilst in my hands.
    Exeunt Frederick and Florinda
BLUNT And, sirrah, upon your life, say I am not at home, or that I
am asleep, or—or anything: away, I'll prevent their coming this
way.
    [*Blunt*] *locks the door,° and exeunt*

5.1

Blunt's chamber

After a great knocking as at his chamber door,° enter Blunt,
softly crossing the stage, in his shirt and drawers as before

[VOICES] (*call within*) Ned, Ned Blunt, Ned Blunt!

BLUNT The rogues are up in arms: 'adsheartlikins, this villainous Frederick has betrayed me; they have heard of my blessed fortune.

[VOICES] (*calling and knocking within*) Ned Blunt, Ned, Ned!   5

BELVILE [*within*] Why, he's dead sir, without dispute dead; he has not been seen today: let's break open the door.—Here, boy—

BLUNT Ha, break open the door? 'Adsheartlikins, that mad fellow will be as good as his word.

BELVILE [*within*] Boy, bring something to force the door.   10

A great noise within, at the door again

BLUNT So, now must I speak in my own defence; I'll try what rhetoric will do.—Hold, hold, what do you mean, gentlemen, what do you mean?

BELVILE (*within*) Oh, rogue, art alive? Prithee open the door and convince us.   15

BLUNT Yes, I am alive, gentlemen; but at present a little busy.

BELVILE (*within*) How, Blunt grown a man of business? Come, come, open and let's see this miracle.

BLUNT No, no, no, no, gentlemen, 'tis no great business, but—I am—at—my devotion; 'adsheartlikins, will you not allow a man   20 time to pray?

BELVILE (*within*) Turned religious! A greater wonder than the first; therefore open quickly, or we shall unhinge, we shall.

BLUNT This won't do.—Why, hark'ee, colonel, to tell you the plain truth, I am about a necessary affair of life: I have a wench with me;   25 you apprehend me?—The devil's in't if they be so uncivil as to disturb me now.

WILLMORE [*within*] How, a wench! Nay then, we must enter and partake, no resistance; unless it be your lady of quality, and then we'll keep our distance.   30

BLUNT So, the business is out.

WILLMORE [*within*] Come, come, lend's more hands to the door; now heave altogether; so, well done my boys.

[Willmore] breaks open the door. Enter Belvile, Willmore,
Frederick, and Pedro. Blunt looks simply;° they all laugh at
him; he lays his hand on his sword, and comes up to Willmore

BLUNT Hark'ee, sir, laugh out your laugh quickly, d'ye hear, and
    begone. I shall spoil your sport else, 'adsheartlikins, sir, I shall; the   35
    jest has been carried on too long. (*Aside*) A plague upon my tailor.

WILLMORE 'Sdeath, how the whore has dressed him!—Faith sir, I'm
    sorry.

BLUNT Are you so, sir? Keep't to yourself then, sir, I advise you,
    d'ye hear; for I can as little endure your pity as his mirth. (*Lays*   40
    his hand on's sword)

BELVILE Indeed, Willmore, thou wert a little too rough with Ned
    Blunt's mistress: call a person of quality whore? And one so young,
    so handsome, and so eloquent! Ha, ha, he.

BLUNT Hark'ee, sir, you know me, and know I can be angry; have a   45
    care, for 'adsheartlikins, I can fight too, I can, sir, do you mark me;
    no more.

BELVILE Why so peevish, good Ned? Some disappointments, I'll
    warrant. What, did the jealous count her husband return just in
    the nick?   50

BLUNT Or the devil, sir. (*They laugh*) D'ye laugh? Look ye settle me
    a good sober countenance, and that quickly too, or you shall know
    Ned Blunt is not—

BELVILE —Not everybody, we know that.

BLUNT Not an ass to be laughed at, sir.   55

WILLMORE Unconscionable sinner, to bring a lover so near his
    happiness, a vigorous passionate lover, and then not only cheat him
    of his moveables, but his very desires too.

BELVILE Ah, sir, a mistress is a trifle with Blunt; he'll have a dozen
    the next time he looks abroad: his eyes have charms, not to be   60
    resisted; there needs no more than to expose that taking person to
    the view of the fair, and he leads 'em all in triumph.

PEDRO Sir, though I'm a stranger to you, I am ashamed at the
    rudeness of my nation; and could you learn who did it, would assist
    you to make an example of 'em.   65

BLUNT Why aye, there's one speaks sense now, and handsomely; and
    let me tell you, gentlemen, I should not have showed myself like
    a jack pudding thus to have made you mirth, but that I have
    revenge within my power: for know, I have got into my possession
    a female, who had better have fallen under any curse, than the ruin   70
    I design her. 'Adsheartlikins, she assaulted me here in my own

lodgings, and had doubtless committed a rape upon me, had not
this sword defended me.

FREDERICK I know not that, but o' my conscience thou hadst
ravished her, had she not redeemed herself with a ring; let's see it,   75
Blunt.

Blunt shows the ring

BELVILE [*aside*] Ha, the ring I gave Florinda, when we exchanged
our vows.—Hark'ee, Blunt—

[*Belvile*] *goes to whisper to* [*Blunt*]

WILLMORE No whispering, good colonel, there's a woman in the
case; no whispering.   80

BELVILE [*aside to Blunt*] Hark'ee, fool, be advised, and conceal both
the ring and the story for your reputation's sake; do not let people
know what despised cullies we English are: to be cheated and
abused by one whore, and another rather bribe thee than be kind
to thee, is an infamy to our nation.   85

WILLMORE Come, come, where's the wench? We'll see her; let her
be what she will, we'll see her.

PEDRO Aye, aye, let us see her; I can soon discover whether she be
of quality, or for your diversion.

BLUNT She's in Fred's custody.   90

WILLMORE (*to Frederick*) Come, come, the key.

[*Frederick*] *gives* [*Willmore*] *the key;* [*Willmore, Frederick,*
Blunt, and Don Pedro] *are going*

BELVILE [*aside*] Death, what shall I do?—Stay, gentlemen.—[*Aside*]
Yet if I hinder 'em I shall discover all.°—Hold, let's go one at
once;° give me the key.

WILLMORE Nay, hold there, colonel; I'll go first.   95

FREDERICK Nay, no dispute; Ned and I have the propriety of her.°

WILLMORE Damn propriety; then we'll draw cuts.

Belvile goes to whisper [*to*] *Willmore*

—Nay, no corruption, good colonel; come, the longest sword
carries her.

They all draw, forgetting Don Pedro, being as a Spaniard,
had the longest

BLUNT I yield up my interest to you, gentlemen, and that will be   100
revenge sufficient.

WILLMORE (*to Pedro*) The wench is yours. [*Aside*] Pox of his toledo,
I had forgot that.

FREDERICK Come, sir, I'll conduct you to the lady.

Exeunt Frederick and Pedro

BELVILE (*aside*) To hinder him will certainly discover her. (*To   105
Willmore, [who is] walking up and down out of humour*) Dost know,
dull beast, what mischief thou hast done?

WILLMORE Aye, aye; to trust our fortune to lots! A devil on't, 'twas
madness, that's the truth on't.

BELVILE Oh, intolerable sot!   110

  Enter Florinda, running, masked, Pedro after her: Willmore
  gazing round her

FLORINDA (*aside*) Good heaven, defend me from discovery.

PEDRO 'Tis but in vain to fly me; you're fallen to my lot.

BELVILE (*aside*) Sure she's undiscovered yet, but now I fear there is
no way to bring her off.

WILLMORE Why, what a pox, is not this my woman, the same I   115
followed but now?

PEDRO (*talking to Florinda, who walks up and down*) As if I did not
know ye, and your business here.

FLORINDA (*aside*) Good heaven, I fear he does indeed.

PEDRO Come, pray be kind; I know you meant to be so when you   120
entered here, for these are proper gentlemen.

WILLMORE But, sir, perhaps the lady will not be imposed upon;
she'll choose her man.

PEDRO I am better bred, than not to leave her choice free.

  Enter Valeria, and is surprised at sight of Don Pedro

VALERIA (*aside*) Don Pedro here! There's no avoiding him.   125

FLORINDA (*aside*) Valeria! then I'm undone.

VALERIA (*to Pedro, running to him*) Oh, have I found you, sir? The
strangest accident—if I had breath—to tell it.

PEDRO Speak: is Florinda safe? Hellena well?

VALERIA Aye, aye, sir; Florinda—is safe—[*aside*] from any fears of   130
you.

PEDRO Why, where's Florinda? Speak.

VALERIA Aye, where indeed sir, I wish I could inform you; but to
hold you no longer in doubt—

FLORINDA (*aside*) Oh, what will she say?   135

VALERIA —She's fled away in the habit—of one of her pages, sir; but
Callis thinks you may retrieve her yet; if you make haste away,
she'll tell you, sir, the rest—(*aside*) if you can find her out.

PEDRO Dishonourable girl, she has undone my aim. [*To Belvile*] Sir,
you see my necessity of leaving you, and hope you'll pardon it; my   140
sister, I know, will make her flight to you; and if she do, I shall
expect she should be rendered back.

BELVILE I shall consult my love and honour, sir.
    Exit Pedro
FLORINDA (*to Valeria*) My dear preserver, let me embrace thee.
WILLMORE What the devil's all this?   145
BLUNT Mystery, by this light.
VALERIA Come, come, make haste and get yourselves married quickly,
    for your brother will return again.
BELVILE I'm so surprised with fears and joys, so amazed to find you
    here in safety, I can scarce persuade my heart into a faith of what   150
    I see.
WILLMORE Hark'ee, colonel, is this that mistress who has cost you
    so many sighs, and me so many quarrels with you?
BELVILE It is. (*To Florinda*) Pray give him the honour of your hand.
WILLMORE (*kneels° and kisses her hand*) Thus it must be received   155
    then; and with it give your pardon too.
FLORINDA The friend to Belvile may command me anything.
WILLMORE (*aside*) Death, would I might; 'tis a surprising beauty.
BELVILE Boy, run and fetch a father° instantly.
    Exit page
FREDERICK So, now do I stand like a dog, and have not a syllable to   160
    plead my own cause with. By this hand, madam, I was never
    thoroughly confounded before, nor shall I ever more dare look up
    with confidence, till you are pleased to pardon me.
FLORINDA Sir, I'll be reconciled to you on one condition: that you'll
    follow the example of your friend, in marrying a maid that does   165
    not hate you, and whose fortune, I believe, will not be unwelcome
    to you.
FREDERICK Madam, had I no inclinations that way, I should obey
    your kind commands.
BELVILE Who, Fred marry? He has so few inclinations for woman-   170
    kind, that had he been possessed of paradise, he might have
    continued there to this day, if no crime but love could have
    disinherited him.
FREDERICK Oh, I do not use to boast of my intrigues.
BELVILE Boast? Why, thou dost nothing but boast; and I dare swear,   175
    wert thou as innocent from the sin of the grape, as thou art from
    the apple, thou might'st yet claim that right in Eden which our
    first parents lost by too much loving.
FREDERICK I wish this lady would think me so modest a man.
VALERIA She would be sorry then, and not like you half so well; and   180
    I should be loth to break my word with you, which was that if your

friend and mine agreed, it should be a match between you and I.
(*Gives him her hand*)

FREDERICK (*kisses her hand*) Bear witness, colonel, 'tis a bargain.

BLUNT (*to Florinda*) I have a pardon to beg too, but 'adsheartlikins,   185
I am so out of countenance, that I'm a dog if I can say anything
to purpose.

FLORINDA Sir, I heartily forgive you all.

BLUNT That's nobly said, sweet lady.—Belvile, prithee present her
her ring again; for I find I have not courage to approach her   190
myself.

> [*Blunt*] *gives* [*Belvile*] *the ring;* [*Belvile*] *gives it to Florinda.*
> *Enter page*

PAGE Sir, I have brought the father that you sent for.

BELVILE 'Tis well.—And now, my dear Florinda, let's fly to complete that mighty joy we have so long wished and sighed for.—
Come, Fred, you'll follow?   195

FREDERICK —Your example, sir: 'twas ever my ambition in war, and
must be so in love.

WILLMORE And must not I see this juggling knot° tied?

BELVILE No, thou shalt do us better service, and be our guard, lest
Don Pedro's sudden return interrupt the ceremony.   200

WILLMORE Content; I'll secure this pass.

> *Exeunt Belvile, Florinda, Frederick, and Valeria. Enter page*

PAGE (*to Willmore*) Sir, there's a lady without would speak to you.

WILLMORE Conduct her in; I dare not quit my post.

PAGE [*to Blunt*] And sir, your tailor waits you in your chamber.

BLUNT Some comfort yet; I shall not dance naked at the wedding.   205

> *Exeunt Blunt and page. Enter again the page, conducting in*
> *Angellica in a masking habit and a vizard. Willmore runs to*
> *her*

WILLMORE [*aside*] This can be none but my pretty gipsy. [*To*
Angellica] Oh, I see you can follow as well as fly. Come, confess
thyself the most malicious devil in nature; you think you have done
my business with Angellica.

ANGELLICA Stand off, base villain.   210

> [*Angellica*] *draws a pistol, and holds* [*it*] *to* [*Willmore's*] *breast*

WILLMORE [*aside*] Ha, 'tis not she.—Who art thou? and what's thy
business?

ANGELLICA One thou hast injured, and who comes to kill thee for't.

WILLMORE What the devil canst thou mean?

ANGELLICA By all my hopes, to kill thee.   215

[Angellica] holds still the pistol to [Willmore's] breast, he going back, she following still

WILLMORE   Prithee, on what acquaintance? For I know thee not.

ANGELLICA   (*pulls off her vizard*) Behold this face, so lost to thy
    remembrance,
  And then call all thy sins about thy soul,
  And let 'em die with thee.

WILLMORE   Angellica!   220

ANGELLICA   Yes, traitor,
  Does not thy guilty blood run shivering through thy veins?
  Hast thou no horror at this sight, that tells thee,
  Thou hast not long to boast thy shameful conquest?

WILLMORE   Faith, no, child; my blood keeps its old ebbs and flows   225
  still, and that usual heat too, that could oblige thee with a kindness,
  had I but opportunity.

ANGELLICA   Devil! dost wanton with my pain? Have at thy heart.

WILLMORE   Hold, dear virago! Hold thy hand a little; I am not now
  at leisure to be killed; hold and hear me. (*Aside*) Death, I think   230
  she's in earnest.

ANGELLICA   (*aside, turning from him*) Oh, if I take not heed,
  My coward heart will leave me to his mercy.
  —What have you, sir, to say? But should I hear thee,
  Thou'dst talk away all that is brave about me: 235
  (*Follows him with the pistol to his breast*)
  And I have vowed thy death, by all that's sacred.

WILLMORE   Why then, there's an end of a proper handsome fellow,
  that might 'a lived to have done good service yet; that's all I can
  say to't.

ANGELLICA   (*pausingly*) Yet, I would give thee—time for—penitence.   240

WILLMORE   Faith, child, I thank God, I have ever took care to lead
  a good sober, hopeful life, and am of a religion that teaches me to
  believe, I shall depart in peace.

ANGELLICA   So will the devil! tell me,
  How many poor believing fools thou hast undone?   245
  How many hearts thou hast betrayed to ruin?
  Yet these are little mischiefs to the ills
  Thou'st taught mine to commit: thou'st taught it love.

WILLMORE   Egad, 'twas shrewdly hurt the while.

ANGELLICA   Love, that has robbed it of its unconcern,   250
  Of all that pride that taught me how to value it.
  And in its room

A mean submissive passion was conveyed,
That made me humbly bow, which I ne'er did
To anything but heaven.   255
Thou, perjured man, didst this, and with thy oaths,
Which on thy knees thou didst devoutly make,
Softened my yielding heart, and then, I was a slave;
Yet still had been content to've worn my chains,
Worn 'em with vanity and joy forever,   260
Hadst thou not broke those vows that put them on.
'Twas then I was undone.

   All this while follows him with the pistol to his breast

WILLMORE Broke my vows! Why, where hast thou lived?
  Amongst the gods? for I never heard of mortal man,
  That has not broke a thousand vows.   265

ANGELLICA Oh, impudence!

WILLMORE Angellica, that beauty has been too long tempting, not to
  have made a thousand lovers languish, who, in the amorous fever,°
  no doubt have sworn like me: did they all die in that faith, still
  adoring? I do not think they did.   270

ANGELLICA No, faithless man: had I repaid their vows, as I did
  thine, I would have killed the ingrateful that had abandoned me.

WILLMORE This old general has quite spoiled thee: nothing makes a
  woman so vain as being flattered; your old lover ever supplies the
  defects of age with intolerable dotage, vast charge,° and that which   275
  you call constancy; and attributing all this to your own merits, you
  domineer, and throw your favours in's teeth, upbraiding him still
  with the defects of age, and cuckold him as often as he deceives
  your expectations. But the gay, young, brisk lover, that brings his
  equal fires, and can give you dart for dart, you'll find will be° as   280
  nice as you sometimes.

ANGELLICA All this thou'st made me know, for which I hate thee.
  Had I remained in innocent security,
  I should have thought all men were born my slaves,
  And worn my power like lightning in my eyes,   285
  To have destroyed at pleasure when offended:
  But when love held the mirror, the undeceiving glass
  Reflected all the weakness of my soul, and made me know
  My richest treasure being lost, my honour,
  All the remaining spoil could not be worth   290
  The conqueror's care or value.
  Oh, how I fell, like a long worshipped idol,

Discovering all the cheat.
Would not the incense and rich sacrifice,
Which blind devotion offered at my altars,   295
Have fallen to thee?
Why wouldst thou then destroy my fancied power?

WILLMORE By heaven thou'rt brave, and I admire thee strangely.
I wish I were that dull, that constant thing
Which thou wouldst have, and nature never meant me: 300
I must, like cheerful birds, sing in all groves,
And perch on every bough,
Billing the next kind she that flies to meet me;
Yet, after all, could build my nest with thee,
Thither repairing when I'd loved my round,   305
And still reserve a tributary flame.
To gain your credit, I'll pay you back your charity,
And be obliged for nothing but for love.
          Offers her a purse of gold°

ANGELLICA Oh, that thou wert in earnest!
So mean a thought of me   310
Would turn my rage to scorn, and I should pity thee,
And give thee leave to live;
Which for the public safety of our sex,
And my own private injuries, I dare not do.
Prepare: (*follows still, as before*)   315
I will no more be tempted with replies.

WILLMORE Sure—

ANGELLICA Another word will damn thee! I've heard thee talk too
  long.
          She follows him with the pistol ready to shoot; he retires still
          amazed. Enter Don Antonio, his arm in a scarf, and lays
          hold on the pistol

ANTONIO Ha, Angellica!   320

ANGELLICA Antonio! What devil brought thee hither?

ANTONIO Love and curiosity, seeing your coach at door. Let me
  disarm you of this unbecoming instrument of death. (*Takes away*
  the pistol) Amongst the number of your slaves, was there not one
  worthy the honour to have fought your quarrel? [*To Willmore*] 325
  Who are you, sir, that are so very wretched to merit death from
  her?

WILLMORE One, sir, that could have made a better end of an
  amorous quarrel without you, than with you.

ANTONIO Sure 'tis some rival. Ha! The very man took down her   330
picture yesterday; the very same that set on me last night; blest
opportunity!

     [Antonio] offers to shoot [Willmore]

ANGELLICA Hold, you're mistaken, sir.

ANTONIO By heaven, the very same!—Sir, what pretensions have
you to this lady?   335

WILLMORE Sir, I do not use to be° examined, and am ill at all
disputes but this.

     [Willmore] draws; Antonio offers to shoot

ANGELLICA (*to Willmore*) Oh, hold! you see he's armed with certain
death;

  —And you, Antonio, I command you hold,

By all the passion you've so lately vowed me.   340

     Enter Don Pedro, sees Antonio, and stays

PEDRO (*aside*) Ha, Antonio! and Angellica!

ANTONIO When I refuse obedience to your will,

May you destroy me with your mortal hate.

By all that's holy, I adore you so,

That even my rival, who has charms enough   345

To make him fall a victim to my jealousy,

Shall live, nay and have leave to love on still.

PEDRO (*aside*) What's this I hear?

ANGELLICA (*pointing to Willmore*) Ah thus, 'twas thus, he talked, and
I believed.

Antonio, yesterday,   350

I'd not have sold my interest in his heart,

For all the sword has won and lost in battle.

[*To Willmore*] But now to show my utmost of contempt,

I give thee life, which if thou wouldst preserve,

Live where my eyes may never see thee more;   355

Live to undo someone whose soul may prove

So bravely constant to revenge my love.

     [Angellica] goes out. Antonio follows, but Pedro pulls him back

PEDRO Antonio, stay.

ANTONIO Don Pedro!

PEDRO What coward fear was that prevented thee   360

From meeting me this morning on the Molo?

ANTONIO Meet thee?

PEDRO Yes, me; I was the man that dared thee to't.

ANTONIO Hast thou so often seen me fight in war,

To find no better cause to excuse my absence?   365
I sent my sword and one to do thee right,
Finding myself uncapable to use a sword.

PEDRO But 'twas Florinda's quarrel that we fought,
And you, to show how little you esteemed her,
Sent me your rival, giving him your interest.   370
But I have found the cause of this affront,
And when I meet you fit for the dispute,
I'll tell you my resentment.

ANTONIO I shall be ready, sir, ere long to do you reason.
        Exit Antonio

PEDRO If I could find Florinda, now whilst my anger's high, I think   375
I should be kind, and give her to Belvile in revenge.

WILLMORE Faith, sir, I know not what you would do, but I believe
the priest within has been so kind.

PEDRO How! My sister married?

WILLMORE I hope by this time he is, and bedded too, or he has not   380
my longings about him.

PEDRO Dares he do this? Does he not fear my power?

WILLMORE Faith, not at all; if you will go in, and thank him for the
favour he has done your sister, so; if not, sir, my power's greater
in this house than yours: I have a damned surly crew here, that   385
will keep you till the next tide, and then clap you on board for
prize.° My ship lies but a league off the Molo, and we shall show
your donship a damned Tramontana rover's trick.
        Enter Belvile

BELVILE [*aside*] This rogue's in some new mischief. Ha, Pedro
returned!   390

PEDRO Colonel Belvile, I hear you have married my sister?

BELVILE You have heard truth, then, sir.

PEDRO Have I so; then, sir, I wish you joy.

BELVILE How!

PEDRO By this embrace I do, and I am glad on't.   395

BELVILE Are you in earnest?

PEDRO By our long friendship, and my obligations to thee, I am: the
sudden change I'll give you reasons for anon. Come, lead me to
my sister, that she may know I now approve her choice.
        Exit Belvile with Pedro. Willmore goes to follow them. Enter
        Hellena, as before in boy's clothes, and pulls him back

WILLMORE [*aside*] Ha, my gipsy! [*To Hellena*] Now, a thousand   400
blessings on thee for this kindness. Egad, child, I was e'en in

despair of ever seeing thee again; my friends are all provided for
within, each man his kind woman.

HELLENA [*aside*] Ha! I thought they had served me some such trick!

WILLMORE And I was e'en resolved to go aboard, and condemn   405
myself to my lone cabin, and the thoughts of thee.

HELLENA And could you have left me behind? Would you have been
so ill-natured?

WILLMORE Why, 'twould have broke my heart, child; but since we
are met again, I defy foul weather to part us.   410

HELLENA And would you be a faithful friend, now, if a maid should
trust you?

WILLMORE For a friend I cannot promise; thou art of a form so
excellent, a face and humour too good for cold dull friendship; I
am parlously afraid of being in love, child, and you have not forgot   415
how severely you have used me?

HELLENA That's all one; such usage you must still look for: to find
out all your haunts, to rail at you to all that love you, till I have
made you love only me in your own defence, because nobody else
will love.   420

WILLMORE But hast thou no better quality, to recommend thyself
by?

HELLENA Faith, none, captain: why, 'twill be the greater charity to
take me for thy mistress. I am a lone child, a kind of orphan lover;
and why I should die a maid, and in a captain's hands too, I do   425
not understand.

WILLMORE Egad, I was never clawed away with broadsides° from
any female before. Thou hast one virtue I adore, good nature. I
hate a coy demure mistress, she's as troublesome as a colt; I'll
break none: no, give me a mad mistress when mewed, and in flying   430
one° I dare trust upon the wing, that whilst she's kind will come
to the lure.°

HELLENA Nay, as kind as you will, good captain, whilst it lasts, but
let's lose no time.

WILLMORE My time's as precious to me as thine can be: therefore,   435
dear creature, since we are so well agreed, let's retire to my
chamber, and if ever thou wert treated with such savoury love!
Come, my bed's prepared for such a guest, all clean and sweet as
thy fair self. I love to steal a dish and a bottle with a friend, and
hate long graces: come, let's retire and fall to.   440

HELLENA 'Tis but getting my consent, and the business is soon
done: let but old gaffer Hymen and his priest say amen to't, and I

dare lay my mother's daughter by as proper a fellow as your
father's son, without fear or blushing.

WILLMORE Hold, hold, no bug words, child. Priest and Hymen?   445
Prithee add a hangman to 'em to make up the consort. No, no,
we'll have no vows but love, child, nor witness but the lover: the
kind deity enjoin naught but love and enjoy! Hymen and priest
wait still upon portion, and jointure; love and beauty have their
own ceremonies. Marriage is as certain a bane to love, as lending   450
money is to friendship: I'll neither ask nor give a vow; though
I could be content to turn gipsy, and become a left-handed
bridegroom,° to have the pleasure of working that great miracle of
making a maid a mother, if you durst venture; 'tis upse gipsy that,
and if I miss, I'll lose my labour.   455

HELLENA And if you do not lose, what shall I get? A cradle full of noise
and mischief, with a pack of repentance at my back? Can you teach
me to weave incle to pass my time with? 'Tis upse gipsy that too.

WILLMORE I can teach thee to weave a true love's knot better.

HELLENA So can my dog.   460

WILLMORE Well, I see we are both upon our guards, and I see
there's no way to conquer good nature, but by yielding: here, give
me thy hand; one kiss and I am thine.

HELLENA One kiss! How like my page he speaks. I am resolved you
shall have none, for asking such a sneaking sum: he that will be   465
satisfied with one kiss, will never die of that longing. Good friend
single-kiss, is all your talking come to this? A kiss, a caudle!
Farewell, captain single-kiss.

    [Hellena is] going out; [Willmore] stays her

WILLMORE Nay, if we part so, let me die like a bird upon a bough,
at the sheriff's charge.° By heaven, both the Indies shall not buy   470
thee from me. I adore thy humour and will marry thee, and we are
so of one humour, it must be a bargain. Give me thy hand. (Kisses
her hand) And now let the blind ones, love and fortune, do their
worst.

HELLENA Why, God-a-mercy, captain!   475

WILLMORE But hark'ee: the bargain is now made; but is it not fit we
should know each other's names? That when we have reason to
curse one another hereafter, and people ask me who 'tis I give to
the devil, I may at least be able to tell, what family you came of.

HELLENA Good reason, captain; and where I have cause (as I doubt   480
not but I shall have plentiful), that I may know at whom to throw
my—blessings—I beseech ye your name.

WILLMORE I am called Robert the constant.

HELLENA A very fine name; pray was it your faulkner or butler
 that christened you? Do they not use to whistle when they call   485
 you?°

WILLMORE I hope you have a better, that a man may name without
 crossing himself;° you are so merry with mine.

HELLENA I am called Hellena the inconstant.

   Enter Pedro, Belvile, Florinda, Frederick, [and] Valeria

PEDRO Ha, Hellena!   490

FLORINDA Hellena!

HELLENA The very same. Ha, my brother! Now, captain, show your
 love and courage; stand to your arms, and defend me bravely, or
 I am lost forever.

PEDRO What's this I hear? False girl, how came you hither, and   495
 what's your business? Speak.

   *[Pedro] goes roughly to [Hellena]. [Willmore] puts himself
   between [them]*

WILLMORE Hold off, sir, you have leave to parley only.

HELLENA I had e'en as good tell it, as you guess it. Faith, brother,
 my business is the same with all living creatures of my age: to love,
 and be beloved; and here's the man.   500

PEDRO Perfidious maid, hast thou deceived me too, deceived thyself
 and heaven?

HELLENA 'Tis time enough to make my peace with that;
 Be you but kind, let me alone with heaven.

PEDRO Belvile, I did not expect this false play from you. Was't not   505
 enough you'd gain Florinda (which I pardoned) but your lewd
 friends too must be enriched with the spoils of a noble family?

BELVILE Faith, sir, I am as much surprised at this as you can be. Yet,
 sir, my friends are gentlemen, and ought to be esteemed for their
 misfortunes, since they have the glory to suffer with the best of   510
 men and kings: 'tis true, he's a rover of fortune,
 Yet a prince, aboard his little wooden world.°

PEDRO What's this to the maintenance of a woman of her birth and
 quality?

WILLMORE Faith, sir, I can boast of nothing but a sword which does   515
 me right where'er I come, and has defended a worse cause than a
 woman's; and since I loved her before I either knew her birth or
 name, I must pursue my resolution, and marry her.

PEDRO And is all your holy intent of becoming a nun, debauched
 into a desire of man?   520

HELLENA Why, I have considered the matter, brother, and find, the three hundred thousand crowns° my uncle left me, and you cannot keep from me,° will be better laid out in love than in religion, and turn to as good an account. [*To the others*] Let most voices carry it: for heaven or the captain?   525

ALL (*cry*) A captain! a captain!

HELLENA Look ye sir, 'tis a clear case.

PEDRO Oh, I am mad! (*Aside*) If I refuse, my life's in danger. [*To Willmore*] Come, there's one motive induces me.
         [*Don Pedro*] *gives* [*Hellena*] *to* [*Willmore*]
     Take her: I shall now be free from fears of her honour; guard it   530
     you now, if you can; I have been a slave to't long enough.

WILLMORE Faith, sir, I am of a nation that are of opinion a woman's honour is not worth guarding when she has a mind to part with it.

HELLENA Well said, captain.

PEDRO (*to Valeria*) This was your plot, mistress, but I hope you have   535
     married one that will revenge my quarrel to you.

VALERIA There's no altering destiny, sir.

PEDRO Sooner than a woman's will: therefore I forgive you all, and wish you may get my father's pardon as easily, which I fear.
         Enter Blunt dressed in a Spanish habit, looking very
         ridiculously; his man adjusting his band

MAN 'Tis very well, sir.   540

BLUNT Well, sir? 'Adsheartlikins, I tell you 'tis damnable ill, sir. A Spanish habit, good lord! Could the devil and my tailor devise no other punishment for me, but the mode of a nation I abominate?

BELVILE What's the matter, Ned?

BLUNT (*turns round*) Pray view me round, and judge.   545

BELVILE I must confess thou art a kind of an odd figure.

BLUNT In a Spanish habit with a vengeance! I had rather be in the Inquisition for Judaism,° than in this doublet and breeches; a pillory were an easy collar to this, three handfuls high; and these shoes too, are worse than the stocks, with the sole an inch shorter   550
     than my foot. In fine, gentlemen, methinks I look altogether like a bag of bays° stuffed full of fool's flesh.

BELVILE Methinks 'tis well, and makes thee look *en cavalier*. Come, sir, settle your face, and salute our friends. [*Turns to Hellena*] Lady—

BLUNT Ha! (*To Hellena*) Say'st thou so, my little rover?° Lady, if   555
     you be one, give me leave to kiss your hand, and tell you, 'adsheartlikins, for all I look so, I am your humble servant. [*Aside*] A pox of my Spanish habit.

Music is heard to play

WILLMORE Hark, what's this?

Enter page

PAGE Sir, as the custom is, the gay people in masquerade, who make   560
every man's house their own, are coming up.

Enter several men and women in masking habits, with music;
they put themselves in order and dance

BLUNT 'Adsheartlikins, would 'twere lawful to pull off their false
faces, that I might see if my doxy were not amongst 'em.

BELVILE (*to the maskers*) Ladies and gentlemen, since you are come
so apropos, you must take a small collation with us.   565

WILLMORE (*to Hellena*) Whilst we'll to the good man within, who
stays to give us a cast of his office.° Have you no trembling at the
near approach?

HELLENA No more than you have in an engagement or a tempest.

WILLMORE Egad, thou'rt a brave girl, and I admire thy love and   570
courage.

Lead on, no other dangers they can dread,
Who venture in the storms o'th' marriage bed.

Exeunt

Epilogue

The banished cavaliers! A roving blade!
A popish carnival! A masquerade!
The devil's in't if this will please the nation,
In these our blessèd times of reformation,
When conventicling is so much in fashion.°   5
And yet:
That mutinous tribe less factions do beget,°
Than your continual differing in wit;
Your judgement's (as your passion's) a disease:
Nor muse nor miss your appetite can please;   10
You're grown as nice as queasy consciences,
Whose each convulsion, when the spirit moves,°
Damns everything that maggot disapproves.°

With canting rule you would the stage refine,
And to dull method all our sense confine.   15
With th'insolence of commonwealths you rule,
Where each gay fop, and politic grave fool
On monarch wit impose, without control.
As for the last, who seldom sees a play,
Unless it be the old Blackfriars way,°   20
Shaking his empty noddle o'er bamboo,°
He cries, 'Good faith, these plays will never do.
Ah, sir, in my young days, what lofty wit,
What high strained scenes of fighting there were writ:
These are slight airy toys. But tell me, pray,   25
What has the House of Commons done today?'
Then shows his politics, to let you see,
Of state affairs he'll judge as notably,
As he can do of wit and poetry.
The younger sparks, who hither do resort,   30
Cry, 'Pox o' your genteel things, give us more sport;
Damn me, I'm sure 'twill never please the court.'

Such fops are never pleased, unless the play
Be stuffed with fools, as brisk and dull as they:
Such might the half-crown spare, and in a glass°   35
At home, behold a more accomplished ass,
Where they may set their cravats, wigs and faces,

And practise all their buffoonry grimaces;
See how this huff becomes, this dammee stare,°
Which they at home may act, because they dare,   40
But must with prudent caution do elsewhere.
Oh, that our Nokes, or Tony Leigh, could show°
A fop but half so much to th'life as you.

POSTSCRIPT

This play had been sooner in print, but for a report about the town
(made by some either very malicious or very ignorant) that 'twas
Thomaso altered;° which made the booksellers fear some trouble from
the proprietor° of that admirable play, which indeed has wit enough
to stock a poet, and is not to be pieced or mended by any but the   5
excellent author himself. That I have stolen some hints from it, may
be a proof that I valued it more than to pretend to alter it, had I had
the dexterity of some poets, who are not more expert in stealing than
in the art of concealing, and who even that way out-do the Spartan
boys.° I might have appropriated all to myself, but I, vainly proud of   10
my judgement, hang out the sign of Angellica (the only stolen object)°
to give notice where a great part of the wit dwelt; though if the play
of *The Novella*° were as well worth remembering as *Thomaso*, they
might (bating the name) have as well said, I took it from thence. I
will only say the plot and business (not to boast on't) is my own: as   15
for the words and characters, I leave the reader to judge and compare
'em with *Thomaso*, to whom I recommend the great entertainment of
reading it; though had this succeeded ill, I should have had no need
of imploring that justice from the critics, who are naturally so kind to
any that pretend to usurp their dominion, especially of our sex,° they   20
would doubtless have given me the whole honour on't. Therefore I
will only say in English what the famous Virgil does in Latin: I make
verses, and others have the fame.°

THE FEIGNED COURTESANS,

or

A Night's Intrigue

The Play was first performed at the the Dorset Garden Theatre, no later than March 1679, with the following cast:

ITALIANS

Morosini° (an old count, uncle to Julio)	*Mr Norris*
Julio (his nephew, a young count, contracted to Laura Lucretia)	*Mr Crosby*
Octavio (a young count contracted to Marcella; deformed, revengeful°)	*Mr Gillow*
Crapine (Morosini's man)	
Petro (supposed pimp to the two courtesans)	*Mr Leigh*
[Silvio° (page to Laura Lucretia)]	
[Antonio (attendant to Laura Lucretia)]	
[Page to Julio]	

ENGLISH

Sir Harry Fillamour (in love with Marcella)	*Mr Smith*
Mr Galliard (in love with Cornelia)	*Mr Betterton*
Sir Signal Buffoon (a fool)	*Mr Nokes*
Mr Tickletext (his governor)	*Mr Underhill*
Jack (Sir Signal's man)	
[Page to Fillamour]	

WOMEN

Laura Lucretia (a young lady of quality, contracted to Julio, in love with Galliard, and sister to Octavio)	*Mrs Lee*
Marcella	*Mrs Currer*
Cornelia	*Mrs Barry*
(sisters to Julio, and nieces to Morosini, pass for courtesans by the names of Euphemia and Silvianetta)	
Philippa (their woman)	*Mrs Norris*
Sabina (confidant to Laura Lucretia)	*Mrs Seymour*
Pages, music, footmen, and bravos	

THE SCENE

Rome

THE EPISTLE DEDICATORY

To Mrs Ellen Gwyn°

Madam,

'Tis no wonder that hitherto I followed not the good example of the believing poets, since less faith and zeal than you alone can inspire had wanted power to have reduced me to the true worship: your permission, madam, has enlightened me, and I with shame look back on my past ignorance, which suffered me not to pay an adoration long since where there was so very much due. Yet even now, though secure in my opinion, I make this sacrifice with infinite fear and trembling, well knowing that so excellent and perfect a creature as yourself differs only from the divine powers in this: the offerings made to you ought to be worthy of you, whilst they accept the will alone; and how, madam, would your altars be loaded, if like heaven you gave permission to all that had a will and desire to approach 'em, who now at distance can only wish and admire?—which all mankind agree to do, as if, madam, you alone had the patent from heaven to engross all hearts; and even those distant slaves, whom you conquer with your fame, pay an equal tribute to those that have the blessing of being wounded by your eyes, and boast the happiness of beholding you daily; insomuch that succeeding ages who shall with joy survey your history shall envy us who lived in this, and saw those charming wonders which they can only read of, and whom we ought in charity to pity, since all the pictures pens or pencils can draw, will give 'em° but a faint idea of what we have the honour to see in such absolute perfection. They can only guess she was infinitely fair, witty, and deserving, but to what vast degrees in all, they can only judge who lived to gaze and listen; for besides, madam, all the charms and attractions and powers of your sex, you have beauties peculiar to yourself, an eternal sweetness, youth and air, which never dwelt in any face but yours, of which not one unimitable grace could be ever borrowed or assumed, though with never so much industry, to adorn another. They cannot steal a look or smile from you to enhance their own beauties' price, but all the world will know it yours, so natural and so fitted are all your charms and excellencies to one another, so entirely designed and created to make up in you alone the most perfect lovely thing in the world. You never appear but you glad the

hearts of all that have the happy fortune to see you, as if you were   35
made on purpose to put the whole world into good humour whenever
you look abroad; and when you speak, men crowd to listen with that
awful reverence as to holy oracles or divine prophecies, and bear° away
the precious words, to tell at home to all the attentive family the
graceful things you uttered, and cry, 'but oh she spoke with such an   40
air, so gay, that half the beauty's lost in the repetition.' 'Tis this that
ought to make your sex vain enough to despise the malicious world
that will allow a woman no wit, and bless ourselves for living in an age
that can produce so wondrous an argument as your undeniable self, to
shame those boasting talkers who are judges of nothing but faults.   45

But how much in vain, madam, I endeavour to tell you the sense of
all mankind with mine, since to the utmost limits of the universe your
mighty conquests are made known: and who can doubt the power of
that illustrious beauty, the charms of that tongue, and the greatness of
that mind, who has subdued the most powerful and glorious monarch   50
of the world? And so well you bear the honours you° were born for,
with a greatness so unaffected, an affability so easy, an humour so soft,
so far from pride or vanity, that the most envious and most disaffected
can find no cause or reason to wish you less; nor can heaven give you
more, who has expressed a particular care of you every way, and above   55
all in bestowing, on the world and you, two noble branches,° who have
all the greatness and sweetness of their royal and beautiful stock; and
who give us too a hopeful prospect of what their future braveries will
perform, when they shall shoot up and spread themselves to that
degree, that all the lesser world may find repose beneath their shades;   60
and whom you have permitted to wear those glorious titles° which you
yourself generously neglected, well knowing with the noble poet, 'tis
better far to merit titles than to wear 'em.

Can you then blame my ambition, madam, that lays this at your feet,
and begs a sanctuary where all pay so great a veneration? 'Twas   65
dedicated yours before it had a being, and overbusy° to render it
worthy of the honour, made it less grateful; and poetry like lovers often
fares the worse by taking too much pains to please; but under so
gracious an influence my tender laurels may thrive, till they become fit
wreaths to offer to the rays that improve their growth: which, madam,   70
I humbly implore, you still permit her ever to do, who is, madam,

> Your most humble,
> and most obedient servant,
> A. Behn

The Prologue

Spoken by Mrs Currer°

The devil take this cursèd plotting age,°
'T has ruined all our plots upon the stage;
Suspicions, new elections, jealousies,
Fresh informations, new discoveries,
Do so employ the busy fearful town,   5
Our honest calling here is useless grown;
Each fool turns politician now, and wears
A formal face, and talks of state-affairs;
Makes acts, decrees, and a new model draws
For regulation both of church and laws;   10
Tires out his empty noddle to invent
What rule and method's best in government;
But wit, as if 'twere Jesuitical,°
Is an abomination to ye all.
To what a wretched pass will poor plays come?   15
This must be damned, the plot is laid in Rome.°
'Tis hard—yet—
Not one amongst ye all, I'll undertake,
E'er thought that we should suffer for religion's sake:
Who would have thought that would have been th'occasion,   20
Of any contest in our hopeful nation?
For my own principles, faith, let me tell ye
I'm still of the religion of my cully;
And till these dangerous times they'd none to fix on,
But now are something in mere contradiction,   25
And piously pretend, these are not days
For keeping mistresses and seeing plays.
Who says this age a reformation wants,
When Betty Currer's lovers all turn saints?
In vain, alas, I flatter, swear, and vow,   30
You'll scarce do any thing for charity now:
Yet I am handsome still, still young and mad,
Can wheedle, lie, dissemble, jilt—egad,
As well and artfully as e'er I did;
Yet not one conquest can I gain or hope,   35

No prentice, not a foreman of a shop,
So that I want extremely new supplies;
Of my last coxcomb, faith, these were the prize;
And by the tattered ensigns you may know,°
These spoils were of a victory long ago: 40
Who would have thought such hellish times to've seen,
When I should be neglected at eighteen?
That youth and beauty should be quite undone!
A pox upon the whore of Babylon.°

1.1

[A street]

*Enter Laura Lucretia and Silvio, richly dressed; Antonio
attending, coming all in in haste*

SILVIO Madam, you need not make such haste away; the stranger
that followed us from St Peter's church° pursues us no longer, and
we have now lost sight of him. Lord, who would have thought the
approach of a handsome cavalier should have possessed Donna
Laura Lucretia with fear?   5

LAURA LUCRETIA I do not fear, my Silvio, but I would have this new
habitation, which I've designed for love, known to none but him
to whom I've destined my heart. (*Aside*) Ah, would he know the
conquest he has made!—Nor went I this evening to church with
any other devotion, but that which warms my heart for my young   10
English cavalier, whom I hoped to have seen there; and I must find
some way to let him know my passion, which is too high for souls
like mine to hide.

SILVIO Madam, the cavalier's in view again, and hot in the pursuit.

LAURA LUCRETIA Let's haste away then; and Silvio, do you lag   15
behind; 'twill give him an opportunity of enquiring, whilst I get
out of sight. Be sure you conceal my name and quality, and tell
him—anything but truth—tell him I am la Silvianetta, the young
Roman courtesan, or what you please, to hide me from his
knowledge.   20

*Exeunt Laura Lucretia [and Antonio]. Enter Julio and page,
in pursuit*

JULIO Boy, fall you into discourse with that page, and learn his lady's
name, whilst I pursue her farther.

*Exit Julio. Page salutes Silvio, who returns it; they go out as
talking to each other. Enter Sir Harry Fillamour and Galliard*

FILLAMOUR He follows her close, whoe'er they be: I see this trade
of love goes forward still.

GALLIARD And will whilst there's difference in sexes. But Harry, the   25
women, the delicate women I was speaking of?

FILLAMOUR Prithee tell me no more of thy fine women, Frank; thou
hast not been in Rome above a month, and thou'st been a dozen
times in love, as thou call'st it. To me there is no pleasure like
constancy.   30

GALLIARD Constancy! And wouldst thou have me one of those dull lovers who believe it their duty to love a woman till her hair and eyes change colour, for fear of the scandalous name of an inconstant! No, my passion, like great victors, hates the lazy stay, but having vanquished, prepares for new conquests.   35

FILLAMOUR Which you gain as they do towns by fire, lose 'em even in the taking; thou wilt° grow penitent, and weary of these dangerous follies.

GALLIARD But I am yet too young for both. Let old age and infirmity bring repentance, there's her feeble province; and even then, too,   40 we find no plague like being deprived of dear womankind.

FILLAMOUR I hate playing about a flame that will consume me.

GALLIARD Away with your antiquated notions, and let's once hear sense from thee. Examine but the whole world, Harry, and thou wilt find a beautiful woman the desire of the noblest, and the   45 reward of the bravest.

FILLAMOUR And the common prize of coxcombs: times are altered now, Frank; why else should the virtuous be cornuted, the coward be caressed, the villain roll with six,° and the fool lie with her ladyship?   50

GALLIARD Mere accident, sir, and the kindness of fortune; but a pretty witty young creature, such as this Silvianetta, and Euphemia, is certainly the greatest blessing this wicked world can afford us.

FILLAMOUR I believe the lawful enjoyment of such a woman, and   55 honest too, would be a blessing.

GALLIARD Lawful enjoyment! Prithee what's lawful enjoyment, but to enjoy 'em according to the generous indulgent law of nature; enjoy 'em as we do meat, drink, air and light, and all the rest of her common blessings? Therefore, prithee, dear knight, let me   60 govern thee but for a day, and I will show thee such a signora, such a beauty; another manner of piece than your so admired Viterboan,° Donna Marcella, of whom you boast so much.

FILLAMOUR And yet this rare piece is but a courtesan; in coarse plain English, a very whore!   65
Who filthily exposes all her beauties
To him can give her most, not love her best.°

GALLIARD Why, faith, to thy comfort be it spoken, she does distribute her charms at that easy rate.

FILLAMOUR Oh, the vast distance between an innocent passion, and   70 a poor faithless lust!

GALLIARD Innocent passion at Rome! Oh, 'tis not to be named but in some northern climate: to be an anchorite here, is to be an epicure in Greenland; impossibilities,° Harry! Sure, thou hast been advising with Sir Signal Buffoon's governor, that formal piece of nonsense and hypocrisy. 75

FILLAMOUR No, faith, I brought the humour along with me to Rome, and for your governor I have not seen him yet, though he lodge in this same house with us, and you promised to bring me acquainted with him° long since. 80

GALLIARD I'll do't this very minute!

FILLAMOUR No, I'm obliged not to engage myself this evening, because I expect the arrival of Count Julio, whose last letters assured me would be tonight.

GALLIARD Julio! What, the young Italian count you made me 85 acquainted with last summer in England?

FILLAMOUR The same; the ambassador's nephew, a good youth, and one I esteem.

   Enter Julio

JULIO I hope my page will bring intelligence° who this beauty is.

FILLAMOUR Ha, Julio! Welcome, dear friend. 90

   [*Fillamour*] *embraces* [*Julio*]

JULIO Sir Harry Fillamour! How glad am I to meet you in a country where I have power to repay you all those friendships I received when I was a stranger to yours. Monsieur Galliard, too; nay, then I'm sure to want no diversion whilst I stay in Rome.

   [*Julio*] *salutes Galliard*

FILLAMOUR But pray, what made you leave England so soon? 95

JULIO E'en the great business of mankind, matrimony. I have an uncle here, who has provided me fetters which I must put on; he says they will be easy. I liked the character° of my mistress well enough—a brave masculine lady, a Roman of quality, Donna Laura Lucretia—till, as luck would have it, at my arrival this evening, 100 stepping into St Peter's church, I saw a woman there that fired my heart, and whom I followed to her house; but meeting none that could inform me who she was, I left my page to make the discovery, whilst I with equal impatience came to look out you, whose sight I prefer even to a new amour; resolving not to visit 105 home, to which I have been a stranger this seven years, till I had kissed your hands, and gained your promise to accompany me to Viterbo.

FILLAMOUR Viterbo! Is that your place of residence?

JULIO Yes; 'tis a pretty town, and many noble families inhabit there;   110
stored too with beauties, at least 'twas wont to be: have you not
seen it?

GALLIARD Yes; and a beauty there, too lately for his repose, who has
made him sigh, and look so like an ass, ever since he came to
Rome.   115

JULIO I'm glad you have so powerful an argument to invite you back;
I know she must be rare, and of quality, that could engage your
heart.

FILLAMOUR She's both; it most unluckily fell out, that I was
recommended by a person of quality in England to a nobleman at   120
Viterbo, who, being a man of a temper frank and gallant, received
me with less ceremony than is usual in Italy. I had the freedom of
the house, one of the finest villas belonging to Viterbo, and the
pleasure to see and converse at a distance with one of the loveliest
persons in the world, a niece of this old count's.   125

JULIO Very well, and could you see her but at distance, sir?

FILLAMOUR Oh no, 'twas all I durst desire, or she durst give. I came
too late to hope, she being before promised in marriage to a more
happy man, the consummation of which waits only the arrival of
a brother of hers, who is now at the court of France, and every   130
day expected.

Enter Petro like a barber

GALLIARD Ha! Signor Petro.

FILLAMOUR *[to Julio]* Come, sir, we'll take a turn i'th'° gallery, for
this pimp never appears but Francis desires to be in private.

GALLIARD Thou wrong'st an honest ingenious fellow, to call him   135
pimp.

PETRO Ah, signor, what his worship pleases!

GALLIARD That thou art, I'll be sworn, or what any man's worship
pleases: for let me tell ye, Harry, he is capacitated to oblige in any
quality; for, sir, he's your brokering Jew, your fencing, dancing   140
and civility-master, your linguist, your antiquary, your bravo, your
pathic, your whore, your pimp, and a thousand more excellencies
he has to supply the necessities of the wanting stranger. *[To Petro]*
Well, sirrah; what design now upon Sir Signal and his wise
governor? What do you represent now?   145

PETRO A barber, sir.

GALLIARD And why a barber, good Signor Petro?

PETRO Oh, sir, the sooner to take the heights of their judgements; it
gives handsome opportunities to commend their faces; for if they

are pleased with flattery, the certain sign of a fool's to be most   150
tickled when most commended, I conclude 'em the fitter for my
purpose. They already put great confidence in me, will have no
masters but of my recommending, all which I supply myself, by
the help of my several disguises; by which, and my industry, I
doubt not but to pick up a good honest painful° livelihood, by   155
cheating these two reverend coxcombs.

GALLIARD How the devil got'st thou this credit with 'em?

PETRO Oh, easily sir, as knaves get estates, or fools employments.

FILLAMOUR I hope amongst all your good qualities you forgot not
your more natural one of pimping.   160

PETRO No, I assure you, sir; I have told Sir Signal Buffoon that no
man lives here without his inamorata, which very word has so fired
him, that he's resolved to have an inamorata whatever it cost him,
and as in all things else I have in that too promised my assistance.

GALLIARD If you assist him no better than you have done me, he   165
may stay long enough for his inamorata.

PETRO Why, faith sir, I lie at° my young lady night and day, but she
is so loth to part with that same maidenhead of hers yet; but
tomorrow night, sir, there's hopes.

GALLIARD Tomorrow night! Oh, 'tis an age in love! Desire knows no   170
time but the present: 'tis now I wish, and now I would enjoy; a
new day ought to bring a new desire.

PETRO Alas sir, I'm but an humble bravo.

GALLIARD Yes, thou'rt a pimp; yet want'st the art to procure a
longing lover the woman he adores, though but a common   175
courtesan. Oh, confound her maidenhead! She understands her
trade too well to have that badge of innocence.

PETRO I offered her her price, sir.

GALLIARD Double it, give anything, for that's the best recipe° I ever
found to soften women's hearts.   180

PETRO Well, sir, she will be this evening in the garden of Medici's
Villa;° there you may get an opportunity to advance your interest.
I must step and trim Mr Tickletext, and then am at your service.
        Exit Petro

JULIO What is this knight and his governor, who have the blessed
fortune to be managed by this squire?   185

FILLAMOUR Certain fools Galliard makes use on when he has a mind
to laugh, and whom I never thought worth a visit since I came to
Rome; and he's like to profit much by his travels, who keeps
company with all the English, especially the fops.°

99

GALLIARD Faith, sir, I came not abroad to return with the formality 190
of a judge; and these are such antidotes against melancholy as
would make thee fond of fooling. Our knight's father is even the
first gentleman of his house, a fellow who having the good fortune
to be much a fool and knave, had the attendant blessing of getting
an estate of some eight thousand a year, with this coxcomb to 195
inherit it, who (to aggrandize the name and family of the Buffoons)
was made a knight; but, to refine throughout and make a complete
fop, was sent abroad under the government of one Mr Tickletext,
his zealous father's chaplain, as arrant a blockhead as a man would
wish to hear preach; the father wisely foreseeing the eminent 200
danger that young travellers are in of being perverted to popery.

JULIO 'Twas well considered.

GALLIARD But for the young spark, there is no description can reach
him; 'tis only to be done by himself; let it suffice 'tis a pert, saucy,
conceited animal, whom you shall just now go see and admire, for 205
he lodges in the house with us.

JULIO With all my heart, I never longed more for a new acquaintance.

FILLAMOUR And in all probability shall sooner desire to be rid on't.
Allons.°
Exeunt

1.2

*Draws off [to Tickletext's room] and discovers° Mr Tickletext
a-trimming,° his hair under a cap, [and] a cloth before him.
Petro snaps his fingers, takes away the basin, and [begins]
wiping [Tickletext's] face*

PETRO Ah *che bella*!° *bella*! I swear by these sparkling eyes, and these
soft plump dimpled cheeks, there's not a signora in all Rome,
could she behold 'em, were able to stand their temptations; and for
la Silvianetta, my life on't, she's your own.

TICKLETEXT *Teze,*° *teze*, speak softly! But, honest Barberacho,° do 5
I, do I indeed look plump, and young, and fresh and——ha?

PETRO Aye, sir, as the rosy morn, young as old time in his infancy,
and plump as the pale-faced moon.

TICKLETEXT Hee; why, this travelling must needs improve a man.
(*Aside*) Why, how admirably spoken your very barbers are here!—— 10
But, Barberacho, did the young gentlewoman say she liked me?
Did she, rogue? Did she?

PETRO 'A° doted on you, signor, doted on you.

TICKLETEXT (*aside*) Why, and that's strange now, in the autumn of
my age too, when nature began to be impertinent, as a man may   15
say, that a young lady should fall in love with me.—Why,
Barberacho, I do not conceive any great matter of sin only in
visiting a lady that loves a man, ha?

PETRO Sin, sir! 'Tis a frequent thing nowadays in persons of your
complexion.   20

TICKLETEXT Especially here at Rome, too, where 'tis no scandal.

PETRO Aye signor, where the ladies are privileged, and fornication
licensed.

TICKLETEXT Right: and when 'tis licensed 'tis lawful, and when 'tis
lawful it can be no sin. Besides, Barberacho, I may chance to turn   25
her, who knows?

PETRO Turn her, signor? Alas, any way, which way you please.

TICKLETEXT Hee, hee, hee! There thou wert knavish, I doubt; but I
mean convert her; nothing else, I profess, Barberacho.

PETRO True, signor, true, she's a lady of an easy nature, and an   30
indifferent argument well handled will do't. Ha, (*combing out
[Tickletext's] hair*) here's your head of hair, here's your natural
frizz!° And such an air it gives the face! So, signor; now you have
the utmost my art can do.

[*Petro*] *takes away the cloth, and bows*

TICKLETEXT Well, signor, and where's your looking-glass?   35

PETRO My looking-glass?

TICKLETEXT Yes, signor, your looking-glass! An English barber
would as soon have forgotten to have snapped his fingers, made his
leg, or taken his money, as have neglected his looking-glass.

PETRO Aye, signor, in your country the laity have so little honesty, 40
they are not to be trusted with the taking off your beard unless you
see't done; but here's a glass, sir.

Gives him the glass. Tickletext sets himself° *and smirks in the
glass, Petro standing behind him, making horns*° *and grimaces
which Tickletext sees in the glass. [Tickletext] gravely rises
[and] turns towards Petro*

TICKLETEXT Why how now, Barberacho, what monstrous faces are
you making there?

PETRO Ah, my belly, my belly, signor: ah, this wind-colic, this   45
hypocondriac° does so torment me! Ah!

TICKLETEXT Alas, poor knave; *certo*, I thought thou hadst been
somewhat uncivil with me, I profess I did.

PETRO Who, I sir, uncivil? I abuse my patron? I that have almost
made myself a pimp to serve you?   50

TICKLETEXT *Teze, teze*, honest Barberacho! No, no, no, all's well,
all's well: but hark'ee, you will be discreet and secret in this
business now, and above all things conceal the knowledge of this
gentlewoman from Sir Signal and Mr Galliard.

PETRO The rack, signor, the rack shall not extort it.   55

TICKLETEXT Hold thy hand; there's somewhat for thee; (*gives him
money*) but shall I, rogue, shall I see her tonight?

PETRO Tonight sir, meet me in the Piazza di Spagna,° about ten o'
clock. I'll meet you there; but 'tis fit, signor, that I should provide
a collation; 'tis the custom here, sir.   60

TICKLETEXT Well, well, what will it come to? Here's an angel.
     [*Tickletext gives Petro money*]

PETRO Why, sir, 'twill come to—about (for you would do't handsomely) some twenty crowns.

TICKLETEXT How, man, twenty crowns?

PETRO Aye, signor, thereabouts.   65

TICKLETEXT Twenty crowns! Why, 'tis a sum, a portion,° a revenue.

PETRO Alas, signor, 'tis nothing with her; she'll look it out in an
hour. Ah, such an eye! so sparkling, with an amorous twire:
thus, sir [*adopts an amorous expression*]. Then she'll kiss it out in
a moment: such a lip, so red, so round, and so plump, so soft,   70
and so—

TICKLETEXT Why, has she, has she, sirrah? Ha; here, here, prithee
take money, here, and make no words on't. Go, go your way, go;
but to entertain Sir Signal with other matter, pray send his masters
to him: if thou canst help him to masters, and me to mistresses,   75
thou shalt be the good genius of us both. But see where he comes.
     Enter Sir Signal

SIR SIGNAL Ha! Signor *Illustrissimo*° Barberacho; let me hug thee,
my little Miphistophiloucho.° D'ye see here, how fine your
brokering Jew has made me, Signor Rabbi Manaseth-Ben-Nebiton,°
and so forth, ha? View me round.   80
     [*Sir Signal*] *turns round*

TICKLETEXT I profess 'tis as fit as if it had been made for you.

SIR SIGNAL Made for me? Why, sir, he swore to me by the old law,°
that 'twas never worn but once, and that but by one High German
prince; I have forgot his name, for the devil can never remember
these damned Hogan-Mogan titles.   85
     A fart°

TICKLETEXT No matter, sir.

SIR SIGNAL Aye, but I should be loth to be in any man's clothes, were he never so high a German prince, except I knew his name though.

TICKLETEXT Sir, I hold his name unnecessary to be remembered, so long as 'twas a princely pennyworth.—Barberacho, get you gone, and send the masters.

    Exit Petro

SIR SIGNAL Why, how now, governor! How now, Signor Tickletext! Prithee, how cam'st thou so transmogrified, ha? Why, thou look'st like any new-fledged Cupid.

TICKLETEXT Do I? Away, you flatter; do I?

SIR SIGNAL As I hope to breathe, your face shines through your powdered hairs like you know what on a barn-door, in a frosty morning.

TICKLETEXT What a filthy comparison's there for a man of my coat!

SIR SIGNAL What, angry? *Corpo di me,*° I meant no harm. Come, shall's to a bona-roba, where thou shalt part with thy pucelage, and that of thy beard, together?

TICKLETEXT How mean you sir, a courtesan, and a Romish courtesan?

SIR SIGNAL Now my tutor's up, ha, ha, ha; and ever is when one names a whore. Be pacified, man, be pacified; I know thou hat'st 'em worse than beads or holy water.

TICKLETEXT Away, you are such another knight; but leave this naughty discourse, and prepare for your fencing and civility-masters, who are coming.

SIR SIGNAL Aye, when, governor, when? Oh, how I long for my civility-master, that I may learn to out-compliment all the dull knights and squires in Kent, with a 'Servitore,° Hulichimo';°—no: 'Signora Bellissima, base le mane de vossignoria,° scusa mi,° Illustrissimo, cospetto di Bacco',° and so I'll run on; ha, governor, ha! Won't this be pure?

TICKLETEXT Notably ingenious, I profess!

SIR SIGNAL Well, I'll send my *staffiere*° for him *incontanente.*°—Hey, Jack—a—*cazzo,*° what a damned English name is Jack? Let me see; I will call him—Giovanni, which is as much as to say John.—Hey, Giovanni!

    Enter Jack

TICKLETEXT Sir, by your favour, his English Protestant-name is John Pepper; and I'll call him by ne'er a Popish name in Christendom.

SIR SIGNAL I'll call my own man, sir, by what name I please, sir; and   125
let me tell you, Reverend Mr Tickletext, I scorn to be served by any
man whose name has not an *-acho*, or an *-oucho*,° or some *Italiano* at
the end on't; [*to Jack*] therefore Giovanni Peperacho is the name by
which you shall be distinguished and dignified hereafter.

TICKLETEXT Sir Signal, Sir Signal, let me tell you, that to call a man   130
out of his name is unwarrantable, for Peter is called Peter, and
John, John; and I'll not see the poor fellow wronged of his name
for ne'er a Giovanni in Rome.

SIR SIGNAL Sir, I tell you that one Italian name is worth any two
English names in Europe, and I'll be judged by my civility-master.   135

TICKLETEXT Who shall end the dispute, if he be of my opinion?

SIR SIGNAL *Molto volentieri*,° which is as much as to say, with all my
heart.

JACK But sir, my grandmother would never own me if I should
change the cursen name° she gave me with her own hands, an't   140
please your worship.

SIR SIGNAL Hey, *bestia*!° I'll have no more of your worship, sirrah,
that old English sir-reverence; let me have you call me Signor
Illustrissimo, or *padrone mio*°—or—

TICKLETEXT Aye, that I like well enough now: but hold, sure this is   145
one of your masters.

Enter Petro, dressed like a French dancing-master

PETRO Signor Barberacho has sent me to teach you de Art of
Fencing.

SIR SIGNAL *Illustrissimo* Signor Monsieur, I am the person who am
to learn.   150

TICKLETEXT Stay, sir, stay: let me ask him some few questions first,
for, sir, I have played at back-sword,° and could have handled ye
a weapon as well as any man of my time in the university.

SIR SIGNAL Say ye so, Mr Tickletext? And i'faith, you shall have a
bout with him.   155

Tickletext gravely goes to Petro

TICKLETEXT Hum—hum—Mr Monsieur; pray, what are the
guards° that you like best?

PETRO Monsieur, eder de *quart* or de *tierce*, dey be both French and
Italian; den° for your *parades*, *degagements*, your *advancements*, your
elongements, and *retierments*:° dey be de same.   160

TICKLETEXT Cart and horse, what new-found inventions and words
have we here? Sir, I would know whether you like St George's
guard° or not.

PETRO *Alors*; monsieur, *mettez-vous en garde!*° Take de fleuret.

SIR SIGNAL Nay, faith and troth, governor, thou shalt have a   165
rubbers° with him.

Tickletext, smiling, refuses

TICKLETEXT Nay, *certo*, Sir Signal—and yet you shall prevail. (*Takes
the fleuret. [To Petro]*) Well, sir, come your ways.

PETRO Set your right foot forward, turn up your hand so: dat be de
quart. Now turn it dus: and dat be de *tierce*.   170

TICKLETEXT Hocus-pocus, Hicksius-doxius; here be de cart and
here be de horse! Why, what's all this for, ha, sir; and where's your
guard all this while?

SIR SIGNAL Aye, sir, where's your guard, sir, as my governor says,
sir, ha?   175

TICKLETEXT Come, come, sir, I must instruct you, I see. Come your
ways, sir.

PETRO A tande, a tande um pew:° trust° de right hand and de right
leg forward together.

TICKLETEXT Aye, marry sir, that's a good one indeed! What shall   180
become of my head then, sir; what guard have I left for that, good
Mr Monsieur, ha?

PETRO Ah, *morbleu*, is not dis for everyting?

TICKLETEXT No, marry is it not, sir; St George's guard is the best
for your head whilst you live: as thus, sir.   185

PETRO Dat, sir? Ha, ha; dat be guard for de back-sword.

TICKLETEXT Back-sword, sir; yes, back-sword, what should it be
else?

PETRO And dis be de single-rapier.°

TICKLETEXT Single-rapier with a vengeance, there's a weapon for a   190
gentleman indeed; is all this stir about single-rapier?

PETRO Single-rapier! What will you have for de gentleman, de
cudgel for de gentleman?

TICKLETEXT No, sir, but I would have it for de rascally Frenchman,
who comes to abuse persons of quality with paltry single-rapier.   195
Single rapier! Come, sir, come; put yourself in your cart and your
horse as you call it, and I'll show you the difference.

*[Tickletext] undresses himself till he appears in a ridiculous
posture*

PETRO Ah, monsieur, me sall run you two three times through de
body, and den you break a me head, what care I for dat? (*Aside*)
Pox on his ignorance!   200

TICKLETEXT Oh ho, sir, do your worst, sir, do your worst, sir.

*They put themselves into several guards, and Tickletext beats
Petro about the stage. Enter Galliard, Fillamour, and Julio*

PETRO Ah, monsieur, monsieur, will you kill a me?

TICKLETEXT Ah, monsieur, where be your carts now, and your
horse, Mr Monsieur, ha? and your single-rapier, Mr Monsieur, ha?

GALLIARD Why, how now Mr Tickletext, what mortal wars are   205
these? Ajax and Ulysses contending for Achilles his armour?°

PETRO (*aside*) If I be not revenged on him, hang me.

SIR SIGNAL Aye; why, who the devil would have taken my governor
for so tall a man of hands?° But *corpo di me*, ° Mr Galliard, I have
not seen his fellow.   210

TICKLETEXT Ah, sir, time was, I would have played ye a match at
cudgels with e'er a sophister° in the college, but verily I have
forgotten it; but here's an impudent Frenchman that would have
passed single-rapier upon us.

GALLIARD How? Nay, o' my word, then, he deserved to be chastised 215
for't. But now all's at peace again, pray know my kinsman, Sir
Harry Fillamour.

SIR SIGNAL [*to Galliard*] *Yo baco les manos*,° Signor *Illustrissimo
Cavaliero*—[*to Fillamour and Julio*] and yours, signors, who are
multo bien venito.°   220

TICKLETEXT ([*to Fillamour*], *dressing himself whilst he talks*) Oh lord,
sir, you take me, sir, in such a posture, sir, as I protest I have not
been seen in this many years.

FILLAMOUR Exercise is good for health, sir.

GALLIARD Sir Signal, you are grown a perfect Italian!—Well, Mr   225
Tickletext, you will carry him home a most accomplished gentleman, I see!

TICKLETEXT Hum, verily, sir, though I say it, for a man that never
travelled before, I think I have done reasonably well. I'll tell you,
sir: it was by my directions and advice that he brought over with   230
him two English knives, a thousand of English pins, four pair of
jersey stockings, and as many pair of buckskin gloves.

SIR SIGNAL Aye, sir, for good gloves, you know, are very scarce
commodities in this country.

JULIO Here, sir, at Rome, as you say, above all other places.   235

TICKLETEXT *Certo*, mere hedging-gloves° sir, and the clouterlest
seams.

FILLAMOUR Very right, sir; and now he talks of Rome, pray, sir, give
me your opinion of the place. Are there not noble buildings here?
Rare statues, and admirable fountains?   240

TICKLETEXT Your buildings are pretty buildings, but not com-
parable to our university-buildings; your fountains I confess are
pretty springs, and your statues reasonably well carved, but sir,
they are so ancient they are of no value! Then your churches are
the worst that ever I saw, that ever I saw.   245

GALLIARD How sir, the churches? Why, I thought Rome had been
famous throughout all Europe for fine churches.

FILLAMOUR What think you of St Peter's church, sir, is it not a
glorious structure?

TICKLETEXT St Peter's church, sir? You may as well call it St Peter's   250
Hall, sir; it has neither pew, pulpit, desk, steeple, nor ring of bells,°
and call you this a church, sir? No, sir, I'll say that for little
England, and a fig for't, for churches, easy pulpits—

SIR SIGNAL And sleeping pews—

TICKLETEXT —they are as well ordered as any churches in Christen-   255
dom: and finer rings of bells, sir, I am sure were never heard.

JULIO Oh, sir, there's much in what you say.

FILLAMOUR But then, sir, your rich altars, and excellent pictures of
the greatest masters of the world, your delicate music, and voices,
make some amends for the other wants.   260

TICKLETEXT How, sir! tell me of your rich altars, your gewgaws and
trinkets, and popish fopperies, with a deal of singsong; when I say,
give me, sir, five hundred close changes° rung by a set of good
ringers, and I'll not exchange 'em for all the anthems in Europe:
and for the pictures, sir, they are superstition, idolatrous, and flat   265
popery.

FILLAMOUR I'll convince you of that error that persuades you
harmless pictures are idolatrous.

TICKLETEXT How, sir, how, sir? Convince me; talk to me of being
convinced, and that in favour of popery? No, sir, by your favour,   270
I shall not be convinced. Convinced, quotha! No, sir, fare you well
an you be for convincing.—Come away, Sir Signal.—Fare you
well, sir, fare you well.—Convinced!
    [*Tickletext*] *goes out*

SIR SIGNAL Ha, ha, ha, so now is my governor gone in a fustian-
fume!° Well, he is ever thus when one talks of whoring and   275
religion; but come, sir, walk in, and I'll undertake my tutor shall
beg your pardon and renounce his English ill-bred opinion, nay,
his English churches, too, all but his own vicarage.

FILLAMOUR I have better diversion, sir, I thank you.—Come, Julio,
are you for a walk in the garden of Medici's Villa? 'Tis hard by.   280

JULIO I'll wait on you.
>   *Exeunt Fillamour and Julio*

SIR SIGNAL How, in the garden of Medici's Villa? But hark'ee, Galliard, will the ladies be there, the courtesans? The bona-robas, the inamoratas, and the *bell' ingrato*s,° ha?

GALLIARD Oh, doubtless, sir.   285
>   *Exit Galliard*

SIR SIGNAL I'll e'en bring my governor thither to beg his pardon, on purpose to get an opportunity to see the fine women; it may be I may get a sight of my new mistress, Donna Silvianetta, whom Petro is to bring me acquainted with.
>   *Exeunt*

2.1

[The garden of Medici's villa]°

Enter Morosini and Octavio

OCTAVIO By heaven, I will not eat, nor sleep, nor pray for anything
but swift and sure revenge, till I have found Marcella, that false
deceiving beauty, or her lover, my hated rival Fillamour, who,
wanton in the arms of the fair fugitive, laughs at my shameful
easiness, and cries, 'These joys were never meant for tame   5
Octavio!'

Enter Crapine

MOROSINI How now, Crapine! What, no news, no news of my nieces
yet, Marcella nor Cornelia?

CRAPINE None, sir.

OCTAVIO That's wondrous strange; Rome's a place of that general   10
intelligence,° methinks thou might'st have news of such trivial
things as women, amongst the cardinals' pages. I'll undertake to
learn the *ragion di stato*,° and present juncture of all affairs in Italy,
of° a common courtesan.

MOROSINI Sirrah, sirrah, let it be your care to examine all the   15
nunneries: for my own part, not a petticoat shall escape me.

OCTAVIO *(aside)* My task shall be for Fillamour.

MOROSINI I'll only make a visit to your sister Donna Laura Lucretia,
and deliver her a letter from my nephew Julio, and return to you
presently.   20

Going out, [Morosini] is stayed by Octavio

OCTAVIO Stay, sir. Defer your visit to my sister Laura: she is not yet
to know of my being in town. 'Tis therefore I have taken a lodging
in an obscure street, and am resolved never to be myself again till
I've redeemed my honour. Come, sir, let's walk.

*Enter to them as they are going out, Marcella and Cornelia,
dressed like courtesans,° [with] Philippa and attendance*°

MOROSINI Stay, stay, what women are these?   25

OCTAVIO Whores, sir, and so 'tis ten to one are all the kind; only
these differ from the rest in this, they generously own their trade
of sin, which others deal by stealth in: they are courtesans.

Exeunt [Morosini and Octavio]

MARCELLA The evening's soft and calm, as happy lovers'
thoughts;

And here are groves where the kind meeting trees   30
Will hide us from the amorous gazing crowd.

CORNELIA What should we do there: sigh till our wandering
    breath
Has raised a gentle gale amongst the boughs,
To whose dull melancholy music, we,
Laid on a bed of moss and new-fall'n leaves,   35
Will read the dismal tale of Echo's love?°
— No, I can make better use of famous Ovid!°
    [*Cornelia*] *snatches a little book from* [*Marcella*]
And prithee, what a pox have we to do with trees, flowers,
fountains, or naked statues?

MARCELLA But prithee, mad Cornelia, let's be grave and wise, at   40
least enough to think a little.

CORNELIA On what? Your English cavalier, Fillamour, of whom you
tell so many dull stories of his making love! Oh, how I hate a civil
whining coxcomb!

MARCELLA And so do I, I'll therefore think of him no more.   45

CORNELIA Good lord! What a damnable wicked thing is a virgin
grown up to woman.

MARCELLA Why, art thou such a fool to think I love this Fillamour?

CORNELIA It may be not at Rome, but at Viterbo, where men are
scarce, you did; and did you follow him to Rome, to tell him you   50
could love no more?

MARCELLA A too forward maid, Cornelia, hurts her own fame, and
that of all her sex.

CORNELIA Her sex! A pretty consideration; by my youth (an oath I
shall not violate this dozen year) my sex should excuse me, if, to   55
preserve their fame, they expected I should ruin my own quiet, in
choosing an ill-favoured husband such as Octavio before a young
handsome lover, such as you say Fillamour is.

MARCELLA I would fain persuade myself to be of thy mind; but the
world, Cornelia!   60

CORNELIA Hang the malicious world.

MARCELLA And there's such charms in wealth and honour, too!

CORNELIA None half so powerful as love, in my opinion: 'life, sister,
thou art beautiful, and hast a fortune too, which before I would
lay out upon so shameful a purchase, as such a bedfellow for life   65
as Octavio, I would turn arrant keeping courtesan,° and buy my
better fortune.

MARCELLA That word, too, startles me.

CORNELIA What, courtesan! Why, 'tis a noble title, and has more
  votaries than religion; there's no merchandise like ours, that of   70
  love, my sister; and can you be frighted with the vizor° which you
  yourself put on?

MARCELLA 'Twas the only disguise that could secure us from the
  search of my uncle and Octavio. Our brother Julio is by this too
  arrived, and I know they'll all be diligent; and some honour I was   75
  content to sacrifice to my eternal repose.

CORNELIA Spoke like my sister: a little impertinent honour we may
  chance to lose, 'tis true; but our right-down honesty, I perceive
  you are resolved we shall maintain through all the dangers of love
  and gallantry; though, to say truth, I find enough to do to defend   80
  my heart against some of those members that nightly serenade us,
  and daily show themselves before our window, gay as young
  bridegrooms, and as full of expectation.

MARCELLA But is't not wondrous, that amongst all these crowds we
  should not once see Fillamour? I thought the charms of a fair   85
  young courtesan might have obliged him to some curiosity at least.

CORNELIA Aye; and an English cavalier too, a nation so fond of all
  new faces.

MARCELLA Heaven, if I should never see him, and I frequent all
  public places to meet him; or if he be gone from Rome, if he have   90
  forgot me, or some other beauty have employed his thoughts!

CORNELIA Why, if all these ifs and ors come to pass, we have no
  more to do than to advance in this same glorious profession, of
  which now we only seem to be; in which, to give it its due, there
  are a thousand satisfactions to be found, more than in a dull   95
  virtuous life! Oh, the world of dark-lantern men° we should have;
  the serenades, the songs, the sighs, the vows, the presents, the
  quarrels; and all for a look or a smile, which you have been hitherto
  so covetous of, that Petro swears our lovers begin° to suspect us
  for some honest jilts, which by some is accounted much the lewder   100
  scandal of the two; therefore I think, faith, we must e'en be kind
  a little, to redeem our reputations.

MARCELLA However we may rally, certainly there's nothing so hard
  to woman, as to expose herself to villainous man.

CORNELIA Faith, sister, if 'twere but as easy to satisfy the nice   105
  scruples of religion and honour, I should find no great difficulty in
  the rest. Besides, another argument I have, our money's all gone,
  and without a miracle can hold out no longer honestly.

MARCELLA Then we must sell our jewels!

CORNELIA When they are gone, what jewel will you part with next?   110
MARCELLA Then we must—
CORNELIA What, go home to Viterbo, ask the old gentleman pardon,
and be received to grace again; you to the embraces of the amiable
Octavio, and I to St Teresa's,° to whistle through a grate like a
bird in a cage? For I shall have little heart to sing. But come, let's   115
leave this sad talk; here's men. Let's walk and gain new conquest;
I love it dearly.
> [*Marcella and Cornelia*] *walk down the garden.*° *Enter*
> *Galliard, Fillamour, and Julio,* [*and*] *see the women*

GALLIARD Women! and by their garb for our purpose, too. They're
courtesans; let's follow 'em.
FILLAMOUR What shall we get by gazing but disquiet? If they are   120
fair and honest, we look and perhaps may sigh in vain; if beautiful
and loose, they are not worth regarding.
GALLIARD Dear notional knight, leave your satirical fopperies, and
be at least good-humoured, and let's follow 'em.
JULIO I'll leave you in the pursuit, and take this opportunity to write   125
my uncle word of my arrival; and wait on you here anon.
FILLAMOUR Prithee do so. Ha, who's that with such an equipage?
> [*Exeunt*] *Julio, Fillamour and Galliard going after. Marcella*
> *and Cornelia meet, just entering, Laura Lucretia with her*
> *equipage, dressed like a man*

GALLIARD Pox, let the tradesmen ask, who cringe for such gay
customers, and follow us the women!
> [*Exeunt*] *Fillamour and Galliard down the scene,*° *Laura*
> *Lucretia looking after them*

LAURA LUCRETIA 'Tis he, my cavalier, my conqueror! Antonio, let   130
the coaches wait!—And stand at distance, all!—Now, Silvio, on thy
life, forget my sex and quality, forget my useless name of Laura
Lucretia, and call me count of—
SILVIO What, madam?
LAURA LUCRETIA Madam! Ah, foolish boy, thy feminine courage   135
will betray us all; but—call me—Count—Sans Cœur;° and tell me,
Silvio, how is it I appear?
How dost thou like my shape, my face and dress,
My mien and equipage; may I not pass for man?
Looks it *en prince*, and masculine?   140
SILVIO Now, as I live, you look all over what you wish, and such as
will beget a reverence and envy in the men, and passion in the
women; but what's the cause of all this transformation?

LAURA LUCRETIA Love! Love! Dull boy, couldst thou not guess
'twas love? That dear *Inglese*° I must enjoy, my Silvio.   145
SILVIO What, he that adores the fair young courtesan?
LAURA LUCRETIA That very he.°
My window joins to hers, and 'twas with charms
Which he'd prepared for her, he took this heart,
Which met the welcome arrows in their flight,   150
And saved her from their dangers.
Oft I've returned the vows he's made to her
And sent him pleased away;
When through the errors of the night, and distance,
He has mistook me for that happy wanton,   155
And gave me language of so soft a power,
As ne'er was breathed in vain to listening maids.
SILVIO But with permission, madam, how does this change of
petticoat for breeches, and shifting houses too, advance that love?
LAURA LUCRETIA This habit, besides many opportunities 'twill give   160
me of getting into his acquaintance, secures me too from being
known by any of my relations in Rome; then I have changed my
house for one so near to that of Silvianetta's, and so like it too,
that even you and I have oft mistook the entrance; by which means
love, fortune, or chance, may with my industry contrive some kind   165
mistake that may make me happier than the rest of womankind.
SILVIO But what shall be reserved then for Count Julio, whose last
letters promise his arrival within a day or two, and whom you're
then to marry?
LAURA LUCRETIA Reserved for him? A wife! A wife, my Silvio,   170
That unconcerned domestic necessary,
Who rarely brings a heart, or takes it soon away.
SILVIO But then your brother, Count Octavio, do you not fear his
jealousy?
LAURA LUCRETIA Octavio! Oh, nature has set his soul and mine at
odds,   175
And I can know no fear, but where I love.
SILVIO And then that thing that ladies call their honour—
LAURA LUCRETIA Honour, that hated idol, even by those
That set it up to worship? No,
I have a soul, my boy, and that's all love;   180
And I'll the talent which heaven lent improve.
    Going out, [Laura Lucretia] meets Marcella and Cornelia,
    followed by Galliard and Fillamour

SILVIO Here be the courtesans, my lord.

LAURA LUCRETIA Ha, Silvianetta and Euphemia! Pursued, too, by
my cavalier. I'll round the garden, and mix myself amongst 'em.

Exeunt [Laura Lucretia, Silvio, and] her train

MARCELLA Prithee, sister, let's retire into the grove, to avoid the   185
pursuit of these cavaliers.

CORNELIA Not I, by these killing eyes! I'll stand my ground were
there a thousand, all armed with conquering beauty.

MARCELLA Ha! Now, on my conscience, yonder's Fillamour!

CORNELIA Ha! Fillamour?   190

MARCELLA My courage fails me at the sight of him. I must retire.

CORNELIA And I'll to my *Art of Love*.

*Marcella retires and leans against a tree. Cornelia walks
about, reading*

GALLIARD 'Tis she, 'tis Silvianetta! Prithee advance, that thou mayst
behold her and renounce all honest women, since in that one
young sinner there are charms that would excuse, even to thee, all   195
frailty.

FILLAMOUR The forms of angels could not reconcile me
To women of her trade.

GALLIARD This is too happy an opportunity, to be lost in convincing
thy singularity.   200

*Galliard goes bowing by the side of Cornelia; Fillamour
walks about in the scene.° [Galliard addresses Cornelia]*

If creatures so fair and charming as yourself had any need of
prayer, I should believe, by your profound attention, you were at
your evening's devotion.

CORNELIA That you may find your mistake, in the opinion of my
charms, pray believe I am so, and ought not to be interrupted.   205

GALLIARD I hope a man may have leave to make his devotions by
you, at least, without danger or offence?

CORNELIA I know not that. I have reason to fear your devotion may
be ominous: like a blazing star, it comes but seldom, but ever
threatens mischief; pray heaven I share not in the calamity.   210

GALLIARD Why, I confess madam, my fit of zeal does not take me
often; but when it does, 'tis very harmless and wondrous hearty.

CORNELIA You may begin then; I shall not be so wicked as to disturb
your orisons.

GALLIARD Would I could be well assured of that, for mine's devotion   215
of great necessity, and the blessing I pray infinitely for, conserves
me; therefore in Christian charity keep down your eyes, and do not

ruin a young man's good intentions, unless they would agree to
send kind looks, and save me the expense of prayer.

CORNELIA Which would be better laid out, you think, upon some   220
other blessing.

GALLIARD Why faith, 'tis good to have a little bank° upon occasion,
though I hope I shall have no great need hereafter; if the charming
Silvianetta be but kind, 'tis all I ask of heaven.

CORNELIA You're very well acquainted with my name, I find.   225

GALLIARD Your name! 'Tis all I have to live on!
Like cheerful birds, 'tis the first tune I sing,
To welcome in the day:
The groves repeat it, and the fountains purl it,
And every pretty sound that fills my ear,   230
Turns all to Silvianetta!
       Fillamour looks awhile on Marcella

FILLAMOUR Galliard, look there; look on that lovely woman; 'tis
Marcella, the beautiful Marcella!
       [Fillamour] offers to run to [Marcella]; Galliard holds him

GALLIARD Hold! Marcella, where?

FILLAMOUR That lady there! Didst ever see her equal?   235

GALLIARD Why, faith, as you say, Harry, that lady is beautiful, and
(make us thankful) kind: why, 'tis Euphemia, sir, the very courtesan I would have showed you.

FILLAMOUR Forbear, I am not fit for mirth.

GALLIARD Nor I in humour to make you merry; I tell ye, yonder   240
woman is a courtesan.

FILLAMOUR Do not profane, nor rob heaven of a saint.

GALLIARD Nor you rob mankind of such a blessing, by giving it to
heaven before its time. I tell thee, 'tis a whore, a fine desirable
expensive whore.   245

FILLAMOUR By heaven, it cannot be! I'll speak to her, and call her
my Marcella, and undeceive thy lewd opinion.
       [Fillamour] offers to go; [Galliard] holds him

GALLIARD Do, salute her in good company for an honest woman, do,
and spoil her markets: 'twill be a pretty civil spiteful compliment,
and no doubt well taken. Come, I'll convince ye, sir.   250
       [Galliard] goes and pulls Philippa
—Hark'ee, thou kind help-meet for man, thou gentle child of
night: what is the price of a night or two of pleasure with yonder
lady? Euphemia, I mean, that Roman courtesan.

FILLAMOUR Oh, heavens! A courtesan!

PHILIPPA Sure you're a great stranger in Rome, that cannot tell her   255
price.

GALLIARD I am so; name it, prithee, here's a young English purchaser.—Come forward, man, and cheapen for yourself.

    [*Galliard*] *pulls* [*Fillamour*]

PHILIPPA Oh, spare your pains, she wants no customers.°

    [*Philippa*] *flings away* [*and goes back to Marcella*]

FILLAMOUR No, no, it cannot, must not be, Marcella;   260
She has too much divinity about her,
Not to defend her from all imputation;
Scandal would die to hear her name pronounced.

PHILIPPA Believe me, madam, he knows you not; I overheard all he
said to that cavalier, and find he's much in love.   265

MARCELLA Not know me, and in love! Punish him, heaven, for
falsehood; but I'll contribute to deceive him on, and ruin him with
perjury.

FILLAMOUR I am not yet convinced; I'll try her farther.

    [*Fillamour*] *goes to* [*Marcella*], *bowing*

—But, madam, is that heavenly beauty purchasable? I'll pay a   270
heart, rich with such wounds and flames—

GALLIARD Not forgetting the money, too, good lad, or your wounds
and flames will be of little use!

    Galliard goes to Cornelia

MARCELLA He tells you truth, sir; we are not like the ladies of your
country, who tire out their men with loving upon the square,°   275
heart for heart, till it becomes as dull as matrimony. To women of
our profession there's no rhetoric like ready money, nor billet-
doux like bill of exchange.

FILLAMOUR [*aside*] Oh, that heaven should make two persons so
resembling,
And yet such different souls. (*Looks on* [*Marcella*])   280
'Sdeath, how she darts me through with every look,
But if she speak, she heals the wound again.

    Enter Octavio, with followers

OCTAVIO Ha, my rival Fillamour here! Fall on. [*To Fillamour*] Draw,
sir; and say I gave you one advantage more, and fought thee fairly.

    *Draws on Fillamour. Fillamour fights him out. The ladies run
    off. Galliard falls on the followers, with whom whilst he is
    engaged, enters Julio, draws and assists him; and* [*enter*]
    *Laura Lucretia at the same time on the other side. Enter
    Petro dressed like a civility-master, Sir Signal, and*

> *Tickletext. Sir Signal climbs a tree;*° *Tickletext runs his head*
> *in a bush,*° *and lies on his hands and knees*

LAURA LUCRETIA Ha, my cavalier engaged amongst the slaves!   285
> [*Laura Lucretia draws and assists Galliard*]

PETRO My ladies' lovers, and set upon by Octavio! We must be
diligent in our affairs.
> *Petro assists Galliard and fights out the bravos.* [*Exeunt*
> *Petro, Galliard, Julio, Laura Lucretia, and bravos*].
> *Re-enter Petro*

Sir Signal, where are ye? Signor Tickletext! I hope they have not
miscarried in the fray.

SIR SIGNAL Oh *vot servitor, vossignoria;*° miscarried? No, the fool has   290
wit enough to keep out of harm's way.
> [*Sir Signal*] *comes down from the tree*

PETRO Oh, very discreetly done, signor.
> [*Petro*] *sees Tickletext in a bush,* [*and*] *pulls him out by the*
> *heels*

SIR SIGNAL Why, how now, governor; what, afraid of swords?

TICKLETEXT No, sir, I am not afraid of swords, but I am afraid of
danger.   295
> *Enter Galliard, embracing Laura Lucretia; after them, Julio*
> *and Fillamour. Fillamour looks about*

GALLIARD This bravery, sir, was wondrous!

LAURA LUCRETIA 'Twas only justice, sir, you being oppressed with
odds.

FILLAMOUR She's gone, she's gone in triumph with my soul.

JULIO What was the matter, sir, how came this mischief?   300

FILLAMOUR Oh, easily, sir; I did but look, and infinitely loved!

JULIO And therefore were you drawn upon, or was it some old
pique?

FILLAMOUR I know not, sir. Oh, tell not me of quarrels. The
woman, friend, the woman has undone me!   305

GALLIARD Oh, a blessed hearing! I'm glad of the reformation, sir;
you were so squeamish, forsooth, that a whore would not down
with ye; no, 'twould spoil your reputation.

FILLAMOUR A whore! Would I could be convinced she were so;
'twould call my virtue home, and make me man again.   310

GALLIARD Thou liest; thou'rt as weak a brother as the best on's; and
believe me, Harry, these sort of damsels are like witches: if they
once get hold of a man, he's their own till the charm be ended;
you guess what that is, sir?

FILLAMOUR Oh, Frank, hadst thou then felt how tenderly she   315
pressed my hand in hers, as if she would have kept it° there
forever, it would have made thee mad, stark mad in love—(*aside*)
and nothing but Marcella could have charmed me.

GALLIARD Aye, gad, I'll warrant thee; well, thou shalt this night
enjoy her.   320

FILLAMOUR How!

GALLIARD How? Why, faith, Harry, e'en the old way; I know
no other. Why, thou shalt lie with her, man! Come, let's to
her.

FILLAMOUR Away, let's follow her instantly.   325
    Going out, [Fillamour is] stopped by Sir Signal. Enter Sir
    Signal, Tickletext, [and] Petro

SIR SIGNAL Signor, I have brought Mr Tickletext, to beg your
pardon: sir?

FILLAMOUR I've other business, sir.
    [Fillamour] goes out

GALLIARD [*to Laura Lucretia*] Come, let's follow him; and you, my
generous cavalier, must give me leave to beg the honour of your   330
friendship.

LAURA LUCRETIA My inclinations, sir, have given you more. Pray
let me wait on you to your lodgings, lest a farther insolence should
be offered you.

GALLIARD Sir, you oblige too fast.   335
    [Galliard and Laura Lucretia] go out

SIR SIGNAL Ah, *che diavolo*° ails these hot-brained fellows; sure
they're drunk.

PETRO Oh fie, signor: drunk, for a man of quality? 'Tis intolerable.

SIR SIGNAL Aye, why how so, Signor Morigoroso?

PETRO *Imbriaco*,° had made it a fine speech indeed.   340

SIR SIGNAL Why, faith, and so it had; as thus: 'ah, *che diavolo*° ails
these hot-brained fellows, sure they are *imbriaco*'.—Now would not
I be drunk for a thousand crowns: *imbriaco* sounds *cinquat par cent*°
better. Come, noble signor, let's *andiamo a casa*,° which is as much
as to say, let's amble home.   345

TICKLETEXT In troth, wondrous expert. [*To Petro*] *Certo*, signor, he's
an apt scholar.

SIR SIGNAL Ah, sir, you shall see, when I come to my civilities.

PETRO Where the first lesson you shall learn, is how to give, and how
to receive, with a *bonne grâce*.°   350

TICKLETEXT That receiving lesson I will learn my self.

PETRO This unfrequented part of the garden, signor, will fit our purpose as well as your lodgings. First then, signors, your address.°

[Petro] puts himself in the middle. Petro bows on both sides; they do the like

Very well; that's at the approach of any person of quality, after which you must take out your snuff-box.   355

SIR SIGNAL Snuff-box? Why, we take no snuff, signor.

PETRO Then, sir, by all means you must learn; for besides the mode and gravity of it, it inviveates the pericranium,° that is, sapientiates° the brain, that is, inspires wit, thought, invention, understanding, and the like; (*bowing*) you conceive° me, signors?   360

SIR SIGNAL (*bowing*) Most profoundly, signor.

PETRO Then, signors, it keeps you in confidence, and countenance; and whilst you gravely seem to take a snush, you gain time to answer to the purpose, and in a politic posture, as thus—[*pretends to take snuff*] to any intricate question.   365

TICKLETEXT Hum; *certo*, I like that well, and 'twere admirable if a man were allowed to take it when he's out in's sermon.

PETRO Doubtless, signor, you might, it helps the memory better than rosemary: therefore I have brought each of you a snuff-box.

SIR SIGNAL By no means. Excuse me, signor.   370

[Sir Signal] refuses to take the [snuff-boxes]

PETRO Ah, *bagatelles*, signor, *bagatelles*; and now, signors, I'll teach you how to take it with a handsome grace. Signor, your hand—and yours, signor. (*Lays snuff on their hands*) So, now draw your hand to and fro under your noses, and snuff it hard up. Excellent well.

[Sir Signal and Ticktext] daub all their noses, and make grimaces and sneeze

SIR SIGNAL Methinks, signor, this snuff stinks most damnably: Pray   375
what scent do you call this?

PETRO *Caccamerda orangate*:° a rare perfume, I'll assure ye, sir.

SIR SIGNAL *Caccamerda orangate*; an 'twere not for the name of *caccamerda*, and so forth, a man had as good have a sir-reverence at his nose.   380

[Sir Signal] sneezes often; [Petro] cries 'bonprovache'°

PETRO *Bonprovache*—signor, you do not understand it yet— *bonprovache*.

SIR SIGNAL (*sneezing*) Why, sir, 'tis impossible to endure this same *caccamerda*; why, assafoetida is odoriferous to it.

PETRO 'Tis your right *dulce piquante*,° believe me; but come, signors,   385
wipe your noses, and proceed to your giving lesson.

SIR SIGNAL As how, signor?

PETRO Why, present me° with something—that diamond on your
finger—to show the manner of giving handsomely.

    Sir Signal gives him [*a diamond ring*]

    Oh fie, signor: between your finger and thumb, thus, with your   390
other fingers at a distance; with a speech, and a bow.

SIR SIGNAL *Illustrissimo* signor, the manifold obligations—

PETRO Now, a fine turn of your hand, thus. Oh, that sets off the
present, and makes it sparkle in the eyes of the receiver.

SIR SIGNAL (*turning his hand*) Which you have heaped upon me—   395

PETRO There flourish° again.

SIR SIGNAL (*flourishing*) Obliges me to beg your acceptance of this
small present, which will receive a double lustre from your fair
hand.

    [*Sir Signal*] *gives* [*the ring to Petro*]

PETRO Now, kiss your fingers' ends, and retire back with a bow.   400

TICKLETEXT Most admirably performed.

SIR SIGNAL Nay, sir, I have docity in me, though I say't. Come,
governor, let's see how you can out-do me in the art of presenting.

TICKLETEXT [*to Petro*] Well, sir, come, your snuff-box will serve
instead of my ring, will it not?   405

PETRO By no means, sir; there is such a certain relation between a
finger and a ring, that no present becomes either the giving or the
receiving hand half so well.

SIR SIGNAL Why, 'twill be restored again, 'tis but to practise by.

PETRO Aye, signor; the next thing you are to learn is to receive.   410

TICKLETEXT Most worthy signor, I have so exhausted the cornucopia of your favours, (*flourishes*) and tasted so plenteously of the
fullness of your bounteous liberality, that to retaliate with this
small gem, is but to offer a spark, where I have received a beam of
superabundant sunshine.   415

    [*Tickletext*] *gives* [*a ring to Petro*]

SIR SIGNAL Most rhetorically performed, as I hope to breathe; tropes
and figures° all over.

TICKLETEXT Oh lord, Sir Signal.

PETRO Excellent. Now let's see if you can refuse as civilly as you
gave, which is by an obstinate denial: stand both together.   420
Illustrious signors, upon my honour, my little merit has not
entitled me to the glory of so splendid an offering, trophies worthy
to be laid only at your magnanimous feet.

SIR SIGNAL Ah, signor, no no.

PETRO Signor Tickletext.   425

    [Petro] offers [the rings]; they refuse, going backward

TICKLETEXT Nay, *certo*, signor!

PETRO With what confidence can I receive so rich a present? Signor Tickletext, ah—signor.

SIR SIGNAL I vow, signor, I'm ashamed you should offer it.

TICKLETEXT In verity, and so am I.   430

    [Sir Signal and Tickletext] still going back, [Petro] follows

PETRO *Perdio*, Bacchus,° most incomparable.

TICKLETEXT But when, signor, are we to learn to receive again?

PETRO Oh, sir, that's always a lesson of itself; but now, signors, I'll teach you how to act a story.

SIR SIGNAL How! How, signor, to act a story?   435

PETRO Aye, sir: no matter for words or sense, so the body perform its part well.

SIR SIGNAL How, tell a story without words! Why, this were an excellent device for Mr Tickletext, when he's to hold forth to the congregation, and has lost his sermon-notes. Why, this is wonderful. 440

PETRO Oh, sir, I have taught it men born deaf and blind. Look ye stand close together, and observe: closer yet.

    [Petro] gets between [Sir Signal and Tickletext]

A certain *ecclesiastico*,° plump, and rich—(*makes a sign of being fat*) riding along the road—(*galloping about the stage*) meets a *povero*° *strapiao*.° 'Un povero strapiao, povero strapiao; strapiao, strapiao, 445
strapiao!'

    [Petro] puts himself in the posture of a lean beggar, his hands
    right down by his sides, and picks both their pockets

'Elemosina° per un povero strapiao, per amour° de dievos!'° At last he begs a julio.—(*Makes the fat bishop*) 'Niente!'—Then—(*lean*) the *povero strapiao* begs a *mezzo*° julio.—(*Fat*) 'Niente!'—(*Lean*) 'Un bacio.'—(*Fat*) 'Niente!'—At last he begs his blessing; and see how 450
willingly the *ecclesiastico* gave his benediction.

    Opening his arms, [Petro] hits them both in the face

(*Begs their pardon*) Scusa,° scusa, miei padroni.°

SIR SIGNAL Yes, very willingly, which by the way he had never done had it been worth a farthing.

TICKLETEXT Marry, I would he had been a little sparing of that too, 455
at this time. (*Sneezes*) A shame on't, it has stirred this same *caccamerda* again most foully.

PETRO Your pardon, signor. But come, Sir Signal, let's see how you will make this silent relation. Come, stand between us two.

SIR SIGNAL Nay, let me alone for a memory; come.   460

PETRO [aside] I think I have revenged my backsword-beating.

       [Petro] goes off

SIR SIGNAL *Un povero strapado*,° plump and rich—no, no, the
ecclesiastico meets *un povero strapado*, and begs a julio.

TICKLETEXT Oh no, sir, the *strapado* begs the julio.

SIR SIGNAL Aye, aye, and the *ecclesiastico*—(*snaps his nail*) cries   465
niente. '*Un mezzo*° *julio*!'—'*Niente.*'—'*Un bacio.*'°—'*Niente.*'—
'Your blessing, then, *signor ecclesiastico.*'

       [Sir Signal] spreads out his arms to give his blessing, and hits
       Tickletext

TICKLETEXT Adds me,° you are all a little too liberal of this same
benediction.

SIR SIGNAL Ha; but where's Signor Morigoroso? What, is he gone?   470
But now I think on't, 'tis a point of good manners to go without
taking leave.

TICKLETEXT It may be so, but I wish I had my ring again. I do not
like the giving lesson without the taking one; why, this is picking
a man's pocket, *certo*.   475

SIR SIGNAL Not so, governor, for then I had had a considerable loss.
Look ye here;—how—(*feeling in his pocket*) how—(*in another*)
how—gone? Gone, as I live! My money, governor! All the gold
Barberacho received of my merchant today, all gone!

TICKLETEXT Ha; and mine; all my stock. (*Aside*) The money which   480
I thought to have made a present to the gentlewoman Barberacho
was to bring me to!—Undone, undone; villains, cutpurses, cheats!
Oh, run after him.

SIR SIGNAL A pox of all silent stories! Rogue, thief! Undone!

       [Exeunt]

3.1

[*A street*]°

Enter Julio and his page

JULIO How, the lady whom I followed from St Peter's church, a courtesan?

PAGE A courtesan, my lord, fair as the morning, and as young.

JULIO I know she's fair and young, but is she to be had, boy?

PAGE My lord, she is: her footman told me she was a *zitèlla*. 5

JULIO How, a *zitèlla*, a virgin? 'Tis impossible.

PAGE I cannot swear it, sir, but so he told me. He said she had a world of lovers. Her name is Silvianetta, sir, and her lodgings—

JULIO I know't, are on the Corso.° A courtesan, and a *zitèlla* too? A pretty contradiction; but I'll bate her the last, so I might enjoy her 10
as the first; whate'er the price be, I'm resolved upon the adventure, and will this minute prepare myself.

[*As Julio is*] *going off, enter Morosini and Octavio*

Ha; does the light deceive me, or is that indeed my uncle, in earnest conference with a cavalier? 'Tis he; I'll step aside till he's past, lest he hinders this night's diversion. 15

[*Julio*] *goes aside*

MOROSINI I say 'twas rashly done, to fight him unexamined.

OCTAVIO I need not ask; my reason has informed me, and I'm convinced, where'er he has concealed her, that she is fled with Fillamour.

JULIO [*aside*] Who is't they speak of? 20

MOROSINI Well, well, sure my ancestors committed some horrid crime against nature, that she sent this pest of womankind into our family. Two nieces for my share: by heaven, a proportion sufficient to undo six generations.

JULIO (*aside*) Ha! Two nieces, what of them? 25

MOROSINI I am like to give a blessed account of 'em to their brother Julio, my nephew, at his return; there's a new plague now; but my comfort is, I shall be mad, and there's an end on't.

[*Morosini*] *weeps*

JULIO [*aside*] My curiosity must be satisfied. [*To Morosini*] Have patience, noble sir. 30

MOROSINI Patience is a flatterer, sir, and an ass, sir, and I'll have none on't; ha, what art thou?

JULIO Has five or six years made ye lose the remembrance of your
nephew Julio?

MOROSINI Julio! Would I had met thee going to thy grave. (*Weeps*) 35

JULIO Why so, sir?

MOROSINI Your sisters, sir, your sisters are both gone. (*Weeps*)

JULIO How, gone, sir?

MOROSINI Run away, sir, flown, sir.

JULIO Heavens! Which way? 40

MOROSINI Nay, who can tell the ways of fickle women? In short, sir,
your sister Marcella was to have been married to this noble
gentleman; nay, was contracted to him, fairly contracted in
my own chapel; but no sooner was his back turned, but in a
pernicious moon-light night she shows me a fair pair of heels, 45
with the young baggage your other sister Cornelia, who was just
come from the monastery where I bred her, to see her sister
married.

JULIO A curse upon the sex! Why must man's honour
Depend upon their frailty? 50
Come, give me but any light which way they went,
And I will trace 'em with that careful vengeance—

OCTAVIO Spoke like a man that understands his honour;
And I can guess how we may find the fugitives.

JULIO Oh, name it quickly, sir! 55

OCTAVIO There was a young cavalier, some time at Viterbo,
Who I confess had charms heaven has denied to me:
That trifle, beauty, which was made to please
Vain foolish woman, which the brave and wise
Want leisure to design. 60

JULIO And what of him?

OCTAVIO This fine gay thing came in your sister's way,
And made that conquest nature meant such fools for,
And, sir, she's fled with him.°

JULIO Oh, show me the man, the daring hardy villain, 65
Bring me but in the view of my revenge,
And if I fail to take it,
Brand me with everlasting infamy.

OCTAVIO That we must leave to fortune, and our industry.
Come, sir, let's walk and think best what to do. 70

> [*As Julio, Octavio, and Morosini are*] *going down the scene,
> enter Fillamour and Galliard*

FILLAMOUR Is not that Julio?—Boy, run and call him back.
    [*Exeunt Julio, Octavio, and Morosini.*] *Exit boy,* [*and*]
    re-enter with Julio

JULIO Oh, Fillamour, I've heard such killing news since last I left
    thee.

FILLAMOUR What, prithee?

JULIO I had a sister, friend, dear as my life, 75
    And bred with all the virtues of her sex;
    No vestals at the holy fire employed themselves
    In innocenter business than this virgin,
    Till love, the fatal fever of her heart,
    Betrayed her harmless hours; 80
    And, just upon the point of being married,
    The thief stole in, and robbed us of this treasure:
    She's left her husband, parents, and her honour,
    And's fled with the base ruiner of her virtue.

FILLAMOUR And lives the villain durst affront ye thus? 85

JULIO He does!

GALLIARD Where, in what distant world?

JULIO I know not.

FILLAMOUR What is he called?

JULIO I know not neither. 90
    Some god direct me to the ravisher,
    And if he 'scape my rage,
    May cowards point me out, for one of their tame herd.

FILLAMOUR In all your quarrels I must join my sword.

GALLIARD And if you want, here's another, sir, that though it be not 95
    often drawn in anger, nor cares to be, shall not be idle in good
    company.

JULIO I thank ye both, and if I have occasion, will borrow their
    assistance; but I must leave you for a minute. I'll wait on you anon.
    They all three walk as down the street° *talking. Enter Laura*
    Lucretia, with [*Silvio and*] *her equipage*

LAURA LUCRETIA Beyond my wish, I'm got into his friendship, 100
    But oh, how distant friendship is from love!
    That's all bestowed on the fair prostitute.
    —Ah, Silvio, when he took me in his arms,
    Pressing my willing bosom to his breast,
    Kissing my cheek, calling me lovely youth, 105
    And wondering how such beauty and such bravery

Met in a man so young! Ah then, my boy,
Then in that happy minute,
How near was I to telling all my soul!
My blushes and my sighs were all prepared,   110
My eyes cast down, my trembling lips just parting,
But still, as I was ready to begin,
He cries out, 'Silvianetta!'
And, to prevent mine, tells me all his love!
But see, he's here.   115

   Fillamour and Galliard coming up the scene°

GALLIARD Come, lay by all sullen unresolves, for now the hour of the
  berger° approaches: night, that was made for lovers!—Ha! my dear
  Sans Cœur, my life, my soul, my joy! Thou art of my opinion?

LAURA LUCRETIA I'm sure I am, whate'er it be.

GALLIARD Why, my friend here and I have sent and paid our fine°   120
  for a small tenement° of pleasure, and I'm for taking present
  possession. But hold: if you should be a rival, after all!

LAURA LUCRETIA Not in your Silvianetta! My love has a nice
   appetite,
  And must be fed with high uncommon delicates.
  I have a mistress, sir, of quality,   125
  Fair as imagination paints young angels,
  Wanton and gay as was the first Corinna°
  That charmed our best of poets,
  Young as the spring, and cheerful as the birds
  That welcome in the day,   130
  Witty as fancy makes the revelling gods,
  And equally as bounteous, when she blesses.

GALLIARD Ah, for a fine young whore, with all these charms! But
  that same quality allays the joy; there's such a damned ado with
  the obligation, that half the pleasure's lost in ceremony.   135
  Here, for a thousand crowns, I reign alone,
  Revel all day in love without control.
  But come, to our business. I have given order for music, dark
  lanterns, and pistols.

   This while Fillamour stands studying

FILLAMOUR (*pausing, aside*) Death, if it should not be Marcella   140
  now!

GALLIARD Prithee, no more considering; resolve, and let's about
  it.

FILLAMOUR I would not tempt my heart again; for love,
    Whate'er it may be in another's breast,   145
    In mine, 'twill turn to a religious fire.
    And so to burn for her, a common mistress,
    Would be an infamy below her practice!°

GALLIARD Oh, if that be all, doubt not, Harry, but an hour's
conversation with Euphemia will convert it to as lewd a flame as a   150
man would wish.

LAURA LUCRETIA What a coil's here about a courtesan! What ado to
persuade a man to a blessing all Rome is languishing for in vain.
Come, sir, we must deal with him, as physicians do with peevish
children, force him to take what will cure him.   155

FILLAMOUR And like those damned physicians, kill me for want of
method; no, I know my own distemper best, and your applications
will make me mad.

GALLIARD Pox on't, that one cannot love a woman like a man, but
one must love like an ass.   160

LAURA LUCRETIA 'Sheart, I'll be bound to lie with all the women in
Rome, with less ado than you are brought to one.

GALLIARD Hear ye that, Henry? 'Sdeath, art not ashamed to be
instructed by one so young? But see, the star there appears, the
star that conducts° thee to the shore of bliss.   165
    Marcella and Cornelia [appear] above°
She comes; let's feel thy heart; she comes!°
So breaks the day on the glad eastern hills,
Or the bright god of rays from Thetis'° lap.
—A rapture, now, dear lad, and then fall to, for thou art old dog
at a long grace.°   170

FILLAMOUR *(aside)* Now I'm mere man again, with all his frailties.
[*To Marcella*] Bright lovely creature!

GALLIARD Damn it, how like my lady's eldest son° was that!

FILLAMOUR May I hope my sacrifice may be accepted by you?
(Aside) By heaven, it must be she! Still she appears more like.   175

MARCELLA I've only time to tell you night approaches,
    And then I will expect you.
    Enter Crapine, [and] gazes on the ladies

CRAPINE [*aside*] 'Tis she; Donna Marcella, on my life, with the
young wild Cornelia! Ha; yonder's the English cavalier, too. Nay,
then by this hand, I'll be paid for all my fruitless jaunts for this   180
good news. Stay, let me mark the house.°

MARCELLA [*aside*] Now to my disguise!
    Exit Marcella

GALLIARD And have you no kind message to send to my heart? Cannot this good example instruct you how to make me happy?

CORNELIA Faith, stranger, I must consider first; she's skilful in the   185
merchandise of hearts, and has dealt in love with so good success hitherto, she may lose one° venture, and never miss it in her stock; but this is my first, and should it prove to be a bad bargain, I were undone for ever.

GALLIARD I dare secure the goods sound—°   190

CORNELIA And I believe will not lie long upon my hands.

GALLIARD Faith, that's according as you'll dispose on't, madam: for let me tell you, gad, a good handsome proper fellow is as staple a commodity as any's in the nation; but I would be reserved for your own use! Faith, take a sample tonight, and as you like it, the whole   195
piece, and that's fair and honest dealing I think, or the devil's in't.

CORNELIA Ah, stranger, you have been so over-liberal of those same samples of yours, that I doubt they have spoiled the sale of the rest. Could you not afford, think ye, to throw in a little love and   200
constancy, to inch out that want of honesty of yours?

GALLIARD Love? Oh, in abundance!
By those dear eyes, by that soft smiling mouth,
By every secret grace thou hast about thee,°
I love thee with a vigorous, eager passion;   205
Be kind, dear Silvianetta, prithee do,
Say you believe, and make me blest tonight!

CRAPINE [*aside*] Silvianetta! So, that's the name she has rifled for Cornelia, I perceive.

CORNELIA If I should be so kind-hearted, what good use would you   210
make of so obliging an opportunity?

GALLIARD That which the happy night was first ordained for.

CORNELIA Well, signor, 'tis coming on, and then I'll try what courage the darkness will inspire me with. Till then, farewell.

GALLIARD (*blowing up kisses to her*) Till then, a thousand times adieu.   215

PHILIPPA [*aside to Cornelia*] Ah, madam, we're undone: yonder's Crapine, your uncle's valet.

CORNELIA [*aside*] Now, a curse on him; shall we not have one night with our cavaliers? [*To Philippa*] Let's retire, and continue to out-wit him, or never more pretend to't. [*To Galliard*] Adieu,   220
signor cavalier; remember night.

GALLIARD Or may I lose my sense to all eternity.
        [*Galliard*] *kisses his fingers and bows;* [*Cornelia*] *returns it*
        for a while

LAURA LUCRETIA (*aside*) Gods, that all this, that looks at least like
        love,
    Should be dispensed to one insensible!
    Whilst every syllable of that dear value,   225
    Whispered to me, would make my soul all ecstasy.
    [*To Galliard*] Oh, spare that treasure for a grateful purchase,
    And buy that common ware with trading gold;
    Love is too rich a price. (*Aside*) I shall betray myself.

GALLIARD Away, that's an heretical opinion, and which this certain   230
    reason must convince thee of:
    That love is love wherever beauty is,
    Nor can the name of whore make beauty less.
        Enter Marcella like a man, with a cloak about her

MARCELLA Signor, is your name Fillamour?

FILLAMOUR It is; what would you, sir?   235

MARCELLA I have a letter for you, from Viterbo, and your Marcella,
    sir.
        [*Marcella*] *gives* [*Fillamour a letter*]

FILLAMOUR Ha; Viterbo, and Marcella!
    It shocks me like the ghost of some forsaken mistress,
    That met me in the way to happiness   240
    With some new longed-for beauty!
        [*Fillamour*] *opens* [*the letter, and*] *reads*

MARCELLA (*aside*) Now I shall try thy virtue, and my fate.

FILLAMOUR What is't that checks the joy, that should surprise me
    at the receipt of this?

GALLIARD How now! What's the cold fit coming on?   245

FILLAMOUR (*paus[ing]*) I have no power to go—where this—invites
    me,
    By which I prove, 'tis no increase of flame that warms my heart,
    But a new fire just kindled from those—eyes,
    Whose rays I find more piercing than Marcella's.

GALLIARD Aye, gad, a thousand times; prithee, what's the matter?   250

MARCELLA (*aside*) Oh this false-souled man; would I had leisure°
    To be revenged for this inconstancy!
        [*Marcella retires a short distance; the others talk among*
        themselves]

FILLAMOUR But still she wants that virtue I admire!

GALLIARD Virtue! 'Sdeath, thou art always fumbling upon that dull
string that makes no music. What letter's that? (*Reads*) 'If the first   255
confession I ever made of love be grateful to you, come armed
tonight, with a friend or two; and behind the garden of the
fountains, you will receive'—ha, 'Marcella'! Oh damn it, from your
honest woman! Well, I see the devil's never so busy with a man,
as when he has resolved upon any goodness. 'Sdeath, what a rub's   260
here in a fair cast;°—how is't, man? *Alegremente!*° Bear up, defy
him and all his works.°

FILLAMOUR But I have sworn, sworn that I loved Marcella! And
honour, friend, obliges me to go, take her away and marry her; and
I conjure thee to assist me, too.   265

GALLIARD What, tonight, this night, that I have given to Silvianetta,
and you have promised to the fair Euphemia!

LAURA LUCRETIA (*aside*) If he should go, he ruins my design.—Nay,
if your word, sir, be already past—

FILLAMOUR 'Tis true, I gave my promise to Euphemia, but that, to   270
women of her trade, is easily absolved.

GALLIARD Men keep not oaths for the sakes of the wise magistrates
to whom they're made, but their own honour, Harry; and is't not
much a greater crime to rob a gallant, hospitable man of his niece,
who has treated you with confidence, and friendship, than to keep   275
touch with a well-meaning whore, my conscientious friend?

LAURA LUCRETIA Infinite degrees, sir!

GALLIARD Besides, thou'st an hour or two good, between this and
the time required to meet Marcella.

LAURA LUCRETIA Which an industrious lover would manage to the   280
best advantage.

GALLIARD That were not given over to virtue and constancy, two the
best excuses I know for idleness.

FILLAMOUR Yes, I may see this woman—

GALLIARD Why, God a mercy,° lad!   285

FILLAMOUR —And break my chains, if possible.

GALLIARD Thou wilt give a good essay to that, I'll warrant thee,
before she part with thee. Come, let's about it.

> [*Galliard and Laura Lucretia*] *go out on either side of
> Fillamour, persuading him*

MARCELLA (*aside*) He's gone! The courtesan has got the day.
Vice has the start of virtue, every way,   290
And for one blessing honest wives obtain,
The happier mistress does a thousand gain!

I'll home, and practise all their art, to prove
That nothing is so cheaply gained as love!
          Exit [Marcella]

GALLIARD ([*as the others are*] *offering to go*) Stay, what farce is this? 295
  Prithee, let's see a little.
          Enter Sir Signal, Mr Tickletext, with his cloak tied about
          him, a great ink-horn tied at his girdle, and a great folio
          under his arm, [and] Petro dressed like an antiquary°
  —How now, Mr Tickletext; what, dressed as if you were going a
  pilgrimage to Jerusalem?

TICKLETEXT I make no such profane journeys, sir.

GALLIARD But where have you been, Mr Tickletext?   300

SIR SIGNAL Why, sir, this most reverend and renowned antiquary
  has been showing us monumental rarities and antiquities.

GALLIARD [*aside*] 'Tis Petro, that rogue.

FILLAMOUR [*to Tickletext*] But what folio have you gotten there, sir,
  Knox, or Cartwright?°   305

PETRO (*aside*) Nay, if he be got into that heap of nonsense, I'll steal
  off and undress.
          Exit Petro

TICKLETEXT (*opening the book*) A small volume, sir, into which I
  transcribe the most memorable and remarkable transactions° of
  the day.   310

LAURA LUCRETIA That doubtless must be worth seeing.

FILLAMOUR (*reads*) 'April the twentieth, arose a very great storm of
  wind, thunder, lightning, and rain; which was a shrewd sign of foul
  weather. The twenty-second, nine of our twelve chickens, getting
  loose, flew over-board; the other three miraculously escaping, by   315
  being eaten by me that morning for breakfast.'

SIR SIGNAL Hark'ee, Galliard, thou art my friend, and 'tis not like a
  man of honour to conceal anything from one's° friend. Know then,
  I am the most fortunate rascal that ever broke bread: I am this
  night to visit, sirrah, the finest, the most delicious young harlot   320
  (mum, under the rose) in all Rome; of Barberacho's acquaintance.

GALLIARD [*aside*] Ha, my woman, on my life!—And will she be kind?

SIR SIGNAL Kind? Hang kindness, man, I'm resolved upon conquest
  by parley or by force.

GALLIARD Spoke like a Roman of the first race, when noble rapes,   325
  not whining courtship, did the lover's business.

SIR SIGNAL Pshaw, rapes, man! I mean by force of money, pure dint
  of gold, faith and troth; for I have given five hundred crowns

entrance already, and *perdio*,° Bacchus, 'tis *tropo caro*,° *tropo caro*,   330
Mr Galliard.

GALLIARD And what's this high-prized lady's name, sir?

SIR SIGNAL La Silvianetta; and lodges on the Corso, not far from St
James's of the Incurables,° very well situated in case of° disaster,
ha!

GALLIARD Very well; and did not your wise worship know, this   335
Silvianetta was my mistress?

SIR SIGNAL [*aside*] How! His mistress! What a damned noddy was I
to name her!

GALLIARD D'ye hear, fool? Renounce me this woman instantly, or
I'll first discover it to your governor, and then cut your throat, sir.   340

SIR SIGNAL Oh, *doucement*, dear Galliard. Renounce her? *Corpo di
me*, that I will, soul and body, if she belong to thee, man.

GALLIARD No more: look to't; look you forget her name, or but to
think of her. Farewell.

    [*Galliard*] *nods at* [*Sir Signal*]

SIR SIGNAL [*aside*] Farewell, quoth ye! 'Tis well I had the art of   345
dissembling, after all; here had been a sweet broil upon the coast
else.

FILLAMOUR [*to Tickletext*] Very well, I'll trouble myself to read no
more, since I know you'll be so kind to the world to make it public.

TICKLETEXT At my return sir, for the good of the nation, I will print   350
it, and I think it will deserve it.

LAURA LUCRETIA [*aside to Fillamour*] This is a precious rogue to
make a tutor of.

FILLAMOUR [*to Laura Lucretia*] Yet these mooncalfs dare pretend to
the breeding of our youth, and the time will come, I fear, when   355
none shall be reputed to travel like a man of quality, who has not
the advantage of being imposed upon by one of these pedantic
novices, who instructs the young heir in what himself is most
profoundly ignorant of.

GALLIARD Come, 'tis dark, and time for our design.—Your servant,   360
signors.

    Exeunt Fillamour [*and*] *Galliard*

LAURA LUCRETIA I'll home, and watch the kind deceiving minute,
that may conduct him by mistake to me.

    Exit Laura Lucretia. Enter Petro, [*dressed as*] *Barberacho,
    just as Tickletext and Sir Signal are going out*

SIR SIGNAL Oh, Barberacho! We are undone! Oh, the *diavolo* take
that master you sent me.   365

PETRO Master, what master?

SIR SIGNAL Why, Signor Morigoroso!

PETRO Mor—oso—what should he be?

SIR SIGNAL A civility-master he should have been, to have taught us
    good manners; but the cornuto cheated us most damnably, and, by   370
    a willing mistake, taught us nothing in the world but wit.

PETRO Oh, abominable knavery! Why, what kind of man was he?

SIR SIGNAL Why, much such another as yourself.

TICKLETEXT Higher, signor, higher.

SIR SIGNAL Aye, somewhat higher; but just of his pitch.°   375

PETRO Well, sir, and what of this man?

SIR SIGNAL Only picked our pockets, that's all.

TICKLETEXT Yes, and cozened us of our rings.

SIR SIGNAL Aye, and gave us *caccamerda orangate* for snuff.

TICKLETEXT And his blessing to boot when he had done.   380

SIR SIGNAL A vengeance on't, I feel it still.

PETRO Why, this 'tis to do things of your own heads, for I sent no
    such Signor Moroso; but I'll see what I can do to retrieve 'em. I
    am now a little in haste; farewell.

> [*Petro*] *offers to go. Tickletext goes out by him, and jogs him*

TICKLETEXT Remember to meet me. Farewell, Barberacho.   385

> [*Tickletext*] *goes out. Sir Signal pulls* [*Petro*]

SIR SIGNAL Barberacho, is the lady ready?

[PETRO] Is your money ready?

SIR SIGNAL (*aside*) Why now, though I am threatened, and killed,
    and beaten, and kicked about, this intrigue I must advance.—But
    dost think there's no danger?   390

PETRO What, in a delicate young amorous lady, signor?

SIR SIGNAL No, no, mum, I don't much fear the lady, but this same
    mad fellow Galliard, I hear, has a kind of a hankering after her.
    (*Aside*) Now dare not I tell him what a discovery I have made.

PETRO Let me alone to secure you; meet me in the Piazza di Spagna,   395
    as soon as you can get yourself in order—(*aside*) where the two
    fools shall meet, and prevent either's coming.

SIR SIGNAL Enough. Here's a bill for five hundred crowns more
    upon my merchant; you know him by a good token. I lost the last
    sum you received for me; a pox of that handsel. Away, here's   400
    company.

> *Exit Petro. Enter Octavio*

Now will I disguise myself, according to the mode of the Roman
inamoratos; and deliver myself upon the place appointed.

Exit Sir Signal

OCTAVIO On the Corso didst thou see 'em?

CRAPINE On the Corso, my lord, in discourse with three cavaliers, 405
one of which has given me many a pistole to let him into the
garden o' nights at Viterbo, to talk with Donna Marcella from her
chamber window; I think I should remember him.

OCTAVIO (*aside*) Oh, that thought fires me with anger fit for my
revenge.—And they're to serenade 'em, thou say'st? 410

CRAPINE I did, my lord; and if you can have patience till they
come, you will find your rival in this very place, if he keep his
word.

OCTAVIO I do believe thee, and have prepared my bravos to attack
him: if I can act but my revenge tonight, how shall I worship 415
fortune! [*Calls offstage to bravos*] Keep out of sight, and when I
give the word, be ready all.—I hear some coming; let's walk off a
little.

> *Enter Marcella in man's clothes, and Philippa as a woman,
> with a lantern.° [Exeunt] Octavio and Crapine the other way*

MARCELLA Thou canst never convince me but if Crapine saw us, and
gazed so long upon us, he must know us, too; and then what 420
hinders but by a diligent watch about the house, they will surprise
us ere we have secured ourselves from 'em?

PHILIPPA And how will this exposing youself to danger prevent 'em?

MARCELLA My design now is, to prevent Fillamour's coming into
danger, by hindering his approach to this house. I would preserve 425
the kind ingrate with any hazard of my own; and 'tis better to die
than fall into the hands of Octavio. I'm desperate with that
thought, and fear no danger. However, be you ready at the door,
and when I ring, admit me.

> [*Philippa gives Marcella the lantern. Exit Philippa*]

Ha, who comes here? 430

> *Enter Tickletext with a periwig and cravat of Sir Signal's, a
> sword by his side, and a dark lantern. [Marcella] opens her
> [lantern],° looks on him, and goes out*

TICKLETEXT A man! Now am I, though an old sinner, as timorous
as a young thief. 'Tis a great inconvenience in these popish
countries, that a man cannot have liberty to steal to a wench
without danger; not that I need fear who sees me except Galliard,
who suspecting my business, will go near to think I am wickedly 435
inclined; Sir Signal I have left hard at his study, and Sir Henry is
no nocturnal inamorato, unless like me he dissemble it. Well, *certo*

'tis a wonderful pleasure to deceive the world; and as a learned
man well observed, that the sin of wenching lay in the habit° only,
I having laid that aside, Timothy Tickletext, principal holder-forth   440
of the Covent Garden conventicle,° chaplain of Buffoon Hall in the
county of Kent, is free to recreate himself.

Enter Galliard with a dark lantern

GALLIARD Where the devil is this Fillamour? And the music? Which
way could he go to lose me thus? (*Looks towards the door*) He is
not yet come.   445

TICKLETEXT Not yet come? That must be Barberacho! (*Groping
towards Galliard*) Where are ye, honest Barberacho, where are ye?

GALLIARD Ha, Barberacho? That name I am sure is used by none
but Sir Signal and his coxcomb tutor; it must be one of those.—
Where are ye, signor, where are ye?   450

*[Galliard] goes towards [Tickletext], opens the lantern, and
shuts it straight°*

—Oh, 'tis the knight.—Are you there, signor?

TICKLETEXT Oh, art thou come, honest rascal? Conduct me quickly,
conduct me to the beautiful and fair Silvianetta!

[Tickletext] gives [Galliard] his hand

GALLIARD Yes, when your dogship's damned; Silvianetta! 'Sdeath,
is she a whore for fools?   455

[Galliard] draws

TICKLETEXT [*aside*] Ha; Mr Galliard, as the devil would have it! I'm
undone if he sees me.

[Tickletext] retires hastily; Galliard gropes for him

GALLIARD Where are you, fop, buffoon, knight?

*Tickletext, retiring hastily, runs against Octavio, who is just
entering, [and] almost beats him down. Octavio strikes him a
good blow, beats him back, and draws. Tickletext gets close up
in a corner of the stage. Octavio gropes for him as Galliard
does, and both meet and fight with each other*

What, dare you draw? You have the impudence to be valiant then,
in the dark. ([*Octavio and Galliard*] *pass*)° I would not kill the   460
rogue.—Death, you can fight, then, when there's a woman in the
case!

OCTAVIO (*aside*) I hope 'tis Fillamour.—You'll find I can, and
possibly may spoil your making love tonight!

GALLIARD [*aside*] Egad, sweetheart, and that may be, one civil thrust   465
will do't; and 'twere a damned rude thing to disappoint so fine a
woman; therefore I'll withdraw whilst I'm well.

> *[Galliard] slips out. Enter Sir Signal, with a masquerading*
> *coat over his clothes, without a wig or cravat, with a dark*
> *lantern*

SIR SIGNAL Well, I have most neatly escaped my tutor; and in this disguise defy the devil to claim his own.

> *Advancing softly, and groping with his hands, meets the point*
> *of Octavio's sword, as he is groping for Galliard*

Ah, *cospetto di diavolo!*° What's that?   470

OCTAVIO Traitor, darest thou not stand my sword?

SIR SIGNAL Ha, swords! No, signor; *scusa mi*, signor.

> *[Sir Signal] hops to the door, and feeling for his way with*
> *his out-stretched arms, runs his lantern in Julio's face, who is*
> *just entering. [Sir Signal] finds he's opposed with a good push*
> *backward, and slips aside into a corner over against*
> *Tickletext. Julio meets Octavio and fights him. Octavio falls.*
> *Julio opens his lantern and sees his mistake*

JULIO Is it you, sir?

OCTAVIO Julio! From what mistake grew all this violence?

JULIO That I should ask of you, who meet you armed against me.   475

OCTAVIO I find the night has equally deceived us; and you are fitly come, to share with me the hopes of dear revenge.

> *[Octavio] gropes for his lantern, which is dropped*

JULIO I'd rather have pursued my kinder passion,
Love, and desire, that brought me forth tonight.

OCTAVIO I've learnt where my false rival is to be this evening; and   480
if you'll join your sword, you'll find it well employed.

JULIO Lead on, I'm as impatient of revenge as you.

OCTAVIO Come this way then, you'll find more aids to serve us.

> *[Julio and Octavio] go out*

TICKLETEXT So; thanks be praised, all's still again. This fright were enough to mortify any lover of less magnanimity than myself.   485
Well, of all sins, this itch of whoring is the most hardy: the most impudent in repulses; the most vigilant in watching, most patient in waiting, most frequent in dangers; in all disasters but disappointment, a philosopher! Yet if Barberacho come not quickly, my philosophy will be put to't, *certo*.   490

> *This while Sir Signal is venturing from his post, listening and*
> *slowly advancing towards the middle of the stage*

SIR SIGNAL The coast is once more clear, and I may venture my carcase forth again, though such a salutation as the last, would make me very unfit for the matter in hand. The baton I could bear

with the fortitude and courage of a hero,° but these dangerous
sharps I never loved. What different rancounters have I met withal   495
tonight, *corpo di me*! A man may more safely pass the Gulf of
Lions,° than convoy himself into a bawdy house in Rome; but I
hope all's past, and I will say with Alexander, '*Vivat esperance en
despetto del fatto*'.°

> [*Sir Signal*] *advances a little*

TICKLETEXT Sure I heard a noise.—No, 'twas only my surmise.   500

> *They both advance softly, meeting just in the middle of the*
> *stage; and coming close up to each other, both cautiously start*
> *back, and stand a-tiptoe in the posture of fear. Then, gently*
> *feeling for each other, (after listening and hearing no noise)*
> [*they*] *draw back their hands at touching each other's, and*
> *shrinking up their shoulders, make grimaces of more fear*

TICKLETEXT *Che è questo?*°

SIR SIGNAL (*aside*) Ha, a man's voice! I'll try if I can fright him
hence. (*In a horrible tone*) *Un maledetto spirito incarnato*!°

TICKLETEXT Ha, *spirito incarnato*? (*Aside*) That devil's voice I should
know.   505

SIR SIGNAL (*in the same tone*) *Sì*, signor! *Una spirito*! Which is to say,
uno spiritello, immortale, incorporale, inanimate, immateriale, philo-
sophical, invisible, unintelligible—*diavolo*!°

TICKLETEXT [*aside*] Aye, aye, 'tis my hopeful pupil; upon the same
design with me, my life on't. Cunning young whoremaster! I'll   510
cool your courage.—Good signor *diavolo*! If you be the *diavolo*, I
have *una certaina immateriale invisible conjuratione*, that will so
neatly lay your *inanimate unintelligible diavolo*-ship.°

> [*Tickletext*] *pulls out his wooden sword*

SIR SIGNAL How! He must needs be valiant indeed that dares fight
with the devil.   515

> [*Sir Signal*] *endeavours to get away. Tickletext beats him*
> *about the stage*

—Ah, signor, signor *mio*;° ah, *cospetto di* Bacchus!°—Hey, cornuto,
I am a damned silly devil, that have no dexterity in vanishing.

> [*Sir Signal*] *gropes and finds the door. Going out,* [*he*] *meets,*
> *just entering, Fillamour* [*and*] *Galliard with* [*a singer and*
> *musicians*]. *He retires and stands close*

Ha, what have we here, new mischief?

> *Tickletext and he stand*° *against each other, on either side of*
> *the stage*

FILLAMOUR Prithee, how came we to lose ye?

GALLIARD I thought I had followed ye; but 'tis well we are met   520
    again. Come, tune your pipes.
        [The musicians] play a little. Enter Marcella, [dressed] as
        before
MARCELLA This must be he.
        [Marcella] goes up to [Fillamour and Galliard]
GALLIARD *[to singer]* Come, come, your song, boy, your song.
        Whilst 'tis singing, enter Octavio, Julio, Crapine, and bravos

THE SONG°

> Crudo Amore, Crudo Amore, } bis
> Il mio core non fa per te.   525
> Suffrir non vo tormenti°
> Senza mai sperar mercè.°
> Beltà che sia tiranna,°
> Beltà che sia tiranna,
> Del mio affetto recetto non è.°   530
> Il tuo rigor s'inganna,°
>   Se le pene
>   Le catene
> Tenta avvolgere al mio piè.°
> Sì sì, Crudel Amore,°   535
> Il mio core non fa per te. } bis
>
> Lusinghiero, Lusinghiero, } bis
> Più non credo alla tua fè.°
> L'incendio del tuo foco
> Nel mio core più vivo non è.°   540
> Beltà che li diè luoco,°
> Beltà che li diè luoco,
> Ma il rigor l'ardore sbande.°
> Io non fo lo tuo gioco;°
>   Ch'il veleno
>   Del mio seno   545
> Vergognoso fuggito se n'è.°
> Sì sì, Crudel Amore,
> Il mio core non fa per te. } bis

OCTAVIO 'Tis they we look for, draw and be ready.   550
TICKLETEXT *(aside)* Ha, draw? Then there's no safety here, *certo.*
        Octavio, Julio, and their party draw, and fight with
        Fillamour and Galliard. Marcella engages on their side. All

*fight, the music° confusedly amongst them. Galliard loses his
sword, and in the hurry gets a bass viol, and happens to strike
Tickletext, who is getting away. [Tickletext's] head breaks its
way quite through, and it hangs about his neck.° [The others
exeunt] fight[ing]. Enter Petro with a lantern. Sir Signal
stands close still*

TICKLETEXT Oh, undone, undone; where am I, where am I?

PETRO Ha; that's the voice of my amorous Ananias,° or I am
mistaken. What the devil's the matter? (*Opens his lantern*)—Where
are ye, sir? Ha, cuts so,° what new-found pillory° have we here?   555

TICKLETEXT Oh, honest Barberacho, undo me, undo me quickly.

PETRO So I design sir, as fast as I can—[*aside*] or lose my aim.—
There, sir, there; all's well, I have set you free. Come, follow me
the back way,° into the house.

> *Exeunt Petro and Tickletext. Enter Fillamour and Marcella,
> with their swords drawn; Galliard after them*

GALLIARD A plague upon 'em, what a quarter's here for a wench, as   560
if there were no more i'th' nation. Would I'd my sword again.
(*Gropes for it*)

MARCELLA [*aside*] Which way shall I direct him to be safer? [*To
Fillamour*] How is it, sir? I hope you are not hurt.

FILLAMOUR Not that I feel; what art thou ask'st so kindly?   565

MARCELLA A servant to the Roman courtesan, who sent me forth to
wait your coming, sir; but finding you in danger, shared it with
you. Come, let me lead you into safety, sir.

FILLAMOUR Thou'st been too kind to give me cause to doubt thee.

MARCELLA Follow me, sir; this key will give us entrance through the   570
garden.°

> *Exeunt [Marcella and Fillamour]. Enter Octavio with his
> sword in his hand*

OCTAVIO Oh, what damned luck had I, so poorly to be vanquished!
When all is hushed, I know he will return: therefore I'll fix me
here, till I become a furious statue, but I'll reach his heart.

SIR SIGNAL Oh, *lamentivolo fato*,° what bloody villains these popish   575
Italians are!

> *Enter Julio*

OCTAVIO Ha; I hear one coming this way. Ha, the door opens, too;
and he makes towards it. Pray heaven he be the right, for this I'm
sure's the house. Now, luck, an't be thy will.

> [*Octavio*] *follows Julio towards the door, softly*

JULIO The rogues are fled, but how secure I know not,   580

And I'll pursue my first design of love;
And if this Silvianetta will be kind—

> *Enter Laura Lucretia from the house° in a nightgown*

LAURA LUCRETIA Whist; who is't names Silvianetta?

JULIO A lover, and her slave.

> *[Laura Lucretia] takes [Julio] by the hand*

LAURA LUCRETIA Oh, is it you; are you escaped unhurt?   585
Come to my bosom, and be safe for ever.

JULIO *[aside]* 'Tis love that calls, and now revenge must stay. This
hour is thine, fond boy; the next that is my own I'll give to anger.

OCTAVIO Oh, ye pernicious pair; I'll quickly change the scene of love
into a rougher and more unexpected entertainment.   590

> *[Laura Lucretia] leads Julio in. Octavio follows close.*
> *[Exeunt Laura Lucretia, Julio, and Octavio], shut[ting] the*
> *door [behind] them. Sir Signal thrusts out his head to harken,*
> *hears nobody, and advances*

SIR SIGNAL Sure the devil reigns tonight; would I were sheltered,
and let him rain fire and brimstone, for pass the streets I dare not.
This should be the house; or hereabouts, I'm sure 'tis. Ha, what's
this? A string; of a bell, I hope. I'll try to enter; and if I am
mistaken, 'tis but crying *con licenzia*!°   595

> *[Sir Signal] rings [the bell]. Enter Philippa*

PHILIPPA Who's there?

SIR SIGNAL 'Tis I, 'tis I; let me in quickly.

PHILIPPA Who, the English cavalier?

SIR SIGNAL The same. *[Aside]* I am right; I see I was expected.

PHILIPPA I'm glad you're come. Give me your hand.   600

SIR SIGNAL I am fortunate at last; and therefore will say with the
famous poet:

> No happiness like that achieved with danger,°
> Which once o'ercome, I'll lie at rack and manger.°
> *Exeunt*

4.1

Silvianetta's apartment°

Enter Fillamour and Galliard

FILLAMOUR How splendidly these common women live;
How rich is all we meet with in this palace,
And rather seems th'apartment of some prince,
Than a receptacle for lust and shame.

GALLIARD You see, Harry, all the keeping fools are not in our 5
dominions; but this grave, this wise people, are mistress-ridden,
too.

FILLAMOUR I fear we have mistook the house, and the youth that
brought us in may have deceived us, on some other design.
However, whilst I've this (*draws [his sword]*), I cannot fear. 10

GALLIARD A good caution, and I'll stand upon my guard with this.
(*Pulls a pistol out of his pocket*) But see, here's one will put us out
of doubt.

Enter Marcella, richly and loosely dressed

FILLAMOUR Ha! the fair enchantress!

MARCELLA What, on your guard, my lovely cavalier? 15
Lies there a danger in this face and eyes,
That needs that rough resistance?°
Hide, hide that mark of anger from my sight,
And if thou wouldst be absolute conqueror here,
Put on soft looks, with eyes all languishing, 20
Words tender, gentle sighs, and kind desires.

GALLIARD Death, with what unconcern he hears all this! Art thou
possessed? Pox, why dost not answer her?

MARCELLA (*aside*) I hope he will not yield. [*Pauses a moment.*] He
stands unmoved.

[*To Fillamour*] Surely I was mistaken in this face, 25
And I believe in charms that have no power.

GALLIARD [*to Fillamour*] 'Sdeath, thou deservest not such a noble
creature. (*Aside*) I'll have 'em both myself.

FILLAMOUR (*pausingly*) Yes, thou hast wondrous power,
And I have felt it long. 30

MARCELLA How!

[FILLAMOUR] I've often seen that face, but 'twas in dreams,
And sleeping, loved extremely;

And waking, sighed to find it but a dream.
The lovely phantom vanished with my slumbers,   35
But left a strong idea on my heart,
Of what I find in perfect beauty here;
But with this difference, she was virtuous too!

MARCELLA What silly she was that?

FILLAMOUR She whom I dreamt I loved.   40

MARCELLA You only dreamt that she was virtuous, too.
Virtue itself's a dream, of so slight force
The very fluttering of love's wings destroys it;
Ambition, or the meaner hope of interest,
Wakes it to nothing; in men, a feeble beauty   45
Shakes the dull slumber off.°

GALLIARD Egad, she argues like an angel, Harry!

FILLAMOUR What haste thou'st made, to damn thyself so young!
Hast thou been long thus wicked?
Hast thou sinned past repentance?°   50
Heaven may do much, to save so fair a criminal;
Turn yet, and be forgiven!

GALLIARD What a pox dost thou mean by all this canting?

MARCELLA A very pretty sermon, and from a priest so gay,
It cannot choose but edify.   55
Do holy men of your religion, signor, wear all this habit?
Are they thus young, and lovely? Sure if they are,
Your congregation's all composed of ladies;
The laity must come abroad for mistresses.

FILLAMOUR Oh, that this charming woman were but honest.   60

GALLIARD 'Twere better thou wert damned: honest!
Pox, thou dost come out with things so *mal-à-propos*!

MARCELLA Come, leave this mask of foolish modesty,
And let us haste where love and music calls;
Music, that heightens love, and makes the soul   65
Ready for soft impressions.

GALLIARD [*aside*] So, she will do his business with a vengeance.

FILLAMOUR Plague of this tempting woman, she will ruin me!
I find weak virtue melt from round my heart,
To give her tyrant image a possession;   70
So the warm sun thaws rivers' icy tops,
Till in the stream he sees his own bright face.

GALLIARD [*aside*] Now he comes on apace. [*To Fillamour*] How is't,
my friend?

Thou standst as thou'dst forgot thy business here!
The woman, Harry, the fair courtesan!   75
Canst thou withstand her charms? I've business of my own;
Prithee fall to, and talk of love to her.

FILLAMOUR Oh, I could talk eternity away,
In nothing else but love, couldst thou be honest.

MARCELLA Honest! Was it for that you sent two thousand
    crowns,   80
Or did believe that trifling sum sufficient
To buy me to the slavery of honesty?

GALLIARD Hold there, my brave virago.

FILLAMOUR No, I would sacrifice a nobler fortune,
To buy thy virtue home.   85

MARCELLA What should it idling there?

FILLAMOUR Why, make thee constant to some happy man,
That would adore thee for't.

MARCELLA Unconscionable! Constant at my years?
Oh, 'twere to cheat a thousand,   90
Who, between this and my dull age of constancy,
Expect the distribution of my beauty.

GALLIARD (aside) 'Tis a brave wench.

FILLAMOUR Yet charming as thou art, the time will come
When all that beauty, like declining flowers,   95
Will wither on the stalk; but with this difference—
The next kind spring brings youth to flowers again,
But faded beauty never more can bloom.
If interest make thee wicked, I can supply thy pride.

MARCELLA Curse on your necessary trash, which I despise, but as   100
'tis useful to advance our love.

FILLAMOUR Is love thy business: who is there born so high,
But love and beauty equals?
And thou mayst choose from all the wishing world.
This wealth together would enrich one man,   105
Which dealt to all would scarce be charity.

MARCELLA Together? 'Tis a mass would ransom kings!
Was all this beauty given for one poor petty conquest?
I might have made a hundred hearts my slaves,
In this lost time of bringing one to reason.   110
Farewell, thou dull philosopher in love;
When age has made me wise, I'll send for you again.

    [Marcella] offers to go; Galliard holds her

GALLIARD By this good light, a noble glorious whore!

FILLAMOUR Oh, stay.

    [*Aside*] I must not let such beauty fall: a whore!   115

    [*To Marcella*] Consider yet the charms of reputation;°

    The ease, the quiet and content of innocence;

    The awful reverence all good men will pay thee,

    Who as thou art, will gaze without respect,

    And cry, 'what pity 'tis she is—a whore'.°   120

MARCELLA Oh, you may give it what coarse name you please;

    But all this youth and beauty ne'er was given,

    Like gold to misers, to be kept from use.

    Exit Marcella

FILLAMOUR Lost, lost, past all redemption.

GALLIARD Nay, gad, thou shalt not lose her so. I'll fetch her back,   125

    and thou shalt ask her pardon.°

    [*Galliard*] *runs out after* [*Marcella*]

FILLAMOUR By heaven, 'twas all a dream, an airy dream!

    The visionary pleasure disappears, and I'm myself again;

    I'll fly, before the drowsy fit o'ertake me.

    [*As Fillamour is*] *going out, enter Galliard, and then Marcella*

GALLIARD Turn back: she yields, she yields to pardon thee.   130

    [*Exit Fillamour*]

    Gone! Nay, hang me if ye part.

    [*Galliard*] *runs after* [*Fillamour*], *still* [*with*] *his pistol in his*

    hand

MARCELLA Gone! I have no leisure now for more dissembling.

    [*Marcella*] *takes the candle and goes in. Enter Petro, leading*

    in Mr Tickletext, as by dark

PETRO Remain here, signor, whilst I step and fetch a light.

TICKLETEXT Do so, do so, honest Barberacho!

    [*Exit Petro*]

    Well, my escape even now from Sir Signal was miraculous, thanks   135

    to my prudence and prowess; had he discovered me, my dominion

    had ended, and my authority been of none effect,° *certo*.

    Philippa at the door puts in Sir Signal

PHILIPPA Now, signor, you're out of danger; I'll fetch a candle, and

    let my lady know of your being here.

    Exit Philippa. Sir Signal advances a little. Enter Petro with

    a light, goes between [*Sir Signal and Tickletext*], *and starts*

TICKLETEXT Sir Signal!   140

SIR SIGNAL My governor!

PETRO [*aside*] The two fools met! A pox of all ill luck. Now shall I
lose my credit with both my wise patrons; my knight I could have
put off with a small harlot of my own,° but my levite° having seen
my lady Cornelia, that is la Silvianetta, none but that Susanna   145
would satisfy his eldership;° but now they have both saved me the
labour of a farther invention to dispatch 'em.

SIR SIGNAL [*aside*] I perceive my governor's as much confounded as
my self; I'll take advantage by the forelock,° be very impudent, and
put it upon him, faith.——Ah, governor, will you never leave your   150
whoring; never be staid, sober and discreet, as I am?

TICKLETEXT [*aside*] So, so; undone, undone; just my documents to
him.

[*Tickletext*] *walks about; Sir Signal follows*

SIR SIGNAL And must I neglect my precious studies to follow you,
in pure zeal and tender care of your person? Will you never   155
consider where you are? In a lewd papish country, amongst the
Romish heathens! And for you, a governor, a tutor, a director of
unbridled youth, a gownman, a politician; for you, I say, to be
taken at this unrighteous time of the night, in a flaunting cavaliero
dress, an unlawful weapon by your side, going the high way to   160
Satan to a courtesan! And to a Romish courtesan! Oh, abomination, oh, *scandalum infiniti.*°

TICKLETEXT [*aside*] Paid in my own coin!

PETRO [*aside*] So, I'll leave the devil to rebuke sin, and to my young
lady, for a little of her assistance, in the management of this affair.   165

[*Exit Petro*]

TICKLETEXT I do confess. I grant ye I am in the house of a
courtesan, and that I came to visit a courtesan, and do intend to
visit each night a several courtesan, till I have finished my work—

SIR SIGNAL Every night one! Oh, glutton!

TICKLETEXT —My great work of conversion, upon the whole nation,   170
generation, and vocation, of this wicked provoking sort of womankind, called courtesans. I will turn 'em, yes, I will turn 'em; for
'tis a shame that man should bow down to those that worship idols!
And now I think, sir, I have sufficiently explained the business in
hand, as honest Barberacho is my witness! And for you—to—scan-   175
dalize—me—with so naughty an interpretation—afflicteth me
wonderfully. (*Pulls out his handkerchief and weeps*)

SIR SIGNAL [*aside*] Alas, poor Mr Tickletext; now as I hope to be
saved, it grieves my heart to see him weep. [*To Tickletext*] Faith
and troth, now, I thought thou hadst some carnal assignation; but   180

ne'er stir, I beg thy pardon, and think thee as innocent as myself, that I do. But see, the lady's here; 'slife, dry your eyes, man!

Enter Cornelia, Philippa, and Petro

CORNELIA [*to Philippa*] I could beat thee for being thus mistaken; and am resolved to flatter him into some mischief, to be revenged on 'em for this disappointment. Go you and watch for my cavalier   185
the while.

[*Exit Philippa*]

TICKLETEXT Is she come? Nay then, turn me loose to her.

CORNELIA (*to Sir Signal*) My cavalier!

Tickletext pulls [*Sir Signal*] *by*°

TICKLETEXT Lady—

SIR SIGNAL You, sir, why who the devil made you a cavalier?—Most   190
potentissimo° signora, I am the man of title, by name Sir Signal
Buffoon, sole son and heir to eight thousand pound a year.

TICKLETEXT Oh, sir, are you the man she looks for?

SIR SIGNAL I sir? No, sir; I'd have ye to know, sir, I scorn any
woman, be she never so fair, unless her design be honest and   195
honourable.

CORNELIA The man of all the world I've chosen out, from all the
wits and beauties I have seen—[*aside*] to have most finely beaten.

SIR SIGNAL (*aside*) How, in love with me already? She's damnable
handsome, too; now would my tutor were hanged a little for an   200
hour or two, out of the way.

[*Cornelia*] *approach*[*es*], *Sir Signal shunning* [*her*]

CORNELIA Why fly you not into my arms,
These arms that were designed for soft embraces?

SIR SIGNAL Aye, and if my tutor were not here, the devil take him
that would hinder 'em; and I think that's civil, egad!   205

TICKLETEXT (*aside to Petro*) Why, how now, Barberacho; what, am I
cozened then, and is Sir Signal the man in favour?

PETRO Lord, signor, that so wise a man as you cannot perceive her
meaning—(*aside*) for the devil take me if I can.—Why, this is done
to take off all suspicion from you, and lay it on him; don't you   210
conceive it, signor?

TICKLETEXT Yes, honest rogue. Oh, the witty wagtail! I have a part
to play too, that shall confirm it.—Young gentlewoman—

CORNELIA Ah, *bell' ingrato*,° is't thus you recompense my suffering
love? To fly this beauty so adored by all, that slights° the ready   215
conquest of the world, to trust a heart with you? Ah, *traditor
cruella.*°

SIR SIGNAL [aside] Poor heart, it goes to the very soul of me to be
  so coy and scornful to her, that it does; but a pox on't, her
  over-fondness will discover all.   220

TICKLETEXT Fly, fly, young man! Whilst yet thou hast a spark of
  virtue shining in thee, fly the temptations of this young hypocrite;
  the love that she pretends with so much zeal and ardour is
  indecent, unwarrantable, and unlawful! First, indecent, as she is
  woman—for thou art woman—and beautiful woman, yes, very   225
  beautiful woman, on whom nature hath showed her height of
  excellence in the out-work, but left the in unfinished, imperfect
  and impure.

CORNELIA Heavens, what have we here?

SIR SIGNAL A pox of my Sir Dominie; now he is beside his text,°   230
  and will spoil all.

TICKLETEXT Secondly, unwarrantable; [to Cornelia] by what authority dost thou seduce with the allurements of thine eyes, and the
  conjurements of thy tongue, the waftings of thy hands, and the
  tinklings of thy feet, the young men in the villages?   235

CORNELIA [to Petro] Sirrah, how got this madman in? Seize him, and
  take him hence.

SIR SIGNAL Corpo di me, my governor tickles her notably, i'faith;
  but had he let the care of my soul alone tonight, and have let
  me taken care of my body, 'twould have been more material at   240
  this time.

TICKLETEXT Thirdly, unlawful—

CORNELIA Quite distracted! In pity take him hence, and lead him
  into darkness, 'twill suit his madness best.

TICKLETEXT [aside to Petro] How, distracted? Take him hence?   245

PETRO [aside to Tickletext] This was lucky; I knew she would come
  again. Take him hence; yes, into her bed-chamber; pretty device
  to get you to herself, signor.

TICKLETEXT Why, but is it? Nay, then I will facilitate my departure;
  ([to Cornelia,] beginning to preach again) therefore I say, oh most   250
  beautiful and tempting woman—

CORNELIA Away with him, give him clean straw and darkness,
  And chain him fast for fear of further mischief.

PETRO She means for fear of losing ye.

TICKLETEXT Ah, baggage! As fast as she will, in those pretty arms.   255
      [Petro goes] to lead [Tickletext] off

SIR SIGNAL Hold, hold, man. Mad, said ye? Ha, ha, ha, mad! Why,
  we have a thousand of these in England that go loose about the

streets, and pass with us for as sober discreet religious persons—
[*aside*] as a man shall wish to talk nonsense withal.

PETRO You are mistaken, signor; I say he is mad, stark mad.   26c

SIR SIGNAL [*aside to Petro*] Prithee, Barberacho, what dost thou
mean?

PETRO [*aside to Sir Signal*] To rid him hence, that she may be alone
with you. 'Slife, sir, you're madder than he; don't you conceive?

SIR SIGNAL Aye, aye!—Nay, I confess, *illustrissima* signora, my   265
governor has a fit that takes him now and then, a kind of a frenzy,
a vagary,° a whimsy, a maggot that bites always at naming of
popery.

[*Exeunt Petro and Tickletext*]

—So, he's gone.—*Bellissimo* signora, you have most artificially
removed him, and this extraordinary proof of your affection is a   27c
sign of some small kindness towards me, and though I was
something coy and reserved before my governor, *excellentissimo*
signora, let me tell you, your love is not cast away.

CORNELIA Oh, sir, you bless too fast; but will you ever love me?

SIR SIGNAL Love thee! Aye, and lie with thee too, most magnani-   275
mous signora, and beget a whole race of Roman Julius Caesars
upon thee; nay, now we're alone, turn me loose to impudence,
i'faith.

[*Sir Signal*] ruffles [*Cornelia*]. *Enter Philippa in haste,*
shutting the door after her

PHILIPPA Oh, madam, here's the young mad English cavalier got
into the house, and will not be denied seeing you.   28c

CORNELIA [*aside*] This was lucky!

SIR SIGNAL [*aside*] How, the mad English cavalier! If this should be
our young Count Galliard, now, I were in a sweet taking. Oh, I
know by my fears 'tis he. [*To Philippa*] Oh, prithee what kind of
a manner of man is he?   285

PHILIPPA A handsome, resolute, brave, bold—

SIR SIGNAL Oh, enough, enough!—Madam, I'll take my leave. I see
you are—something busy at present, and I'll—

CORNELIA Not for the world!—Philippa, bring in the cavalier—that
you may see there's none here fears him, signor.   29c

SIR SIGNAL Oh hold, hold.—Madam, you are mistaken in that point,
for to tell you the truth, I do fear, having—a certain—aversion or
antipathy—to—madam—a gentleman—why, madam, they're the
very monsters of the nation, they devour every day a virgin.

CORNELIA Good heavens; and is he such a fury?   295

SIR SIGNAL Oh, and the veriest Beelzebub.° Besides, madam, he
vowed my death, if ever he catch me near this house, and he ever
keeps his word in cases of this nature.

Knocking [is heard] at the door

Oh, that's he, I know it by a certain trembling instinct about me.
Oh, what shall I do?   300

CORNELIA Why, I know not: can you leap a high window?

SIR SIGNAL He knocks again! I protest I'm the worst vaulter° in
Christendom. Have ye no moderate danger, between the two
extremes of the window or the mad count? No closet? Fear has
dwindled me to the scantling of a mousehole.°   305

CORNELIA Let me see. (*Aside*) I have no leisure to pursue my revenge
farther, and will rest satisfied with this, for this time.—Give me the
candle, and whilst Philippa is conducting the cavalier to the alcove
by dark, you may have an opportunity to slip out. [*Aside*] Perhaps
there may be danger in his being seen. Farewell, fool.   310

*Exit Cornelia with the candle. Philippa goes to the door
[and] lets in Galliard*

GALLIARD Pox on't, my knight's bound for Viterbo, and there's no
persuading him into safe harbour again. He has given me but two
hours to dispatch matters here; and then I'm to embark with him
upon this new discovery of honourable love, as he calls it, whose
adventurers are fools, and the returning cargo, that dead com-   315
modity called a wife! A voyage very suitable to my humour!—
Who's there?

[Philippa] takes [Galliard] by the hand

PHILIPPA A slave of Silvianetta's, sir; give me your hand.

*Exeunt [Philippa and Galliard] over the stage. Sir Signal
goes out softly*

[4.2]

*The scene changes to a bed-chamber alcove,° Petro leading in
Tickletext*

PETRO Now, signor, you're safe and happy, in the bed-chamber of
your mistress, who will be here immediately, I'm sure. I'll fetch a
light and put you to bed in the meantime.

TICKLETEXT Not before supper, I hope, honest Barberacho!

PETRO Oh, signor, that you shall do lying, after the manner of the   5
ancient Romans.

TICKLETEXT *Certo*, and that was a marvellous good lazy custom.
  Exit Petro. Enter Philippa, with Galliard, by dark

PHILIPPA My lady will be with you instantly.
  [*Philippa*] *goes out*

TICKLETEXT Ha, sure I heard somebody come softly in at the door:
  I hope 'tis the young gentlewoman!   10
  [*Tickletext*] *advances forward*

GALLIARD (*in a soft tone*) Silence and night, love, and dear oppor-
    tunity,
  Join all your aids to make my Silvia kind;
  For I am filled with the expecting bliss,
      Tickletext thrusts his head out to listen
  And much delay or disappointment kills me.

TICKLETEXT Disappointment kills me? And me, too, *certo*. 'Tis she.   15
  [*Tickletext*] *gropes about*

GALLIARD Oh, haste, my fair, haste to my longing arms;
  Where are you, dear and loveliest of your sex?

TICKLETEXT (*groping and speaking low*) That's I, that's I. *Mi alma,*
  mea core, mea vita!°

GALLIARD Ha; art thou come, my life, my soul, my joy?   20
  [*Galliard*] *goes to embrace Tickletext; they meet and kiss*
  —'Sdeath, what's this, a bearded mistress? Lights, lights there,
  quickly, lights!—Nay, curse me if thou 'scap'st me.
      Tickletext struggles to get away. [*Galliard*] *holds him by the*
      cravat and periwig. Enter Petro with a candle

GALLIARD (*groping*) Barberacho; confound him, 'tis the fool whom I
  found this evening about the house, hovering to roost him here!
  Ha, what the devil have I caught, a tartar?° Escaped again! The   25
  devil's his confederate.
      Petro puts out the candle, comes to Tickletext [*and*] *unties his*
      cravat behind. [*Tickletext*] *slips his head out of the periwig*
      and gets away, leaving both in Galliard's hand

PETRO Give me your hand, I'll lead you a back pair of stairs through
  the garden.

TICKLETEXT Oh, any way to save my reputation; oh!
  [*Exeunt Petro and Tickletext*]

GALLIARD Let me but once more grasp thee, and thou shalt   30
  find more safety in the devil's clutches. None but my mistress
  serve ye?
      [*Galliard*] *gropes out after* [*Tickletext*]. [*Re-enter*] *Petro with*
      Tickletext, running over the stage, [*and*] *Galliard after 'em,*

*with the cravat and periwig in one hand, his pistol in the
other. [Exeunt all three.] Enter Philippa with a light*

PHILIPPA Mercy upon us, what's the matter? What noise is this?
(*A pistol goes off*) Ha, a pistol; what can this mean?
       Enter Sir Signal, running

SIR SIGNAL Oh, save me, gentle devil, save me; the stairs are fortified   35
with cannons and double culverins; I'm pursued by a whole
regiment of armed men! Here's gold, gold in abundance; save me!

PHILIPPA What cannons? What armed men?

SIR SIGNAL Finding myself pursued as I was groping my way
through the hall, and not being able to find the door, I made   40
towards the stairs again, at the foot of which I was saluted with a
great gun; a pox of the courtesy.

GALLIARD (*without*) Where are ye, knight, buffoon, dog of Egypt?

SIR SIGNAL Thunder and lightning! 'Tis Galliard's voice.

PHILIPPA Here, step behind this hanging; there's a chimney which   45
may shelter ye till the storm be over,—[*aside*] if you be not
smothered before.

      *Puts him behind the arras. Enter Galliard as before, and
      Cornelia at the other door*

CORNELIA Heavens! what rude noise is this?

GALLIARD Where have you hid this fool, this lucky fool?
He whom blind chance, and more ill-judging woman,   50
Has raised to that degree of happiness
That witty men must sigh and toil in vain for?

CORNELIA What fool, what happiness?

GALLIARD Cease, cunning false one, to excuse thyself,
See here, [*shows the wig and cravat*] the trophies of your shameful
   choice,
    55
And of my ruin, cruel, fair deceiver!

CORNELIA Deceiver, sir, of whom; in what despairing minute did I
swear to be a constant mistress? To what dull whining lover did I
vow, and had the heart to break it?

GALLIARD Or if thou hadst, I know of no such dog as would believe   60
thee; no, thou art false to thy own charms, and hast betrayed 'em
To the possession of the vilest wretch
That ever fortune cursed with happiness;
False to thy joys, false to thy wit and youth,
All which thou'st damned with so much careful industry   65
To an eternal fool,
That all the arts of love can ne'er redeem thee!

SIR SIGNAL (*peeping out of the chimney, his face blacked*) Meaning me, meaning me.

CORNELIA A fool? What indiscretion have you seen in me, should 70
make ye think I would choose a witty man for a lover? Who,
perhaps, loves out his month in pure good husbandry, and in that
time does more mischief than a hundred fools. Ye conquer without
resistance, ye treat without pity, and triumph without mercy; and
when you're gone, the world cries, 'she had not wit enough to keep 75
him', when indeed you are not fool enough to be kept. Thus we
forfeit both our liberties and discretion with you villainous witty
men; for wisdom is but good success in things, and those that fail
are fools.

GALLIARD Most gloriously disputed! 80
You're grown a Machiavellian in your art.

CORNELIA Oh, necessary maxims only, and the first politics we learn
from observation. I've known a courtesan grown infamous, despised, decayed, and ruined, in the possession of you witty men,
who when she had the luck to break her chains, and cast her net 85
for fools, has lived in state, finer than brides upon their wedding-
day, and more profuse than the young amorous coxcomb that set
her up an idol.

SIR SIGNAL (*peeping out with a face more smutted*) Well argued of my
side, I see the baggage loves me! 90

GALLIARD And hast thou (oh, but prithee jilt me on,
And say thou hast not) destined all thy charms
To such a wicked use?
Is that dear face and mouth for slaves to kiss?
Shall those bright eyes be gazed upon, and serve 95
But to reflect the images of fools?

SIR SIGNAL (*peeping, more black*) That's I still.

GALLIARD Shall that soft tender bosom be approached
By one who wants a soul to breathe in languishment,
At every kiss that presses it? 100

SIR SIGNAL Soul! What a pox care I for soul, as long as my person
is so amiable?

GALLIARD No, renounce that dull discretion that undoes thee;
Cunning is cheaply to be wise, leave it to those that have
No other powers to gain a conquest by; 105
It is below thy charms.
Come, swear (and be forsworn most damnably)
Thou hast not yielded yet; say 'twas intended only,

And though thou liest, by heaven I must believe thee.
Say, hast thou—given him—all?   110
CORNELIA I've done as bad; we have discoursed th'affair,
And 'tis concluded on.
GALLIARD As bad? By heaven, much worse! Discoursed with him!
Wert thou so wretched, so deprived of sense,
To hold discourse with such an animal?   115
Damn it, the sin is ne'er to be forgiven.
Hadst thou been wanton to that lewd degree,
By dark he might have been conducted to thee,
Where silently he might have served thy purpose,
And thou hadst had some poor excuse for that;   120
But bartering words with fools admits of none.
CORNELIA I grant ye, had I talked sense to him, which had been
enough to have lost him for ever.
SIR SIGNAL (aside) Poor devil, how fearful 'tis of losing me!
GALLIARD That's some atonement for thy other sins. Come, break   125
thy word, and wash it quite away.
SIR SIGNAL [aside] That cogging won't do, my good friend, that
won't do.
GALLIARD Thou shalt be just and perjured, and pay my heart the
debt of love you owe it.   130
CORNELIA And would you have the heart, to make a whore of me?
GALLIARD With all my soul, and the devil's in't if I can give thee a
greater proof of my passion.
CORNELIA I rather fear you would debauch me into that dull slave
called a wife.   135
GALLIARD A wife! Have I no conscience, no honour in me?
Prithee believe I would not be so wicked.
No, my desires are generous, and noble,
To set thee up that glorious insolent thing,
That makes mankind such slaves: almighty courtesan!   140
Come, to thy private chamber let us haste,
The sacred temple of the god of love,
And consecrate thy power.
     [Galliard] offers to bear [Cornelia] off
CORNELIA Stay, do you take me then for what I seem?
GALLIARD I'm sure I do, and would not be mistaken for a
kingdom;   145
But if thou art not, I can soon mend that fault,
And make thee so. Come, I'm impatient to begin the experiment.

Offers again to carry her off

CORNELIA Nay, then I am in earnest. Hold, mistaken stranger! I am
of noble birth; and should I in one hapless loving minute destroy
the honour of my house, ruin my youth and beauty, and all that   150
virtuous education my hoping parents gave me?

GALLIARD Pretty dissembled pride and innocence, and wounds no
less than smiles! Come, let us in, where I will give thee leave to
frown and jilt; such pretty frauds advance the appetite.

Offers again [to carry her off]

CORNELIA By all that's good, I am a maid of quality,   155
Blest with a fortune equal to my birth!

GALLIARD I do not credit thee, or if I did,
For once I would dispense with quality,
And, to express my love, take thee with all these faults!

CORNELIA And being so, can you expect I'll yield?   160

GALLIARD The sooner for that reason, if thou'rt wise;
The quality will take away the scandal.
Do not torment me longer.

Offers to lead her again

CORNELIA Stay, and be undeceived, I do conjure ye.

GALLIARD Art thou no courtesan?   165

CORNELIA Not on my life, nor do intend to be.

GALLIARD No prostitute! Nor dost intend to be?

CORNELIA By all that's good, I only feigned to be so!

GALLIARD No courtesan! Hast thou deceived me then?
Tell me, thou wicked-honest cozening beauty!   170
Why didst thou draw me in with such a fair pretence,
Why such a tempting preface to invite,
And the whole piece so useless and unedifying?
Heavens! Not a courtesan!
Why from thy window didst thou take my vows,   175
And make such kind returns? Oh damn your quality,
What honest whore but would have scorned thy cunning?

CORNELIA I, make ye kind returns?

GALLIARD Persuade me out of that, too; 'twill be like thee.

CORNELIA By all my wishes, I never held discourse with you, but   180
this evening, since I first saw your face.

GALLIARD (*in passion*) Oh, the impudence of honesty and quality in
woman!
A plague upon 'em both, they have undone me.
Bear witness, oh thou gentle queen of night,

Goddess of shades, adored by lovers most,   185
How oft under thy covert she has damned herself,
With feignèd love to me!

CORNELIA (*angry*) Heavens! This is impudence. That power I call to
witness, too, how damnably thou injur'st me.

GALLIARD You never from your window talked of love to me?   190

CORNELIA Never.

GALLIARD So; nor you're no courtesan?

CORNELIA No, by my life!

GALLIARD So; nor do intend to be, by all that's good?

CORNELIA By all that's good, never.   195

GALLIARD So; and you are real honest, and of quality?

CORNELIA Or may I still be wretched!

GALLIARD So; then farewell, honesty and quality. 'Sdeath, what a night,
what hopes, and what a mistress, have I all lost for honesty and quality!

> *Offers to go*

CORNELIA Stay.   200

GALLIARD (*in fury*) I will be wrecked first; let go thy hold! (*In a soft
tone*) Unless thou wouldst repent.

CORNELIA I cannot of my fixed resolves for virtue.
But if you could but—love me—honourably,
For I assumed this habit and this dress—   205

GALLIARD To cheat me of my heart the readiest way!
And now, like gaming rooks, unwilling to give o'er till you have
hooked in my last stake, my body, too, you cozen me with honesty.
Oh, damn the dice. I'll have no more on't, I; the game's too deep
for me, unless you played upon the square, or I could cheat like   210
you. Farewell, quality!

> [*Galliard*] *goes out*

CORNELIA He's gone: Philippa, run and fetch him back;
I have but this short night allowed for liberty,
Perhaps tomorrow I may be a slave.

> *Exit Philippa*

Now, o' my conscience, there never came good of this troublesome   215
virtue. Hang't, I was too serious; but a devil on't, he looks so
charmingly, and was so very pressing, I durst trust my gay humour
and good nature no farther.

> [*Cornelia*] *walks about. Sir Signal peeps and then comes out*

SIR SIGNAL He's gone! So; ha, ha, ha; as I hope to breathe, madam,
you have most neatly despatched him; poor fool, to compare his   220
wit and his person to mine.

CORNELIA [*aside*] Ha, the coxcomb here still.

SIR SIGNAL Well, this countenance of mine never failed me yet.
      [*Cornelia*], *looking about on him, sees his face black*

CORNELIA (*squeaks*) Ah!
      [*Cornelia*] *runs away*

SIR SIGNAL [*aside*] Ah; why what the *diavolo*'s that for? [*Calls after*   225
   Cornelia] Why, 'tis I, 'tis I, most *serenissimo*° signora!
      Galliard returns [*with*] *Philippa*

GALLIARD What noise is that; or is't some new design
   To fetch me back again?

SIR SIGNAL How, Galliard returned?

GALLIARD Ha, what art thou, a mortal or a devil?   230

SIR SIGNAL [*aside*] How, not know me? Now might I pass upon him
   most daintily for a devil, but that I have been beaten out of one
   devilship already, and dare venture no more conjurationing.

GALLIARD Dog, what art thou; not speak? Nay, then I'll inform
   myself, and try if you be flesh and blood.   235
      [*Galliard*] *kicks* [*Sir Signal, who*] *avoids*

SIR SIGNAL No matter for all this: 'tis better to be kicked than
   discovered, for then I shall be killed; and I can sacrifice a limb or
   two to my reputation at any time.

GALLIARD [*aside*] Death, 'tis the fool, the fool for whom I am abused
   and jilted. 'Tis some revenge to disappoint her cunning, and drive   240
   the slave before me.—Dog, were you her last reserve?
      [*Galliard*] *kicks* [*Sir Signal, who*] *keeps in his cry*

SIR SIGNAL Still I say mum.

GALLIARD The ass will still appear through all disguises,
   Nor can the devil's shape secure the fool.
      [*Galliard*] *kicks* [*Sir Signal, who*] *runs out, as Cornelia*
      enters, and holds Galliard

CORNELIA Hold, tyrant.   245

GALLIARD Oh women, women, fonder in your appetites
   Than beasts; and more unnatural!
   For they but couple with their kind, but you
   Promiscuously shuffle your brutes together:
   The fop of business with the lazy gownman,   250
   The learnèd ass with the illiterate wit;
   The empty coxcomb with the politician,
   As dull and insignificant as he;
   From the gay fool, made more a beast by fortune,
   To all the loathed infirmities of age!   255

Farewell; I scorn to crowd with the dull herd,
Or graze upon the common where they batten.
          [*Galliard*] *goes out*

PHILIPPA I know he loves, by this concern I know it,
And will not let him part dissatisfied.
          [*Philippa*] *goes out*

CORNELIA By all that's good, I love him more each moment, and   260
know he's destined to be mine.
          Enter Marcella
—What hopes, Marcella? What is't we next shall do?

MARCELLA Fly to our last reserve: come, let's haste, and dress in that
disguise we took our flight from Viterbo in; and something I
resolve!   265

CORNELIA My soul informs me what: I ha't! A project worthy of us
both, which, whilst we dress, I'll tell thee; and by which,
                    My dear Marcella, we will stand or fall,
                    'Tis our last stake we set; and have at all.

5.1

[*A courtyard*]°

Enter Petro [*and*] *Tickletext, from the garden*°
[*of Silvianetta's house*]

TICKLETEXT Haste, honest Barberacho, before the day discover us to the wicked world, and that more wicked Galliard!

PETRO Well signor, of a bad turn 'twas a good one, that he took you for Sir Signal: the scandal lies at his door now, sir. So the ladder's fast,° you may now mount and away.   5

TICKLETEXT Very well; go your ways, and commend me, honest Barberacho, to the young gentlewoman, and let her know as soon as I may be certain to run no hazard in my reputation, I'll visit her again.

PETRO I'll warrant ye, signor, for the future.   10

TICKLETEXT So; now, get you gone, lest we be discovered.

PETRO Farewell, signor, *à bon voyage*.°

Exit Petro. Tickletext descends°

TICKLETEXT (*groping*) 'Tis marvellous dark, and I have lost my lantern in the fray. Ha, whereabouts am I? Hum, what have we here?   15

[*Tickletext*] *stumbles at the well, gets hold of the rope, and slides down in the bucket*°

Ah, help, help, help! I shall be drowned! Fire, fire, fire; for I have water enough! Oh, for some house, some street, nay, would Rome itself were a second time in flames, that my deliverance might be wrought by the necessity for water; but no human help is nigh; oh!

Enter Sir Signal, [*his face blacked*] *as before*

SIR SIGNAL Did ever any knight adventurer run through so many   20
disasters in one night? My worshipful carcase has been cudgelled most plentifully: first banged for a coward, which by the way was none of my fault, I cannot help nature; then clawed away for a *diavolo*! There I was the fool; but who can help that, too? Frighted, with Galliard's coming, into an ague; then chimneyed into a fever,   25
where I had a fine regale of soot, a perfume which nothing but my *caccamerda orangate* could excel, and which I find by (*snuffs*) my smelling, has defaced nature's image, and a second time made me be suspected for a devil. Let me see.

[*Sir Signal*] *opens his lantern and looks on his hands*

158

'Tis so; I am in a cleanly pickle!° If my face be of the same piece, 30
I am fit to scare away old Beelzebub himself, i'faith. (*Wipes his face*)
Aye, 'tis so; like to like, quoth the devil to the collier!° Well, I'll
home, scrub myself clean if possible, get me to bed, devise a
handsome lie to excuse my long stay to the governor; and all's well,
and the man has his mare again.° 35

> [*Sir Signal*] *shuts his lantern and gropes away.* [*He*] *runs*
> *against the well*

Che è questo?° (*Feels gently*) Make me thankful, 'tis substantial
wood! By your leave—(*opens his lantern*) how, a well; sent by
providence that I may wash myself, lest people smoke me by the
scent, and beat me anew for stinking.

> [*He*] *sets down his lantern, pulls off his masking coat, and*
> *goes to draw water*

'Tis a damnable heavy bucket; now do I fancy I shall look, when 40
I am washing myself, like the sign of the labour-in-vain.°

TICKLETEXT So, my cry is gone forth, and I am delivered by miracle
from this dungeon of death and darkness, this cold element of
destruction.

SIR SIGNAL Ha, sure I heard a dismal hollow voice. 45

> *Tickletext appears in the bucket, above the well*°

TICKLETEXT What art thou com'st in charity?

SIR SIGNAL Ah, *le diavolo, le diavolo, le diavolo!*

> [*Sir Signal*] *lets go of the bucket, and is running frighted*
> *away. Enter Fillamour and page.* [*Sir Signal*] *returns*

How, a man! Was ever wretched wight so miserable; the devil at
one hand, and a Roman night-walker at the other! Which danger
shall I choose? 50

> [*Sir Signal*] *gets to the door of the house*

TICKLETEXT So, I am got up at last; thanks to my knight, for I am
sure 'twas he. Ha, he's here; I'll hear his business.

> [*Tickletext*] *goes near to Fillamour*

FILLAMOUR Confound this woman, this bewitching woman;
I cannot shake her from my sullen heart;
Spite of my soul I linger hereabouts, 55
And cannot to Viterbo.

TICKLETEXT Very good! A dainty rascal this!

> *Enter Galliard with a lantern, as from Silvianetta's house,*
> *held by Philippa*

FILLAMOUR Ha, who's this coming from her house? Perhaps 'tis
Galliard.

GALLIARD [to Philippa] No argument shall fetch me back, by heaven.   60
FILLAMOUR 'Tis the mad rogue!
TICKLETEXT [aside] Oh lord, 'tis Galliard, and angry, too; now could
    I but get off and leave Sir Signal to be beaten, 'twere a rare project;
    but 'tis impossible without discovery.
PHILIPPA [to Galliard] But will you hear her, signor?   65
GALLIARD That is, will I lose more time about her? Plague on't, I
    have thrown away already such songs, and sonnets, such madrigals
    and posies, such night walks, sighs, and direful lover's looks, as
    would have mollified any woman of conscience and religion; and
    now to be popped i'th' mouth° with quality! Well, if ever you   70
    catch me lying with any but honest well-meaning damsels here-
    after, hang me. Farewell, old secret, farewell!
        Exit Philippa
    Now am I ashamed of being cozened so damnably. Fillamour, that
    virtuous rascal, will so laugh at me! 'Sheart, could I but have
    debauched him, we had been on equal terms; but I must help   75
    myself with lying, and swear I have—a—
FILLAMOUR You shall not need, I'll keep your counsel, sir.
GALLIARD Ha, êtes-vous là?°
TICKLETEXT [aside] How, Fillamour all this while? Some comfort
    yet, I am not the only professor° that dissembles; but how to get   80
    away?
GALLIARD Oh Harry, the most damnably defeated!
        A noise of swords
FILLAMOUR Hold, what noise is that? Two men coming this way, as
    from the house of the courtesans.
        Enter Julio, backwards, fighting Octavio and bravos
GALLIARD Ha, one retreating; 'sdeath, I've no sword!   85
        Julio and Octavio [come nearer], fighting
FILLAMOUR Here's one! I'll take my page's!
        [Fillamour gives Galliard his sword, and] takes the boy's
        sword
GALLIARD Now am I mad for mischief; here, hold my lantern, boy!
        [Fillamour and Galliard] fight on Julio's side, and fight
        Octavio out at the other side, [and exeunt]. Enter Laura
        Lucretia and Sabina at the fore-door where Sir Signal
        stands. Tickletext, groping up that way, finds Sir Signal
        just entering in [through the door, on his way offstage].
        Laura Lucretia and Sabina pass over the stage
        [and exeunt]

SIR SIGNAL Ha, a door open; I care not who it belongs to, 'tis better
    dying within doors like a man, than in the street like a dog.
        [*As Sir Signal is*] *going in, Tickletext in great fear comes up*
        and pulls him

TICKLETEXT Signor, ah, gentle signor, whoe'er ye are that owns this   90
    mansion, I beseech you to give protection to a wretched man, half
    dead with fear and injury!

SIR SIGNAL [*aside*] Nay, I defy the devil to be more dead with fear
    than I!—Signor, you may enter. [*Aside*] Perhaps 'tis somebody that
    will make an excuse for us both.—But hark, they return!   95
        [*Sir Signal and Tickletext*] *go in. Just after, Laura*
        Lucretia and Sabina [*and Silvio*]° *enter*

LAURA LUCRETIA He's gone, he's gone, perhaps for ever gone.—
    Tell me, thou silly manager of love, how got this ruffian° in? How
    was it possible, without thy knowledge, he could get admittance?

SABINA Now, as I hope to live and learn, I know not, madam, unless
    he followed you when you let in the cavalier, which being by dark,   100
    he easily concealed himself; no doubt some lover of the Silvia-
    netta's, who mistaking you for her, took him, too, for a rival.

LAURA LUCRETIA 'Tis likely, and my fortune is to blame,
    My cursèd fortune, who, like misers, deals
    Her scanty bounties with so slow a hand,   105
    That or we die before the blessing falls,
    Or have it snatched ere we can call it ours.
    (*Raving*) To have him in my house, to have him kind!
    Kind as young lovers when they meet by stealth;
    As fond as age to beauty, and as soft   110
    As love and wit could make impatient youth,
    Preventing even my wishes and desires;°
    Oh Gods, and then, even then, to be defeated,
    Then from my o'erjoyed arms to have him snatched,
    Then, when our vows had made our freedom lawful!   115
    What maid could suffer a surprise so cruel?
    —The day begins to break: go, search the streets,
    And bring me news he's safe, or I am lost.
        [*Exit Sabina.*] *Enter Galliard, Fillamour, and Julio*

FILLAMOUR Galliard, where art thou?

GALLIARD Here, safe, and by thy side.   120

LAURA LUCRETIA [*aside*] 'Tis he!

JULIO Whoe'er he were, the rogue fought like a fury, and but for
    your timely aid, I'd been in some danger.

FILLAMOUR But Galliard, thou wert telling me thy adventure with Silvianetta; there may be comfort in't.   125

LAURA LUCRETIA (*aside*) So, now I shall hear with what concern he speaks of me.

GALLIARD Oh, damn her, damn her!

LAURA LUCRETIA [*aside*] Ha!

GALLIARD The veriest jilt that ever learnt the art.   130

LAURA LUCRETIA [*aside*] Heavens!

GALLIARD Death, the whore took me for some amorous English elder brother, and was for matrimony, in the devil's name! Thought me a loving fool, that ne'er had seen so glorious a sight before, and would at any rate enjoy.   135

LAURA LUCRETIA (*aside*) Oh heavens! I am amazed! How much he differs from the thing he was but a few minutes since.

GALLIARD And to advance her price, set up for quality; nay, swore she was a maid, and that she did but act the courtesan!

LAURA LUCRETIA [*aside*] Which then he seemed to give a credit to;   140 oh, the forsworn dissembler.

GALLIARD But when I came to the matter then in debate, she was for honourable love, forsooth, and would not yield—no, marry, would she—not under a licence from the parson of the parish.   145

JULIO Who was it, prithee? 'Twere a good deed to be so revenged on her!

GALLIARD Pox on her, no; I'm sure she's a damned gipsy, for at the same time she had her lovers in reserve, lay hid in her bed-chamber.   150

LAURA LUCRETIA [*aside*] 'Twas that he took unkindly,
And makes me guilty of that rude address.

FILLAMOUR Another lover, had she?

GALLIARD Yes, our coxcomb knight buffoon, laid by for a relishing bit, in case I proved not seasoned to her mind.   155

LAURA LUCRETIA [*aside*] Ha, he knew him° then!

GALLIARD But damn her, she passes with the night, the day will bring new objects.

FILLAMOUR Oh, I do not doubt it, Frank!

LAURA LUCRETIA (*aside to Silvio*) False and inconstant! Oh, I shall   160 rave, Silvio.

    Enter Cornelia, in man's clothes, with a letter

CORNELIA [*aside*] Here be the cavaliers. Give me, kind heaven, but hold of him, and if I keep him not, I here renounce my charms of

wit and beauty!—Signors, is there a cavalier amongst ye called
Fillamour?   165

FILLAMOUR I own that name; what would you, sir?

CORNELIA Only deliver this, signor.

> *Fillamour goes aside, opens his lantern, and reads.*
> *Julio and Galliard talk aside*

FILLAMOUR (*reads*) 'I'll only tell you I am brother to that Marcella
whom you have injured, to oblige you to meet me an hour hence,
in the Piazza di Spagna; I need not say with your sword in your   170
hand, since you will there meet—Julio Sebastiano Morosini.'
(*Aside*) Ha, her brother, sure, returned from travel. (*To Cornelia*)
Signor, I will not fail to answer it as he desires. (*Aside, going out*)
I'll take this opportunity to steal off undiscovered.

> [*Exit Fillamour*]

CORNELIA [*aside*] So, I've done my sister's business; now for my   175
own.

GALLIARD [*to Julio*] But, my good friend, pray what adventure have
you been on tonight?

JULIO Faith, sir, 'twas like to have proved a pleasant one; I came just
now from the Silvianetta, the fair young courtesan.   180

CORNELIA (*aside*) Ha, what said the man, came from me?

GALLIARD How, sir, you with Silvianetta! When?

JULIO Now, all the dear livelong night.

CORNELIA (*aside*) A pox take him, who can this be?

GALLIARD This night! This night that is not yet departed?   185

JULIO This very happy night. I told you I saw a lovely woman at
St Peter's church.

GALLIARD You did so.

JULIO I told you too I followed her home, but could learn neither
her name nor quality; but my page, getting into the acquaintance   190
of one of hers, brought me news of both: her name Silvianetta, her
quality a courtesan!

CORNELIA [*aside*] I at church yesterday! Now, hang me if I had any
such devout thoughts about me; why, what a damned scandalous
rascal this.   195

JULIO Filled with hopes of success, at night I made her a visit, and
under her window had a skirmish with some rival, who was then
serenading her.

GALLIARD (*aside*) Was't he that fought us then? But it seems you
were not mistaken in the house.—On with your story, pray. (*Aside*) 200
Death, I grow jealous now.—You came at night, you said?

JULIO Yes, and was received at the door by the kind Silvianetta, who softly whispered me, 'come to my bosom, and be safe for ever'; and doubtless took me for some happier man.

LAURA LUCRETIA (*aside, raving*) Confusion on him, 'twas my very   205
language!

JULIO Then led me by dark into her chamber.

CORNELIA (*aside*) Oh, this damned lying rascal! I do this?

JULIO But oh, the things, the dear obliging things, the kind, the fair young charmer, said and did.   210

GALLIARD To thee!

JULIO To me.

GALLIARD Did Silvianetta do this, Silvianetta the courtesan?

JULIO That passes, sir, for such, but is indeed of quality.

CORNELIA This stranger is the devil! How should he know that   215
secret else?

JULIO She told me, too, 'twas for my sake alone, whom from the first minute she saw, she loved, she had assumed that name and that disguise, the sooner to invite me.

LAURA LUCRETIA [*aside*] 'Tis plain, the things I uttered! Oh, my   220
heart!

GALLIARD [*aside*] Curse on the public jilt; the very flattery she would have passed on me.

CORNELIA (*aside*) Pox take him, I must draw on him, I cannot hold!

GALLIARD [*aside*] Was ever such a whore?   225

LAURA LUCRETIA (*aside*) Oh, that I knew this man, whom by mistake
I lavished all the secrets of my soul to!

JULIO I pressed for something more than dear expressions,
And found her yield apace,
But, sighing, told me of a fatal contract   230
She was obliged to make to one she never saw,
And yet if I would vow to marry her, when she could prove°
To merit it, she would deny me nothing.

LAURA LUCRETIA [*aside*] 'Twas I, by heaven, that heedless fool was I.

JULIO Which I with lover's eager joy performed,   235
And on my knees uttered the hasty words,
Which she repeated o'er, and gave me back.

GALLIARD (*aside*) So, he has swallowed with a vengeance the very bait she had prepared for me, or anybody that would bite.

JULIO But ere I could receive the dear reward of all my vows, I was   240
drawn upon, by a man that lay hid in her chamber (whether by

chance or design I know not), who fought me out, and was the same you found me engaged with.°

CORNELIA [*aside*] A pleasant rascal this, as e'er the devil taught his lesson to!   245

GALLIARD [*aside*] So, my comfort is she has jilted him, too, most damnably.

CORNELIA [*aside*] 'Slife, I have anger enough to make me valiant, why should I not make use on't, and beat this lying villain whilst the fit holds?   250

GALLIARD And you design to keep these vows, though you're contracted to another woman?

JULIO I neither thought of breaking those, or keeping these; My soul was all employed another way.

LAURA LUCRETIA [*aside*] It shall be so.—Silvio, I've thought upon a   255
way that must redeem all; hark, and observe me.

      [*Laura Lucretia*] *takes Silvio* [*aside*], *and whispers to him*

JULIO But I'm impatient to pursue my adventure, which I must endeavour to do, before the light discover the mistake. Farewell, sir.

      Exit Julio

GALLIARD Go, and be ruined quite; she has the knack of doing it.   260

SILVIO I'll warrant ye, madam, for my part.

      Exit Laura Lucretia

GALLIARD I have a damned hankering after this woman. Why could not I have put the cheat on her, as Julio has? I stand as little on my word as he! A good round oath or two had done the business; but a pox on't, I loved too well to be so wise.°   265

      Silvio comes up to him

SILVIO° *Con licenzia*, signor! Is your name Galliard?

GALLIARD I am the man, sweetheart; let me behold thee. Ha, Sans Cœur's page.

SILVIO (*aside*) A deuce of his lantern, what shall I say now?—Softly, signor; I am that page, whose chiefest business is to attend my   270
lord's mistress, sir.

CORNELIA (*aside, listening close*) His mistress! Whose mistress, what mistress? 'Slife, how that little word has nettled me!

GALLIARD (*aside, hugging himself*) Upon my life, the woman that he boasted of; a fair, young, amorous, noble, wanton, a—[*to Silvio*]   275
and she would speak with me, my lovely boy?

SILVIO You have prevented the commands I had; but should my lord know of it—

GALLIARD Thou wert undone; I understand thee, and will be as
secret as a confessor, as lonely shades, or everlasting night. Come,   280
lead the way.

CORNELIA (*aside*) Where I will follow thee, though to the bed of her
thou'rt going to, and even prevent thy very business there.
    Exeunt

[5.2]

A chamber

Enter Laura Lucretia, as before, in a night-gown

LAURA LUCRETIA Now for a power that never yet was known,
    To charm this stranger quickly into love;
    Assist my eyes, thou god of kind desires;
    Inspire my language with a moving force,
    That may at once gain and secure the victory.   5
        Enter Silvio°

SILVIO Madam, your lover's here; your time's but short. Consider,
too, Count Julio may arrive.

LAURA LUCRETIA Let him arrive!
    Having secured myself of what I love,
    I'll leave him to complain his unknown loss   10
    To careless winds, as pitiless as I.
    Silvio, see the rooms be filled with lights,°
    Whilst I prepare myself to entertain him.
    Darkness shall ne'er deceive me more.
        [*Exit Laura Lucretia*]. *Enter, to Silvio, Galliard, gazing
        about him, [followed by] Cornelia, [still in man's clothes,]
        peeping at the door*

GALLIARD All's wondrous rich, gay as the court of love,   15
    But still and silent as the shades of death.
        Soft music [is heard, and continues] whilst they speak
    Ha, music, and excellent! Pox on't, but where's the woman? I need
    no preparation.

CORNELIA [*aside*] No, you are always provided for such encounters,
and can fall to sans ceremony; but I may spoil your stomach.   20
        A song tuning

GALLIARD A voice, too, by heaven, and 'tis a sweet one;
    Grant she be young, and I'll excuse the rest,

Yet vie for pleasure with the happiest Roman.

> *The song as by Laura Lucretia,° after which soft music till*
> *she enters*

THE SONG
by a person of quality

> *Farewell the world and mortal cares,°*
> *The ravished Strephon cried,*
> *As, full of joy and tender tears,*   25
> *He lay by Phillis' side:*
> *Let others toil for wealth and fame,*
> *Whilst not one thought of mine*
> *At any other bliss shall aim,*
> *But those dear arms, but those dear arms of thine.*   30
>
> *Still let me gaze on thy bright eyes,*
> *And hear thy charming tongue,*
> *I nothing ask t'increase my joys*
> *But thus to feel 'em long;*
> *In close embraces let us lie,*   35
> *And spend our lives to come;*
> *Then let us both together die,*
> *And be each other's, be each other's tomb.*

GALLIARD Death, I am fired already with her voice.

CORNELIA [*aside*] So, I am like to thrive.   40

> *Enter Julio*

JULIO What mean these lights in every room, as if to make the day without the sun, and quite destroy my hopes? Ha, Galliard here!

CORNELIA [*aside*] A man! Grant it some lover, or some husband, heaven, or anything that will but spoil the sport. The lady! Oh, blast her, how fair she is.   45

> *Enter Laura Lucretia, with her lute, dressed in a careless rich*
> *dress, followed by Sabina, to whom she gives her lute*

JULIO Ha, 'tis the same woman!

> [*Laura Lucretia*] *sees Julio, and starts*

LAURA LUCRETIA [*aside*] A stranger here! What art can help me now? (*She pauses*)

GALLIARD By all my joys, a lovely woman 'tis.

LAURA LUCRETIA [*aside*] Help me, deceit, dissembling, all that's woman!

> *She starts, and gazes on Galliard, pulling Silvio*

CORNELIA [*aside*] Sure I should know that face.   50

LAURA LUCRETIA Ah, look, my Silvio! Is't not he? It is!
That smile, that air, that mien, that bow is his!
'Tis he, by all my hopes, by all my wishes!

GALLIARD He? Yes, yes, I am a he, I thank my stars,
And never blessed 'em half so much for being so,   55
As for the dear variety of woman.

CORNELIA Curse on her charms, she'll make him love in earnest.
   [*Exit Silvio*]°

LAURA LUCRETIA (*going towards* [*Galliard*]) It is my brother, and
   report was false!

GALLIARD [*aside*] How, her brother? Gad, I'm sorry we're so near
akin with all my soul, for I am damnably pleased with her!°   60

LAURA LUCRETIA Ah, why do ye shun my arms; or are ye air,
And not to be enclosed in human twines?
Perhaps you are the ghost of that dead lord,
That comes to whisper vengeance to my soul.

GALLIARD (*aside*) 'Sheart, a ghost! This is an odd preparative to love.   65

CORNELIA [*aside*] 'Tis Laura, my brother Julio's mistress, and sister
   to Octavio.

GALLIARD Death, madam, do not scare away my love with tales of
ghosts, and fancies of the dead: I'll give ye proofs I'm living, loving
man, as arrant and° amorous a mortal as heart can wish.—(*Aside*)   70
I hope she will not jilt me, too.

CORNELIA [*aside*] So, he's at his common proof for all arguments. If she should take him at his word, now; and she'll be sure
to do't.

LAURA LUCRETIA Amiable stranger, pardon the mistake,   75
And charge it on my passion for a brother!
Devotion was not more retired than I,
Vestals, or widowed matrons when they weep,
Till, by a fatal chance, I saw in you
The dear resemblance of a murdered brother! (*Weeps*)   80

JULIO (*aside*) What the devil can she mean by this?

LAURA LUCRETIA (*weeping*) I durst not trust my eyes, yet still I
   gazed,
And that increased my faith you were my brother;
But since they erred, and he indeed is dead,
Oh, give me leave to pay you all that love,   85
That tenderness and passion, that was his!

CORNELIA [*aside*] So, I knew she would bring matters about some
way or other. Oh, mischief, mischief, help me! 'Slife, I can be

wicked enough when I have no use on't, and now I have, I'm as
harmless as a fool.   90

> *As Galliard is earnestly talking to Laura Lucretia, Julio pulls*
> *him by the sleeve*

LAURA LUCRETIA Oh, save me, save me from the murderer!

JULIO Ha!

GALLIARD A murderer, where?

LAURA LUCRETIA I faint, I die with horror of the sight.

GALLIARD Ha, my friend a murderer? Sure you mistake him,   95
madam, he saw not Rome till yesterday; an honest youth, madam,
and one that knows his distance, upon occasion. [*Aside to Julio*]
'Slife, how cam'st thou here? Prithee begone, and leave us!

JULIO Why, do you know this lady, sir?

GALLIARD Know her! A—aye, aye, man, and all her relations; she's   100
of quality. Withdraw, withdraw.—Madam—a—he is my friend,
and shall be civil.

LAURA LUCRETIA I have an easy faith for all you say; but yet,
however innocent he be, or dear to you, I beg he would depart. He
is so like my brother's murderer, that one look more would kill me.   105

JULIO A murderer! Charge me with cowardice, with rapes, or
treasons; gods, a murderer!

CORNELIA [*aside*] A devil on her! She has robbed the sex of all their
arts of cunning.

GALLIARD [*to Julio*] Pox on't, thou'rt rude; go, in good manners, go.   110

LAURA LUCRETIA [*to Julio*] I do conjure ye, torture me no more;
If you would have me think you're not that murderer,
Be gone, and leave your friend to calm my heart
Into some kinder thoughts.

GALLIARD Aye, aye, prithee go! I'll be sure to do thy business for   115
thee.

CORNELIA [*aside*] Yes, yes, you will not fail to do a friendly part, no
doubt.

JULIO [*aside*] 'Tis but in vain to stay; I see she did mistake her man
last night, and 'twas to chance I am in debt for that good   120
fortune.—I will retire, to show my obedience, madam.

> *Exit Julio, Galliard going to the door with him*

LAURA LUCRETIA (*aside*) He's gone, and left me mistress of my wish.
Descend, ye little wingèd gods of love,
Descend and hover round our bower of bliss,
Play all in various forms about the youth,   125
And empty all our quivers at his heart.

Galliard returns. She takes him by the hand
—Advance, thou dearer to my soul than kindred,
Thou more than friend or brother.
Let meaner souls, born base, conceal the god;
Love owns his monarchy within my heart:°   130
So kings that deign to visit humble roofs,
Enter disguised; but in a noble palace,
Own their great power, and show themselves in glory.

GALLIARD I am all transport with this sudden bliss,
And want some kind allay, to fit my soul for recompense.   135

CORNELIA [*aside*] Yes, yes, my forward friend, you shall have
an allay, if all my art can do't, to damp thee even to disappointment.

GALLIARD My soul's all wonder now; let us retire,
And gaze till I have softened it to love.   140

[Galliard], going out, is met by Cornelia

CORNELIA Madam!

LAURA LUCRETIA (*turns*) More interruption? Ha!

CORNELIA My master, the young Count Julio—

LAURA LUCRETIA Julio!

GALLIARD (*aside*) What of him?   145

CORNELIA Being just now arrived at Rome—

LAURA LUCRETIA (*aside*) Heavens, arrived!

CORNELIA Sent me to beg the honour of waiting on you—

LAURA LUCRETIA Sure, stranger, you mistake!

CORNELIA If, madam, you are Laura Lucretia?   150

GALLIARD (*aside*) Laura Lucretia! By heaven, the very woman he's
to marry.

LAURA LUCRETIA (*aside*) This would surprise a virgin less resolved,
But what have I to do with aught but love?
—And can your lord imagine this an hour   155
To make a ceremonious visit in?

GALLIARD (*aside*) Riddles, by love; or is't some trick again?

CORNELIA Madam, where vows are past, the want of ceremony may
be pardoned.

LAURA LUCRETIA I do not use to have my will disputed;   160
Begone, and let him know I'll be obeyed.

CORNELIA (*aside*) 'Slife, she'll out-wit me yet.
—Madam, I see this niceness is not general;
You can except some lovers.

GALLIARD My pert young confidant, depart, and let your master   165

know he'll find a better welcome from the fair vain courtesan, la
Silvianetta, where he has passed the night, and given his vows.

LAURA LUCRETIA (*aside, smiling*) Dearly devised, and I must take the
hint.

CORNELIA (*aside*) He knows me, sure, and says all this to plague   170
me.—My lord, my master with a courtesan? He's but just now
arrived.

GALLIARD A pretty, forward, saucy, lying boy, this, and may do well
in time!—Madam, believe him not, I saw his master yesterday;
conversed with him; I know him, he's my friend. 'Twas he that   175
parted hence just now; he told me all his passion for a courtesan,
scarce half an hour since.

CORNELIA So!

LAURA LUCRETIA I do not doubt it. [*Aside*] Oh, how I love him for
this seasonable lie.   180
  (*To Cornelia*) And can you think I'll see a perjured man,
  Who gives my interest in him to another?
  (*Aside, laughing, to Galliard*) Do I not help ye out most artfully?

CORNELIA [*aside*] I see they are resolved to out-face me.

GALLIARD Nay, vowed to marry her!   185

LAURA LUCRETIA Heavens, to marry her!

CORNELIA (*aside*) To be conquered at my own weapon, too, lying:
'tis a hard case!

GALLIARD Go, boy, you may be gone; you have your answer, child,
and may depart.—Come, madam, let us leave him.   190
        [*Galliard and Laura Lucretia begin to depart*]

CORNELIA [*aside*] Gone! No help? Death, I'll quarrel with him; nay,
fight him, damn him, rather than lose him thus. ([*She*] *pulls
[Galliard]*) Stay, signor; you call me boy, but you may find
yourself mistaken, sir; and know, I've that about me may convince
ye; (*showing [her] sword*) 't has done some execution!   195

GALLIARD Prithee, on whom or what, small village curs? The
barking of a mastiff would unman thee.
        [*Galliard*] *offers to go*

CORNELIA Hold: follow me from the refuge of her arms!
  As thou'rt a man, I do conjure thee, do't.
  (*Aside*) I hope he will; I'll venture beating for't.   200

GALLIARD Yes, my brisk—little rascal—I will—a—

LAURA LUCRETIA By all that's good, you shall not stir from hence.—
  Ho, who waits there, Antonio, Silvio, Gaspero!
        Enter [Silvio and other attendants]

Take that fierce youth, and bear him from my sight.

CORNELIA You shall not need. [*Aside*] 'Slife, these rough rogues will   205
be too hard for me. I've one prevention left. [*To Galliard*]
Farewell;
Mayst thou supply her with as feeble art,
As I should do, were I to play thy part.
　　　[*Cornelia*] *goes out with* [*Silvio and the other attendants*]

GALLIARD He's gone! Now, let's redeem our blessed minutes lost.   210
　　　[*Galliard and Laura Lucretia*] *go in*

[5.3]

The street. Piazza di Spagna

Enter Julio, alone

JULIO Now, by this breaking daylight, I could rave. I knew she
mistook me last night, which made me so eager to improve my
lucky minutes. Sure Galliard is not the man? I long to know the
mystery. Ha, who's here? Fillamour.

　　　*Enter Fillamour, met by Marcella in man's clothes. They pass
　　　by each other, cock, and jostle* [*each other*]

MARCELLA I take it you are he I look for, sir!   5

FILLAMOUR My name is Fillamour.

MARCELLA Mine, Julio Sebastiano Morosini.

JULIO (*aside*) Ha, my name, by heaven!

FILLAMOUR I doubt it not, since in that lovely face,
I see the charming image of Marcella.   10

JULIO [*aside*] Ha!

MARCELLA You might, ere travel ruffled me to man.°
I should return thy praise whilst I survey thee,
But that I came not here for compliment: draw.
　　　[*Marcella*] *draws* [*her sword*]

FILLAMOUR Why, 'cause thou'rt like Marcella?   15

MARCELLA That were sufficient reason for thy hate,
But mine's because thou hast betrayed her basely.
She told me all the story of her love,
How well you meant, how honestly you swore;
And with a thousand tears, employed my aid   20
To break the contract she was forced to make

T'Octavio, and give her to your arms.
I did, and brought you word of our design.
I need not tell ye what returns you made;
Let it suffice my sister was neglected,   25
Neglected for a courtesan, a whore!
I watched, and saw each circumstance of falsehood.

JULIO Damnation! What means this?

FILLAMOUR I scorn to save my life by lies or flatteries;
But credit me, the visit that I made,   30
I durst have sworn had been to my Marcella!
Her face, her eyes, her beauty was the same,
Only the business of her language differed,
And undeceived my hope.

MARCELLA In vain thou think'st to flatter me to faith.   35
When thou'dst my sister's letter in thy hand,
Which ended that dispute, even then I saw
With what regret you read it; what care you took
To disobey it, too. The shivering maid,
Half dead with fears, and terrors of the night,   40
In vain expected a relief from love or thee.
Draw, that I may return her the glad news I have revenged her.

JULIO Hold, much mistaken youth! 'Tis I am Julio.—Thou, Fillamour, know'st my name; know'st I arrived but yesterday at Rome,
and heard the killing news of both my sisters' flights, Marcella and   45
Cornelia;—(to Marcella) and thou art some imposture.

MARCELLA [aside] If this now should be true, I were in a fine
condition.

FILLAMOUR Fled! Marcella fled!

JULIO 'Twas she I told thee yesterday was lost;   50
But why art thou concerned? Explain the mystery!

FILLAMOUR I loved her more than life, nay even than heaven,
And dost thou question my concern for her?
Say how, and why, and whither is she fled?

JULIO Oh, would I knew, that I might kill her in her lover's arms;   55
or if I found her innocent, restore her to Octavio!°

FILLAMOUR To Octavio! And is my friendship of so little worth you
cannot think I merit her?°

JULIO [aside] This is some trick between 'em! [To Fillamour] But I have
sworn most solemnly, have sworn by heaven and my honour, to resign   60
her, and I will do't or die; (to Marcella) therefore declare quickly,
declare where she is,° or I will leave thee dead upon the place.

MARCELLA [*aside*] So, death or Octavio, a pretty hopeful choice this!

FILLAMOUR Hold!

> [*Fillamour*] *puts himself between* [*Marcella and Julio, and*]
> *draws*

By heaven, you shall not touch a single hair;   65
Thus will I guard the secret in his bosom.

JULIO 'Tis plain thou'st injured me, and to my honour
I'll sacrifice my friendship: follow me.

> [*Exeunt Julio and Fillamour*]. *Enter Petro and Cornelia*

MARCELLA Ah, Petro, fly, fly, swift, and rescue him!

> *Exit Petro, with his sword in his hand*

CORNELIA Oh, have I found thee? Fit for my purpose, too! Come,   70
haste along with me: thou must present my brother Julio instantly,
or I am lost, and my project's lost, and my man's lost, and all's
lost.

> *Enter Petro*

PETRO *Victoria*,° *Victoria*, your cavalier's the° conqueror! The other,
wounded in his sword–hand, was easily disarmed.   75

MARCELLA Then let's retire; if I am seen, I'm lost.—Petro, stay here
for the cavalier, and conduct him to me to this house.—I must be
speedy now.

CORNELIA (*pointing to Marcella*) Remember, this is Julio!

PETRO I know your design, and warrant ye my part. Ha, Octavio!   80

> *Enter Octavio, Morosini, and Crapine*

OCTAVIO Now cowardice, that everlasting infamy, dwell ever on my
face, that men may point me out° that hated lover, that saw his
mistress false; stood tamely by whilst she repeated vows; nay, was
so infamous, so dully tame, to hear her swear her hatred and
aversion; yet still I calmly listened, though my sword were ready,   85
and did not cut his throat for't!

MOROSINI I thought you'd said you'd fought?

OCTAVIO Yes, I did rouse at last, and waked my wrongs;
But like an ass, a patient fool of honour,
I gave him friendly notice I would kill him;   90
And fought like prizers, not as angry rivals.

MOROSINI Why, that was handsome; I love fair play. What would
you else have done?

OCTAVIO Have fallen upon him like a sudden storm,
Quick, unexpected, in his height of love.   95

> *Enter Petro and Fillamour.* [*They cross the stage and leave*
> *by the door leading to Laura Lucretia's house*]

See, see yonder! Or I'm mistaken by this glimmering day, or that
is Fillamour now entering at her door. 'Tis he, by my revenge!
What say you, sir?

MOROSINI By th'mass, I think it was he.

    Enter Julio

OCTAVIO Julio, I've caught the wantons in their toil;° I have 'em fast,   100
thy sister and her lover.

    [Octavio] embraces [Julio]

JULIO Eternal shame light on me if they 'scape, then!

OCTAVIO Follow me quick, whilst we can get admittance.

JULIO Where, here?

OCTAVIO Here: come all, and see her shame and my revenge.   105

JULIO And are you not mistaken in the house?

OCTAVIO Mistaken! I saw the ravisher enter just now; thy uncle saw
it too. Oh, my excessive joy! Come, if I lie, say I'm a dog, a villain!

    Exeunt as into [Laura Lucretia's] house

[5.4]

    [Laura Lucretia's] chamber

    Enter Sir Signal, a little groping

SIR SIGNAL There's no finding my way out; and now does fear make
me fancy this some enchanted castle—

    Enter Tickletext, listening

TICKLETEXT Ha, an enchanted castle!

SIR SIGNAL Belonging to a monstrous giant, who having spirited away
the king of Tropicipopican's daughter,° keeps her here enclosed; and   5
that I, wandering knight, am by fickle fortune sent to her deliverance.

    Tickletext listens

TICKLETEXT (*aside*) How's that! Spirited away the king of
Tropicipopican's daughter? Bless me, what unlawful wickedness is
practised in this Romish heathenish country!

SIR SIGNAL And yet the devil of any dwarf, squire, or damsel, have   10
I met with yet. Would I were cleanlily off o' this business. Ha,
lights, as I live; and people coming this way! Bless me from the
giant; oh lord, what shall I do?

    [Sir Signal] falls on his knees

TICKLETEXT [*aside*] I fear no giants, having justice on my side, but
reputation makes me tender of my person. Ha, what's this? A   15
curtain: I'll wind myself in this, it may secure me.

        [Tickletext] winds himself in a window curtain°

SIR SIGNAL They're entering; what shall I do? Ha, here's a corner; defend me from a chimney.

        [Sir Signal] creeps to the corner of the window, and feels a
        space between Tickletext's legs and the corner, creeps in and
        stands just behind Tickletext. Enter Galliard, leading Laura
        Lucretia; Sabina, with lights; [and] just after them, Julio,
        Octavio, Morosini, and Crapine

OCTAVIO Just in the happy minute!

GALLIARD I've sworn by every god, by every power divine, to marry thee, and save thee from the tyranny of a forced contract. *[Aside]*   20
Nay, gad, if I lose a fine wench for want of oaths this bout, the devil's in me.

OCTAVIO What think ye now, sir?

JULIO Damnation on her, set my rage at liberty, that I may kill 'em both!   25

        Morosini holds [Octavio]

MOROSINI I see no cause for that; she may be virtuous yet.

OCTAVIO D'ye think as such to pass her off on me,
Or that I'll bear the infamy of your family?
No, I scorn her now, but can revenge my honour on a rival!

MOROSINI Nay, then I'll see fair play. *[To Galliard]* Turn, and   30
defend thy life.

        [Morosini] goes to Galliard, who turns

JULIO Whilst I do justice on the prostitute. (*He gazes [on Laura
Lucretia]*) Ha! Defend me, 'tis the woman that I love.

        [Laura Lucretia] runs to Galliard

LAURA LUCRETIA Octavio!

OCTAVIO Laura! My sister! Perfidious, shameful—   35

        [Octavio] offers to kill [Laura Lucretia]

JULIO Hold! Thy sister, this, that sister I'm to marry?

LAURA LUCRETIA Is this then Julio, and do all the powers conspire to make me wretched?

OCTAVIO May I be dumb for ever!

        [Octavio] holds his sword down and looks sadly. Julio holds   40
        Laura Lucretia by one hand [and] pleads with Octavio with
        the other. Enter Fillamour and Petro

FILLAMOUR Ha, Galliard; in danger, too!

        [Fillamour] draws, [and] steps to them; Morosini puts
        [himself] between [Fillamour and Octavio]

OCTAVIO Fillamour here? How now, what's the matter, friend?

They talk whilst enter Marcella and Cornelia

CORNELIA Ha, new broils, sure the devil's broke loose tonight. My uncle, as I live!

Morosini pleads between Fillamour and Octavio

MARCELLA And Octavio! Where shall we fly for safety?   45

CORNELIA I'll e'en trust to my breeches; 'tis too late to retreat. 'Slife, here be our cavaliers too; nay then, ne'er fear falling into the enemies' hands!

FILLAMOUR I, I fled with Marcella? Had I been blessed with so much love from her, I would have boasted on't i'th' face of heaven.   50

MOROSINI (*to Octavio*) La ye,° sir.

FILLAMOUR The lovely maid I own I have a passion for,
But by the powers above, the flame was sacred,
And would no more have passed the bounds of honour,
Or hospitality, than I would basely murder;   55
And were she free, I would from all the world
Make her for ever mine.

MOROSINI Look ye sir, a plain case this.

GALLIARD He tells ye simple truth, sir.

OCTAVIO Was it not you, this scarce-past night, I fought with, here,   60
in the house, by dark; just when you had exchanged your vows with her?

LAURA LUCRETIA [*aside*] Heavens! Was it he?

FILLAMOUR This minute was the first I ever entered here.

JULIO 'Twas I, sir, was that interrupted lover; and this the lady.   65

LAURA LUCRETIA [*aside*] And must I yield at last?

OCTAVIO Wonders and riddles!

GALLIARD (*slyly,* [*to Julio*]) And was this the Silvianetta, sir, you told the story of?

JULIO The same whom inclination, friends and destiny,   70
Conspire to make me blessed with.

GALLIARD So many disappointments in one night, would make a man turn honest in spite of nature.

Sir Signal peeps from behind [*the curtain*]

SIR SIGNAL Some comfort yet, that I am not the only fool defeated. Ha! Galliard.   75

OCTAVIO (*to Fillamour*) I'm satisfied. (*To Galliard*) But what could move you, sir, to injure me, one of my birth and quality!

GALLIARD Faith, sir, I never stand upon ceremony when there's a woman in the case, nor knew I 'twas your sister; or if I had, I should a' liked her ne'er the worse for that, had she been kind.   80

JULIO It is my business to account with him, and I am satisfied he
has not injured me; he is my friend.

GALLIARD That's frankly said; and, uncompelled, I swear she's
innocent.

OCTAVIO If you're convinced, I too am satisfied,   85
And give her to you, whilst that faith continues.
       [Octavio] gives [Laura Lucretia to Julio]

LAURA LUCRETIA (*aside*) And must I, must I force my heart to
yield?
And yet his generous confidence obliges me.

OCTAVIO And here I vow, (*kneels*) by all the sacred powers
That punish perjury, never to set my heart   90
On faithless woman; never to love nor marry! (*Rises*)
Travel shall be my business, (*to Julio*) thou my heir.°

SIR SIGNAL [*peeping out*] So, poor soul, I warrant he has been
defeated, too.

MARCELLA [*stepping towards Octavio*] Marcella, sir, will take ye at   95
your word.

FILLAMOUR Marcella!

MARCELLA Who owns with blushes truths should° be concealed, but
to prevent more mischief. (*To Octavio*) That I was yours, sir, was
against my will; my soul was Fillamour's ere you claimed a right   100
in me, though I ne'er saw or held discourse with him, but at an
awful distance, nor knew he of my flight.

OCTAVIO I do believe, and give thee back my claim. I scorn the
brutal part of love, the noblest body, where the heart is wanting.
      They all talk aside. Cornelia comes up to Galliard

CORNELIA Why, how now, cavalier! How like a discarded favourite   105
do you look now, who whilst your authority lasted, laid about ye,
domineered, huffed and blustered, as if there had been no end on't.
Now a man may approach ye without terror! You see the meat's
snatched out of your mouth, sir; the lady's disposed on, whose
friends and relations you were so well acquainted with.   110

GALLIARD Peace, boy, I shall be angry else.

CORNELIA Have you never a cast mistress that will take compassion
on you; faith, what think you of the little courtesan now?

GALLIARD As ill as e'er I did! What's that to thee?

CORNELIA Much more than you're aware on, sir; and, faith, to tell   115
you truth, I'm no servant to Count Julio, but e'en a little
mischievous instrument she sent hither to prevent your making
love to Donna Laura.

GALLIARD (*aside*) 'Tis she herself; how could that beauty hide itself
so long from being known!—Malicious little dog in a manger, that   120
would neither eat, nor suffer the hungry to feed themselves; what
spiteful devil could move thee to treat a lover thus? But I am pretty
well revenged on ye.

CORNELIA On me!

GALLIARD You think I did not know those pretty eyes, that lovely   125
mouth I have so often kissed in cold imagination!

CORNELIA Softly, tormentor!
        [*Cornelia and Galliard*] *talk aside*

MARCELLA In this disguise we parted from Viterbo, attended only
by Petro and Philippa; at Rome we took the title and habit of two
courtesans; both to shelter us from knowledge, and to oblige   130
Fillamour to visit us, which we believed he would in curiosity, and
yesterday it so fell out as we desired.

FILLAMOUR Howe'er my eyes might be imposed upon, you see my
heart was firm to its first object; can you forget and pardon the
mistake?   135

JULIO She shall; and with Octavio's, and my uncle's, leave, thus
make your title good.
        [*Julio*] *gives* [*Marcella*] *to Fillamour*

OCTAVIO 'Tis vain to strive with destiny!
        [*Octavio*] *gives* [*Marcella to Fillamour*]

MOROSINI With all my heart; but where's Cornelia all this while?

GALLIARD Here's the fair straggler, sir.   140
        [*Galliard*] *leads* [*Cornelia*] *to Morosini*, [*who*] *holds his cane*
        up at her

MOROSINI Why, thou baggage, thou wicked contriver of mischief,
what excuse hadst thou for running away? Thou hadst no lover.

CORNELIA 'Twas therefore, sir, I went, to find one; and if I am not
mistaken in the mark, 'tis this cavalier I pitch upon for that use
and purpose.   145

GALLIARD Gad, I thank ye for that; I hope you'll ask my leave first;
I'm finely drawn in, i'faith! Have I been dreaming all this night of
the possession of a new-gotten mistress, to wake and find myself
noosed to a dull wife in the morning?

FILLAMOUR Thou talk'st like a man that never knew the pleasures   150
thou despisest; faith, try it Frank, and thou wilt hate thy past loose
way of living.

CORNELIA And to encourage a young setter-up, I do here promise to
be the most mistress-like wife. You know, signor, I have learnt the

trade, though I had not stock to practise, and will be as expensive,   155
insolent, vain, extravagant, and inconstant, as if you only had the
keeping part, and another the amorous assignations; what think ye,
sir?

FILLAMOUR Faith, she pleads well, and ought to carry the cause.

GALLIARD She speaks reason, and I'm resolved to trust good na-   160
ture.—Give me thy dear hand.

  They all join to give [Galliard Cornelia's] hand; he kisses it

MOROSINI And now you are both sped, pray give me leave to ask ye
a civil question: are you sure you have been honest? If you have,
I know not by what miracle you have lived.

PETRO Oh, sir, as for that, I had a small stock of cash, in the hands   165
of a couple of English bankers, one Sir Signal Buffoon—

SIR SIGNAL (*peeping*) Sir Signal Buffoon! What a pox, does he mean
me, trow?

PETRO And one Mr Tickletext.

TICKLETEXT How, was that—*certo*, my name!   170

  [Tickletext] peeps out and [he and Sir Signal] see each other,
  their faces being close together, one at one side of the curtain,
  and the other at the other

GALLIARD AND FILLAMOUR Ha, ha, ha!

SIR SIGNAL And have I caught you, i'faith, Mr Governor? Nay,
ne'er put in your head for the matter, here's none but friends,
mun.

GALLIARD How now, what have we here?   175

SIR SIGNAL Speak of the devil, and he appears.

  [Sir Signal] pulls his governor forward

TICKLETEXT I am undone; but, good Sir Signal, do not cry whore
first, as the old proverb says.

SIR SIGNAL And good Mr Governor, as another old proverb says, do
not let the kettle call the pot black-arse.   180

FILLAMOUR How came you hither, gentlemen?

SIR SIGNAL Why, faith, sir, divining of a wedding or two forward, I
brought Mr Chaplain to give you a cast of his office, as the saying
is.

FILLAMOUR What, without book, Mr Tickletext?   185

CORNELIA How now, sure you mistake; these are two lovers of mine.

SIR SIGNAL How, sir, your lovers? We are none of those,° sir, we are
Englishmen!

GALLIARD You mistake, Sir Signal; this is Silvianetta.

SIR SIGNAL AND TICKLETEXT (*aside*) How!   190

GALLIARD Here's another spark of your acquaintance; do you know
  him?

TICKLETEXT How, Barberacho? Nay, then all will out.

GALLIARD Yes, and your fencing and civility-master.

SIR SIGNAL Aye? [*To Petro*] Why, what was it you that picked our   195
  pockets then, and cheated us?

GALLIARD Most damnably; but since 'twas for the supply of two fair
  ladies, all shall be restored again.

TICKLETEXT Some comfort that.

FILLAMOUR Come, let's in, and forgive all; 'twas but one night's   200
  intrigue, in which all were a little faulty.

SIR SIGNAL And, governor, pray let me have no more domineering
  and usurpation; but as we have hitherto been honest brothers in
  iniquity, so let's wink hereafter at each other's frailties:
    Since love and women easily betray man,   205
    From the grave gownman to the busy layman.

The Epilogue

Spoken by Mr Smith°

So hard the times are, and so thin the town,
Though but one playhouse, that must too lie down;°
And when we fail, what will the poets do?
They live by us as we are kept by you:
When we disband, they no more plays will write,   5
But make lampoons, and libel ye in spite;
Discover each false heart that lies within,
Nor man nor woman shall in private sin;
The precise whoring husband's haunts betray,
Which the demurer lady, to repay,   10
In his own coin does the just debt defray.
The brisk young beauty linked to lands and age,
Shuns the dull property, and strokes the youthful page;
And if the stripling apprehend not soon,
Turns him aside and takes the brawny groom,   15
Whilst the kind man so true a husband proves,
To think all's well done by the thing he loves;
Knows he's a cuckold, yet content to bear
Whate'er heaven sends, or horns or lusty heir;
Fops of all sorts he draws more artfully,   20

Than ever on the stage did Nokes or Leigh.°
And heaven be praised, when these are scarce, each brother
O'th' pen contrives to set on one another.
   These are the effects of angry poets' rage,
Driven from their winter-quarters on the stage;° 25
And when we go, our women vanish too;
What will the well-fledged keeping gallant do?
And where but here can he expect to find,
A gay young damsel managed to his mind,
Who ruins him and yet seems wondrous kind? 30
One insolent and false, and what is worse,
Governs his heart and manages his purse;
Makes him whate'er she'd have him to believe,
Spends his estate, then learns him how to live;
I hope these weighty considerations will 35
Move ye to keep us all together still;
To treat us equal to our great desert,
And pay your tributes with a franker heart,
If not, th'aforesaid ills will come, and we must part.

THE LUCKY CHANCE,

or
An Alderman's Bargain

The play was first performed at Drury Lane, by mid-April 1686, with the following cast:

MEN

Sir Feeble Fainwould (an old alderman to be married to Leticia)	*Mr Leigh*
Sir Cautious Fulbank (an old banker married to Julia)	*Mr Nokes*
Mr Gayman (a spark of the town, lover of Julia)	*Mr Betterton*
Mr Belmour (contracted to Leticia; disguised, and passes° for Sir Feeble's nephew)	*Mr Kynaston*
Mr Bearjest (nephew to Sir Cautious; a fop)	*Mr Jevon*
Captain Noisy (his companion)	*Mr Harris*
Mr Bredwell (prentice to Sir Cautious, and brother to Leticia; in love with Diana)	*Mr Boman*
Rag (footman to Gayman)	
Ralph (footman to Sir Feeble)	
Dick (footman to Sir Cautious)	
[Jingle (a music master)]	

WOMEN

Lady Fulbank (in love with Gayman; honest and generous)	*Mrs Barry*
Leticia (contracted to Belmour, married to Sir Feeble; young and virtuous)	*Mrs Cooke*
Diana (daughter to Sir Feeble, in love with Bredwell; virtuous)	*Mrs Mountfort*
Pert (Lady Fulbank's woman)	
Gammer Grime (landlady to Gayman; a smith's wife in Alsatia)	*Mrs Powell*
[Susan (servant to Sir Feeble)]	
[Phillis (Leticia's woman)]	
A parson, [a postman, a servant; two porters;] fiddlers, dancers, and singers	

THE SCENE

London

THE EPISTLE DEDICATORY

To the Right Honourable Laurence, Lord Hyde,° Earl of Rochester, one of his Majesty's most honourable Privy Council, Lord High Treasurer of England, and Knight of the Noble Order of the Garter.

My Lord,

When I consider how ancient and honourable a date plays have borne, how they have been the peculiar care of the most illustrious persons of Greece and Rome, who strove as much to outdo each other in magnificence, when by turns they managed the great business of the stage, as if they had contended for the victory of the universe; I say, my lord, when I consider this, I with the greater assurance most humbly address this comedy to your lordship, since, by right of ancient custom, the patronage of plays belonged only to the great men, and chiefest magistrates. Cardinal Richelieu,° that great and wise statesman, said that there was no surer testimony to be given of the flourishing greatness of a state, than public pleasures and divertisements: for they are, says he, the schools of virtue, where vice is always either punished, or disdained. They are secret instructions to the people, in things that 'tis impossible to insinuate into them any other way. 'Tis example that prevails above reason or divine precepts (philosophy not understood by the multitude); 'tis example alone that inspires morality, and best establishes virtue. I have myself known a man,° whom neither conscience nor religion could persuade to loyalty, who, with beholding in our theatre a modern politician set forth in all his colours, was converted, renounced his opinion, and quitted the party.

The abbot of Aubignac,° to show that plays have been ever held most important to the very political part of government, says the philosophy of Greece, and the majesty and wisdom of the Romans, did equally concern their great men, in making them venerable, noble and magnificent: venerable, by their consecration to their gods: noble, by being governed by their chiefest men; and their magnificency was from the public treasury, and the liberal contributions of their noblemen.

It being undeniable then, that plays and public diversions were thought, by the greatest and wisest of states, one of the most essential parts of good government, and in which so many great persons were

interested, suffer me to beg your lordship's patronage for this little
endeavour; and believe it not below the grandeur of your birth and
state, the illustrious places you so justly hold in the kingdom, nor
your illustrious relation to the greatest monarch of the world, to afford 35
it the glory of your protection, since it is the product of a heart and
pen that always faithfully served that royal cause, to which your
lordship is by many ties so firmly fixed. It approaches you with that
absolute veneration, that all the world is obliged to pay you; and has
no other design than to express my sense of those excellent virtues, 40
that make your lordship so truly admired and loved. Amongst which
we find those two so rare in a great man and a statesman, those of
gracious speech and easy access; and I believe none were ever sent
from your presence dissatisfied. You have an art to please even when
you deny; and something in your look and voice has an air so greatly 45
good, it recompenses even for disappointment, and we never leave
your lordship but with blessings. It is no less our admiration, to
behold with what serenity and perfect conduct that great part of the
nation's business is carried on, by one single person; who having to
do with so vast numbers of men of all qualities, interests and 50
humours, nevertheless all are well satisfied, and none complain of
oppression; but all is done with gentleness and silence, as if (like the
first creator) you could finish all by a word. You have, my lord, a
judgement so piercing and solid, a wisdom so quick and clear, and a
fortitude so truly noble, that those fatigues of state, that would even 55
sink a spirit of less magnitude, is by yours accomplished without toil,
or any appearance of that harsh and crabbed austerity that is usually
put on by the busy great. You, my lord, support the globe as if you
did not feel its weight, nor so much as seem to bend beneath it; your
zeal for the glorious monarch you love and serve makes all things a 60
pleasure that advance his interest, which is so absolutely your care.
You are, my lord, by your generous candour, your unbiased justice,
your sweetness, affability and condescending goodness (those never-
failing marks of greatness), above that envy which reigns in courts,
and is aimed at the most elevated fortunes and noblest favourites of 65
princes: and when they consider, your lordship, with all the abilities
and wisdom of a great counsellor, your unblemished virtue, your
unshaken loyalty, your constant industry for the public good; how all
things under your part of sway have been refined and purged from
those grossnesses, frauds, briberies, and grievances, beneath which so 70
many of his majesty's subjects groaned; when we see merit established
and preferred, and vice discouraged; it imposes silence on malice

itself, and compels 'em to bless his majesty's choice of such a pillar of the state, such a patron of virtue.

Long may your lordship live to remain in this most honourable   75
station, that his majesty may be served with an entire fidelity, and the nation be rendered perfectly happy; since from such heads and hearts the monarch reaps his glory, and the kingdom receives its safety and tranquillity. This is the unfeigned prayer of, my Lord,   80

> Your Lordship's most humble,
> and most obedient servant,
> A. Behn.

PREFACE

The little obligation I have to some of the witty sparks and poets of the town, has put me on a vindication of this comedy from those censures° that malice and ill nature have thrown upon it, though in vain. The poets I heartily excuse, since there is a sort of self-interest in their malice, which I should rather call a witty way they have in this age of railing at everything they find (with pain) successful, and never to show good nature and speak well of anything; but when they are sure 'tis damned, then they afford it that worse scandal, their pity. And nothing makes them so through-stitched° an enemy as a full third day;° that's crime enough to load it with all manner of infamy; and when they can no other way prevail with the town, they charge it with the old never-failing scandal—that 'tis not fit for the ladies: as if (if it were as they falsely give it out) the ladies were obliged to hear indecencies only from their pens and plays; and some of them have ventured to treat 'em as coarsely as 'twas possible, without the least reproach from them; and in some of their most celebrated plays have entertained 'em with things that, if I should here strip from their wit and occasion that conducts 'em in and makes them proper, their fair cheeks would perhaps wear a natural colour° at the reading them; yet are never taken notice of, because a man writ them, and they may hear that from them they blush at from a woman. But I make a challenge to any person of common sense and reason—that is not wilfully bent on ill nature, and will° in spite of sense wrest a *double entendre* from everything, lying upon the catch for a jest or a quibble,° like a rook for a cully; but any unprejudiced person that knows not the author—to read any of my comedies and compare 'em with others of this age, and if they find one word that can offend the chastest ear, I will submit to all their peevish cavils: but, right or wrong, they must be criminal because a woman's; condemning them without having the Christian charity to examine whether it be guilty or not, with reading, comparing, or thinking; the ladies taking up any scandal on trust from some conceited sparks, who will in spite of nature be wits and beaux, then scatter it for authentic all over the town and court, poisoning of others' judgement with their false notions, condemning it to worse than death, loss of fame. And to fortify their detraction, charge me with all the plays that have ever been offensive; though I wish, with all their faults, I had been the author of some of those they have honoured me with.

For the farther justification of this play: it being a comedy of intrigue, Dr Davenant,° out of respect to the commands he had from court, to take great care that no indecency should be in plays, sent for it and nicely looked it over, putting out anything he but imagined the critics would play with. After that, Sir Roger L'Estrange° read it and licensed it, and found no such faults as 'tis charged with. Then Mr Killigrew,° who, more severe than any, from the strict order he had, perused it with great circumspection; and lastly, the master players, who you will, I hope, in some measure esteem judges of decency and their own interest, having been so many years prentice to the trade of judging.

I say, after all these supervisors, the ladies may be convinced they left nothing that could offend, and the men of their unjust reflections on so many judges of wit and decencies. When it happens that I challenge any one to point me out the least expression of what some have made their discourse, they cry, that Mr Leigh opens his night gown,° when he comes into the bride-chamber; if he do, which is a jest of his own making, and which I never saw, I hope he has his clothes on underneath? And if so, where is the indecency? I have seen in that admirable play of *Oedipus*,° the gown opened wide, and the man shown in his drawers and waistcoat, and never thought it an offence before. Another cries, 'why, we know not what they mean, when the man takes a woman off the stage, and another is thereby cuckolded'; is that any more than you see in the most celebrated of your plays? As *The City Politics*:° the Lady Mayoress, and the old lawyer's wife, who goes with a man she never saw before, and comes out again the joyfullest woman alive, for having made her husband a cuckold with such dexterity; and yet I see nothing unnatural nor obscene; 'tis proper for the characters. So in that lucky play of *The London Cuckolds*,° not to recite particulars. And in that good comedy of *Sir Courtly Nice*,° the tailor to the young lady; in the famed *Sir Fopling*,° Dorimant and Bellinda, see the very words; in *Valentinian*,° see the scene between the court bawds, and Valentinian all loose and ruffled a moment after the rape; and all this you see without scandal, and a thousand others. *The Moor of Venice*° in many places. *The Maid's Tragedy*,° see the scene of undressing the bride, and between the king and Amintor, and after between the king and Evadne. All these I name as some of the best plays I know. If I should repeat the words expressed in these scenes I mention, I might justly be charged with coarse ill manners, and very little modesty; and yet they so naturally fall into the places they are designed for, and so are proper for the business, that there is not the least fault to be found with them; though, I say, those things in any of mine would damn the whole piece, and alarm the town. Had I a day or two's time, as I have scarce so many hours to write this in (the play being all printed off and the press waiting), I would sum up all your beloved plays, and all the things in them that are passed with such silence by—because written by men: such masculine strokes in me, must not be allowed. I must conclude those women (if there be any such) greater critics in that sort of conversation than myself, who find any of that sort in mine, or anything that can justly be reproached. But 'tis in vain by dint of reason or comparison to convince the obstinate critics, whose business is to find fault, if not by a loose and gross imagination to create them, for they must either find the jest, or make it; and those of this sort fall to my share; they find faults of another kind for the men writers. And this one thing I will venture to say, though against my nature, because it has a vanity in it: that had the plays I have writ come forth under any man's name, and never known to have been mine, I appeal to all unbiased judges of sense, if they had not said that person had made as many good comedies, as any one man that has writ in our age; but a devil on't, the woman damns the poet.

Ladies, for its further justification to you, be pleased to know that the first copy of this play was read by several ladies of very great quality and unquestioned fame, and received their most favourable opinion, not one charging it with the crime that some have been pleased to find in the acting. Other ladies who saw it more than once, whose quality and virtue can sufficiently justify anything they design to favour, were pleased to say they found an entertainment in it very far from scandalous; and for the generality of the town, I found by my receipts° it was not thought so criminal. However, that shall not be an encouragement to me to trouble the critics with new occasion of affronting me for endeavouring, at least, to divert; and at this rate, both the few poets that are left, and the players who toil in vain, will be weary of their trade.

I cannot omit to tell you, that a wit of the town,° a friend of mine at Will's coffee-house,° the first night of the play, cried it down as much as in him lay, who before had read it and assured me he never saw a prettier comedy. So complaisant one pestilent wit will be to another, and in the full cry make his noise too; but since 'tis to the witty few I speak, I hope the better judges will take no offence, to whom I am obliged for better judgements; and those I hope will be so kind to me, knowing my conversation not at all addicted to the

indecencies alleged, that I would much less practise it in a play, that 120
must stand the test of the censuring world. And I must want common
sense, and all the degrees of good manners—renouncing my fame, all
modesty and interest for a silly saucy fruitless jest, to make fools
laugh, and women blush, and wise men ashamed; myself all the while,
if I had been guilty of this crime charged to me, remaining the only 125
stupid insensible.° Is this likely, is this reasonable to be believed, by
anybody but the wilfully blind? All I ask, is the privilege for my
masculine part the poet in me (if any such you will allow me) to tread
in those successful paths my predecessors have so long thrived in, to
take those measures that both the ancient and modern writers have 130
set me, and by which they have pleased the world so well. If I must
not, because of my sex, have this freedom, but that you will usurp all
to yourselves, I lay down my quill, and you shall hear no more of
me—no, not so much as to make comparisons, because I will be
kinder to my brothers of the pen than they have been to a defenceless 135
woman—for I am not content to write for a third day only. I value
fame as much as if I had been born a hero; and if you rob me of that,
I can retire from the ungrateful world, and scorn its fickle favours.

Prologue

Spoken by Mr Jevon°

Since with old plays you have so long been cloyed,°
As with a mistress many years enjoyed,
How briskly dear variety you pursue;
Nay, though for worse ye change, ye will have new.
Widows take heed: some of you in fresh youth   5
Have been th'unpitied martyrs of this truth,
When, for a drunken sot, that had kind hours,
And taking their own freedoms, left you yours,
'Twas your deliberate choice your days to pass
With a damned, sober, self-admiring ass,   10
Who thinks good usage for the sex unfit,
And slights ye out of sparkishness and wit.
But you can fit him: let a worse fool come,
If he neglect, to officiate in his room.
Vain amorous coxcombs everywhere are found;   15
Fops for all uses, but the stage, abound.
Though you should change them oftener than your fashions,
There still would be enough for your occasions;
But ours are not so easily supplied,
All that could e'er quit cost, we have already tried.°   20
Nay, dear sometimes have bought the frippery stuff.
This, widows, you—I mean the old and tough—
Will never think, be they but fool enough.
    Such will with any kind of puppies play,
But we must better know for what we pay;   25
We must not purchase such dull fools as they.
Should we show each her own particular dear,
What they admire at home, they would loathe here.
Thus, though the Mall, the Ring, the pit is full,°
And every coffee-house still swarms with fool,   30
Though still by fools all other callings live,
Nay, our own women by fresh cullies thrive;
Though your intrigues, which no lampoon can cure,
Promise a long succession to ensure,
And all your matches plenty do presage,   35

Dire is the dearth and famine on the stage.
Our store's quite wasted, and our credit's small,
Not a fool left to bless ourselves withal.
We're forced at last to rob (which is great pity,
Though 'tis a never-failing bank) the city.   40
  We show you one today entirely new,
And of all jests, none relish like the true.
Let that the value of our play enhance,
Then it may prove indeed the lucky chance.

1.1

The street at break of day

Enter Belmour, disguised in a travelling habit

BELMOUR Sure, 'tis the day that gleams in yonder east;°
The day that all but lovers blest by shade
Pay cheerful homage to—
Lovers, and those pursued, like guilty me,
By rigid laws, which put no difference°   5
'Twixt fairly killing in my own defence,
And murders bred by drunken arguments,
Whores, or the mean revenges of a coward.
(*Looking about*) This is Leticia's father's house,
And that the dear balcony   10
That has so oft been conscious of our loves;
From whence she's sent me down a thousand sighs,
A thousand looks of love, a thousand vows!
O thou dear witness of those charming hours,
How do I bless thee, how am I pleased to view thee   15
After a tedious age of six months' banishment.

Enter [Mr Jingle° and] several with music

FIDDLER But hark'ee, Mr Jingle, is it proper to play before the wedding?
JINGLE Ever while you live; for many a time, in playing after the first
night, the bride's sleepy, the bridegroom tired, and both so out of
humour that perhaps they hate anything that puts 'em in mind   20
they are married.

[The musicians] play and sing

SONG

Rise, Cloris, charming maid, arise
And baffle breaking day,
Show the adoring world thy eyes
Are more surprising gay;   25
The gods of love are smiling round,
And lead the bridegroom on,
And Hymen has the altar crowned;
While all thy sighing lovers are undone.

To see thee pass they throng the plain;   30
The groves with flowers are strown,

> *And every young and envying swain*
>> *Wishes the hour his own.*
> *Rise then, and let the god of day,*
>> *When thou dost to the lover yield,*   35
> *Behold more treasure given away*
>> *Than he in his vast circle e'er beheld.*

Enter Phillis in the balcony, and throws them money

BELMOUR Ha, Phillis, Leticia's woman!

JINGLE Fie, Mrs Phillis, do ye take us for fiddlers that play for hire?
I came to compliment Mrs Leticia on her wedding morning   40
because she is my scholar.

PHILLIS She sends it only to drink her health.

JINGLE Come, lads, let's to the tavern then.
Exit music

BELMOUR Ha, said he Leticia?
Sure, I shall turn to marble at this news: 45
I harden, and cold damps pass through my senseless pores.
—Ha, who's here?
Enter Gayman, wrapped in his cloak

GAYMAN 'Tis yet too early, but my soul's impatient,
And I must see Leticia.
[Gayman] goes to the door

BELMOUR Death and the devil, the bridegroom!—Stay, sir; by   50
heaven, you pass not this way.
*[Bellmour] goes to the door as [Gayman] is knocking, pushes
him away, and draws*

GAYMAN Ha, what art thou, that durst forbid me entrance? Stand off.
*[Bellmour and Gayman] fight a little, and closing° view each
other*

BELMOUR Gayman!

GAYMAN My dearest Belmour!

BELMOUR Oh, thou false friend, thou treacherous base deceiver!   55

GAYMAN Ha, this to me, dear Harry?

BELMOUR Whither is honour, truth and friendship fled?

GAYMAN Why, there ne'er was such a virtue. 'Tis all a poet's
dream.°

BELMOUR I thank you, sir.   60

GAYMAN I am sorry for't, or that ever I did anything that could
deserve it. Put up your sword: an honest man would say how he's
offended, before he rashly draws.

BELMOUR Are not you going to be married, sir?

GAYMAN No, sir, as long as any man in London is so, that has but   65
a handsome wife, sir.

BELMOUR Are not you in love, sir?

GAYMAN Most damnably, and would fain lie with the dear jilting
gipsy.

BELMOUR Ha, who would you lie with, sir?   70

GAYMAN You catechize me roundly: 'tis not fair to name, but I am
no starter,° Harry; just as you left me, you find me; I am for the
faithless Julia still, the old alderman's wife. 'Twas high time the
city should lose their charter,° when their wives turn honest. But
pray, sir, answer me a question or two.   75

BELMOUR Answer me first: what make you here this morning?

GAYMAN Faith, to do you service. Your damned little jade of a
mistress has learned of her neighbours the art of swearing and
lying in abundance, and is——

BELMOUR (*sighing*) To be married!   80

GAYMAN Even so, God save the mark; and she'll be a fair one° for
many an arrow besides her husband's, though he's° an old
Finsbury hero° this threescore years.

BELMOUR Who mean you?

GAYMAN Why, thy cuckold that shall be, if thou be'st wise.   85

BELMOUR Away, who is this man? Thou dalliest with me.

GAYMAN Why, an old knight, and alderman here o'th' city, Sir
Feeble Fainwould: a jolly old fellow, whose activity is all got into
his tongue; a very excellent teaser, but neither youth nor beauty
can grind his dudgeon to an edge.   90

BELMOUR Fie, what stuff's here!

GAYMAN Very excellent stuff, if you have but the grace to improve
it.

BELMOUR You banter me; but in plain English, tell me, what made
you here thus early, entering yon house with such authority?°   95

GAYMAN Why, your mistress Leticia, your contracted wife, is this
morning to be married to old Sir Feeble Fainwould, induced to't
I suppose by the great jointure he makes her, and the improbability
of your ever gaining your pardon for your high duel. Do I speak
English now, sir?   100

BELMOUR Too well; would I had never heard thee.

GAYMAN Now I, being the confidant in your amours, the jack-go-
between, the civil pimp, or so, you left her in charge with me at
your departure.

BELMOUR I did so.   105

GAYMAN I saw her every day; and every day
　　She paid the tribute of a shower of tears
　　To the dear lord of all her vows, young Belmour;°
　　Till, faith, at last, for reasons manifold,
　　I slacked my daily visits.   110

BELMOUR And left her to temptation; was that well done?

GAYMAN Now must I afflict you and myself with a long tale of causes
　　why, or be charged with want of friendship.°

BELMOUR You will do well to clear that point to me.

GAYMAN I see you're peevish, and you shall be humoured. You know   115
　　my Julia° played me e'en such another prank as your false one is
　　going to play you, and married old Sir Cautious Fulbank here i'th'
　　city; at which you know I stormed, and raved, and swore, as thou
　　wilt° now, and to as little purpose. There was but one way left,
　　and that was cuckolding him.   120

BELMOUR Well, that design I left thee hot upon.

GAYMAN And hotly have I pursued it. Swore, wept, vowed, wrote,
　　upbraided, prayed and railed; then treated lavishly, and presented°
　　high, till between you and I, Harry, I have presented the best part
　　of eight hundred a year into her husband's hands, in mortgage.   125

BELMOUR This is the course you'd have me steer, I thank you.

GAYMAN No, no, pox on't, all women are not jilts. Some are honest,
　　and will give as well as take; or else there would not be so many
　　broke i'th' city.° In fine, sir, I have been in tribulation,° that is to
　　say, moneyless, for six tedious weeks, without either clothes or   130
　　equipage to appear withal; and so not only my own love affair lay
　　neglected, but thine too, and I am forced to pretend to my lady
　　that I am i'th' country with a dying uncle, from whom, if he were
　　indeed dead, I expect two thousand a year.

BELMOUR But what's all this to being here this morning?   135

GAYMAN Thus have I lain concealed like a winter fly, hoping for
　　some blessed sunshine to warm me into life again, and make me
　　hover my flagging wings; till the news of this marriage (which fills
　　the town) made me crawl out this silent hour, to upbraid the fickle
　　maid.   140

BELMOUR Didst thou? Pursue thy kind design. Get me to see her,
　　and sure, no woman, even possessed with a new passion, grown
　　confident even to prostitution,° but when she sees the man to
　　whom she's sworn so very, very much, will find remorse and
　　shame.   145

GAYMAN For your sake, though the day be broke upon us,
   And I'm undone if seen, I'll venture in.
       [*Gayman*] *throws his cloak over* [*his head, concealing his*
       face]. *Enter Sir Feeble Fainwould, Sir Cautious Fulbank,*
       Bearjest, and Noisy, [*who*] *pass over the stage and go in*
GAYMAN Ha, see, the bridegroom! And with him my destined
   cuckold, old Sir Cautious Fulbank. Ha, what ail'st thou, man?
BELMOUR The bridegroom!   150
   Like Gorgon's head he 'as turned me into stone.°
GAYMAN Gorgon's head? A cuckold's head; 'twas made to graft
   upon.°
BELMOUR By heaven, I'll seize her even at the altar!
   And bear her thence in triumph.   155
GAYMAN Aye, and be borne to Newgate in triumph, and be hanged
   in triumph. 'Twill be cold comfort celebrating your nuptials in the
   press yard,° and be waked the next morning like Mr Barnardine
   in the play:° 'will you please to rise and be hanged a little, sir?'
BELMOUR What wouldst thou have me do?   160
GAYMAN As many an honest man has done before thee: cuckold him,
   cuckold him.
BELMOUR What, and let him marry her! She that's mine by sacred
   vow already? By heaven, it would be flat adultery in her!
GAYMAN She'll learn the trick, and practise it the better with thee. 165
BELMOUR Oh heavens! Leticia marry him, and lie with him! Here
   will I stand and see this shameful woman, see if she dares pass by
   me to this wickedness.
GAYMAN Hark'ee, Harry; in earnest, have a care of betraying your-
   self, and do not venture sweet life for a fickle woman, who perhaps 170
   hates you.
BELMOUR You counsel well; but yet, to see her married!
   How every thought of that shocks all my resolution!
   But hang it, I'll be resolute and saucy,
   Despise a woman who can use me ill,   175
   And think myself above her.
GAYMAN Why, now thou art thyself, a man again.
   But see, they're coming forth; now stand your ground.
       Enter Sir Feeble, Sir Cautious, Bearjest, Noisy, Leticia, sad,
       Diana, [*and*] *Phillis.* [*They*] *pass over the stage*
BELMOUR 'Tis she; support me, Charles, or I shall sink to earth.
   Methought in passing by she cast a scornful glance at me: 180
   Such charming pride I've seen upon her eyes,

When our love-quarrels armed 'em with disdain.
I'll after 'em, if I live she shall not 'scape me.
    [Belmour] offers to go. Gayman holds him

GAYMAN Hold; remember you're proscribed, and die if you are taken.°   185

BELMOUR I've done, and I will live, but he shall ne'er enjoy her.
Who's yonder; Ralph, my trusty confidant?
    Enter Ralph
Now, though I perish, I must speak to him.
—Friend, what wedding's this?

RALPH One that was never made in heaven, sir: 'tis Alderman   190
Fainwould, and Mrs Leticia Bredwell.

BELMOUR Bredwell? I've heard of her; she was mistress—°

RALPH —To fine Mr Belmour, sir. Aye, there was a gentleman; but
rest his soul, he's hanged, sir. (*Weeps*)

BELMOUR How! hanged?   195

RALPH Hanged, sir, hanged; at the Hague in Holland.

GAYMAN I heard some such news, but did not credit it.

BELMOUR For what, said they, was he hanged?

RALPH Why, e'en for high treason, sir: he killed one of their kings.

GAYMAN Holland's a commonwealth,° and is not ruled by kings.   200

RALPH Not by one, sir, but by a great many; this was a cheesemonger.
They fell out over a bottle of brandy, went to snicker snee;°
Mr Belmour cut his throat, and was hanged for't; that's all, sir.

BELMOUR And did the young lady believe this?

RALPH Yes, and took on most heavily. The doctors gave her over,   205
and there was the devil to do to get her to consent to this marriage;
but her fortune was small, and the hope of a ladyship, and a gold
chain at the spittle sermon,° did the business; and so, your servant,
sir.
    Exit Ralph

BELMOUR So, here's a hopeful account of my sweet self now.   210
    Enter postman with letters

POSTMAN Pray, sir, which is Sir Feeble Fainwould's?

BELMOUR What would you with him, friend?

POSTMAN I have a letter here from the Hague for him.

BELMOUR [*aside*] From the Hague! Now have I a curiosity to see it.
    [*To postman*] I am his servant; give it me.   215
    [Postman] gives [the letter to Belmour], and exit[s]
Perhaps here may be the second part of my tragedy. I'm full of
mischief, Charles, and have a mind to see this fellow's secrets. For

from this hour I'll be his evil genius: haunt him at bed and board, he shall not sleep nor eat; disturb him at his prayers, in his embraces; and tease him into madness.   220

(*Opening the letter*) Help me invention, malice, love and wit;
Ye gods and little fiends, instruct my mischief.

(*Reads*) 'Dear brother, according to your desire I have sent for my son from St Omer's,° whom I have sent to wait on you in England; he is a very good accountant and fit for business, and much pleased   225
he shall see that uncle to whom he's so obliged, and which is so gratefully acknowledged by, dear brother, your affectionate brother, Francis Fainwould.' Hum—hark'ee, Charles, do you know who I am now?

GAYMAN Why, I hope a very honest friend of mine, Harry Belmour.   230
BELMOUR No, sir, you are mistaken in your man.
GAYMAN It may be so.
BELMOUR I am, d'ye see, Charles, this very individual, numerical young Mr—what ye call um—Fainwould, just come from St Omer's into England, to my uncle the alderman. I am, Charles,   235
this very man.
GAYMAN I know you are, and will swear't upon occasion.
BELMOUR This lucky thought has almost calmed my mind. And if I don't fit you, my dear uncle, may I never lie with my aunt.
GAYMAN Ah, rogue! But prithee, what care have you taken about   240
your pardon?° 'Twere good you should secure that.
BELMOUR There's the devil, Charles; had I but that—but I have had a very good friend at work: a thousand guineas, that seldom fails; but yet in vain, I being the first transgressor since the act against duelling. But I, impatient to see this dear delight of my soul, and   245
hearing from none of you this six weeks, came from Brussels in this disguise—for the Hague I have not seen, though hanged there. But come, let's away, and complete me a right St Omer's spark, that I may present myself as soon as they come from church.°

Exeunt

200

1.2

Sir Cautious Fulbank's House

Enter Lady Fulbank, Pert, and Bredwell. Bredwell gives
[Lady Fulbank] a letter

LADY FULBANK (*reads*) 'Did my Julia know how I languish in this
cruel separation, she would afford me her pity, and write oftener.
If only the expectation of two thousand a year kept me from you,
ah, Julia, how easily would I abandon that trifle for your more
valued sight; but that I know a fortune will render me more   5
agreeable to the charming Julia, I should quit all my interest here,
to throw myself at her feet, to make her sensible how I am° entirely
her adorer, Charles Gayman.'—Faith, Charles, you lie. You are as
welcome to me now,
Now, when I doubt thy fortune is declining,   10
As if the universe were thine.

PERT That, madam, is a noble gratitude. For if his fortune be
declining, 'tis sacrificed to his passion for your ladyship. 'Tis all
laid out on love.

LADY FULBANK I prize my honour more than life,   15
Yet I had rather have given him all he wished of me,
Than be guilty of his undoing.

PERT And I think the sin were less.

LADY FULBANK I must confess, such jewels, rings and presents as
he made me must needs decay his fortune.   20

BREDWELL Aye, madam; his very coach at last was turned into a
jewel for your ladyship. Then, madam, what expenses his despairs
have run him on: as drinking and gaming, to divert the thought of
your marrying my old master.

LADY FULBANK And put in wenching, too.   25

BREDWELL No, assure yourself, madam—

LADY FULBANK Of that I would be better satisfied;—(*to Bredwell*)
and you, too, must assist me, as e'er you hope I should be kind to
you in gaining you Diana.

BREDWELL Madam, I'll die to serve you.   30

PERT Nor will I be behind in my duty.

LADY FULBANK Oh, how fatal are forced marriages!
How many ruins one such match pulls on:
Had I but kept my sacred vows to Gayman,
How happy had I been, how prosperous he!   35

Whilst now I languish in a loathed embrace,
Pine out my life with age, consumptuous coughs.
—But dost thou fear that Gayman is declining?

BREDWELL You are my lady, and the best of mistresses;
Therefore I would not grieve you, for I know   40
You love this best, but most unhappy, man.

LADY FULBANK You shall not grieve me: prithee on.

BREDWELL My master sent me yesterday to Mr Crap° his scrivener,
to send to one Mr Wasteall, to tell him his first mortgage was out,
which is two hundred pounds a year—and who has since engaged   45
five or six hundred more to my master; but if this first be not
redeemed, he'll take the forfeit on't, as he says a wise man ought.

LADY FULBANK That is to say, a knave, according to his notion of
a wise man.

BREDWELL Mr Crap, being busy with a borrowing lord, sent me to 50
Mr Wasteall, whose lodging is in a nasty place, called Alsatia,° at
a blacksmith's.

LADY FULBANK But what's all this to Gayman?

BREDWELL Madam, this Wasteall was Mr Gayman.

LADY FULBANK Gayman? Saw'st thou Gayman?   55

BREDWELL Madam, Mr Gayman, yesterday.

LADY FULBANK When came he to town?

BREDWELL Madam, he has not been out of it.

LADY FULBANK Not at his uncle's in Northamptonshire?

BREDWELL Your ladyship was wont to credit me.   60

LADY FULBANK Forgive me—you went to a blacksmith's—

BREDWELL Yes, madam; and at the door encountered the beastly
thing he calls a landlady, who looked as if she'd been of her own
husband's making, composed of moulded smith's dust. I asked for
Mr Wasteall, and she began to open,° and did so rail at him, that   65
what with her Billingsgate,° and her husband's hammers, I was
both deaf and dumb. At last the hammers ceased, and she grew
weary, and called down Mr Wasteall; but he not answering, I was
sent up a ladder rather than a pair of stairs; at last I scaled the top,
and entered the enchanted castle; there did I find him, spite of the   70
noise below, drowning his cares in sleep.

LADY FULBANK Whom found'st thou, Gayman?

BREDWELL He, madam; whom I waked, and seeing me, heavens,
what confusion seized him; which nothing but my own surprise
could equal. Ashamed, he would have turned away, but when he   75
saw, by my dejected eyes, I knew him, he sighed, and blushed, and

heard me tell my business. Then begged I would be secret, for, he
vowed, his whole repose and life depended on my silence. Nor had
I told it now, but that your ladyship may find some speedy means
to draw him from this desperate condition.°   80

LADY FULBANK Heavens, is't possible?

BREDWELL He's driven to the last degree of poverty. Had you but
seen his lodgings, madam!

LADY FULBANK What were they?

BREDWELL 'Tis a pretty convenient tub, madam. He may lie along   85
in't; there's just room for an old joined stool besides the bed, which
one cannot call a cabin,° about the largeness of a pantry bin, or a
usurer's trunk; there had been dornex curtains to't in the days of
yore, but they were now annihilated, and nothing left to save his
eyes from the light, but my landlady's blue apron, tied by the   90
strings before the window, in which stood a broken sixpenny
looking-glass, that showed as many faces as the scene in *Henry
VIII*,° which could but just stand upright, and then the comb-case
filled it.

LADY FULBANK What a lewd description hast thou made of his   95
chamber!

BREDWELL Then for his equipage, 'tis banished to one small monsieur, who (saucy with his master's poverty) is rather a companion
than a footman.

LADY FULBANK But what said he to the forfeiture of his land?   100

BREDWELL He sighed, and cried, 'why, farewell, dirty acres.
It shall not trouble me, since 'twas all but for love!'

LADY FULBANK How much redeems it?

BREDWELL Madam, five hundred pounds.

LADY FULBANK Enough; you shall in some disguise convey this   105
money to him, as from an unknown hand: I would not have him
think it comes from me, for all the world; that nicety and virtue
I've professed, I am resolved to keep.°

PERT If I were your ladyship, I would make use of Sir Cautious his
cash: pay him in his own coin.   110

BREDWELL Your ladyship would make no scruple of it, if you
knew how this poor gentleman has been used by my unmerciful
master.

LADY FULBANK I have a key already to his counting-house; it being
lost, he had another made, and this I found and kept.   115

BREDWELL Madam, this is an excellent time for't, my master being
gone to give my sister Leticia at church.

LADY FULBANK 'Tis so; I'll go and commit the theft, whilst you prepare to carry it, and then we'll to dinner with your sister the bride.   120

    Exeunt

1.3

    The house of Sir Feeble

    Enter Sir Feeble, Leticia, Sir Cautious, Bearjest, Diana,
    Noisy. Sir Feeble sings and salutes them

SIR FEEBLE Welcome, Joan Sanderson,° welcome, welcome.

    [Sir Feeble] kiss[es] the bride

Od's bobs, and so thou art, sweetheart.

    The rest [of the company kiss Leticia]°

BEARJEST Methinks my lady bride is very melancholy.

SIR CAUTIOUS Aye, aye; women that are discreet are always thus upon their wedding-day.   5

SIR FEEBLE Always by daylight, Sir Cautious.

>   *[Sings] But when bright Phoebus does retire*
>   *To Thetis' bed to quench his fire,°*
>   *And do the thing we need not name,*
>   *We mortals by his influence do the same.*   10
>   *Then, then, the blushing maid lays by°*
>   *Her simpering, and her modesty;*
>   *And round the lover clasps and twines*
>   *Like ivy, or the circling vines.*

—Here, Ralph, the bottle, rogue, of sack, ye rascal! Hadst thou   15
been a butler worth hanging, thou wouldst have met us at the door
with it. *[To Leticia]* Od's bobs, sweetheart, thy health.

BEARJEST Away with it, to the bride's haunce in kelder.°

SIR FEEBLE God so;° go to, rogue, go to, that shall be, knave, that
shall be, by the morrow morning; hee, od's bobs, we'll do't,   20
sweetheart; here's to't. *(Drinks again)*

LETICIA *[aside]* I die but to imagine it; would I were dead indeed.

SIR FEEBLE Ha, hum, how's this? Tears upon your wedding-day?
Why, why, you baggage you, ye little ting,° fool's-face! Away, you
rogue, you're naughty, you're naughty. *(Patting, and playing, and*   25
following her) Look, look, look now; buss it, buss it, and friends.

Did'ums, did'ums beat its nown° silly baby? Away, you little
hussy, away, and pledge me.

    [Leticia] drinks a little

SIR CAUTIOUS A wise discreet lady, I'll warrant her: my lady would
prodigally have took it off all.   30

SIR FEEBLE Dere's° its nown dear Fubs;° buss again, buss again,
away, away. Od's bobs, I long for night. Look, look, Sir Cautious;
what an eye's there!

SIR CAUTIOUS Aye, so there is, brother, and a modest eye too.

SIR FEEBLE Adad, I love her more and more.—Ralph, call old Susan   35
hither.—Come, Mr Bearjest, put the glass about. Od's bobs, when
I was a young fellow, I would not let the young wenches look pale
and wan; but would rouse 'em, and touse 'em, and blowze 'em,°
'till I put a colour in their cheeks like an apple-John,° affacks.°
Nay, I can make a shift still, and pupsey shall not be jealous.   40

    Enter Susan. Sir Feeble whispers [to] her; she goes out

LETICIA Indeed, not I, sir. I shall be all obedience.

SIR CAUTIOUS A most judicious lady; would my Julia had a little of
her modesty; but my lady's a wit.

    Enter Susan with a box

SIR FEEBLE Look here, my little puskin,° here's fine playthings for
its nown little coxcomb. Go, get ye gone, get ye gone, and off with   45
this Saint Martin's trumpery,° these playhouse glass baubles, this
necklace, and these pendants, and all this false ware; od's bobs, I'll
have no counterfeit gear about thee, not I. See, these are right as
the blushes on thy cheeks, and these as true as my heart, my girl.
Go, put 'em on and be fine.   50

    [Sir Feeble] gives [the jewels to Leticia]

LETICIA Believe me, sir, I shall not merit this kindness.

SIR FEEBLE Go to! More of your love, and less of your ceremony:
give the old fool a hearty buss, and pay him that way. Hee, ye little
wanton tit, I'll steal up, and catch ye and love ye; adod I will. Get
ye gone, get ye gone.   55

LETICIA *[aside]* Heavens, what a nauseous thing is an old man turned
lover.

    Exeunt Leticia and Diana

SIR CAUTIOUS How, steal up, Sir Feeble? I hope not so; I hold it
most indecent before the lawful hour.

SIR FEEBLE Lawful hour! Why, I hope all hours are lawful with a   60
man's own wife.

SIR CAUTIOUS But wise men have respect to times and seasons.

SIR FEEBLE Wise young men, Sir Cautious, but wise old men must
nick their inclinations—(*singing and dancing*) 'for it is not as 'twas
wont to be, for it is not as 'twas wont to be.'   65
      Enter Ralph
RALPH Sir, here's a young gentleman without would speak with you.
SIR FEEBLE Hum, I hope it is not that same Belmour come to forbid
the banns. If it be, he comes too late: therefore bring me first my
long sword, and then the gentleman.
      Exit Ralph
BEARJEST Pray, sir, use mine; it is a travelled blade, I can assure you,   70
sir.
      [*Bearjest gives Sir Feeble a sword*]
SIR FEEBLE I thank you, sir.
      Enter Ralph, and Belmour, disguised. [*Belmour*] *gives* [*Sir
      Feeble*] *a letter; he reads*
—How, my nephew, Francis Fainwould? (*Embraces* [*Belmour*])
BELMOUR [*aside*] I am glad he has told me my christian name.
SIR FEEBLE Sir Cautious, know my nephew. 'Tis a young Saint   75
Omer's scholar; but none of the witnesses.°
SIR CAUTIOUS Marry, sir, the wiser he, for they got nothing by't.
BEARJEST Sir, I love and honour you because you are a traveller.
SIR FEEBLE A very proper young fellow, and as like old Frank
Fainwould as the devil to the collier;° but, Francis, you are come   80
into a very lewd town, Francis, for whoring and plotting and
roaring and drinking; but you must go to church, Francis, and
avoid ill company, or you may make damnable havoc in my cash,
Francis. What, you can keep merchants' books?
BELMOUR 'T has been my study, sir.   85
SIR FEEBLE And you will not be proud, but will be commanded by
me, Francis?
BELMOUR I desire not to be favoured as a kinsman, sir, but as your
humblest servant.
SIR FEEBLE Why, thou'rt an honest fellow, Francis; and thou'rt   90
heartily welcome; and I'll make thee fortunate!—But come, Sir
Cautious, let you and I take a turn i'th' garden, and beget a right
understanding between your nephew Mr Bearjest and my daughter
Di.
SIR CAUTIOUS Prudently thought on, sir; I'll wait on you.   95
      Exeunt Sir Feeble and Sir Cautious
BEARJEST You are a traveller, sir, I understand?
BELMOUR I have seen a little part of the world, sir.

BEARJEST So have I, sir, I thank my stars, and have performed most
of my travels on foot, sir.

BELMOUR You did not travel far then, I presume, sir.   100

BEARJEST No, sir, it was for my diversion indeed; but I assure you
I travelled into Ireland a-foot, sir.

BELMOUR Sure, sir, you go by shipping into Ireland?

BEARJEST That's all one sir, I was still a-foot: ever walking on the
deck.   105

BELMOUR Was that your farthest travel, sir?

BEARJEST Farthest? Why, that's the end of the world; and sure a man
can go no further.

BELMOUR Sure, there can be nothing worth a man's curiosity?

BEARJEST No, sir? I'll assure you, there are the wonders of the world, 110
sir; I'll hint you this one. There is a harbour which since the
creation was never capable of receiving a lighter, yet by another
miracle, the king of France was to ride there with a vast fleet of
ships, and to land a hundred thousand men.°

BELMOUR This is a swingeing wonder; but are there store of mad   115
men there, sir?

BEARJEST That's another rarity, to see a man run out of his wits.

NOISY Marry, sir, the wiser they, I say.

BEARJEST Pray, sir, what store of miracles have you at St Omer's?

BELMOUR None, sir, since that of the wonderful Salamanca doc-   120
tor,° who was both here and there at the same instant of time.

BEARJEST How, sir! Why, that's impossible.

BELMOUR That was the wonder sir, because 'twas impossible.

NOISY But 'twas a greater, sir, that 'twas believed.

Enter Lady Fulbank and Pert, Sir Cautious and Sir Feeble

SIR FEEBLE Enough, enough, Sir Cautious, we apprehend one   125
another.—Mr Bearjest, your uncle here and I have struck the
bargain: the wench is yours with three thousand pound present and
something more after death,° which your uncle likes well.

BEARJEST Does he so, sir? I'm beholding to him; then 'tis not a pin
matter whether I like or not, sir.   130

SIR FEEBLE How, sir, not like my daughter Di?

BEARJEST Oh Lord, sir, die or live, 'tis all one for that, sir. I'll stand
to the bargain my uncle makes.

PERT (*aside* [*to Bearjest*]) Will you so, sir? You'll have very good luck
if you do.   135

BEARJEST [*aside to Pert*] Prithee, hold thy peace, my lady's
woman.°

LADY FULBANK [*to Sir Feeble*] Sir, I beg your pardon for not waiting
on you to church; I knew you would be private.

    Enter Leticia, fine, in jewels

SIR FEEBLE [*to Lady Fulbank*] You honour us too highly now,   140
madam.

    [*Sir Feeble*] *presents his wife, who salutes* [*Lady Fulbank*]

LADY FULBANK Give you joy, my dear Leticia!—I find, sir, you
were resolved for youth, wit and beauty.

SIR FEEBLE Aye, madam, to the comfort of many a hoping coxcomb;—but Letty, rogue Letty, thou wouldst° not make me free   145
o'th' city° a second time. Wouldst thou entice the rogues with the
twire and wanton leer? The amorous simper that cries 'come kiss
me'? Then the pretty round lips are pouted out; hee, rogue, how
I long to be at 'em!—Well, she shall never go to church more, that
she shall not.   150

LADY FULBANK How, sir, not to church, the chiefest recreation of a
city lady?

SIR FEEBLE That's all one, madam; that tricking and dressing and
prinking and patching is not your devotion to heaven, but to the
young knaves that are licked and combed, and are minding you   155
more than the parson. Od's bobs, there are more cuckolds destined
at church than are made out of it.

SIR CAUTIOUS Ha, ha, ha! (*To his lady*) He tickles ye, i-faith,
ladies.

BELMOUR [*aside*] Not one chance look this way; and yet   160
  I can forgive her lovely eyes, because°
They look not pleased with all this ceremony;
And yet methinks some sympathy in love
Might this way glance their beams. I cannot hold.

    [*To Sir Feeble*] Sir, is this fair lady my aunt?   165

SIR FEEBLE Oh, Francis! Come hither, Francis.—Letty, here's a
young rogue has a mind to kiss thee.

    [*Sir Feeble*] *puts them together,* [*Leticia*] *starts back*

Nay, start not, he's my own flesh and blood, my nephew, baby.
[*To the others*] Look, look how the young rogues stare at one
another; like will to like, I see that.   170

LETICIA [*aside*] There's something in his face so like my Belmour, it
calls my blushes up, and leaves my heart defenceless.

    Enter Ralph

RALPH Sir, dinner's on the table.

SIR FEEBLE Come, come, let's in then, gentlemen and ladies,

And share today my pleasures and delight;   175
But—
Ad's bobs, they must be all mine own at night.
Exeunt

2.1

Gayman's lodging

Enter Gayman in a night-cap, and an old campaign coat°
tied about him; very melancholy

GAYMAN Curse on my birth! Curse on my faithless fortune!
Curse on my stars, and cursed be all—but love!
That dear, that charming sin, though 't have pulled
Innumerable mischiefs on my head,
I have not, nor I cannot find repentance for.   5
No: let me die despised, upbraided, poor;
Let fortune, friends and all abandon me,
But let me hold thee, thou soft smiling god,
Close to my heart while life continues there,
Till the last pantings of my vital blood.   10
May the last spark of life and fire be love's!

Enter Rag

—How now, Rag, what's o'clock?

RAG My belly can inform you better than my tongue.

GAYMAN Why, you gourmandising vermin you, what have you done
with the threepence I gave you a fortnight ago?   15

RAG Alas, sir, that's all gone, long since.

GAYMAN You gutling rascal, you are enough to breed a famine in a
land. I have known some industrious footmen, that have not only
gotten their own livings, but a pretty livelihood for their masters
too.   20

RAG Aye, till they came to the gallows, sir.

GAYMAN Very well, sirrah, they died in an honourable calling. But
hark'ee, Rag: I have business, very earnest business abroad this
evening; now, were you a rascal of docity, you would invent a way
to get home my last suit that was laid in lavender,° with the   25
appurtenances thereunto belonging, as periwig, cravat, and so
forth.

RAG Faith, master, I must deal in the black art° then, for no human
means will do't; and now I talk of the black art, master, try your
power once more with my landlady.   30

GAYMAN Oh! name her not, the thought on't turns my stomach. A
sight of her is a vomit, but he's a bold hero that dares venture on
her for a kiss, and all beyond that, sure, is hell itself. Yet there's

my last, last refuge; and I must to this wedding. I know not what,
but something whispers me, this night I shall be happy; and   35
without Julia 'tis impossible!

RAG Julia, who's that, my lady Fulbank, sir?

GAYMAN Peace, sirrah, and call—a—no. Pox on't, come back—and
yet—yes, call my fulsome landlady.

> *Exit Rag*

Sir Cautious knows me not, by name or person. And I will to this   40
wedding; I'm sure of seeing Julia there, and what may come of
that—but here's old Nasty coming. I smell her up.

> *Enter Rag and landlady*

—Ha, my dear landlady, quite out of breath. [*To Rag*] A chair
there for my landlady.

RAG Here's ne'er a one, sir.   45

LANDLADY More of your money and less of your civility, good Mr
Wasteall.

GAYMAN Dear landlady—

LANDLADY Dear me no dears, sir, but let me have my money: eight
weeks' rent last Friday. Besides taverns, ale-houses, chandlers,   50
laundresses' scores,° and ready money out of my purse; you know
it, sir.

GAYMAN Aye, but your husband does not; speak softly.

LANDLADY My husband! What, do you think to fright me with my
husband? I'd have you to know I am an honest woman and care   55
not this—for my husband.° Is this all the thanks I have for my
kindness, for patching, borrowing, and shifting° for you? 'Twas
but last week I pawned my best petticoat, as I hope to wear it again
it cost me six and twenty shillings, besides making; then this
morning my new Norwich mantua° followed, and two 'postle   60
spoons; I had the whole dozen when you came first, but they
dropped, and dropped, till I had only Judas left° for my
husband.

GAYMAN Hear me, good landlady—

LANDLADY Then I've passed my word at the George Tavern° for   65
forty shillings for you; ten shillings at my neighbour Squab's for
ale; besides seven shillings to mother Suds for washing—and do
you fob me off with my husband?

GAYMAN [*aside to Rag*] Here, Rag, run and fetch her a pint of sack,
there's no other way of quenching the fire in her slabber chops.°   70

> *Exit Rag*

—But, my dear landlady, have a little patience.

LANDLADY Patience? I scorn your words, sir; is this a place to trust
in? Tell me of patience, that used to have my money beforehand!
Come, come, pay me quickly, or old Gregory Grime's house shall
be too hot to hold you.   75

GAYMAN Is't come to this, can I not be heard?

LANDLADY No, sir: you had good clothes when you came first, but
they dwindled daily, till they dwindled to this old campaign, with
tanned-coloured lining, once red, but now all colours of the
rainbow; a cloak to skulk in a-nights, and a pair of piss-burned   80
shammy breeches. Nay, your very badge of manhood's gone, too.

GAYMAN How, landlady! Nay then, i-faith, no wonder if you rail so.

LANDLADY Your silver sword, I mean: transmogrified to this two-
handed basket hilt,° this old Sir Guy of Warwick,° which will sell
for nothing but old iron. In fine, I'll have my money sir, or i-faith,   85
Alsatia shall not shelter you.

>   *Enter Rag [with the drink]*

GAYMAN Well, landlady, if we must part, let's drink at parting; here,
landlady, here's to the fool that shall love you better than I have
done.

>   *Sighing, [Gayman] drinks*

LANDLADY Rot your wine! D'ye think to pacify me with wine, sir?   90

>   *[Landlady] refusing to drink, [Gayman] holds open her jaws;*
>   *Rag throws a glass of wine into her mouth*

What, will you force me? No, give me another glass, I scorn to be
so uncivil to be forced; my service to you, sir; but this shan't do,
sir.

>   *[Landlady] drinks; [Gayman], embracing her, sings*

[GAYMAN]   *Ah, Cloris, 'tis in vain you scold,*
>   *Whilst your eyes kindle such a fire.*   95
>   *Your railing cannot make me cold,*
>   *So fast as they a warmth inspire.*

LANDLADY Well, sir, you have no reason to complain of my eyes,
nor my tongue neither, if rightly understood. (*Weeps*)

GAYMAN I know you are the best of landladies, as such I drink your   100
health.° (*Drinks*) But to upbraid a man in tribulation, fie, 'tis not
done like a woman of honour—a man that loves you, too.

LANDLADY I am a little hasty sometimes, but you know my good
nature. (*She drinks*)

GAYMAN I do, and therefore trust my little wants with you. I shall   105
be rich again, and then, my dearest landlady—°

LANDLADY Would this wine might ne'er go through me, if I would not go as they say through fire and water, by night or by day for you. (*She drinks*)

GAYMAN And as this is wine, I do believe thee. (*He drinks*)   110

LANDLADY Well, you have no money in your pocket now, I'll warrant you. Here, here's ten shillings for you old Greg'ry knows not of. (*Opens a great greasy purse*)

GAYMAN I cannot in conscience take it, good faith I cannot: besides, the next quarrel you'll hit me in the teeth with it.   115

LANDLADY Nay, pray no more of that, forget it, forget it. I own I was to blame. Here, sir, you shall take it.

GAYMAN Aye, but what should I do with money in these damned breeches? No, put it up, I can't appear abroad thus; no, I'll stay at home and lose my business.   120

LANDLADY Why, is there no way to redeem one of your suits?

GAYMAN None, none; I'll e'en lay me down and die.

LANDLADY Die! Marry, heavens forbid, I would not for the world— let me see: hum, what does it lie for?

GAYMAN Alas, dear landlady, a sum, a sum.   125

LANDLADY Well, say no more, I'll lay about me.

GAYMAN By this kiss, but you shall not.

        [*Gayman kisses landlady*]

        [*Aside*] Asafoetida, by this light.

LANDLADY Shall not? That's a good one, i-faith: shall you rule, or I?

GAYMAN But should your husband know it—   130

LANDLADY Husband? Marry come up, husbands know wives' secrets? No, sure, the world's not so bad yet. Where do your things lie, and for what?

GAYMAN Five pound equips me. Rag can conduct you; but I say you shall not go; I've sworn—   135

LANDLADY Meddle with your matters! Let me see, the caudle cup° that Molly's grandmother left her will pawn for about that sum; I'll sneak it out. Well, sir, you shall have your things presently; trouble not your head, but expect me.

        Exeunt landlady and Rag

GAYMAN Was ever man put to such beastly shifts? 'Sdeath, how she   140
stunk! My senses are most luxuriously regaled.

        [*The*] *knocking of hammers on an anvil* [*is heard*]

There's my perpetual music, too. The ringing of bells is an ass to't.°

        Enter Rag

RAG Sir, there's one in a coach below would speak to you.

GAYMAN With me, and in a coach? Who can it be?   145

RAG The devil, I think, for he has a strange countenance.

GAYMAN The devil? Show yourself a rascal of parts, sirrah, and wait
on him up with ceremony.

RAG Who, the devil, sir?

GAYMAN Aye, the devil, sir, if you mean to thrive. [*Aside*] Who can   150
this be? But see, he comes to inform me. [*To Rag*] Withdraw.
          Exit Rag. Enter Bredwell, dressed like a devil

BREDWELL I come to bring you this.
          [*Bredwell*] *gives* [*Gayman*] *a letter*

GAYMAN (*reads*) 'Receive what love and fortune present you with; be
grateful and be silent, or 'twill vanish like a dream, and leave you
more wretched than it found you: adieu.'   155
          [*Bredwell*] *gives* [*Gayman*] *a bag of money*
Ha!

BREDWELL Nay, view it, sir, 'tis all substantial gold.

GAYMAN (*aside*) Now dare not I ask one civil question, for fear it
vanish all. [*To Bredwell*] But I may ask how 'tis I ought to pay for
this great bounty.   160

BREDWELL Sir, all the pay is secrecy.

GAYMAN And is this all that is required, sir?

BREDWELL No, you're invited to the shades below.

GAYMAN Hum, shades below? I am not prepared for such a journey,
sir.   165

BREDWELL (*in feigned heroic tone*) If you have courage, youth, or
          love, you'll follow me.
When night's black curtain's drawn around the world,
And mortal eyes are safely locked in sleep,
And no bold spy dares view when gods caress,
Then I'll conduct thee to the banks of bliss.   170
Durst thou not trust me?

GAYMAN Yes, sure, on such substantial security. (*Hugs the bag*)

BREDWELL Just when the day is vanished into night,
And only twinkling stars inform the world,
Near to the corner of the silent wall   175
In fields of Lincoln's Inn, thy spirit shall meet thee.°
Farewell.
          [*Bredwell*] *goes out*

GAYMAN Hum: I am awake, sure, and this is gold I grasp.
I could not see this devil's cloven foot,

Nor am I such a coxcomb to believe   180
But he was as substantial as his gold.
Spirits, ghosts, hobgoblins, furies, fiends and devils,°
I've often heard old wives fright fools and children with,
Which, once arrived to common sense, they laugh at.
No, I am for things possible and natural: 185
Some female devil, old, and damned to ugliness,
And past all hopes of courtship and address,
Full of another devil called desire,
Has seen this face, this shape, this youth,
And thinks it worth her hire. It must be so.   190
I must moil on in the damned dirty road,
And sure such pay will make the journey easy;
And for the price of the dull drudging night,
All day I'll purchase new and fresh delight.
    Exit

2.2

Sir Feeble's house

Enter Leticia, pursued by Phillis

PHILLIS Why, madam, do you leave the garden
  For this retreat to melancholy?

LETICIA Because it suits my fortune and my humour;
  And even thy presence would afflict me now.

PHILLIS Madam, I was sent after you. My Lady Fulbank has   5
  challenged Sir Feeble at bowls, and stakes a ring of fifty pound
  against his new chariot.

LETICIA Tell him I wish him luck in everything,
  But in his love to me.
  Go, tell him I am viewing of the garden.   10
    Exit Phillis. Enter Belmour at a distance behind° [*Leticia*]
  Blessed be this kind retreat, this 'lone occasion
  That lends a short cessation to my torments,
  And gives me leave to vent my sighs and tears! (*Weeps*)

BELMOUR [*aside*] And doubly blessed be all the powers of love,
  That gives me this dear opportunity.   15

LETICIA Where were you, all ye pitying gods of love,
  That once seemed pleased at Belmour's flame and mine,

And smiling joined our hearts, our sacred vows,
And spread your wings, and held your torches high?
BELMOUR Oh!   20
    [Leticia] starts [and] pauses
LETICIA Where were you now, when this unequal marriage,
    Gave me from all my joys, gave me from Belmour?
    Your wings were flagged, your torches bent to earth,
    And all your little bonnets veiled your eyes.
    You saw not, or were deaf and pitiless.   25
BELMOUR Oh, my Leticia!
LETICIA Ha, 'tis there again: that very voice was Belmour's.
    Where art thou, oh thou lovely charming shade?
    For sure thou canst not take a shape to fright me.
    (*Not looking behind her yet, for fear*) What art thou? Speak!   30
BELMOUR (*approaching nearer*) Thy constant true adorer,
    Who all this fatal day has haunted thee
    To ease his tortured soul.
LETICIA (*speaking with signs of fear*) My heart is well acquainted with
    that voice,
    But oh, my eyes dare not encounter thee.   35
BELMOUR Is it because thou'st broken all thy vows?
    Take to thee courage, and behold thy slaughters.
LETICIA Yes, though the sight would blast me, I would view it.
    Turns
    'Tis he, 'tis very Belmour! Or so like,
    I cannot doubt but thou deserv'st this welcome.   40
    [Leticia] embraces [Belmour]
BELMOUR Oh, my Leticia!
LETICIA I'm sure I grasp not air; thou art no phantom.
    My arms return not empty to my bosom,
    But meet a solid treasure.
BELMOUR A treasure thou so easily threw'st away!   45
    A riddle simple love ne'er understood.
LETICIA Alas, I heard, my Belmour, thou wert dead.
BELMOUR And was it thus you mourned my funeral?
LETICIA I will not justify my hated crime:
    But oh, remember I was poor and helpless,   50
    And much reduced, and much imposed upon.
    Belmour weeps
BELMOUR And want compelled thee to this wretched marriage, did it?
LETICIA 'Tis not a marriage, since my Belmour lives:

The consummation were adultery.
I was thy wife before; wouldst thou deny me?   55
BELMOUR No, by those powers that heard our mutual vows,
Those vows that tie us faster than dull priests.°
LETICIA But oh, my Belmour, thy sad circumstances
Permit thee not to make a public claim.
Thou art proscribed, and diest if thou art seen.   60
BELMOUR Alas!
LETICIA Yet I would wander with thee o'er the world,
And share thy humblest fortune with thy love.
BELMOUR Is't possible, Leticia, thou wouldst fly
To foreign shores with me?   65
LETICIA Can Belmour doubt the soul he knows so well?
BELMOUR Perhaps in time the king may find my innocence, and may
extend his mercy. Meantime, I'll make provision for our flight.°
LETICIA But how 'twixt this and that can I defend myself from the
loathed arms of an impatient dotard, that I may come a spotless   70
maid to thee?
BELMOUR Thy native modesty and my industry
Shall well enough secure us.
Feign you nice virgin-cautions all the day;
Then trust at night to my conduct to preserve thee.   75
And wilt thou yet be mine? Oh, swear anew,
Give me again thy faith, thy vows, thy soul:
For mine's so sick with this day's fatal business,
It needs a cordial of that mighty strength;
Swear, swear, so as if thou break'st,   80
Thou mayst be—anything—but damned, Leticia.
LETICIA (kneels) Thus then, and hear me heaven!
BELMOUR (kneels) And thus I'll listen to thee.
          Enter Sir Feeble, Lady Fulbank, [and] Sir Cautious
SIR FEEBLE Letty, Letty, Letty; where are you, little rogue? Letty!
          Belmour snatches [Leticia] to his bosom, as if she [has] fainted
—Ha! Hum, what's here?   85
BELMOUR Oh heavens, she's gone, she's gone!
SIR FEEBLE Gone; whither is she gone? It seems she had the wit to
take good company with her.
          The women go to [Leticia and] take her up
BELMOUR She's gone to heaven, sir, for aught I know.
SIR CAUTIOUS She was resolved to go in a young fellow's arms, I   90
see.

SIR FEEBLE Go to, Francis, go to.

LADY FULBANK Stand back, sir, she recovers.

BELMOUR Alas, I found her dead upon the floor: should I have left
her so? If I had known your mind—°   95

SIR FEEBLE Was it so, was it so? God so, by no means, Francis.

LETICIA Pardon him, sir; for surely I had died,
But for his timely coming.

SIR FEEBLE Alas, poor pupsey, was it sick? Look here, here's a fine
thing to make it well again. [*Shows a jewel*] Come, buss, and it shall   100
have it. [*Kisses Leticia and gives her the jewel*] Oh, how I long for
night.—Ralph, are the fiddlers ready?

RALPH They are tuning in the hall, sir.

SIR FEEBLE That's well, they know my mind. I hate that same
'twang, twang, twang, fum, fum, fum, tweedle, tweedle, tweedle',   105
then 'screw' go the pins, till a man's teeth are on edge; then 'snap'
says a small gut, and there we are at a loss again. I long to be in
bed. (*Dancing, and playing on his stick like a flute*) With a hey
tredodle, tredodle, tredodle—with a hey tredool, tredodle, tredo—

SIR CAUTIOUS A prudent man would reserve himself. Goodfacks,° I   110
danced so on my wedding day, that when I came to bed, to my
shame be it spoken, I fell fast asleep, and slept till morning.

LADY FULBANK Where was your wisdom then, Sir Cautious? But I
know what a wise woman ought to have done.

SIR FEEBLE Od's bobs, that's wormwood, that's wormwood. I shall   115
have my young hussy set agog too; she'll hear there are better
things in the world than she has at home, and then, od's bobs, and
then they'll ha't, adod they will, Sir Cautious. Ever while you live,
keep a wife ignorant, unless a man be as brisk as his neighbours.

SIR CAUTIOUS A wise man will keep 'em from bawdy christenings   120
then, and gossipings.

SIR FEEBLE Christenings and gossipings! Why, they are the very
schools that debauch our wives, as dancing-schools do our daughters.

SIR CAUTIOUS Aye, when the over-joyed good man invites 'em all   125
against that time twelve month: 'Oh, he's a dear man,' cries one;
'Aye, marry,' cries another, 'here's a man indeed: my husband,
God help him—'

SIR FEEBLE Then she falls to telling of her grievance till (half
maudlin) she weeps again. 'Just my condition,' cries a third; so the   130
frolic goes round, and we poor cuckolds are anatomized, and
turned the right sides outwards; ad's bobs we are, Sir Cautious.

SIR CAUTIOUS Aye, aye, this grievance ought to be redressed, Sir
Feeble; the grave and sober part o'th' nation are hereby ridiculed,
aye, and cuckolded too, for aught I know.   135

LADY FULBANK Wise men, knowing this, should not expose their
infirmities, by marrying us young wenches, who, without instruction, find how we are imposed upon.

    Enter fiddlers, playing; Mr Bearjest and Diana, dancing;
    Bredwell and Noisy

LADY FULBANK So, cousin, I see you have found the way to Mrs
Di's heart.   140

BEARJEST Who, I, my dear lady aunt? I never knew but one way to
a woman's heart, and that road I have not yet travelled; for my
uncle, who is a wise man, says matrimony is a sort of a—kind of
a—as it were, d'ye see, of a voyage, which every man of fortune is
bound to make one time or other; and, madam, I am, as it were, a   145
bold adventurer.

DIANA And are you sure, sir, you will venture on me?

BEARJEST Sure? I thank you for that—as if I could not believe my
uncle; for in this case a young heir has no more to do but to come
and see, settle, marry, and use you scurvily.   150

DIANA How, sir, scurvily?

BEARJEST Very scurvily: that is to say, be always fashionably drunk,
despise the tyranny of your bed, and reign absolutely; keep a
seraglio of women, and let my bastard issue inherit; be seen once
a quarter or so with you in the park for countenance,° where we   155
loll two several ways in the gilt coach, like Janus, or a spread-
eagle.°

DIANA And do you expect I should be honest the while?

BEARJEST Heaven forbid, not I; I have not met with that wonder in
all my travels.   160

LADY FULBANK How sir, not an honest woman?

BEARJEST Except my lady aunt. Nay, as I am a gentleman and the
first of my family, you shall pardon me; here, cuff me, cuff me
soundly.

    [Bredwell] kneels to [Lady Fulbank]. Enter Gayman, richly
    dressed

GAYMAN This love's a damned bewitching thing: now, though I   165
should lose my assignation with my devil, I cannot hold from
seeing Julia tonight. Ha! There, and with a fop at her feet. Oh,
vanity of woman!

    [Gayman] softly pulls [Lady Fulbank]

LADY FULBANK Oh, sir, you're welcome from Northampton-
shire.   170

GAYMAN (*aside*) Hum, surely she knows the cheat.

LADY FULBANK You are so gay, you save me, sir, the labour
Of asking if your uncle be alive.

GAYMAN (*aside*) Pray heaven she have not found my circum-
stances!
But if she have, confidence must assist me.   175
[*To Lady Fulbank*] And, madam, you're too gay for me to enquire
Whether you are that Julia which I left you?

LADY FULBANK Oh, doubtless, sir.

GAYMAN But why the devil do I ask? Yes, you are still the same: one
of those hoiting ladies, that love nothing like fool and fiddle;   180
crowds of fops; had rather be publicly, though dully, flattered, than
privately adored; you love to pass for the wit of the company, by
talking all and loud.

LADY FULBANK Rail on, till you have made me think my virtue at
so low ebb, it should submit to you.   185

GAYMAN What, I'm not discreet enough,
I'll babble all in my next high debauch,
Boast of your favours, and describe your charms
To every wishing fool?

LADY FULBANK Or make most filthy verses of me,   190
Under the name of Cloris; you, Philander,
Who, in lewd rhymes, confess the dear appointment;
What hour, and where, how silent was the night,
How full of love your eyes, and wishing, mine.
Faith, no. If you can afford me a lease of your love, till the old   195
gentleman my husband depart this wicked world, I'm for the
bargain.°

SIR CAUTIOUS Hum; what's here, a young spark at my wife?
[*Sir Cautious*] goes [*near to Gayman and Lady Fulbank*]

GAYMAN Unreasonable Julia, is that all
My love, my sufferings, and my vows must hope?   200
Set me an age: say when you will be kind,
And I will languish out in starving wish.
But thus to gape for legacies of love,
Till youth be past enjoyment,
The devil, I will as soon—farewell. (*Offers to go*)   205

LADY FULBANK Stay, I conjure you, stay.

GAYMAN (*aside*) And lose my assignation with my devil.

SIR CAUTIOUS 'Tis so, aye, aye, 'tis so, and wise men will perceive
it. 'Tis here, here in my forehead; it more than buds; it sprouts, it
flourishes.   210

SIR FEEBLE [*aside*] So, that young gentleman has nettled him, stung
him to the quick. I hope he'll chain her up; the gad bee's in his
conundrum.° In charity I'll relieve him.—Come, my Lady
Fulbank, the night grows old upon our hands: to dancing, to
jiggeting. Come, shall I lead your ladyship?   215

LADY FULBANK No, sir, you see I am better provided. (*Takes
Gayman's hand*)

SIR CAUTIOUS Aye, no doubt on't; a pox on him for a young
handsome dog.
    They dance all

SIR FEEBLE Very well, very well; now the posset, and then, od's   220
bobs, and then—

DIANA —And then we'll have t'other dance.°

SIR FEEBLE Away girls, away, and steal the bride to bed; they
have a deal to do upon their wedding nights, and what with the
tedious ceremonies of dressing and undressing, the smutty   225
lectures of the women by way of instruction, and the little
stratagems of the young wenches, od's bobs, a man's cozened of
half his night. Come, gentlemen, one bottle, and then we'll toss
the stocking.°
    *Exeunt all but Lady Fulbank [and] Bredwell, who are
    talking, and Gayman*

LADY FULBANK But dost thou think he'll come?   230

BREDWELL I do believe so, madam.

LADY FULBANK Be sure you contrive it so he may not know whither
or to whom he comes.

BREDWELL I warrant you, madam, for our parts.
    Exit Bredwell. Gayman [is] stealing out

LADY FULBANK How now! What, departing?   235

GAYMAN You are going to the bride-chamber.

LADY FULBANK No matter, you shall stay.

GAYMAN I hate to have you in a crowd.

LADY FULBANK Can you deny me? Will you not give me one lone
hour i'th' garden?   240

GAYMAN Where we shall only tantalize each other with dull kissing,
and part with the same appetite we met. No, madam; besides, I
have business.

LADY FULBANK Some assignation; is it so, indeed?

GAYMAN Away, you cannot think me such a traitor; 'tis most   245
  important business.

LADY FULBANK Oh, 'tis too late for business: let tomorrow serve.

GAYMAN By no means: the gentleman is to go out of town.

LADY FULBANK Rise the earlier then.

GAYMAN But, madam, the gentleman lies dangerously sick, and   250
  should he die—

LADY FULBANK 'Tis not a dying uncle, I hope, sir?

GAYMAN Hum—

LADY FULBANK The gentleman a-dying, and to go out of town
  tomorrow!   255

GAYMAN Aye—a—he goes—in a litter; 'tis his fancy, madam; change
  of air may recover him.

LADY FULBANK So may your change of mistress do me, sir.
  Farewell.

    [*Lady Fulbank*] *goes out*

GAYMAN Stay, Julia!   260
  —Devil be damned, for you shall tempt no more,
  I'll love and be undone.—But she is gone;°
  And if I stay the most that I shall gain
  Is but a reconciling look, or kiss.
  —No, my kind goblin: 265
        I'll keep my word with thee, as the least evil;
        A tantalizing woman's worse than devil.
    Exit

3.1

Sir Feeble's house

The second song° before the entry.° A song made by Mr Cheek°

[SONG]

No more, Lucinda, ah! expose no more
To the admiring world those conquering charms:
In vain all day unhappy men adore,
What the kind night gives to my longing arms.
Their vain attempts can ne'er successful prove,   5
Whilst I so well maintain the fort of love.

Yet to the world with so bewitching arts,
Your dazzling beauty you around display,
And triumph in the spoils of broken hearts,
That sink beneath your feet, and crowd your way: 10
Ah! suffer now your cruelty to cease,
And to a fruitless war prefer a peace.°

Enter Ralph, with light; Sir Feeble; and Belmour, sad

SIR FEEBLE So, so, they're gone. Come, Francis, you shall have the honour of undressing me for the encounter; but 'twill be a sweet one, Francis.   15

BELMOUR *(aside, undressing [Sir Feeble] all the while)* Hell take him, how he teases me!

SIR FEEBLE But is the young rogue laid, Francis; is she stolen to bed? What tricks the young baggages have to whet a man's appetite!

BELMOUR Aye, sir. *[Aside]* Pox on him; he will raise my anger   20
up to madness, and I shall kill him to prevent his going to bed to her.

SIR FEEBLE A pise of those bandstrings!° The more haste the less speed.

BELMOUR *[aside]* Be it so in all things, I beseech thee, Venus!   25

SIR FEEBLE Thy aid a little, Francis.

    [Belmour] pinches [Sir Feeble] by the throat

Oh, oh, thou chokest me. 'Sbobs, what dost mean?

BELMOUR You had so hampered 'em, sir. *(Aside)* The devil's very mischievous in me.

SIR FEEBLE Come, come, quick, good Francis; adod, I'm as yare as a   30
hawk at the young wanton. Nimbly, good Francis, untruss, untruss.

BELMOUR [*aside*] Cramps seize ye! What shall I do? The near
approach distracts me!

SIR FEEBLE So, so, my breeches, good Francis. But well, Francis,
how dost think I got the young jade my wife?   35

BELMOUR With five hundred pounds a year jointure, sir.

SIR FEEBLE No, that would not do: the baggage was damnably in
love with a young fellow they call Belmour; a handsome young
rascal he was, they say, that's truth on't, and a pretty estate; but
happening to kill a man, he was forced to fly.   40

BELMOUR That was great pity, sir.

SIR FEEBLE Pity! Hang him, rogue; 'sbobs, and all the young fellows
in the town deserve it. We can never keep our wives and daughters
honest for rampant young dogs; and an old fellow cannot put in
amongst 'em, under being undone, with presenting,° and the devil   45
and all. But what dost think I did, being damnably in love? I
feigned a letter as from the Hague, wherein was a relation of this
same Belmour's being hanged.

BELMOUR Is't possible, sir? Could you devise such news?

SIR FEEBLE Possible, man? I did it, I did it. She swooned at the   50
news, shut herself up a whole month in her chamber, but I
presented high; she sighed and wept, and swore she'd never marry,
still I presented; she hated, loathed, spit upon me, still, adod, I
presented; till I presented myself effectually in church to her, for
she at last wisely considered her vows were cancelled since   55
Belmour was hanged.

BELMOUR Faith, sir, this was very cruel, to take away his fame, and
then his mistress.

SIR FEEBLE Cruel? Thou'rt an ass, we are but even with the brisk
rogues, for they take away our fame, cuckold us, and take away our   60
wives. So, so, my cap, Francis.

BELMOUR And do you think this marriage lawful, sir?

SIR FEEBLE Lawful? It shall be when I've had livery and seisin of her
body;° and that shall be presently, rogue; quick. Besides this,
Belmour dares as well be hanged as come into England.   65

BELMOUR If he gets his pardon, sir—

SIR FEEBLE Pardon? No, no, I have took care for that, for I have,
you must know, got his pardon already.

BELMOUR How, sir, got his pardon? That's some amends for robbing
him of his wife.   70

SIR FEEBLE Hold, honest Francis; what, dost think 'twas in kindness
to him? No, you fool, I got his pardon myself, that nobody else
should have it; so that if he gets anybody to speak to his majesty
for it, his majesty cries he has granted it; but for want of my
appearance, he's defunct, trussed up, hanged, Francis.   75

BELMOUR This is the most excellent revenge I ever heard of.

SIR FEEBLE Aye, I learned it of a great politician of our times.

BELMOUR But have you got his pardon?

SIR FEEBLE I've done 't, I've done 't; pox on him, it cost me five
hundred pounds, though! Here 'tis, my solicitor brought it me this   80
evening.

>   *[Sir Feeble] gives [Belmour a paper]*

BELMOUR *[aside]* This was a lucky hit; and if it 'scape me, let me be
hanged by a trick indeed.

SIR FEEBLE So, put it into my cabinet: safe, Francis, safe.

BELMOUR Safe, I'll warrant you, sir.   85

SIR FEEBLE My gown, quick, quick—t'other sleeve, man—so, now
my night-cap; well, I'll in, throw open my gown to fright away the
women, and jump into her arms.

>   *Exit Sir Feeble*

BELMOUR He's gone; quickly, oh love, inspire me!

>   *Enter a footman*

FOOTMAN Sir, my master, Sir Cautious Fulbank, left his watch on   90
the little parlour-table tonight, and bid me call for't.

BELMOUR Ha, the bridegroom has it, sir, who is just gone to bed; it
shall be sent him in the morning.

FOOTMAN 'Tis very well, sir. Your servant.

>   *Exit Footman*

BELMOUR Let me see: here is the watch, I took it up to keep for him;   95
but his sending has inspired me with a sudden stratagem, that will
do better than force to secure the poor trembling Leticia, who, I
am sure, is dying with her fears.

>   *Exit*

[3.2]

*The bedchamber;° Leticia in an undress,° by the women at
the table*

Enter to them Sir Feeble Fainwould

SIR FEEBLE What's here? What's here? The prating women still.
Od's bobs, what, not in bed yet? For shame of love, Leticia.

LETICIA For shame of modesty, sir; you would not have me go to
bed before all this company.

SIR FEEBLE What, the women! Why, they must see you laid, 'tis the   5
fashion.

LETICIA What, with a man? I would not for the world. [*Aside*] Oh
Belmour, where art thou, with all thy promised aid?

DIANA Nay, madam, we should see you laid indeed.

LETICIA First in my grave, Diana.   10

SIR FEEBLE Od's bobs, here's a compact amongst the women: high
treason against the bridegroom; therefore, ladies, withdraw, or
adod I'll lock you all in.

*[Sir Feeble] throws open his gown;° [all the women except
Leticia] run away; he locks the door*

—So, so, now we're alone, Leticia; off with this foolish modesty,
and night-gown, and slide into my arms.   15

She runs from him

Hey, my little puskin; what, fly me, my coy Daphne?°

He pursues her. Knocking [is heard]

Ha, who's that knocks?—Who's there?

BELMOUR 'Tis I sir, 'tis I; open the door presently.

SIR FEEBLE Why, what's the matter, is the house o' fire?

BELMOUR Worse sir, worse.   20

LETICIA [*aside*] 'Tis Belmour's voice!

*[Sir Feeble] opens the door; Belmour enters with the watch in
his hand*

BELMOUR Oh, sir, do you know this watch?

SIR FEEBLE This watch?

BELMOUR Aye, sir, this watch.

SIR FEEBLE This watch! Why, prithee, why dost tell me of a watch?   25
'Tis Sir Cautious Fulbank's watch, what then? What a pox, dost
trouble me with watches?

[Sir Feeble] offers to put [Belmour] out; [Belmour] returns

BELMOUR 'Tis indeed his watch, sir, and by this token he has sent
for you to come immediately to his house, sir.

SIR FEEBLE What a devil! Art mad, Francis, or is his worship mad,   30
or does he think me mad? Go, prithee, tell him I'll come to him
tomorrow.

    Goes to put him out

BELMOUR Tomorrow, sir! Why, all our throats may be cut before
tomorrow.

SIR FEEBLE What say'st thou, throats cut?   35

BELMOUR Why, the city's up in arms,° sir, and all the aldermen are
met at Guildhall;° some damnable plot,° sir.

SIR FEEBLE Ha, plot—the aldermen met at Guildhall? Hum: why,
let 'em meet, I'll not lose this night to save the nation.

LETICIA Would you to bed, sir, when the weighty affairs of state   40
require your presence?

SIR FEEBLE Hum, met at Guildhall?—My clothes, my gown again,
Francis, I'll out.

    [*Sir Feeble puts*] *on his gown;* [*then*] *pausing, pulls it off again*
Out, what, upon my wedding night? No, I'll in.

LETICIA For shame, sir; shall the reverend council of the city debate 45
without you?

SIR FEEBLE Aye, that's true, that's true; come, truss again, Francis,
truss again. Yet now I think on't, Francis, prithee run thee to the
hall, and tell 'em 'tis my wedding night, d'ye see, Francis; and let
somebody give my voice° for—   50

BELMOUR What, sir?

SIR FEEBLE Adod, I cannot tell; up in arms, say you? Why, let 'em
fight dog, fight bear; mun, I'll to bed. Go.

LETICIA And shall his majesty's service and his safety° lie unregarded
for a slight woman, sir?   55

SIR FEEBLE Hum, his majesty!—Come, haste, Francis, I'll away and
call Ralph, and the footmen, and bid 'em arm; each man shoulder
his musket, and advance his pike; and bring my artillery implements quick; and let's away.—[*To Leticia*] Pupsey, 'bye, Pupsey,
I'll bring it a fine thing yet before morning, it may be.—[*To*   60
Belmour] Let's away; I shall grow fond, and forget the business of
the nation. Come, follow me, Francis.

    Exit Sir Feeble. Belmour runs to Leticia

BELMOUR Now, my Leticia, if thou e'er didst love,
If ever thou design'st to make me blessed,
Without delay fly this adulterous bed!   65

SIR FEEBLE (*within*) Why, Francis, where are you, knave?

BELMOUR I must be gone, lest he suspect us. I'll lose him, and return
to thee immediately. Get thyself ready.

LETICIA I will not fail, my love.

> *Exit Belmour*
>> Old man, forgive me: thou the aggressor art,   70
>> Who rudely forced the hand without the heart.
>> She cannot from the paths of honour rove,
>> Whose guide's religion, and whose end is love.
> *Exit*

[3.3]

A wash-house, or out-house

*Enter, with [a] dark-lantern,° Bredwell, disguised like a
devil, leading Gayman*

BREDWELL Stay here, till I give notice of your coming.

> *Exit Bredwell. [He] leaves his dark-lantern*

GAYMAN Kind light, a little of your aid. Now must I be peeping,
though my curiosity should lose me all. Ha! Zouns, what's here, a
hovel or a hog-sty? Hum, see the wickedness of man, that I should
find no time to swear in, but just when I'm in the devil's clutches.   5

> *Enter Pert, [disguised] as an old woman, with a staff*

[PERT] Good even to you, fair sir.

GAYMAN [*aside*] Ha, defend me! If this be she, I must rival the devil,
that's certain.

[PERT] Come, young gentleman, dare not you venture?

GAYMAN [*aside*] He must be as hot as Vesuvius, that does. I shall   10
never earn my morning's present.

[PERT] What, do you fear a longing woman, sir?

GAYMAN The devil I do. [*Aside*] This is a damned preparation to love.

[PERT] Why stand you gazing, sir? A woman's passion is like the tide,
it stays for no man when the hour is come.   15

GAYMAN [*aside*] I'm sorry I have took it at the turning. I'm sure
mine's ebbing out as fast.

[PERT] Will you not speak, sir? Will you not on?

GAYMAN I would fain ask a civil question or two first.

[PERT] You know too much curiosity lost paradise.   20

GAYMAN Why, there's it now.

[PERT] Fortune and love invite you, if you dare follow me.
GAYMAN [*aside*] This is the first thing in petticoats that ever dared
  me in vain. Were I but sure she were but human, now, for sundry
  considerations she might down; but I will on.   25
      [*Pert*] *goes,* [*Gayman*] *follows; exeunt*

[3.4]

    A chamber in the apartments of Lady Fulbank

    Enter [*Pert, still as an*] *old woman,*° *followed by Gayman in*
    the dark. Soft music plays. She leaves him
[GAYMAN] Ha, music—and excellent!

        [SONG]°

    Oh, love, that stronger art than wine,
    Pleasing delusion, witchery divine,
    Want to be prized above all wealth,
    Disease that has more joys than health,   5
    Though we blaspheme thee in our pain,
    And of thy tyranny complain,
    We all are bettered by thy reign.

    What reason never can bestow,
    We to this useful passion owe.   10
    Love wakes the dull from sluggish ease,
    And learns a clown the art to please;
    Humbles the vain, kindles the cold,
    Makes misers free, and cowards bold.
    'Tis he reforms the sot from drink,   15
    And teaches airy fops to think.

    When full brute appetite is fed,
    And choked the glutton lies, and dead,
    Thou new spirits dost dispense,°
    And 'finest the gross delights of sense:°   20
    Virtue's unconquerable aid,
    That against nature can persuade,
    And makes a roving mind retire
    Within the bounds of just desire:
    Cheerer of age, youth's kind unrest,   25
    And half the heaven of the blessed.

[GAYMAN] Ah Julia, Julia! if this soft preparation
    Were but to bring me to thy dear embraces,
    What different motions would surround my soul
    From what perplex it now.   30
        [Enter Pert, still disguised.] Enter nymphs and shepherds, and
        dance. Then two dance alone. All go out but Pert and a
        shepherd
If these be devils, they are obliging ones. I did not care if I
ventured on that last female fiend.°

MAN (*sings*)   *Cease your wonder, cease your guess,*
               Whence arrives your happiness;
               Cease your wonder, cease your pain,   35
               Human fancy is in vain.

      [Enter nymphs and shepherds]

CHORUS   *'Tis enough you once shall find,*
               Fortune may to worth be kind;

      [Man] gives [Gayman] gold

               And love can leave off being blind.
PERT (*sings*)   *You, before you enter here,*   40
               On this sacred ring must swear:

      [Pert] puts [the ring] on [Gayman's] finger, holds his hand

               By the figure, which is round,
               Your passion constant and profound;
               By the adamantine stone,
               To be fixed to one alone;   45
               By the lustre, which is true,
               Ne'er to break your sacred vow;
               Lastly, by the gold, that's tried,
               For love all dangers to abide.

      They all dance about [Gayman], while [Pert and the man] sing

MAN   *Once about him let us move,*   50
               To confirm him true to love. (*bis*)
PERT   *Twice with mystic turning feet,*
               Make him silent and discreet. (*bis*)
MAN   *Thrice about him let us tread,*
               To keep him ever young in bed. (*bis*)   55

Gives [Gayman] another part [of gold]

MAN   *Forget Aminta's proud disdain:*
             Taste here, and sigh no more in vain,
             The joy of love without the pain.

PERT   *That god repents his former slights,*
             And fortune thus your faith requites.   60

BOTH   *Forget Aminta's proud disdain:*
             Then taste, and sigh no more in vain,
             The joy of love without the pain,
             The joy of love without the pain.

Exeunt all dancers. [Gayman] looks on himself and feels
about him

GAYMAN What the devil can all this mean? If there be a woman in   65
the case—sure, I have not lived so bad a life, to gain the dull
reputation of so modest a coxcomb, but that a female might down
with me without all this ceremony. Is it care of her honour? That
cannot be; this age affords° none so nice. Nor fiend, nor goddess
can she be, for these I saw were mortal! No, 'tis a woman, I am   70
positive. Not young nor handsome, for then vanity had made her
glory to 'ave been seen. No, since 'tis resolved a woman, she must
be old and ugly, and will not balk my fancy with her sight, but
baits me more with this essential beauty.°

             Well, be she young or old, woman or devil,   75
             She pays, and I'll endeavour to be civil.
[*Exit*]

[3.5]

In the same house. The flat scene of the hall°

After a knocking, enter Bredwell in his masking habit, with
his vizard in one hand and a light in t'other, in haste

BREDWELL Ha, knocking so late at our gate?
             [*Bredwell*] *opens the door. Enter Sir Feeble, dressed and*
             armed cap-a-pie, with a broad waist-belt stuck around with
             pistols, a helmet, scarf, buffcoat, and half pike

SIR FEEBLE How now, how now, what's the matter here?

BREDWELL [*aside*] Matter? What, is my lady's innocent intrigue°
found out? [*To Sir Feeble*] Heavens, sir, what makes you here in
this warlike equipage?   5

SIR FEEBLE What makes you in this showing equipage, sir?

BREDWELL I have been dancing among some of my friends.

SIR FEEBLE And I thought to have been fighting with some of my friends. Where's Sir Cautious? Where's Sir Cautious?

BREDWELL Sir Cautious? Sir, in bed.   10

SIR FEEBLE Call him, call him; quickly, good Edward.

BREDWELL *[aside]* Sure, my lady's frolic is betrayed, and he comes to make mischief. However, I'll go and secure Mr Gayman.

> *Exit Bredwell. Enter Sir Cautious and [Dick, his] boy, with light*

DICK Pray, sir, go to bed, here's no thieves; all's still and well.

SIR CAUTIOUS This last night's misfortune of mine, Dick, has kept   15
me waking, and methought all night I heard a kind of a silent noise. I am still afraid of thieves. Mercy upon me, to lose five hundred guineas° at one clap, Dick! Ha, bless me! What's yonder? Blow the great horn, Dick.—Thieves, murder, murder!

SIR FEEBLE Why, what a pox, are you mad? 'Tis I, 'tis I, man.   20

SIR CAUTIOUS I, who am I? Speak, declare, pronounce.

SIR FEEBLE Your friend, old Feeble Fainwould.

SIR CAUTIOUS How, Sir Feeble? At this late hour, and on his wedding night!—Why, what's the matter, sir? Is it peace or war with you?   25

SIR FEEBLE A mistake, a mistake. Proceed to the business, good brother, for time you know is precious.

SIR CAUTIOUS *(aside)* Some strange catastrophe has happened between him and his wife tonight, that makes him disturb me thus. *[To Sir Feeble]* Come, sit, good brother, and to the business, as you   30
say.

> *[Sir Cautious and Sir Feeble] sit one at one end of the table, the other at the other. Dick sets down the light and goes out. Both sit gaping and staring, and expecting when either should speak*

SIR FEEBLE As soon as you please, sir. *[Aside]* Lord, how wildly he stares! He's much disturbed in's mind. *[To Sir Cautious]* Well, sir, let us be brief.

SIR CAUTIOUS As brief as you please, sir. Well, brother—*(pausing   35
still)*

SIR FEEBLE So, sir.

SIR CAUTIOUS *[aside]* How strangely he stares and gapes: some deep concern!

SIR FEEBLE Hum—hum—

SIR CAUTIOUS I listen to you, advance.   40

SIR FEEBLE Sir?

SIR CAUTIOUS (*aside*) A very distracted countenance! Pray heaven he
  be not mad, and a young wife is able to make any old fellow mad,
  that's the truth on't.

SIR FEEBLE [*aside*] Sure, 'tis something of his lady, he's so loth to   45
  bring it out. [*To Sir Cautious*] I am sorry you are thus disturbed,
  sir.

SIR CAUTIOUS No disturbance to serve a friend.

SIR FEEBLE I think I am your friend indeed, Sir Cautious, or I would
  not have been here upon my wedding night.   50

SIR CAUTIOUS (*aside*) His wedding night: there lies his grief, poor
  heart! Perhaps she has cuckolded him already. [*To Sir Feeble*] Well,
  come, brother, many such things are done.

SIR FEEBLE Done, hum? Come, out with it, brother: what troubles
  you tonight?   55

SIR CAUTIOUS (*aside*) Troubles me, why, knows he I am robbed?

SIR FEEBLE I may perhaps restore you to the rest you've lost.

SIR CAUTIOUS The rest, why, have I lost more since? Why, know
  you then who did it? Oh, how I'll be revenged upon the rascal!

SIR FEEBLE (*aside*) 'Tis jealousy, the old worm that bites. [*To Sir*   60
  Cautious] Who is it you suspect?

SIR CAUTIOUS Alas, I know not whom to suspect, I would I did; but
  if you could discover him, I would so swinge him!

SIR FEEBLE I know him? What, do you take me for a pimp, sir? I
  know him? There's your watch again, sir; I'm your friend, but no   65
  pimp, sir.

    [*Sir Feeble*] *rises in rage*

SIR CAUTIOUS My watch! I thank you, sir; but why pimp, sir?

SIR FEEBLE Oh, a very thriving calling, sir; and I have a young wife
  to practise with. I, know your rogues?

SIR CAUTIOUS (*aside*) A young wife! 'Tis so, his gentlewoman has   70
  been at hot-cockles° without her husband, and he's horn mad
  upon't. I suspected her being so close in with his nephew: in a fit,
  with a pox!—Come, come, Sir Feeble, 'tis many an honest man's
  fortune.

SIR FEEBLE I grant it, sir; but to the business, sir, I came for.   75

SIR CAUTIOUS With all my soul.

    They sit gaping and expecting when either should speak. Enter
    Bredwell and Gayman at the door. Bredwell sees them, and
    puts Gayman back again

BREDWELL [*aside*] Ha, Sir Feeble; and Sir Cautious there! What shall
I do? For this way we must pass, and to carry him back would
discover my lady to him, betray all and spoil the jest. [*To Gayman*]
Retire, sir; your life depends upon your being unseen.   80
      [*Bredwell and Gayman*] *go out*
SIR FEEBLE Well, sir, do you not know that I am married, sir? And
this my wedding night?
SIR CAUTIOUS Very good, sir.
SIR FEEBLE And that I long to be in bed!
SIR CAUTIOUS Very well, sir.   85
SIR FEEBLE Very good sir, and very well sir! Why, then, what the
devil do I make here, sir!
      [*Sir Feeble*] *rises in a rage*
SIR CAUTIOUS Patience, brother, and forward.
SIR FEEBLE Forward! Lend me your hand, good brother, let's feel
your pulse. How has this night gone with you?   90
SIR CAUTIOUS Ha, ha, ha, this is the oddest conundrum. [*Aside*] Sure
he's mad; and yet, now I think on't, I have not slept tonight, nor shall
I ever sleep again till I have found the villain that robbed me. (*Weeps*)
SIR FEEBLE (*aside*) So, now he weeps: far gone; this laughing and
weeping is a very bad sign!—Come, let me lead you to your bed.   95
SIR CAUTIOUS [*aside*] Mad, stark mad.—No, now I'm up 'tis no
matter. Pray, ease your troubled mind; I am your friend. Out with
it: what, was it acted? Or but designed?
SIR FEEBLE How, sir?
SIR CAUTIOUS Be not ashamed: I'm under the same premunire° I   100
doubt, little better than a—but let that pass.
SIR FEEBLE Have you any proof?
SIR CAUTIOUS Proof of what, good sir?
SIR FEEBLE Of what? Why, that you're a cuckold, sir, a cuckold, if
you'll ha't.   105
SIR CAUTIOUS Cuckold, sir: do ye know what ye say?
SIR FEEBLE What I say?
SIR CAUTIOUS Aye, what you say, can you make this out?
SIR FEEBLE I make it out?
SIR CAUTIOUS Aye, sir: if you say it, and cannot make it out,   110
you're a—
SIR FEEBLE What am I, sir? What am I?
SIR CAUTIOUS A cuckold as well as myself, sir, and I'll sue you for
scandalum magnatum: I shall recover swingeing damages with a city
jury.°   115

SIR FEEBLE I know of no such thing, sir.

SIR CAUTIOUS No, sir?

SIR FEEBLE No, sir.

SIR CAUTIOUS Then what would you be at, sir?

SIR FEEBLE I be at, sir! What would you be at, sir?   120

SIR CAUTIOUS Ha, ha, ha! Why, this is the strangest thing: to see an
    old fellow, a magistrate of the city, the first night he's married
    forsake his bride and bed, and come armed cap-a-pie, like
    Gargantua,° to disturb another old fellow and banter him with a
    tale of a tub;° and all to be-cuckold him here! In plain English,   125
    what's your business?

SIR FEEBLE Why, what the devil's your business, an you go to that?

SIR CAUTIOUS My business with whom?

SIR FEEBLE With me sir, with me: what a pox do ye think I do here?

SIR CAUTIOUS 'Tis that I would be glad to know, sir.   130

    Enter Dick

SIR FEEBLE Here, Dick, remember I've brought back your master's
    watch; next time he sends for me o'er night, I'll come to him in
    the morning.

SIR CAUTIOUS Ha, ha, ha: I send for you? Go home and sleep, sir;
    'ad, an° ye keep your wife waking to so little purpose you'll go near 135
    to be haunted with a vision of horns.

SIR FEEBLE Roguery, knavery to keep me from my wife! Look ye,
    this was the message I received.

    [Sir Feeble] tells [Sir Cautious] seemingly.° Enter Bredwell to
    the door, in a white sheet like a ghost, speaking to Gayman,
    who stands within°

BREDWELL Now, sir, we are two to two, for this way you must pass
    or be taken in the lady's lodgings. I'll first adventure out to make 140
    you pass the safer. (*Aside*) And that he may not, if possible, see Sir
    Cautious, whom I shall fright into a trance, I am sure. And Sir
    Feeble—the devil's in't if he know him.

GAYMAN A brave kind fellow this.

    Enter Bredwell, stalking on as a ghost by [Sir Feeble and Sir
    Cautious]

SIR CAUTIOUS Oh, undone, undone! Help, help, I'm dead, I'm dead!   145

    [Sir Cautious] falls down on his face. Sir Feeble stares and
    stands still

BREDWELL (*aside*) As I could wish. (*Turns [to Gayman]*) Come on,
    thou ghastly thing, and follow me.

    Enter Gayman, like a ghost, with a torch

SIR CAUTIOUS Oh Lord, oh Lord!

GAYMAN Ha, old Sir Feeble Fainwould! Why, where the devil am I? 'Tis he, and be it where it will, I'll fright the old dotard for cozening my friend of his mistress. 150

    [Gayman] stalks on

SIR FEEBLE (*trembling*) Oh, guard me, guard me, all ye powers!

GAYMAN Thou call'st in vain, fond wretch: for I am Belmour,
Whom first thou rob'st of fame and life,
And then what dearer was, his wife. 155

    [Gayman] goes out shaking his torch at [Sir Feeble]

SIR CAUTIOUS Oh Lord, oh Lord!

    Enter Lady Fulbank in an undress, and Pert undressed°

LADY FULBANK Heavens, what noise is this? [*Aside*] So, he's got safe out, I see. (*Sees Sir Feeble armed*) Ha, what thing art thou?

SIR FEEBLE Stay, madam, stay. 'Tis I, 'tis I, a poor trembling mortal.

LADY FULBANK Sir Feeble Fainwould? Rise, are you both mad? 160

SIR CAUTIOUS No, no; madam, we have seen the devil.

SIR FEEBLE Aye, and he was as tall as the monument.°

SIR CAUTIOUS With eyes like a beacon, and a mouth, heaven bless us, like London Bridge at a full tide.°

SIR FEEBLE Aye, and roared as loud. 165

LADY FULBANK Idle fancies! What makes you from your bed? And you, sir, from your bride?

    Enter Dick with sack

SIR FEEBLE Oh! that's the business of another day: a mistake only, madam.

LADY FULBANK Away, I'm ashamed to see wise men so weak: the phantoms of the night, or your own shadows, the whimsies of the brain for want of rest—or perhaps Bredwell, your man, who being wiser than his master, played you this trick to fright you both to bed. 170

SIR FEEBLE Hum, adod and that may be, for the young knave, when he let me in tonight, was dressed up for some waggery. 175

SIR CAUTIOUS Ha, ha, ha, 'twas even so, sure enough, brother.

SIR FEEBLE Ad's bobs, but they frighted me at first basely; but I'll home to Pupsey, there may be roguery, as well as here.—Madam, I ask your pardon, I see we're all mistaken.

LADY FULBANK Aye, Sir Feeble; go home to your wife. 180

    Exeunt severally

[3.6]

The street

Enter Belmour at the door, knocks; and enter to him from the house, Phillis

PHILLIS Oh, are you come, sir? I'll call my lady down.

BELMOUR Oh haste, the minutes fly: leave all behind,
And bring Leticia only to my arms.
    [Exit Phillis.] A noise of people
Ha, what noise is that? 'Tis coming this way; I tremble with my
fears. Ha, death and the devil, 'tis he.
    Enter Sir Feeble and his men, armed. [Sir Feeble] goes to the   5
    door [and] knocks
Aye, 'tis he, and I'm undone: what shall I do to kill him now?
Besides, the sin would put me past all hopes of pardoning.

SIR FEEBLE A damned rogue to deceive me thus!
    Enter Leticia and Phillis softly, undressed, with a box

BELMOUR Ha, see, by heaven, Leticia! Oh, we are ruined!

SIR FEEBLE Hum, what's here, two women?
    [Sir Feeble] stands a little off   10

LETICIA Where are you, my best wishes? Lord of my vows, and
charmer of my soul? Where are you?

BELMOUR Oh, heavens! (*Draws his sword half-way*)

SIR FEEBLE (*aside*) Hum, who's here? My gentlewoman: she's monstrous kind of the sudden. But whom is't meant to?

LETICIA Give me your hand, my love, my life, my all. Alas! where   15
are you?

SIR FEEBLE Hum, no, no, this is not to me. I am jilted, cozened,
cuckolded, and so forth.
    Groping, [Leticia] takes hold of Sir Feeble

LETICIA Oh, are you here? Indeed, you frighted me with your
silence. Here, take these jewels, and let us haste away.   20

SIR FEEBLE [*aside*] Hum, are you thereabouts, mistress; was I sent
away with a sham-plot for this? She cannot mean it to me.

LETICIA Will you not speak; will you not answer me? Do you repent
already? Before enjoyment are you cold and false?

SIR FEEBLE [*aside*] Hum, before enjoyment: that must be me. Before   25
enjoyment: aye, aye, 'tis I. (*Merrily*) I see a little prolonging° a
woman's joy, sets an edge upon her appetite.

LETICIA What means my dear? Shall we not haste away?

SIR FEEBLE [*aside*] Haste away? There 'tis again: no, 'tis not me she   30
means. What, at your tricks and intrigues already? Yes, yes, I am
destined a cuckold.

LETICIA Say, am I not your wife; can you deny me?

SIR FEEBLE ([*aside*], *merrily*) Wife! adod, 'tis I she means, 'tis I she
means.   35

LETICIA Oh, Belmour, Belmour!
    Sir Feeble starts back from [Leticia's] hands

SIR FEEBLE Hum, what's that, Belmour?

LETICIA [*aside*] Ha! Sir Feeble! [*To Sir Feeble*] He would not, sir,
have used me thus unkindly.

SIR FEEBLE [*Aside*] Oh, I'm glad 'tis no worse. Belmour, quotha; I   40
thought the ghost was come again.

PHILLIS Why did you not speak, sir, all this while? My lady weeps
with your unkindness.

SIR FEEBLE I did but hold my peace to hear how prettily she prattled
love. But, fags, you are naught to think of a young fellow; ad's bobs   45
you are now.

LETICIA I only said he would not have been so unkind to me.

SIR FEEBLE But what makes ye out at this hour, and with these jewels?

PHILLIS Alas, sir, we thought the city was in arms, and packed up
our things to secure 'em, if there had been a necessity for flight.   50
For had they come to plundering once, they would have begun
with the rich aldermen's wives, you know, sir.

SIR FEEBLE Ad's bobs, and so they would; but there was no arms,
nor mutiny. Where's Francis?

BELMOUR Here, sir.   55

SIR FEEBLE Here, sir! Why, what a story you made of a meeting in
the hall, and arms, and—a—the devil of anything was stirring, but
a couple of old fools, that sat gaping and waiting for one another's
business.

BELMOUR Such a message was brought me, sir.   60

SIR FEEBLE Brought! Thou'rt an ass, Francis; but no more. Come,
come, let's to bed.

LETICIA To bed, sir? What, by daylight? for that's hasting on. I
would not for the world: the night would hide my blushes, but the
day would let me see myself in your embraces.   65

SIR FEEBLE Embraces, in a fiddlestick;° why, are we not married?

LETICIA 'Tis true, sir, and time will make me more familiar with
you, but yet my virgin modesty forbids it. I'll to Diana's chamber;
the night will come again.

SIR FEEBLE For once you shall prevail; and this damned jaunt has   70
pretty well mortified me.—A pox of your mutiny, Francis. Come,
I'll conduct thee to Diana, and lock thee in, that I may have thee
safe, rogue.

      We'll give young wenches leave to whine and blush,
      And fly those blessings which, ad's bobs, they wish.   75
     [*Exeunt*]

4.1

Sir Feeble's house

*Enter Lady Fulbank, Gayman fine, gently pulling her back
by the hand; and Ralph meets 'em*

LADY FULBANK How now, Ralph, let your lady know I am come to
wait on her.

Exit Ralph

GAYMAN Oh, why this needless visit?
Your husband's safe, at least till evening safe.
Why will you not go back?   5
And give me one soft hour, though to torment me.

LADY FULBANK You are at leisure now; I thank you, sir.
Last night, when I with all love's rhetoric pleaded,
And heaven knows what last night might have produced,
You were engaged! False man, I do believe it,   10
And I am satisfied you love me not.

[Lady Fulbank] walks away in scorn

GAYMAN Not love you!
Why do I waste my youth in vain pursuit,
Neglecting interest, and despising power?
Unheeding and despising other beauties?   15
Why at your feet is all my fortune laid,
And why does all my fate depend on you?

LADY FULBANK I'll not consider why you play the fool,
Present me rings and bracelets; why pursue me;
Why watch whole nights before my senseless door,   20
And take such pains to show yourself a coxcomb.

GAYMAN Oh! why all this?
By all the powers above, by this dear hand,
And by this ring, which on this hand I place,
On which I've sworn fidelity to love;   25
I never had a wish or soft desire
To any other woman,
Since Julia swayed the empire of my soul!

LADY FULBANK (*aside*) Ha, my own ring I gave him last night.
—Your jewel, sir, is rich,   30
Why do you part with things of so much value
So easily, and so frequently?

GAYMAN To strengthen the weak arguments of love.

LADY FULBANK And leave yourself undone?

GAYMAN Impossible, if I am blessed with Julia.   35

LADY FULBANK Love's a thin diet, nor will keep out cold.
   You cannot satisfy your dunning tailor,
   To cry, 'I am in love!'
   Though possible you may your seamstress.

GAYMAN Does aught about me speak such poverty?   40

LADY FULBANK I am sorry that it does not, since to maintain this
   gallantry, 'tis said you use base means, below a gentleman.

GAYMAN Who dares but to imagine it's a rascal, a slave, below a
   beating. What means my Julia?

LADY FULBANK No more dissembling; I know your land is gone. I   45
   know each circumstance of all your wants: therefore, as e'er you
   hope that I should love you ever, tell me where 'twas you got this
   jewel, sir.

GAYMAN (aside) Ha, I hope 'tis no stolen goods. [To Lady Fulbank]
   Why on the sudden all this nice examining?   50

LADY FULBANK You trifle with me, and I'll plead no more.

GAYMAN Stay: why, I bought it, madam.

LADY FULBANK Where had you money, sir? You see I am no
   stranger to your poverty.

GAYMAN This is strange! Perhaps it is a secret.   55

LADY FULBANK So is my love, which shall be kept from you.
        [Lady Fulbank] offers to go

GAYMAN (sighing) Stay, Julia: your will shall be obeyed!
   Though I had rather die than be obedient,
   Because I know you'll hate me when 'tis told.

LADY FULBANK By all my vows, let it be what it will,   60
   It ne'er shall alter me from loving you.

GAYMAN I have, of late, been tempted,
   With presents, jewels, and large sums of gold.

LADY FULBANK Tempted! By whom?

GAYMAN The devil, for aught I know.   65

LADY FULBANK Defend me heaven! the devil?
   I hope you have not made a contract with him?

GAYMAN No, though in the shape of woman it appeared.

LADY FULBANK Where met you with it?

GAYMAN By magic art I was conducted, I know not how,   70
   To an enchanted palace in the clouds,
   Where I was so attended:

Young, dancing, singing fiends innumerable!

LADY FULBANK Imagination all.

GAYMAN But for the amorous devil, the old Proserpine—°   75

LADY FULBANK Aye, she: what said she?

GAYMAN Not a word! Heaven be praised, she was a silent devil; but
she was laid in a pavilion, all formed of gilded clouds, which hung
by geometry,° whither I was conveyed, after much ceremony, and
laid in bed with her;° where with much ado,° and trembling with   80
my fears—I forced my arms about her.

LADY FULBANK (*aside*) And sure that undeceived him.

GAYMAN But such a carcase 'twas—deliver me—so rivelled, lean,
and rough: a canvas bag of wooden ladles were a better bedfellow.

LADY FULBANK [*aside*] Now, though I know that nothing is more   85
distant than I from such a monster, yet this angers me. [*To
Gayman*] Death, could you love me, and submit to this?

GAYMAN 'Twas that first drew me in.
The tempting hope of means to conquer you,
Would put me upon any dangerous enterprise: 90
Were I the lord of all the universe,
I am so lost in love,
For one dear night to clasp you in my arms,
I'd lavish all that world, then die with joy.

LADY FULBANK ([*aside*], *walking in a fret*) 'Slife, after all, to seem   95
deformed, old, ugly—

GAYMAN I knew you would be angry when you heard it.
        [*Gayman*] *pursues* [*Lady Fulbank*] *in a submissive posture.*
        Enter Sir Cautious, Bearjest, Noisy, and Bredwell

SIR CAUTIOUS How, what's here? My lady with the spark that
courted her last night! Hum, with her again so soon! Well, this
impudence and importunity undoes more city wives than all their   100
unmerciful finery.

GAYMAN But, madam—

LADY FULBANK (*angry*) Oh, here's my husband; you'd best tell him
your story. [*Aside*] What makes him here so soon?

SIR CAUTIOUS Me his story! I hope he will not tell me he's a mind   105
to cuckold me!

GAYMAN A devil on him, what shall I say to him?

LADY FULBANK (*aside* [*to Gayman*]) What, so excellent at intrigues,
and so dull at an excuse?

GAYMAN Yes, madam, I shall tell him—   110
        Enter Belmour

LADY FULBANK Is my lady at leisure for a visit, sir?

BELMOUR Always to receive your ladyship.

> [*Lady Fulbank*] *goes out*

SIR CAUTIOUS With me, sir, would you speak?

GAYMAN With you, sir, if your name be Fulbank?

SIR CAUTIOUS Plain Fulbank! Methinks you might have had a 115
sir-reverence under your girdle,° sir; I am honoured with another
title, sir.

> [*Sir Cautious*] *goes talking to the rest*

GAYMAN With many, sir, that very well become you.

> [*Gayman*] *pulls* [*Sir Cautious*] *a little aside*

I've something to deliver to your ear.

SIR CAUTIOUS [*aside*] So, I'll be hanged if he do not tell me I'm a 120
cuckold now. I see it in his eyes. [*To Gayman*] My ear, sir? I'd
have you to know I scorn any man's secrets, sir; for aught I know
you may whisper treason to me, sir. (*Aside*) Pox on him, how
handsome he is. I hate the sight of the young stallion.

GAYMAN I would not be uncivil, sir, before all this company. 125

SIR CAUTIOUS Uncivil! [*Aside*] Aye, aye, 'tis so; he cannot be content
to cuckold me, but he must tell me so too.

GAYMAN But since you'll have it, sir, you are—a rascal: a most
notorious villain, sir, d'ye hear?

SIR CAUTIOUS (*laughing*) Yes, yes, I do hear, and am glad 'tis no 130
worse.

GAYMAN Griping as hell, and as insatiable; worse than a brokering
Jew: not all the twelve tribes harbours such a damned extortioner.

SIR CAUTIOUS (*pulling off his hat*) Pray, under favour, sir, who are
you? 135

GAYMAN One whom thou hast undone—

SIR CAUTIOUS (*aside, smiling*) Hum, I'm glad of that, however.

GAYMAN —Racking me up to starving want and misery; then took
advantages to ruin me.°

SIR CAUTIOUS (*aside, smiling*) So, and he'd revenge it on my wife. 140

GAYMAN Do you not know one Wasteall, sir?

> *Enter Ralph with wine,* [*and*] *sets it on a table*

SIR CAUTIOUS Wasteall? Ha, ha, ha; if you are any friend to that
poor fellow, you may return and tell him, sir—d'ye hear?—that the
mortgage of two hundred pound a year is this day out, and I'll not
bate him an hour,° sir. Ha, ha, ha; what, do you think to hector 145
civil magistrates?

GAYMAN Very well, sir, and is this your conscience?

SIR CAUTIOUS Conscience, what, do you tell me of conscience? Why, what a noise's here: as if the undoing a young heir were such a wonder; ods so, I've undone a hundred without half this ado.   150

GAYMAN I do believe thee, and am come to tell you I'll be none of that number: for this minute I'll go and redeem it, and free myself from the hell of your indentures.

SIR CAUTIOUS (*aside*) How, redeem it, sure the devil must help him then! [*To Gayman*] Stay, sir, stay. Lord, sir, what need you put   155 yourself to that trouble? Your land is in safe hands, sir; come, come, sit down, and let us take a glass of wine together, sir.

BELMOUR [*to Gayman*] Sir, my service to you. (*Drinks to him*)

GAYMAN [*to Belmour*] Your servant, sir. [*Aside*] Would I could come to speak to Belmour, which I dare not do in public, lest I betray   160 him. I long to be resolved where 'twas Sir Feeble was last night, if it were he; by which I might find out my invisible mistress.

NOISY Noble Mr Wasteall.

[*Noisy*] *salutes* [*Gayman*]; *so does Bearjest*

BELMOUR Will you please to sit, sir?

GAYMAN I have a little business, sir, but anon I'll wait on you. Your   165 servant, gentlemen. (*Aside*) I'll to Crap the scrivener's.

[*Gayman*] *goes out*

SIR CAUTIOUS (*to Noisy*) Do you know this Wasteall, sir?

NOISY Know him, sir? Aye, too well.

BEARJEST The world's well amended with him, captain, since I lost my money to him and you at the George in Whitefriars.°   170

NOISY Aye, poor fellow: he's sometimes up and sometimes down, as the dice favour him.

BEARJEST Faith, and that's pity; but how came he so fine o'th' sudden? 'Twas but last week he borrowed eighteen pence of me on his waist-belt, to pay his dinner in an ordinary.   175

BELMOUR Were you so cruel, sir, to take it?

NOISY We are not all one man's children; faith sir, we are here today and gone tomorrow.

SIR CAUTIOUS I say 'twas done like a wise man, sir.—But under favour, gentlemen, this Wasteall is a rascal.   180

NOISY A very rascal, sir, and a most dangerous fellow; he cullies in your prentices and cashiers to play,° which ruins so many o'th' young fry i'th' city.

SIR CAUTIOUS Hum, does he so?—Do hear that, Edward?

NOISY Then he keeps a private press, and prints your Amsterdam   185 and Leiden libels.°

SIR CAUTIOUS Aye, and makes 'em too, I'll warrant him; a dangerous fellow.°

NOISY Sometimes he begs for a lame soldier° with a wooden leg.

BEARJEST Sometimes, as a blind man, sells switches in Newmarket 190
road.°

NOISY At other times he runs the country like a gipsy: tells fortunes, and robs hedges when he's out of linen.°

SIR CAUTIOUS [aside] Tells fortunes, too! Nay, I thought he dealt with the devil.—Well, gentlemen, you are all wide o' this matter, 195
for to tell you the truth, he deals with the devil, gentlemen—(aside) otherwise he could never have redeemed his land.

BELMOUR How, sir, the devil?

SIR CAUTIOUS I say the devil. Heaven bless every wise man from the devil. 200

BEARJEST The devil, sha! There's no such animal in nature. I rather think he pads.°

NOISY Oh, sir, he has not courage for that; but he's an admirable fellow at your lock.

SIR CAUTIOUS Lock! My study lock was picked. I begin to suspect 205
him.

BEARJEST I saw him once open a lock with the bone of a breast of mutton, and break an iron bar asunder with the eye of a needle.

SIR CAUTIOUS Prodigious! Well, I say the devil still.

          Enter Sir Feeble

[SIR FEEBLE] Who's this talks of the devil? A pox of the devil, I say. 210
This last night's devil has so haunted me—

SIR CAUTIOUS Why, have you seen it since, brother?

SIR FEEBLE In imagination, sir.

BELMOUR How, sir, a devil?

SIR FEEBLE Aye, or a ghost. 215

BELMOUR Where, good sir?

BEARJEST Aye, where? I'd travel a hundred mile to see a ghost.

BELMOUR Sure, sir, 'twas fancy?

SIR FEEBLE If 'twere a fancy, 'twas a strong one, and ghosts and fancies are all one, if they can deceive. I tell you, if ever I thought 220
in my life, I thought I saw a ghost; aye, and a damnable impudent ghost too; he said he was a—a fellow here—they call Belmour.

BELMOUR How, sir!

BEARJEST Well, I would give the world to see the devil, provided he were a civil affable devil, such an one as Wasteall's acquaint- 225
ance is.

SIR CAUTIOUS He can show him too soon, it may be. I'm sure, as
civil as he is, he helps him to steal my gold, I doubt; and to be
sure—gentlemen, you say he's a gamester: I desire when he comes
anon, that you would propose to sport a die° or so; and we'll fall   230
to play for a tester, or the like; and if he sets any money, I shall
go near to know my own gold, by some remarkable pieces amongst
it; and if he have it, I'll hang him, and then all his six hundred a
year will be my own, which I have in mortgage.

BEARJEST Let the captain and I alone to top upon him.° Meantime,   235
sir, I have brought my music, to entertain my mistress with a song.

SIR FEEBLE Take your own methods, sir (they are at leisure) while
we go drink their healths within. Adod, I long for night; we are
not half in kelter,° this damned ghost will not out of my head yet.
          Exeunt all but Belmour

BELMOUR Ha, a ghost! What can he mean? A ghost, and Bel-
       mour's.   240
Sure my good angel, or my genius,
In pity of my love, and of Leticia—
But see, Leticia comes; but still attended.
          Enter Leticia, Lady Fulbank, [and] Diana
(*Aside to [Leticia], passing by*) Remember, oh remember to be true!
          [*Belmour*] *goes out*

LADY FULBANK I was sick to know with what Christian patience you 245
bore the martyrdom of this night.

LETICIA As those condemned bear the last hour of life.
A short reprieve I had, and by a kind mistake,
Diana only was my bedfellow. (*Weeps*)

DIANA I wish, for your repose, you ne'er had seen my father.
       (*Weeps*)   250

LETICIA And so do I, I fear he has undone me.

DIANA And me, in breaking of his word with Bredwell.

LADY FULBANK So; as Trincalo says, would you were both hanged
for me, for putting me in mind of my husband.° For I have e'en
no better luck than either of you.   255
[*To Diana*] Let our two fates warn your approaching one:
I love young Bredwell and must plead for him.

DIANA I know his virtue justifies my choice.
But pride and modesty forbids I should unloved pursue him.

LETICIA Wrong not my brother so, who dies for you.   260

DIANA Could he so easily see me given away
Without a sigh at parting?

For all the day a calm was in his eyes,
And unconcerned he looked and talked to me;
In dancing never pressed my willing hand, 265
Nor with a scornful glance reproached my falsehood.

LETICIA Believe me, that dissembling was his masterpiece.

DIANA Why should he fear, did not my father promise him?

LETICIA Aye, that was in his wooing time to me;
But now 'tis all forgotten. 270

Music at the door, after which enter Bearjest and Bredwell

LADY FULBANK How now, cousin! Is this high piece of gallantry
from you?

BEARJEST Aye, madam, I have not travelled for nothing.

LADY FULBANK I find my cousin is resolved to conquer: he assails
with all his artillery of charms; we'll leave him to his success, 275
madam.

BEARJEST Oh, lord, madam, you oblige me.

Exeunt Leticia and Lady Fulbank

—Look, Ned, you had a mind to have a full view of my mistress,
sir, and here she is.

[Bredwell] stands gazing [at Diana]

Go, salute her. [*Aside*] Look how he stands now: what a sneaking 280
thing is a fellow who has never travelled and seen the world!
[*To Diana*] Madam, this is a very honest friend of mine, for all he
looks so simply.°

DIANA [*to Bredwell*] Come, he speaks for you, sir.

BEARJEST He, madam! Though he be but a banker's 'prentice, 285
madam, he's as pretty a fellow of his inches° as any i'th' city. He
has made love in dancing schools, and to ladies of quality in the
middle gallery,° and shall joke ye, and repartee with any foreman
within the walls.° [*To Bredwell*] Prithee to her, and commend me;
I'll give thee a new point cravat.° 290

DIANA He looks as if he could not speak to me.

BEARJEST Not speak to you? Yes, Gad, madam, and do anything to
you too.

DIANA ([*to Bearjest*,] *in scorn*) Are you his advocate, sir?

BEARJEST For want of a better. 295

[Bearjest] stands behind [Bredwell], pushing him on

BREDWELL An advocate for love I am,
And bring you such a message from a heart—

BEARJEST Meaning mine, dear madam.

BREDWELL —That when you hear it, you will pity it.

BEARJEST [*aside*] Or the devil's in her.   300

DIANA Sir, I have many reasons to believe
   It is my fortune you pursue, not person.

BEARJEST (*behind him*) There's something in that, I must confess.
   But say what you will, Ned.

BREDWELL May all the mischiefs of despairing love   305
   Fall on me if it be.

BEARJEST That's well enough.

BREDWELL No: were you born an humble village maid
   That fed a flock upon the neighbouring plain,
   With all that shining virtue in your soul,   310
   By heaven, I would adore you, love you, wed you,
   Though the gay world were lost by such a nuptial.
      Bearjest looks on him
   (*Recollecting*) This—I would do, were I my friend the squire.

BEARJEST [*aside*] Aye, if you were me, you might do what you
   pleased; but I'm of another mind.   315

DIANA Should I consent, my father is a man whom interest sways,
   not honour, and whatsoever promises he's made you, he means to
   break 'em all, and I am destined to another.

BEARJEST How, another? His name, his name, madam. Here's Ned
   and I fear ne'er a single man i'th' nation. What is he? What is he?   320

DIANA A fop, a fool, a beaten ass; a blockhead.

BEARJEST What a damned shame's this, that women should be
   sacrificed to fools, and fops must run away with heiresses; whilst
   we men of wit and parts dress and dance, and cock and travel, for
   nothing but to be tame keepers.   325

DIANA But I, by heaven, will never be that victim:
   But where my soul is vowed, 'tis fixed for ever.

BREDWELL Are you resolved, are you confirmed in this?
   Oh, my Diana, speak it o'er again:
      [*Bredwell*] *runs to* [*Diana*] *and embraces her*
   Bless me, and make me happier than a monarch.   330

BEARJEST Hold, hold, dear Ned: that's my part, I take it.

BREDWELL Your pardon, sir, I had forgot myself. But time is short:
   what's to be done in this?

BEARJEST Done? I'll enter the house with fire and sword, d'ye see,
   not that I care this°—but I'll not be fobbed off: what, do they take   335
   me for a fool, an ass?

BREDWELL Madam, dare you run the risk of your father's displeas-
   ure, and run away with the man you love?

DIANA With all my soul.

BEARJEST That's hearty; and we'll do't, Ned and I here; and I love   340
an amour with an adventure in't, like *Amadis de Gaul.*° Hark'ee,
Ned, get a coach and six ready tonight when 'tis dark, at the back
gate.

BREDWELL And I'll get a parson ready in my lodging, to which I
have a key through the garden, by which we may pass unseen.   345

BEARJEST Good. Mum,° here's company.

> *Enter Gayman with his hat with money in't, Sir Cautious in*
> *a rage, Sir Feeble, Lady Fulbank, Leticia, Captain Noisy,*
> *[and] Belmour*

SIR CAUTIOUS A hundred pound lost already! Oh, coxcomb, old
coxcomb, and a wise coxcomb; to turn prodigal at my years, why
I was bewitched!

SIR FEEBLE Pshaw, 'twas a frolic, sir; I have lost a hundred pound as   350
well as you. My lady has lost, and your lady has lost, and the
rest—what, old cows will kick sometimes, what's a hundred pound?

SIR CAUTIOUS A hundred pound, why, 'tis a sum, sir, a sum. Why,
what the devil did I do with a box and dice?

LADY FULBANK Why, you made a shift to lose, sir. And where's the   355
harm of that? We have lost, and he has won, anon it may be your
fortune.

SIR CAUTIOUS Aye, but he could never do it fairly, that's certain.
Three hundred pound! Why, how came you to win so unmerci-
fully, sir?   360

GAYMAN Oh, the devil will not lose a gamester of me, you see, sir.

SIR CAUTIOUS The devil! Mark that, gentlemen.

BEARJEST The rogue has damned luck, sure, he has got a fly.°

SIR CAUTIOUS And can you have the conscience to carry away all our
money, sir?   365

GAYMAN Most assuredly, unless you have the courage to retrieve it.
I'll set it at a throw, or any way; what say you, gentlemen?

SIR FEEBLE Od's bobs, you young fellows are too hard for us every
way, and I am engaged at an old game with a new gamester here,
who will require all an old man's stock.   370

LADY FULBANK Come, cousin, will you venture a guinea?—Come,
Mr Bredwell.

GAYMAN Well, if nobody dare venture on me, I'll send away my
cash.

> *They all go to play at the table but Sir Cautious, Sir Feeble,*
> *and Gayman*

SIR CAUTIOUS (*aside*) Hum, must it all go? A rare sum: if a man were   375
    but sure the devil would but stand neuter, now! [*To Gayman*] Sir,
    I wish I had anything but ready money to stake. Three hundred
    pound: a fine sum!

GAYMAN You have moveables sir, goods; commodities—

SIR CAUTIOUS That's all one, sir; that's money's worth, sir; but if I   380
    had anything that were worth nothing—°

GAYMAN —You would venture it; I thank you, sir. I would your lady
    were worth nothing.

SIR CAUTIOUS Why so, sir?

GAYMAN Then I would set all this against that nothing.   385

SIR CAUTIOUS What, set it against my wife?

GAYMAN Wife, sir; aye, your wife.

SIR CAUTIOUS Hum, my wife against three hundred pounds? What,
    all my wife, sir?

GAYMAN All your wife? Why, sir, some part of her would serve my   390
    turn.

SIR CAUTIOUS (*aside*) Hum, my wife. Why, if I should lose, he could
    not have the impudence to take her.

GAYMAN Well, I find you are not for the bargain, and so I put up.

SIR CAUTIOUS Hold, sir, why so hasty? My wife? No: put up your   395
    money, sir; what, lose my wife, for three hundred pounds!

GAYMAN Lose her, sir! Why, she shall be never the worse for my
    wearing, sir. [*Aside*] The old covetous rogue is considering on't, I
    think. [*To Sir Cautious*] What say you to a night? I'll set it to a
    night. There's none need know it, sir.   400

SIR CAUTIOUS [*aside*] Hum, a night! Three hundred pounds for a
    night! Why, what a lavish whore-master's this: we take money to
    marry our wives, but very seldom part with 'em, and by the
    bargain get money. [*To Gayman*] For a night, say you? (*Aside*)
    Gad, if I should take the rogue at his word, 'twould be a pure jest.   405

SIR FEEBLE You are not mad, brother?

SIR CAUTIOUS No, but I'm wise, and that's as good; let me consider—

SIR FEEBLE What, whether you shall be a cuckold or not?

SIR CAUTIOUS Or lose three hundred pounds: consider that. A cuckold:
    why, 'tis a word, an empty sound, 'tis breath, 'tis air, 'tis nothing; but   410
    three hundred pounds: lord, what will not three hundred pounds do!
    You may chance to be a cuckold for nothing, sir.

SIR FEEBLE It may be so; but she shall do't discreetly then.

SIR CAUTIOUS Under favour, you're an ass, brother: this is the
    discreetest way of doing it, I take it.   415

SIR FEEBLE But would a wise man expose his wife?

SIR CAUTIOUS Why, Cato was a wiser man than I, and he lent his
wife to a young fellow they called Hortensius,° as story says; and
can a wise man have a better precedent than Cato?

SIR FEEBLE I say Cato was an ass, sir, for obliging any young rogue 420
of 'em all.

SIR CAUTIOUS But I am of Cato's mind;—[to Gayman] well, a single
night, you say.

GAYMAN A single night: to have, to hold, possess, and so forth, at
discretion. 425

SIR CAUTIOUS A night; I shall have her safe and sound° i'th'
morning.

SIR FEEBLE Safe, no doubt on't: but how sound?

GAYMAN And for non-performance, you shall pay me three hundred
pounds; I'll forfeit as much if I tell. 430

SIR CAUTIOUS Tell? Why, make your three hundred pounds six
hundred, and let it be put into the *Gazette*,° if you will, man; but
is't a bargain?

GAYMAN Done. Sir Feeble shall be witness, and there stands my hat.
[*Gayman*] *puts down his hat of money, and each of them take
a box and dice, and kneel on the stage. The rest* [*of the
company leave the table, and*] *come about 'em*

SIR CAUTIOUS He that comes first to one and thirty wins. 435
They throw and count. [*Lady Fulbank approaches Sir
Cautious*]

LADY FULBANK What are you playing for?

SIR FEEBLE Nothing, nothing, but a trial of skill between an old man
and a young; and your ladyship is to be judge.

LADY FULBANK I shall be partial, sir.

SIR CAUTIOUS (*throws, and pulls the hat towards him*) Six and five's 440
eleven.

GAYMAN [*throws*] Cater tray:° pox of the dice.

SIR CAUTIOUS [*throws*] Two fives: one and twenty.
[*Sir Cautious*] *sets up,° pulls the hat nearer*

GAYMAN Now, luck. [*Throws*] Doubles of sixes: nineteen.

SIR CAUTIOUS [*throws*] Five and four: thirty. 445
[*Sir Cautious*] *draws the hat to him*

SIR FEEBLE Now, if he wins it, I'll swear he has a fly indeed: 'tis
impossible without doubles of sixes.

GAYMAN Now, fortune, smile; and for the future frown. (*Throws*)

SIR CAUTIOUS Hum, two sixes.

[Sir Cautious] rises and looks dolefully round

LADY FULBANK How now? What's the matter? You look so like an 450
ass: what have you lost?

SIR CAUTIOUS A bauble, a bauble: 'tis not for what I've lost, but
because I have not won.

SIR FEEBLE You look very simply, sir: what think you of Cato now?

SIR CAUTIOUS A wise man may have his failings. 455

LADY FULBANK What has my husband lost?

SIR CAUTIOUS Only a small parcel of ware that lay dead upon my
hands, sweetheart.

GAYMAN But I shall improve 'em, madam, I'll warrant you.

LADY FULBANK Well, since 'tis no worse, bring in your fine dancer, 460
cousin, you say you brought to entertain your mistress with.

Bearjest goes out

GAYMAN Sir, you'll take care to see me paid tonight?

SIR CAUTIOUS Well, sir; but my lady, you must know sir, has the
common frailties of her sex, and will refuse what she even longs
for, if persuaded to't by me. 465

GAYMAN 'Tis not in my bargain to solicit her, sir, you are to procure
her; or three hundred pounds, sir: choose you whether.°

SIR CAUTIOUS Procure her? With all my soul, sir. Alas, you mistake
my honest meaning: I scorn to be so unjust as not to see you a-bed
together; and then agree as well as you can, I have done my part. 470
In order to this, sir, get you but yourself conveyed in a chest to
my house, with a direction upon't for me, and for the rest—

GAYMAN I understand you.

SIR FEEBLE Ralph, get supper ready.

*Enter Bearjest with dancers. [A dance.] All go out but Sir
Cautious*

SIR CAUTIOUS Well, I must break my mind, if possible, to my lady; 475
but if she should be refractory now, and make me pay three
hundred pounds? Why, sure she won't have so little grace. Three
hundred pounds saved, is three hundred pounds got, by our
account: could all

> Who of this city-privilege are free, 480
> Hope to be paid for cuckoldom like me,
> Th'unthriving merchant, whom grey hair adorns,
> Before all ventures would insure his horns;
> For thus, while he but lets spare rooms to hire,
> His wife's cracked credit keeps his own entire.° 485

Exit

5.1

Sir Cautious his house

Enter Belmour alone, sad

BELMOUR The night is come: oh, my Leticia!
  The longing bridegroom hastens to his bed,
  Whilst she, with all the languishment of love
  And sad despair, casts her fair eyes on me,
  Which silently implore I would deliver her.   5
  But how? Aye, there's the question.—Ha—(*pausing*)
  I'll get myself hid in her bed-chamber,
  And something I will do may save us yet;
  If all my arts should fail, I'll have recourse
      ([*Belmour*] *draws a dagger*)
  To this: and bear Leticia off by force.   10
  But see, she comes.
      Enter Lady Fulbank, Sir Cautious, Sir Feeble, Leticia,
      Bearjest, Noisy, [and] Gayman. Exit Belmour

SIR FEEBLE Lights there, Ralph, and my lady's coach there.
      Bearjest goes to Gayman

BEARJEST Well, sir, remember you have promised to grant me my
  diabolical request, in showing me the devil.

GAYMAN I will not fail you, sir.   15
      [*Enter Ralph with a light*]

LADY FULBANK Madam, your servant.—I hope you'll see no more
  ghosts, Sir Feeble.

SIR FEEBLE No more of that, I beseech you, madam:—prithee, Sir
  Cautious, take away your wife.—Madam, your servant.
      [*Lady Fulbank, Sir Cautious, Bearjest, Noisy, and Gayman*]
      go out after [Ralph, who carries] the light
  —Come, Letty, Letty; hasten, rogue, hasten to thy chamber; away,   20
  here be the young wenches coming.
      [*Sir Feeble*] *puts* [*Leticia*] *out; he goes out. Enter Diana,*
      [*and*] *puts on her hood and scarf*

DIANA So, they are gone to bed; and now for Bredwell. The coach
  waits, and I'll take this opportunity.
      Father, farewell; if you dislike my course,
      Blame the old rigid customs of your force.   25
    Goes out

[5.2]

A bed-chamber

Enter Sir Feeble, Leticia, and Phillis

LETICIA Ah, Phillis! I am fainting with my fears,
Hast thou no comfort for me?

[Sir Feeble] undresses to his gown

SIR FEEBLE Why, what art doing there fiddle-faddling? Adod, you
young wenches are so loth to come to; but when your hand's in,
you have no mercy upon us poor husbands.   5

LETICIA Why do you talk so, sir?

SIR FEEBLE Was it an-angered at the fool's prattle? Tum-a-me,
tum-a-me, I'll undress it, effags, I will, roguy.

LETICIA You are so wanton, sir, you make me blush. I will not go to
bed, unless you'll promise me—   10

SIR FEEBLE No bargaining, my little hussy. What, you'll tie my
hands behind me, will you?

[Leticia] goes to the table

LETICIA *[aside to Phillis]* What shall I do? Assist me, gentle maid,
Thy eyes methinks puts on a little hope!

PHILLIS *[aside to Leticia]* Take courage, madam; you guess right: be   15
confident.

SIR FEEBLE No whispering, gentlewoman, and putting tricks into her
head; that shall not cheat me of another night.

*As [Leticia] is at the toilet he looks over her shoulder, and
sees her face in the glass*

Look on that silly little round chitty-face;° look on those smiling,
roguish, loving eyes there; look, look how they laugh, twire and   20
tempt! He, rogue; I'll buss 'em there, and here and everywhere.
Od's bobs: away, this is fooling and spoiling of a man's stomach,
with a bit here, and a bit there. To bed, to bed.

LETICIA Go you first, sir; I will but stay to say my prayers—*(aside)*
which are that heaven would deliver me.   25

SIR FEEBLE Say thy prayers? What, art thou mad, prayers upon thy
wedding night? A short thanksgiving, or so; but prayers, quotha!
'Sbobs, you'll have time enough for that, I doubt.

LETICIA I am ashamed to undress before you, sir; go to bed.

SIR FEEBLE What, was it ashamed to show its little white foots, and   30 its little round bubbies? Well, I'll go, I'll go. ([*Aside,*] *going towards the bed*) I cannot think on't, no I cannot.

> *Belmour comes forth from between the curtains, his coat off, his shirt bloody, a dagger in his hand, and his disguise off*

BELMOUR Stand.

SIR FEEBLE Ha!

LETICIA AND PHILLIS (*squeak*) Oh, heavens!   35

LETICIA (*aside to Phillis*) Why, is it Belmour?

BELMOUR Go not to bed; I guard this sacred place,
And the adulterer dies that enters here.

SIR FEEBLE Oh, why do I shake? Sure I'm a man! What art thou?

BELMOUR I am the wronged, the lost and murdered Belmour.   40

SIR FEEBLE [*aside*] Oh, lord! It is the same I saw last night. [*To Belmour*] Oh! hold thy dread vengeance: pity me, and hear me.—Oh! a parson, a parson! What shall I do? Oh! where shall I hide myself?

BELMOUR I'th' utmost borders of the earth I'll find thee,
Seas shall not hide thee, nor vast mountains guard thee.   45
Even in the depth of hell I'll find thee out,
And lash thy filthy and adulterous soul.

SIR FEEBLE Oh! I am dead, I'm dead; will no repentance save me?
'Twas that young eye that tempted me to sin; oh!

BELMOUR [*to Leticia*] See, fair seducer, what thou'st made me do;   50
Look on this bleeding wound: it reached my heart,
To pluck thy dear tormenting image thence,°
When news arrived that thou hadst broke thy vow.

SIR FEEBLE Oh lord! Oh! [*Aside*] I'm glad he's dead though.

LETICIA Oh, hide that fatal wound; my tender heart faints with a   55
sight so horrid! (*Seems to weep*)

SIR FEEBLE [*aside*] So, she'll clear herself, and leave me in the devil's clutches.

BELMOUR You've both offended heaven, and must repent or die.

SIR FEEBLE Ah, I do confess I was an old fool, bewitched with   60
beauty, besotted with love, and do repent most heartily.

BELMOUR No, you had rather yet go on in sin:
Thou wouldst live on, and be a baffled cuckold.

SIR FEEBLE Oh, not for the world, sir: I am convinced and mortified.

BELMOUR Maintain her fine, undo thy peace to please her, and still   65
be cuckolded on; believe her, trust her, and be cuckold still.

SIR FEEBLE I see my folly, and my age's dotage, and find the devil
was in me; yet spare my age, ah! spare me to repent.

BELMOUR If thou repent'st, renounce her, fly her sight;
    Shun her bewitching charms, as thou wouldst hell: 70
    Those dark eternal mansions of the dead,
    Whither I must descend.

SIR FEEBLE Oh, would he were gone!

BELMOUR Fly; be gone; depart; vanish for ever, from her to some
more safe and innocent apartment.   75

SIR FEEBLE Oh, that's very hard!

    [Sir Feeble] goes back trembling; Belmour follows in, with his
    dagger up; both go out

LETICIA Blessed be this kind release; and yet, methinks, it grieves
me° to consider how the poor old man is frighted.

    Belmour re-enters, puts on his coat

BELMOUR He's gone, and locked himself into his chamber.
    And now, my dear Leticia, let us fly: 80
    Despair till now did my wild heart invade,
    But pitying love has the rough storm allayed.

    Exeunt

[5.3]

    Sir Cautious his garden

    Enter two porters and Rag, bearing Gayman in a chest.
    [They] set it down; he comes forth with a dark lantern

GAYMAN Set down the chest behind yon hedge of roses, and then
put on those shapes I have appointed you; and be sure you
well-favouredly bang both Bearjest and Noisy, since they have a
mind to see the devil.

RAG Oh, sir, leave 'em to us for that, and if we do not play the devil   5
with 'em, we deserve they should beat us. But, sir, we are in Sir
Cautious his garden: will not he sue us for a trespass?

GAYMAN I'll bear you out; be ready at my call.

    Exeunt [Rag and porters]
    Let me see: I have got no ready stuff to banter with, but no matter,
any gibberish will serve the fools. 'Tis now about the hour of ten: 10
But twelve is my appointed lucky minute,
When all the blessings that my soul could wish°
Shall be resigned to me.

    Enter Bredwell

Ha, who's there, Bredwell?

BREDWELL Oh, are you come, sir; and can you be so kind to a poor   15
youth, to favour his designs, and bless his days?

GAYMAN Yes, I am ready here with all my devils, both to secure you
your mistress, and to cudgel your captain and squire, for abusing
me behind my back so basely.

BREDWELL 'Twas most unmanly, sir, and they deserve it. I wonder   20
that they come not?

GAYMAN How durst you trust her with him?

BREDWELL Because 'tis dangerous to steal a city heiress, and let the
theft be his, so the dear maid be mine. Hark, sure they come.

Enter Bearjest; runs against Bredwell

—Who's there, Mr Bearjest?   25

BEARJEST Who's that, Ned? Well, I have brought my mistress. Hast
thou got a parson ready, and a licence?

BREDWELL Aye, aye; but where's the lady?

BEARJEST In the coach, with the captain at the gate. I came before
to see if the coast be clear.   30

BREDWELL Aye, sir; but what shall we do? Here's Mr Gayman come
on purpose to show you the devil, as you desired.

BEARJEST Pshaw! A pox of the devil, man: I can't intend° to speak
with him now.

GAYMAN How, sir? D'ye think my devil of so little quality, to suffer   35
an affront unrevenged?

BEARJEST Sir, I cry his devilship's pardon: I did not know his
quality. I protest, sir, I love and honour him, but I am now just
going to be married, sir; and when that ceremony's past, I'm ready
to go to the devil as soon as you please.   40

GAYMAN I have told him your desire of seeing him, and should you
baffle him?

BEARJEST Who, I, sir? Pray let his worship know I shall be proud of
the honour of his acquaintance; but sir, my mistress and the parson
waits in Ned's chamber.   45

GAYMAN If all the world wait, sir, the prince of hell will stay for no
man.

BREDWELL Oh, sir, rather than the prince of the infernals shall be
affronted, I'll conduct the lady up, and entertain her till you come, sir.

BEARJEST Nay, I have a great mind to kiss his—paw, sir; but I could   50
wish you'd show him me by daylight, sir.

GAYMAN The prince of darkness does abhor the light. But, sir, I will
for once allow your friend the captain to keep you company.

Enter Noisy and Diana

BEARJEST I'm much obliged to you, sir.—Oh, captain—
    [Bearjest] talks to [Noisy]

BREDWELL *[aside to Diana]* Haste, dear; the parson waits,   55
  To finish what the powers designed above.

DIANA Sure nothing is so bold as maids in love!
    They go out

NOISY Pshaw! He conjure! He can fly as soon.

GAYMAN Gentlemen, you must be sure to confine yourselves to this
  circle,° and have a care you neither swear, nor pray.   60

BEARJEST Pray, sir? I dare say neither of us were ever that way gifted.
    A horrid noise

GAYMAN   Cease your horror, cease your haste.
  And calmly as I saw you last,
  Appear! Appear!
  By thy pearls and diamond rocks,   65
  By thy heavy money box,
  By thy shining petticoat,
  That hid thy cloven feet from note,
  By the veil that hid thy face,
  Which else had frightened human race: 70
  Appear, that I thy love may see,
  Appear, kind fiends, appear to me!

    Soft music ceases
  [Aside] A pox of these rascals, why come they not?
    Four enter from the four corners of the stage, to music that
    plays. They dance, and in the dance, dance round [Bearjest
    and Noisy], and kick, pinch, and beat them

BEARJEST Oh, enough, enough! Good sir, lay 'em,° and I'll pay the
  music.   75

GAYMAN I wonder at it: these spirits are in their nature kind and
  peaceable, and you have basely injured somebody: confess,° and
  then they will be satisfied.

BEARJEST Oh, good sir, take your Cerberuses° off. I do confess the
  captain here and I have violated your fame.   80

NOISY Abused you, and traduced you; and thus we beg your pardon.

GAYMAN Abused me? 'Tis more than I know, gentlemen.

BEARJEST But it seems your friend the devil does.

GAYMAN *[aside]* By this time Bredwell's married. *[To devils]* Great
  Pantamogan,° hold, for I am satisfied—   85

Ex[eunt] devils
and thus undo my charm.
  [*Gayman*] *takes away the circle.* [*Bearjest and Noisy*] *run out*
So, the fools are gone, and—(*going*) now to Julia's arms.
  [*Exit*]

[5.4]

Lady Fulbank's antechamber

[*Lady Fulbank is*] *discovered° undressed at her glass.
Sir Cautious* [*is*] *undressed*

LADY FULBANK But why tonight? Indeed, you're wondrous kind,
 methinks.

SIR CAUTIOUS Why, I don't know: a wedding is a sort of an alarm°
 to love; it calls up every man's courage.

LADY FULBANK Aye, but will it come when 'tis called?°   5

SIR CAUTIOUS (*aside*) I doubt you'll find it, to my grief. [*To Lady
 Fulbank*] But I think 'tis all one to thee, thou car'st not for my
 compliment; no, thou'dst rather have a young fellow.

LADY FULBANK I am not used to flatter much; if forty years were
 taken from your age, 'twould render you something more agreeable 10
 to my bed, I must confess.

SIR CAUTIOUS Aye, aye, no doubt on't.

LADY FULBANK Yet you may take my word without an oath: were
 you as old as time, and I were young and gay as April flowers,
 which all are fond to gather,   15
 My beauties all should wither in the shade,
 Ere I'd be worn in a dishonest bosom.

SIR CAUTIOUS Aye, but you're wondrous free, methinks, sometimes,
 which gives shrewd suspicions.

LADY FULBANK What, because I cannot simper, look demure, and 20
 justify my honour when none questions it?
 Cry 'fie', and 'out upon the naughty women',
 Because they please themselves?—and so would I.

SIR CAUTIOUS How, would; what, cuckold me?

LADY FULBANK Yes, if it pleased me better than virtue, sir.   25
 But I'll not change my freedom and my humour,
 To purchase the dull fame of being honest.

SIR CAUTIOUS Aye, but the world, the world—

LADY FULBANK I value not the censures of the crowd.

SIR CAUTIOUS But I am old.   30

LADY FULBANK That's your fault, sir, not mine.

SIR CAUTIOUS But being so, if I should be good-natured, and give
thee leave to love discreetly—?

LADY FULBANK I'd do't without your leave, sir.

SIR CAUTIOUS Do't: what, cuckold me?   35

LADY FULBANK No; love discreetly, sir, love as I ought, love
honestly.

SIR CAUTIOUS What, in love with anybody but your own husband?

LADY FULBANK Yes.

SIR CAUTIOUS Yes, quotha: is that your loving as you ought?   40

LADY FULBANK We cannot help our inclinations, sir,
No more than time or light from coming on;
But I can keep my virtue, sir, entire.

SIR CAUTIOUS What, I'll warrant this is your first love, Gayman?

LADY FULBANK I'll not deny that truth, though even to you.   45

SIR CAUTIOUS Why, in consideration of my age and your youth, I'd
bear a conscience, provided you do things wisely.

LADY FULBANK Do what thing, sir?

SIR CAUTIOUS You know what I mean.

LADY FULBANK Ha, I hope you would not be a cuckold, sir?   50

SIR CAUTIOUS Why—truly in a civil way, or so—

LADY FULBANK There is but one way, sir, to make me hate you;
And that would be tame suffering.

SIR CAUTIOUS [aside] Nay, an she be thereabouts, there's no discovering.   55

LADY FULBANK But leave this fond discourse, and if you must, let
us to bed.

SIR CAUTIOUS Aye, aye. I did but try your virtue, mun; dost think
I was in earnest?

     Enter servant

SERVANT Sir, here's a chest directed to your worship.   60

SIR CAUTIOUS [aside] Hum, 'tis Wasteall: now does my heart fail me.
[To servant] A chest, say you? To me? So late! I'll warrant it comes
from Sir Nicholas Smuggle: some prohibited goods that he has
stolen the custom of, and cheated his majesty. Well, he's an honest
man; bring it in.   65

LADY FULBANK What, into my apartment, sir, a nasty chest!

SIR CAUTIOUS By all means: for if the searchers come, they'll never
be so uncivil to ransack thy lodgings; and we are bound in Christian

charity to do for one another—some rich commodities, I am sure; and some fine knick-knack will fall to thy share, I'll warrant thee. (*Aside*) Pox on him for a young rogue, how punctual he is!

 Enter [men] with the chest

—Go, my dear, go to bed. I'll send Sir Nicholas a receipt for the chest, and be with thee presently.

 Exeunt [Sir Cautious, Lady Fulbank, and the men,] severally.

 Gayman peeps out of the chest, and looks round him wondering

GAYMAN Ha, where am I? By heaven, my last night's vision! 'Tis that enchanted room, and yonder the alcove! Sure, 'twas indeed some witch, who knowing of my infidelity, has by enchantment brought me hither. 'Tis so, I am betrayed. (*Pauses*) Ha! or was it Julia, that last night gave me that lone opportunity? But hark, I hear some coming.

 [Gayman] shuts himself in [the chest]. Enter Sir Cautious

SIR CAUTIOUS (*lifting up the chest lid*) So, you are come, I see.

 [Sir Cautious] goes and locks the door

GAYMAN (*aside*) Ha, he here! Nay, then I was deceived, and it was Julia that last night gave me the dear assignation.

 Sir Cautious peeps into the bedchamber

LADY FULBANK (*within*) Come, Sir Cautious; I shall fall asleep, and then you'll waken me.

SIR CAUTIOUS Aye, my dear, I'm coming. [*To Gayman*] She's in bed; I'll go put out the candle, and then—

GAYMAN Aye, I'll warrant you for my part.

SIR CAUTIOUS Aye, but you may over-act your part, and spoil all; but, sir, I hope you'll use a Christian conscience in this business.

GAYMAN Oh, doubt not, sir, but I shall do you reason.°

SIR CAUTIOUS Aye, sir, but—

GAYMAN Good sir, no more cautions; you, unlike a fair gamester, will rook me out of half my night. I am impatient.

SIR CAUTIOUS Good lord, are you so hasty? If I please, you shan't go at all.

GAYMAN With all my soul, sir; pay me three hundred pound, sir.

SIR CAUTIOUS Lord, sir, you mistake my candid meaning still. I am content to be a cuckold, sir; but I would have things done decently, d'ye mind me?

GAYMAN As decently as a cuckold can be made, sir. But no more disputes, I pray, sir.

SIR CAUTIOUS I'm gone, I'm gone—

 [Sir Cautious], going out, returns

but hark'ee, sir, you'll rise before day?

GAYMAN Yet again!

SIR CAUTIOUS I vanish, sir; but hark'ee: you'll not speak a word, but   105
let her think 'tis I?

GAYMAN Be gone, I say, sir.

[Sir Cautious] runs out

I am convinced last night I was with Julia.

Oh, sot, insensible and dull!

Enter softly Sir Cautious

SIR CAUTIOUS So, the candle's out; give me your hand.   110

[Sir Cautious] leads [Gayman] softly in

[5.5]

A bed-chamber°

*Lady Fulbank supposed in bed. Enter Sir Cautious and
Gayman by dark*

SIR CAUTIOUS Where are you, my dear?

[Sir Cautious] leads [Gayman] to the bed

LADY FULBANK Where should I be? In bed. What, are you by dark?

SIR CAUTIOUS Aye, the candle went out by chance.

*Gayman signs to him to be gone; he makes grimaces as loth to
go, and exit*

[5.6]

*Scene draws over,° and represents another room in the same
house*

Enter parson, Diana, and Pert dressed in Diana's clothes

DIANA I'll swear, Mrs Pert, you look very prettily in my clothes;—
and since you, sir, have convinced me that this innocent deceit is
not unlawful, I am glad to be the instrument of advancing Mrs
Pert to a husband she already has so just a claim to.°

PARSON Since she has so firm a contract, I pronounce it a lawful   5
marriage. But hark, they are coming, sure.

DIANA Pull your hoods down, and keep your face from the light.

Diana runs out. Enter Bearjest and Noisy, disordered

BEARJEST Madam, I beg your pardon: I met with a most devilish
adventure.—Your pardon, too, Mr Doctor, for making you wait;
but the business is this, sir: I have a great mind to lie with this   10
young gentlewoman tonight, but she swears if I do, the parson of
the parish shall know it.

PARSON If I do, sir, I shall keep counsel.

BEARJEST And that's civil, sir; come, lead the way—
  With such a guide, the devil's in't if we can go astray.   15

  Exeunt

[5.7]

Scene changes to the antechamber

Enter Sir Cautious

SIR CAUTIOUS Now cannot I sleep, but am as restless as a merchant
in stormy weather, that has ventured all his wealth in one bottom.
Woman is a leaky vessel: if she should like the young rogue now,
and they should come to a right understanding, why then am I
a—wittol, that's all, and shall be put in print at Snow-hill° with   5
my effigies o'th' top, like the sign of cuckold's haven.° Hum,
they're damnable silent; pray heaven he have not murdered her,
and robbed her. Hum: hark, what's that? A noise: he has broke his
covenant with me, and shall forfeit the money. How loud they are!
Aye, aye, the plot's discovered; what shall I do? Why, the devil is   10
not in her, sure, to be refractory now, and peevish; if she be I must
pay my money yet, and that would be a damned thing. Sure,
they're coming out: I'll retire and harken how 'tis with them.

  [Sir Cautious] retires [a little distance]. Enter Lady Fulbank,
  undressed; Gayman, half undressed, upon his knees, following
  her, holding her gown

LADY FULBANK Oh! you unkind—what have you made me do?
  Unhand me, false deceiver, let me loose.   15

SIR CAUTIOUS (*aside, peeping*) Made her do? So, so, 'tis done; I'm
  glad of that.

GAYMAN Can you be angry, Julia?
  Because I only seized my right of love.

LADY FULBANK And must my honour be the price of it?   20
  Could nothing but my fame reward your passion?
  What, make me a base prostitute, a foul adulteress?

Oh, be gone, be gone, dear robber of my quiet. (*Weeping*)

SIR CAUTIOUS [*aside*] Oh, fearful!

GAYMAN Oh! Calm your rage, and hear me: if you are so,   25
  You are an innocent adulteress.
  It was the feeble husband you enjoyed
  In cold imagination, and no more;
  Shyly you turned away, faintly resigned.°

SIR CAUTIOUS [*aside*] Hum, did she so?   30

GAYMAN Till my excess of love betrayed the cheat.

SIR CAUTIOUS [*aside*] Aye, aye, that was my fear.

LADY FULBANK Away, be gone, I'll never see you more.

GAYMAN You may as well forbid the sun to shine.
  Not see you more! Heavens! I before adored you,   35
  But now I rave! And with my impatient love,
  A thousand mad and wild desires are burning!
  I have discovered now new worlds of charms,
  And can no longer tamely love and suffer.

SIR CAUTIOUS [*aside*] So, I have brought an old house upon my   40
  head:° entailed cuckoldom upon myself.

LADY FULBANK I'll hear no more.—Sir Cautious! Where's my husband?
  Why have you left my honour thus unguarded?

SIR CAUTIOUS [*aside*] Aye, aye, she's well enough pleased, I fear, for
  all that.   45

GAYMAN Base as he is, 'twas he exposed this treasure;
  Like silly Indians bartered thee for trifles.°

SIR CAUTIOUS [*aside*] Oh, treacherous villain!

LADY FULBANK Ha, my husband do this?

GAYMAN He, by love, he was the kind procurer,   50
  Contrived the means, and brought me to thy bed.

LADY FULBANK My husband? My wise husband!
  What fondness in my conduct had he seen,
  To take so shameful and so base revenge?

GAYMAN None: 'twas filthy avarice seduced him to't.   55

LADY FULBANK If he could be so barbarous to expose me,
  Could you who loved me be so cruel too?

GAYMAN What, to possess thee when the bliss was offered,
  Possess thee, too, without a crime to thee?
  Charge not my soul with so remiss a flame,   60
  So dull a sense of virtue, to refuse it.

LADY FULBANK I am convinced the fault was all my husband's;
  (*Kneels*) And here I vow, by all things just and sacred,

To separate for ever from his bed.°

SIR CAUTIOUS [*aside*] Oh, I am not able to endure it! [*To Lady   65
Fulbank*] Hold, oh hold, my dear.
      [*Sir Cautious*] kneels as [*Lady Fulbank*] rises

LADY FULBANK Stand off; I do abhor thee.

SIR CAUTIOUS With all my soul; but do not make rash vows. They
break my very heart. Regard my reputation!°

LADY FULBANK Which you have had such care of, sir, already.   70
Rise, 'tis in vain you kneel.

SIR CAUTIOUS No, I'll never rise again. Alas, madam, I was merely
drawn in; I only thought to sport a die or so; I had only an
innocent design to discover whether this gentleman had stolen my
gold, that so I might have hanged him.   75

GAYMAN A very innocent design, indeed.

SIR CAUTIOUS Aye, sir, that's all, as I'm an honest man.

LADY FULBANK I've sworn, nor are the stars more fixed than I.
      Enter servant.

SERVANT How! my lady and his worship up?—Madam, a gentleman
and a lady below in a coach knocked me up, and say they must   80
speak with your ladyship.

LADY FULBANK This is strange!—Bring 'em up.
      Exit servant
Who can it be at this odd time of neither night nor day?
      Enter Leticia, Belmour, and Phillis

LETICIA Madam, your virtue, charity and friendship to me, has made
me trespass on you for my life's security, and beg you will protect   85
me—and my husband. (*Points at Belmour*)

SIR CAUTIOUS So, here's another sad catastrophe!°

LADY FULBANK Ha: does Belmour live, is't possible?
Believe me, sir, you ever had my wishes,
And shall not fail of my protection now.   90

BELMOUR I humbly thank your ladyship.

GAYMAN I'm glad thou hast her, Harry, but doubt thou durst not
own her; nay, dar'st not own thyself.

BELMOUR Yes, friend, I have my pardon.
      A noise of somebody coming in
But hark, I think we are pursued already;   95
But now I fear no force.

LADY FULBANK However, step into my bed-chamber.
      *Exeunt Leticia, Gayman, and Phillis. Enter Sir Feeble in an
      antic manner*°

SIR FEEBLE (*coming up in a menacing manner to Sir Cautious*) 'Hell shall not hold thee, nor vast mountains cover thee, but I will find thee out, and lash thy filthy and adulterous carcase.'   100

SIR CAUTIOUS How, lash my filthy carcase? I defy thee, Satan.

SIR FEEBLE 'Twas thus he said.

SIR CAUTIOUS Let who's will° say it, he lies in's throat.

SIR FEEBLE How! the ghostly—hush, have a care, for 'twas the ghost of Belmour—oh! hide that bleeding wound, it chills my soul!   105

[*Sir Feeble*] *runs to the Lady Fulbank*

LADY FULBANK What bleeding wound? Heavens, are you frantic, sir?

SIR FEEBLE (*weeps*) No; but for want of rest, I shall ere° morning. She's gone, she's gone, she's gone. (*He weeps*)

SIR CAUTIOUS Aye, aye, she's gone, she's gone indeed.   110

Sir Cautious weeps

SIR FEEBLE But let her go, so I may never see that dreadful vision. Hark'ee sir, a word in your ear: have a care of marrying a young wife.

SIR CAUTIOUS (*weeping*) Aye, but I have married one already.

SIR FEEBLE Hast thou? Divorce her, fly her; quick, depart, be gone: she'll cuckold thee, and still she'll cuckold thee.   115

SIR CAUTIOUS Aye, brother, but whose fault was that? Why, are not you married?

SIR FEEBLE Mum, no words on't, unless you'll have the ghost about your ears; part with your wife, I say, or else the devil will part ye.

LADY FULBANK Pray, go to bed, sir.   120

SIR FEEBLE Yes, for I shall sleep now, I shall lie alone. (*Weeps*) Ah fool, old dull besotted fool, to think she'd love me; 'twas by base means I gained her: cozened an honest gentleman of fame and life.

LADY FULBANK You did so, sir, but 'tis not past redress: you may   125 make that honest gentleman amends.

SIR FEEBLE Oh, would I could, so I gave half my estate.

LADY FULBANK That penitence atones with him and heaven.— Come forth, Leticia, and your injured ghost.

[*Enter Leticia, Belmour, and Phillis*]

SIR FEEBLE Ha, ghost; another sight would make me mad indeed.   130

BELMOUR Behold me, sir, I have no terror now.

SIR FEEBLE Ha, who's that, Francis? My nephew Francis?

BELMOUR Belmour, or Francis; choose you which you like, and I am either.

SIR FEEBLE Ha, Belmour! and no ghost?   135

BELMOUR Belmour, and not your nephew, sir.

SIR FEEBLE But art alive? Od's bobs, I'm glad on't, sirrah. But are you real, Belmour?°

BELMOUR As sure as I'm no ghost.

GAYMAN We all can witness for him, sir.   140

SIR FEEBLE Where be the minstrels? We'll have a dance, adod we will. [*To Leticia*] Ah, art thou there, thou cozening little chits-face? A vengeance on thee, thou madest me an old doting loving coxcomb; but I forgive thee, and give thee all thy jewels,—[*to Belmour*] and you your pardon, sir, so you'll give me mine; for I 145 find you young knaves will be too hard for us.

BELMOUR You are so generous, sir, that 'tis almost with grief I receive the blessing of Leticia.

SIR FEEBLE No, no, thou deserv'st her; she would have made an old fond blockhead of me, and one way or other you would have had 150 her, od's bobs you would.

Enter Bearjest, Diana, Pert, Bredwell, and Noisy

BEARJEST Justice, sir, justice: I have been cheated, abused, assassinated and ravished!

SIR CAUTIOUS How, my nephew ravished!

PERT No, sir, I am his wife.   155

SIR CAUTIOUS Hum, my heir marry a chamber-maid!

BEARJEST Sir, you must know I stole away Mrs Di, and brought her to Ned's chamber here, to marry her.

SIR FEEBLE My daughter Di stolen!

BEARJEST But I being to go to the devil a little, sir, whip—what does 160 he, but marries her himself, sir; and fobbed me off here with my lady's cast petticoat.°

NOISY Sir, she's a gentlewoman, and my sister, sir.

PERT Madam, 'twas a pious fraud, if it were one, for I was contracted to him before. See, here it is.   165

[Pert] gives [a paper to] them

ALL A plain case, a plain case.

SIR FEEBLE (*to Bredwell, who with Diana kneels*) Hark'ee sir, have you had the impudence to marry my daughter, sir?

BREDWELL Yes, sir, and humbly ask your pardon, and your blessing.   170

SIR FEEBLE You will ha't whether I will or not. Rise, you are still too hard for us.—Come, sir, forgive your nephew.

SIR CAUTIOUS Well, sir, I will; but all this while you little think the tribulation I am in: my lady has forsworn my bed.

SIR FEEBLE Indeed sir, the wiser she.   175

SIR CAUTIOUS For only performing my promise to this gentleman.

SIR FEEBLE Aye, you showed her the difference, sir; you're a wise
man. Come, dry your eyes, and rest yourself contented; we are a
couple of old coxcombs, d'ye hear, sir, coxcombs.   180

SIR CAUTIOUS I grant it, sir,—(to Gayman) and if I die, sir, I
bequeath my lady to you, with my whole estate: my nephew has
too much already for a fool.

GAYMAN I thank you, sir.—Do you consent,° my Julia?

LADY FULBANK No, sir: you do not like me. 'A canvas bag of   185
wooden ladles were a better bed-fellow.'

GAYMAN Cruel tormentor! Oh, I could kill myself with shame and
anger!

LADY FULBANK Come hither, Bredwell: witness, for my honour,
that I had no design upon his person, but that of trying of his   190
constancy.

BREDWELL Believe me sir, 'tis true. I feigned a danger near,° just as
you got to bed; and I was the kind devil, sir, that brought the gold
to you.

BEARJEST And you were one of the devils that beat me and the   195
captain here, sir?

GAYMAN No, truly, sir, those were some I hired, to beat you for
abusing me today.

NOISY To make you 'mends sir, I bring you the certain news of the
death of Sir Thomas Gayman, your uncle, who has left you two   200
thousand pounds a year.

GAYMAN I thank you, sir; I heard the news before.°

SIR CAUTIOUS How's this: Mr Gayman, my lady's first lover? I find,
Sir Feeble, we were a couple of old fools indeed, to think at our
age to cozen two lusty young fellows of their mistresses; 'tis no   205
wonder that both the men and the women have been too hard for
us; we are not fit matches for either, that's the truth on't.

> That warrior needs must to his rival yield,
> Who comes with blunted weapons to the field.

Epilogue

Written by a person of quality, spoken by Mr Betterton

Long have we turned the point of our just rage
On the half-wits and critics of the age.
Oft has the soft, insipid sonneteer
In Nice and Flutter, seen his fop-face here.°
Well was the ignorant lampooning pack   5
Of shatterhead rhymers whipped on Craffey's back;°
But such a trouble weed is poetaster,
The lower 'tis cut down, it grows the faster.
Though satire then had such a plenteous crop,
An aftermath of coxcombs is come up,°   10
Who not content false poetry to renew,
By sottish censures would condemn the true.
Let writing, like a gentleman, fine appear,
But must you needs judge too *en cavalier*?°
These whiffling critics 'tis our authoress fears,°   15
And humbly begs a trial by her peers;
Or let a poll of fools her fate pronounce,°
There's no great harm in a good quiet dunce.
But shield her, heaven! from the left-handed blow
Of airy blockheads who pretend to know.   20
On downright dullness let her rather split,
Than be fop-mangled under colour of wit.
  Hear me, ye scribbling beaux:
Why will you in sheer rhyme, without one stroke
Of poetry, ladies' just disdain provoke,   25
And address songs to whom you never spoke?
In doleful hymns for dying felons fit,
Why do you tax their eyes, and blame their wit?
Unjustly of the innocent you complain,
'Tis bulkers give, and tubs must cure your pain.°   30
Why in lampoons will you yourselves revile?
'Tis true, none else will think it worth their while:
But thus you're hid! Oh, 'tis a politic fetch:°
So some have hanged themselves, to ease Jack Ketch.°
Justly your friends and mistresses you blame,   35

For being so they well deserve the shame,
'Tis the worst scandal to have borne that name.
At poetry of late, and such whose skill   *See the late*
Excels your own, you dart a feeble quill;   *satire on*
Well may you rail at what you ape so ill.   *poetry*°   40
With virtuous women, and all men of worth,
You're in a state of mortal war by birth.
Nature in all her atom-fights ne'er knew°
Two things so opposite as them and you.
On such your muse her utmost fury spends,   45
They're slandered worse than any but your friends.
More years may teach you better; the meanwhile,
If you can't mend your morals, mend your style.

THE EMPEROR OF
THE MOON:
A Farce

The play was first performed at the Dorset Garden Theatre in
March or April 1687, with the following cast:

Doctor Baliardo°	*Mr Underhill*
Scaramouch° (his man)	*Mr Leigh*
Pedro (his boy)	
Don Cinthio°	*Young Mr Powell*
Don Charmante	*Mr Mountfort*
(both nephews to the viceroy, and lovers of	
Elaria and Bellemante)	
Harlequin° (Cinthio's man)	*Mr Jevon*
Officer and Clerk	
[Page]	
Elaria° (daughter to the doctor)	*Mrs Cooke*
Bellemante (niece to the doctor)	*Mrs Mountfort*
Mopsophil (governante to the young ladies)	*Mrs Corey*
[Florinda]	

The persons in the moon are Don Cinthio (Emperor); Don Charmante (Prince of Thunderland); their attendants (persons that
represent the court cards)

Kepler and Galileus° (two philosophers)

Twelve persons representing the figures of the twelve signs of the
zodiac

Negroes, and persons that dance

Music, kettledrums, and trumpets

THE SCENE

Naples

THE EPISTLE DEDICATORY

To the Lord Marquess of Worcester, &c.°

My Lord,

It is a common notion, that gathers as it goes, and is almost become a vulgar error, that dedications in our age, are only the effects of flattery, a form of compliment, and no more; so that the great, to whom they are only due, decline those noble patronages that were so generally allowed the ancient poets, since the awful custom has been so scandalized by mistaken addresses; and many a worthy piece is lost for want of some honourable protection, and sometimes many indifferent ones traverse the world with that advantageous passport only.

This humble offering, which I presume to lay at your lordship's feet, is of that critical nature, that it does not only require the patronage of a great title, but of a great man too, and there is often times a vast difference between those two great things; and amongst all the most elevated, there are but very few in whom an illustrious birth and equal parts complete the hero; but among those, your lordship bears the first rank, from a just claim, both of the glories of your race and virtues. Nor need we look back into long past ages, to bring down to ours the magnanimous deeds of your ancestors: we need no more than to behold (what we have so often done with wonder) those of the great Duke of Beauford,° your illustrious father, whose every single action is a glorious and lasting precedent to all the future great ones; whose unshaken loyalty, and all other eminent virtues, have rendered him to us, something more than man, and which alone deserving a whole volume, would be here but to lessen his fame, to mix his grandeurs with those of any other; and while I am addressing to the son, who is only worthy of that noble blood he boasts, and who gives the world a prospect of those coming gallantries that will equal those of his glorious father; already, my lord, all you say and do is admired, and every touch of your pen reverenced; the excellency and quickness of your wit, is the subject that fills the world most agreeably. For my own part, I never presume to contemplate your lordship, but my soul bows with a perfect veneration to your mighty mind; and while I have adored the delicate effects of your uncommon wit, I have wished for nothing more than an opportunity

of expressing my infinite sense of it; and this ambition, my lord, was 35
one motive of my present presumption, in the dedicating this farce to
your lordship.

I am sensible, my lord, how far the word farce might have offended
some, whose titles of honour, a knack in dressing, or his art in writing
a billet doux, had been his chiefest talent, and who, without consider- 40
ing the intent, character, or nature of the thing, would have cried out
upon the language, and have damned it (because the persons in it did
not all talk like heroes) as too debased and vulgar to entertain a man
of quality; but I am secure from this censure, when your lordship
shall be its judge, whose refined sense, and delicacy of judgement, 45
will, through all the humble actions and trivialness of business, find
nature there, and that diversion which was not meant for the
numbers, who comprehend nothing beyond the show and buffoonery.

A very barren and thin hint of the plot I had from the Italian, and
which, even as it was, was acted in France eighty-odd times without 50
intermission.° 'Tis now much altered, and adapted to our English
theatre and genius, who cannot find an entertainment at so cheap a
rate as the French will, who are content with almost any incoherences,
howsoever shuffled together under the name of a farce;° which I have
endeavoured as much as the thing would bear, to bring within the 55
compass of possibility and nature, that I might as little impose upon
the audience as I could; all the words are wholly new,° without one
from the original. 'Twas calculated for his late majesty° of sacred
memory, that great patron of noble poetry, and the stage, for whom
the muses must for ever mourn, and whose loss, only the blessing of 60
so illustrious a successor can ever repair; and 'tis a great pity to see
that best and most useful diversion of mankind, whose magnificence
of old was the most certain sign of a flourishing state, now quite
undone by the misapprehension of the ignorant, and misrepresentings
of the envious, which evidently shows the world is improved in 65
nothing but pride, ill nature, and affected nicety; and the only
diversion of the town now, is high dispute, and public controversies
in taverns, coffee-houses, &c., and those things which ought to be the
greatest mysteries in religion, and so rarely the business of discourse,
are turned into ridicule, and look but like so many fanatical° 70
stratagems to ruin the pulpit as well as the stage. The defence of the
first is left to the reverend gown, but the departing stage can be no
otherwise restored, but by some leading spirits so generous, so public,
and so indefatigable as that of your lordship, whose patronages are
sufficient to support it, whose wit and judgement to defend it, and 75

whose goodness and quality to justify it; such encouragement would
inspire the poets with new arts to please, and the actors with industry.
'Twas this that occasioned so many admirable plays heretofore, as
Shakespeare's, Fletcher's, and Jonson's, and 'twas this alone that
made the town able to keep so many play-houses alive, who now   80
cannot supply one.° However, my lord, I, for my part, will no longer
complain, if this piece find but favour in your lordship's eyes, and
that it be so happy to give your lordship one hour's diversion, which
is the only honour and fame is wished to crown all the endeavours of,

> my lord, your lordship's most humble, and
> most obedient servant,
> A. Behn.

Prologue

spoken by Mr Jevon°

[JEVON] Long, and at vast expense, the industrious stage
    Has strove to please a dull ungrateful age:
    With heroes and with gods we first began,
    And thundered to you in heroic strain:
    Some dying love-sick queen each night you enjoyed,   5
    And with magnificence, at last were cloyed:
    Our drums and trumpets frighted all the women;
    Our fighting scared the beaux and billet-doux men.
    So spark, in an intrigue of quality,
    Grows weary of his splendid drudgery;   10
    Hates the fatigue, and cries, 'a pox upon her,
    What a damned bustle's here with love and honour?'
      In humbler comedy we next appear,
    No fop or cuckold, but slap-dash we had him here;
    We showed you all, but you, malicious grown,   15
    Friends' vices to expose, and hide your own,
    Cry, 'damn it—this is such or such a one'.
    Yet, nettled: 'plague, what does the scribbler mean,
    With his damned characters, and plot obscene?
    No woman without vizard in the nation,°   20
    Can see it twice, and keep her reputation—that's certain.'
    Forgetting—
    That he himself, in every gross lampoon,
    Her lewder secrets spreads about the town;
    Whilst their feigned niceness is but cautious fear   25
    Their own intrigues should be unravelled here.
      Our next recourse was dwindling down to farce,
    Then: ''zounds, what stuff's here? 'tis all o'er my—'
    Well, gentlemen, since none of these has sped,
    'Gad, we have bought a share i'th' speaking head.°   30
    So there you'll save a sice,
    You love good husbandry in all but vice;
    Whoring and drinking only bears a price.
      The head rises upon a twisted post, on a bench, from under
      the stage. After [this] Jevon speaks to its mouth

Oh!—Oh!—Oh!
STENTOR Oh!—Oh!—Oh!   35
    After this it sings 'Sawny',° laughs, [and] cries 'God bless the
    king' in order. [Jevon speaks to its mouth again]
STENTOR (*answers*) Speak louder, Jevon, if you'd have me repeat—
[JEVON]° Plague of this rogue, he will betray the cheat.
    [Jevon] speaks louder, [the head] answers indirectly°
—Hum—There 'tis again,
Pox of your echo with a northern strain.°
Well—this will be but a nine days' wonder too;   40
There's nothing lasting but the puppets' show.°
What lady's heart so hard, but it would move,
To hear Philander and Irene's love?°
Those sisters too, the scandalous wits do say,
Two nameless, keeping beaux have made so gay;   45
But those amours are perfect sympathy,
Their gallants being as mere machines as they.°
Oh! how the city wife, with her nown ninny,°
Is charmed with, 'come into my coach, Miss Jinny, Miss Jinny.'
But, overturning, Fribble cries, 'Adznigs,   50
The juggling rogue has murdered all his kids.'°
The men of war cry, 'pox on't, this is dull,
We are for rough sports: Dog Hector, and the Bull.'°
Thus each in his degree diversion finds,
Your sports are suited to your mighty minds;   55
Whilst so much judgement in your choice you show,
The puppets have more sense than some of you.

1.1

A Chamber

Enter Elaria and Mopsophil

[ELARIA sings]° *A curse upon that faithless maid,*°
 Who first her sex's liberty betrayed;
 Born free as man to love and range,
 Till nobler nature did to custom change:
 Custom, that dull excuse for fools,   5
 Who think all virtue to consist in rules.

 From Love our fetters never sprung,
 That smiling god, all wanton, gay, and young,
 Shows by his wings he cannot be
 Confined to a restless slavery;   10
 But here and there at random roves,
 Not fixed to glittering courts or shady groves.

 Then she that constancy professed,
 Was but a well dissembler at the best;
 And that imaginary sway   15
 She feigned to give, in seeming to abey,
 Was but the height of prudent art,
 To deal with greater liberty her heart.

 After the song Elaria gives her lute to Mopsophil
This does not divert me:
Nor nothing will, till Scaramouch return,   20
And bring me news of Cinthio.

MOPSOPHIL Truly I was so sleepy last night, I know nothing of the
adventure, for which you are kept so close a prisoner today, and
more strictly guarded than usual.

ELARIA Cinthio came with music last night under my window, which 25
my father hearing, sallied out with his myrmidons upon him; and
clashing of swords I heard, but what hurt was done, or whether
Cinthio were discovered to him, I know not; but the billet I sent
him now by Scaramouch, will occasion me soon intelligence.

MOPSOPHIL And see, madam, where your trusty Roger° comes. 30
 Enter Scaramouch peeping on all sides before he enters
[*To Scaramouch*] You may advance, and fear none but your friends.

278

SCARAMOUCH Away, and keep the door.

ELARIA Oh, dear Scaramouch! hast thou been at the viceroy's?

SCARAMOUCH (*in heat*) Yes, yes.

ELARIA And hast thou delivered my letter to his nephew Don 35
Cinthio?

SCARAMOUCH Yes, yes, what should I deliver else?

ELARIA Well, and how does he?

SCARAMOUCH (*fanning himself with his cap*) Lord, how should he do?
Why, what a laborious thing it is to be a pimp! 40

ELARIA Why, well he should do.

SCARAMOUCH So he is, as well as a night-adventuring lover can be:
he has got but one wound, madam.

ELARIA How! Wounded, say you? Oh heavens! 'Tis not mortal?

SCARAMOUCH Why, I have no great skill; but they say it may be 45
dangerous.

ELARIA I die with fear; where is he wounded?

SCARAMOUCH Why, madam, he is run—quite through the—heart;
but the man may live, if I please.

ELARIA Thou please! Torment me not with riddles. 50

SCARAMOUCH Why, madam, there is a certain cordial balsam, called
a fair lady—which, outwardly applied to his bosom, will prove a
better cure than all your weapon-salve,° or sympathetic powder°—
meaning your ladyship.

ELARIA Is Cinthio then not wounded? 55

SCARAMOUCH No otherwise than by your fair eyes, madam; he got
away unseen and unknown.

ELARIA Dost know how precious time is, and dost thou fool it away
thus? What said he to my letter?

SCARAMOUCH What should he say? 60

ELARIA Why, a hundred dear soft things of love, kiss it as often, and
bless me for my goodness.

SCARAMOUCH Why, so he did.

ELARIA Ask thee a thousand questions of my health after my last
night's fright. 65

SCARAMOUCH So he did.

ELARIA Expressing all the kind concern love could inspire, for the
punishment my father has inflicted on me, for entertaining him at
my window last night.

SCARAMOUCH All this he did. 70

ELARIA And for my being confined a prisoner to my apartment,
without the hope or almost possibility of seeing him any more.

SCARAMOUCH There I think you are a little mistaken; for (besides the plot that I have laid to bring you together all this night) there are such stratagems a-brewing, not only to bring you together, but with your father's consent, too; such a plot, madam! 75

ELARIA Aye, that would be worthy of thy brain; prithee what?

SCARAMOUCH Such a device!

ELARIA I'm impatient.

SCARAMOUCH Such a conundrum! Well, if there be wise men and conjurers in the world, they are intriguing lovers. 80

ELARIA Out with it.

SCARAMOUCH You must know, madam, your father, (my master the doctor) is a little whimsical, romantic, or Don Quick-sottish,° or so. 85

ELARIA Or rather mad.

SCARAMOUCH That were uncivil to be supposed by me; but lunatic we may call him without breaking the decorum of good manners, for he is always travelling to the moon.

ELARIA And so religiously believes there is a world there, that he discourses as gravely of the people, their government, institutions, laws, manners, religion and constitution, as if he had been bred a Machiavel° there. 90

SCARAMOUCH How came he thus infected first?

ELARIA With reading foolish books, Lucian's *Dialogue of Icaromenip-pus,*° who flew up to the moon, and thence to heaven; an heroic business called *The Man in the Moon,*° if you'll believe a Spaniard, who was carried thither, upon an engine drawn by wild geese; with another philosophical piece, *A Discourse of the World in the Moon;*° with a thousand other ridiculous volumes too hard to name. 95 100

SCARAMOUCH Aye, this reading of books is a pernicious thing. I was like to have run mad once, reading Sir John Mandeville;° but to the business. I went, as you know, to Don Cinthio's lodgings, where I found him with his dear friend Charmante, laying their heads together for a farce. 105

ELARIA A farce!

SCARAMOUCH Aye, a farce, which shall be called *The World in the Moon*: wherein your father shall be so imposed on, as shall bring matters most magnificently about.

ELARIA I cannot conceive thee, but the design must be good since Cinthio and Charmante own it. 110

SCARAMOUCH In order to this, Charmante is dressing himself like one of the cabalists° of the Rosicrucian order,° and is coming to

prepare my credulous master for the greater imposition. I have his
trinkets here to play upon him, which shall be ready.   115

ELARIA But the farce, where is it to be acted?

SCARAMOUCH Here, here, in this very house; I am to order the
decoration, adorn a stage, and place scenes proper.

ELARIA How can this be done without my father's knowledge?

SCARAMOUCH You know the old apartment next the great orchard,   120
and the worm-eaten gallery, that opens to the river; which place
for several years nobody has frequented; there all things shall be
acted proper for our purpose.

Enter Mopsophil, running

MOPSA Run, run, Scaramouch; my master's conjuring° for you like
mad below: he calls up all his little devils with horrid names, his   125
microscope, his horoscope, his telescope, and all his scopes.°

SCARAMOUCH Here, here: I had almost forgot the letters; here's one
for you, and one for Mrs Bellemante.

*[Scaramouch gives Elaria two letters, and] runs out. Enter
Bellemante, with a book*

BELLEMANTE Here, take my prayer book, oh *ma très chère.*°

[Bellemante] embraces [Elaria]

ELARIA Thy eyes are always laughing, Bellemante.   130

BELLEMANTE And so would yours, had they been so well employed
as mine this morning. I have been at the chapel, and seen so many
beaux, such a number of *plumés,*° I could not tell which I should
look on most; sometimes my heart was charmed with the gay
blonding, then with the melancholy *noir,* anon the amiable bru-   135
nette;° sometimes the bashful, then again the bold; the little now,
anon the lovely tall! In fine, my dear, I was embarrassed on all
sides, I did nothing but deal my heart *tout autour.*°

ELARIA Oh, there was then no danger, cousin.

BELLEMANTE No, but abundance of pleasure.   140

ELARIA Why, this is better than sighing for Charmante.

BELLEMANTE That's when he's present only, and makes his court to
me; I can sigh to a lover, but will never sigh after him; but oh, the
beaux, the beaux, cousin, that I saw at church!

ELARIA Oh, you had great devotion to heaven, then!   145

BELLEMANTE And so I had, for I did nothing but admire its
handiwork; but I could not have prayed heartily if I had been
dying; but a deuce on't, who should come in and spoil all but my
lover Charmante, so dressed, so gallant, that he drew together all
the scattered fragments of my heart, confined my wandering   150

thoughts, and fixed 'em all on him: oh, how he looked, how he was
dressed! (*Sings*)

> *Chevalier, à cheveux blonds,*
> *Plus de mouche, plus de poudre,*
> *Plus de ribbons et cannons.*°   155

Oh, what a dear ravishing thing is the beginning of an amour!

ELARIA Thou'rt still in tune; when wilt thou be tame, Bellemante?

BELLEMANTE When I am weary of loving, Elaria.

ELARIA To keep up your humour, here's a letter from your Charmante.   160

[*Elaria gives Bellemante a letter*]

BELLEMANTE (*reads*) 'Malicious creature, when wilt thou cease to
torment me, and either appear less charming, or more kind? I
languish when from you, and am wounded when I see you, and
yet I am eternally courting my pain. Cinthio and I are contriving
how we shall see you tonight. Let us not toil in vain; we ask but   165
your consent: the pleasure will all be ours, 'tis therefore fit we
suffer all the fatigue. Grant this, and love me, if you will save the
life of your Charmante.'—Live, then, Charmante! Live as long as
love can last!

ELARIA Well, cousin, Scaramouch tells me of rare designs a-hatch-   170
ing, to relieve us from this captivity; here are we mewed up, to be
espoused to two moon-calfs° for aught I know; for the devil of any
human thing is suffered to come near us without our governante,
and keeper,° Mr Scaramouch.

BELLEMANTE Who, if he had no more honesty and conscience than   175
my uncle, would let us pine for want of lovers; but heaven be
praised, the generosity of our cavaliers has opened their obdurate
hearts with a golden key, that lets 'em in at all opportunities.
Come, come, let's in, and answer their billets doux.°

Exeunt

1.2

A garden

*Enter Doctor, with all manner of mathematical instruments
hanging at his girdle; Scaramouch bearing a telescope twenty
(or more) foot long*°

DOCTOR Set down the telescope. Let me see, what hour is it?

SCARAMOUCH About six o'clock, sir.

DOCTOR Then 'tis about the hour that the great monarch of the
upper world enters into his closet. Mount, mount the telescope.

SCARAMOUCH What to do, sir?   5

DOCTOR I understand, of certain moments critical,° one may be
snatched of such a mighty consequence to let the sight into the
secret closet.

SCARAMOUCH How, sir, peep into the king's closet? Under favour,
sir, that will be something uncivil.   10

DOCTOR Uncivil? It were flat treason if it should be known; but thus
unseen, and as wise politicians should, I take survey of all: this is
the statesman's peeping-hole, through which he steals the secrets
of his king, and seems to wink at distance.°

SCARAMOUCH The very key-hole, sir, through which, with half an   15
eye, he sees him even at his devotion, sir.

A knocking at the garden gate

DOCTOR Take care none enter.

Scaramouch goes to the door°

SCARAMOUCH Oh, sir, sir, here's some strange great man come to
wait on you.

DOCTOR Great man! from whence?   20

SCARAMOUCH Nay, from the moon world, for aught I know, for he
looks not like the people of the lower orb.

DOCTOR Ha! and that may be: wait on him in.

*Exit Scaramouch. [Re-]enter Scaramouch bare,° bowing
before Charmante, dressed in a strange fantastical habit,° with
Harlequin.° [Charmante] salutes the doctor. [Exit
Scaramouch]*

CHARMANTE Doctor Baliardo, most learned sir, all hail; hail from the
great cabala°—of Eutopia.°   25

DOCTOR Most reverend bard, thrice welcome. (*Salutes him low*)°

CHARMANTE The fame° of your great learning, sir, and virtue, is
known with joy to the renowned society.°

DOCTOR Fame, sir, has done me too much honour, to bear my name
to the renowned cabala.   30

CHARMANTE You must not attribute it all to fame, sir; they are too
learned and wise to take up things from fame, sir. Our intelligence
is by ways more secret and sublime: the stars, and little demons of
the air, inform us all things, past, present, and to come.

DOCTOR I must confess the Count of Gabalis° renders it plain, from   35
writ divine and human, there are such friendly and intelligent
demons.

CHARMANTE I hope you do not doubt that doctrine,° sir, which
holds that the four elements are peopled with persons of a form
and species more divine than vulgar mortals. Those of the fiery   40
regions we call the salamanders: they beget kings and heroes, with
spirits like their deietical° sires. The lovely inhabitants of the
water, we call nymphs. Those of the earth are gnomes or fairies.
Those of the air are sylphs.° These, sir, when in conjunction with
mortals, beget immortal races: such as the first-born man, which   45
had continued so, had the first man ne'er doted on a woman.

DOCTOR I am of that opinion, sir; man was not made for woman.

CHARMANTE Most certain, sir, man was to have been immortalized
by the love and conversation of these charming sylphs and
nymphs, and woman by the gnomes and salamanders, and to have   50
stocked the world with demi-gods, such as at this day inhabit the
empire of the moon.

DOCTOR Most admirable philosophy and reason. But do these sylphs
and nymphs appear in shapes?°

CHARMANTE Of the most beautiful of all the sons and daughters of   55
the universe. Imagination itself, imagination is not half so charming: and then so soft, so kind! But none but the cabala and their
families are blessed with their divine addresses. Were you but once
admitted into that society—

DOCTOR Aye, sir, what virtues or what merits can accomplish me for   60
that great honour?

CHARMANTE An absolute abstinence from carnal thought,° devout
and pure of spirit; free from sin.

DOCTOR I dare not boast my virtues, sir; is there no way to try my
purity?   65

CHARMANTE Are you very secret?

DOCTOR 'Tis my first principle, sir—

CHARMANTE And one the most material in our Rosicrucian order.
Please you to make a trial?

DOCTOR As how, sir, I beseech you?   70

CHARMANTE If you be thoroughly purged from vice, the optics of
your sight will be so illuminated, that glancing through this
telescope, you may behold one of those lovely creatures, that
people the vast region of the air.

DOCTOR Sir, you oblige profoundly.   75

CHARMANTE Kneel then, and try your strength of virtue, sir. Keep
your eye fixed and open.

> [*Doctor Baliardo*] *looks in the telescope. While he is looking,*
> *Charmante goes to the door to Scaramouch, who waited on*
> *purpose without, and takes a glass with a picture of a nymph*
> *on it, and a light behind it,*° *that as he brings it, it shows to*
> *the audience.* [*Charmante*] *goes to the end of the telescope*

CHARMANTE Can you discern, sir?

DOCTOR Methinks I see a kind of glorious cloud drawn up—and
now—'tis gone again.   80

CHARMANTE Saw you no figure?

DOCTOR None.

CHARMANTE Then make a short prayer to Alikin,° the spirit of the
east; shake off all earthly thoughts, and look again.

> [*Doctor*] *prays. Charmante puts the glass into the mouth of*
> *the telescope*°

DOCTOR Astonished, ravished with delight, I see a beauty young and   85
angel-like, leaning upon a cloud.

CHARMANTE Seems she on a bed? Then she's reposing, and you
must not gaze.

DOCTOR Now a cloud veils her from me.

CHARMANTE She saw you peeping then, and drew the curtain of the   90
air between.

DOCTOR I am all rapture, sir, at this rare vision. Is't possible, sir, that
I may ever hope the conversation of so divine a beauty?

CHARMANTE Most possible, sir; they will court you, their whole
delight is to immortalize: Alexander° was begot by a salamander,   95
that visited his mother in the form of a serpent, because he would
not make King Philip jealous; and that famous philosopher,
Merlin,° was begotten on a vestal nun, a certain king's daughter,
by a most beautiful young salamander; as indeed all the heroes, and
men of mighty minds are.   100

DOCTOR Most excellent!

CHARMANTE The nymph Egeria, enamoured on Numa Pompilius,°
came to him invisible to all eyes else, and gave him all his wisdom

and philosophy. Zoroaster,° Trismegistus,° Apuleius,° Aquinas,°
Albertus Magnus,° Socrates, and Virgil had their Zilphid,° which   105
foolish people called their demon or devil. But you are wise, sir.°

DOCTOR But do you imagine, sir, they will fall in love with an old
mortal?

CHARMANTE They love not like the vulgar; 'tis the immortal part
they dote upon.   110

DOCTOR But, sir, I have a niece and daughter which I love equally;
were it not possible they might be immortalized?

CHARMANTE No doubt on't, sir, if they be pure and chaste.

DOCTOR I think they are, and I'll take care to keep 'em so; for I
confess, sir, I would fain have a hero to my grandson.   115

CHARMANTE You never saw the emperor of the moon, sir, the
mighty Iredonozar?°

DOCTOR Never, sir; his court I have, but 'twas confusedly too.

CHARMANTE Refine your thoughts, sir, by a moment's prayer, and
try again.   120

    [Doctor] prays. Charmante claps the glass with the emperor°
    on it [onto the telescope. Doctor] looks in, and sees it

DOCTOR It is too much, too much for mortal eyes! I see a monarch
seated on a throne; but seems most sad and pensive.

CHARMANTE Forbear then, sir, for now his love-fit's on, and then he
would be private.

DOCTOR His love-fit, sir!   125

CHARMANTE Aye, sir, the emperor's in love with some fair mortal.

DOCTOR And can he not command her?

CHARMANTE Yes, but her quality being too mean, he struggles,
though a king, 'twixt love and honour.

DOCTOR It were too much to know the mortal, sir?   130

CHARMANTE 'Tis yet unknown, sir, to the cabalists, who now are
using all their arts to find her, and serve his majesty; but now my
great affair deprives me of you. Tomorrow, sir, I'll wait on you
again; and now I've tried your virtue, tell you wonders.

DOCTOR I humbly kiss your hands, most learned sir.   135

    Charmante goes out. Doctor waits on him to the door, and
    returns; [enter] to him Scaramouch. All this while Harlequin
    was hid in the hedges,° peeping now and then, and when his
    master went out he was left behind

SCARAMOUCH [aside] So, so, Don Charmante has played his part
most exquisitely; I'll in and see how it works in his pericranium.
[To Doctor] Did you call, sir?

DOCTOR Scaramouch, I have for thy singular wit and honesty, always
    had a tenderness for thee above that of a master to a servant.   140
SCARAMOUCH I must confess it, sir.
DOCTOR Thou hast virtue and merit that deserves much.
SCARAMOUCH Oh lord, sir!
DOCTOR And I may make thee great: all I require, is, that thou wilt
    double thy diligent care of my daughter and my niece, for there   145
    are mighty things designed for them, if we can keep 'em from the
    sight of man.
SCARAMOUCH The sight of man, sir!
DOCTOR Aye, and the very thoughts of man.
SCARAMOUCH What antidote is there to be given to a young wench,   150
    against the disease of love and longing?
DOCTOR Do you your part, and because I know thee discreet and
    very secret, I will hereafter discover wonders to thee. On pain of
    life, look to the girls; that's your charge.
SCARAMOUCH Doubt me not, sir, and I hope your reverence will   155
    reward my faithful service with Mopsophil, your daughter's
    governante, who is rich, and has long had my affection, sir.
HARLEQUIN (*peeping, cries*) Oh, traitor!
DOCTOR Set not thy heart on transitories, mortal,° there are better
    things in store: besides, I have promised her to a farmer for his   160
    son. Come in with me, and bring the telescope.
        Exeunt Doctor and Scaramouch. Harlequin comes out on the
        stage°
HARLEQUIN My mistress Mopsophil to marry a farmer's son!
    What, am I then forsaken, abandoned by the false fair one!
    If I have honour, I must die with rage;
    Reproaching gently, and complaining madly.   165
    It is resolved, I'll hang myself. No: when did I ever hear of a hero
    that hanged himself? No, 'tis the death of rogues. What if I drown
    myself? No: useless dogs and puppies are drowned; a pistol or a
    caper on my own sword° would look more nobly, but that I have
    a natural aversion to pain. Besides, it is as vulgar as rat's-bane, or   170
    the slicing of the weasand. No, I'll die a death uncommon, and
    leave behind me an eternal fame. I have somewhere read in an
    author, either ancient or modern, of a man that laughed to death.
    I am very ticklish, and am resolved to die that death. Oh
    Mopsophil, my cruel Mopsophil!   175
        Pulls off his hat, sword, and shoes
    —And now, farewell the world, fond love, and mortal cares.

*[Harlequin] falls to tickle himself,° his head, his ears, his
arm-pits, hands, sides, and soles of his feet; making ridiculous
cries and noises of laughing several ways, with antic leaps and
skips; at last falls down as dead. Enter Scaramouch*

SCARAMOUCH Harlequin was left in the garden, I'll tell him the news
of Mopsophil.

Going forward, [Scaramouch] tumbles over [Harlequin]
Ha, what's here? Harlequin dead!

[Scaramouch] heaving him up, [Harlequin] flies in a rage

HARLEQUIN Who is't that thus would rob me of my honour?   180

SCARAMOUCH Honour? Why, I thought thou'dst been dead.

HARLEQUIN Why so I was, and the most agreeably dead.

SCARAMOUCH I came to bemoan with thee the common° loss of our
mistress.

HARLEQUIN I know it, sir, I know it, and that thou'rt as false as she: 185
was't not a covenant between us, that neither should take advantage of the other, but both should have fair play? And yet you
basely went to undermine me, and ask her of the doctor! But since
she's gone, I scorn to quarrel for her; but let's, like loving brothers,
hand in hand, leap from some precipice into the sea.   190

SCARAMOUCH What, and spoil all my clothes? I thank you for that;
no, I have a newer way: you know I lodge four pair of stairs high,
let's ascend thither, and after saying our prayers—

HARLEQUIN Prayers! I never heard of a dying hero that ever prayed.

SCARAMOUCH Well, I'll not stand with you° for a trifle. Being come   195
up, I'll open the casement, take you by the heels, and fling you out
into the street; after which, you have no more to do, but to come
up and throw me down in my turn.

HARLEQUIN The achievement's great and new; but now I think on't,
I'm resolved to hear my sentence from the mouth of the perfidious   200
trollop, for yet I cannot credit it.

I'll to the gipsy, though I venture banging,
To be undeceived, 'tis hardly worth the hanging.

Exeunt

[1.3]

The chamber of Bellemante

Enter Scaramouch, groping°

SCARAMOUCH So, I have got rid of my rival, and shall here get an opportunity to speak with Mopsophil, for hither she must come anon, to lay the young ladies' night-things in order; I'll hide myself in some corner till she come.

[Scaramouch] goes on to the further side of the stage.
Enter Harlequin, groping

HARLEQUIN So, I made my rival believe I was gone, and hid myself, 5 till I got this opportunity to steal to Mopsophil's apartment, which must be hereabouts, for from these windows she used to entertain my love.

[Harlequin] advances

SCARAMOUCH Ha, I hear a soft tread: if it were Mopsophil's, she would not come by dark. 10

Harlequin, advancing, runs against a table and almost strikes himself backwards

HARLEQUIN What was that? A table: there I may obscure myself.— (*Groping for the table*) What a devil, is it vanished?

SCARAMOUCH Devil—vanished—what can this mean? 'Tis a man's voice. If it should be my master the doctor, now, I were a dead man! He can't see me; and I'll put myself into such a posture, 15 that if he feel me, he shall as soon take me for a church spout as a man.

[Scaramouch] puts himself into a posture ridiculous, his arms akimbo, his knees wide open, his backside almost touching the ground, his mouth stretched wide, and his eyes staring. Harlequin, groping, thrusts his hand into [Scaramouch's] mouth. [Scaramouch] bites him. [Harlequin] dares not cry out

HARLEQUIN Ha, what's this? All mouth, with twenty rows of teeth. Now dare not I cry out, lest the doctor should come, find me here, and kill me. I'll try if it be mortal. 20

Making damnable faces and signs of pain, [Harlequin] draws a dagger. Scaramouch feels the point of it, and shrinks back, letting go his hand

SCARAMOUCH Who the devil can this be? I felt a poniard, and am glad I saved my skin from pinking.

> [*Scaramouch*] *steals out. Harlequin, groping about, finds the*
> *table, on which there is a carpet, and creeps under it,*
> *listening. Enter Bellemante, with a candle in one hand, and a*
> *book in the other*

BELLEMANTE I am in a *belle* humour for poetry tonight. I'll make
some boremes° on love.

> [*Bellemante*] *writes and studies*

'Out of a great curiosity,   25
A shepherd did demand of me.'
—No, no: 'A shepherd this implored of me'—

> [*She*] *scratches out* [*the words*]*, and writes anew*

Aye, aye, so it shall go.
'Tell me, said he, can you resign?'
—Resign, aye, what shall rhyme to resign? 'Tell me, said he'—   30

> *She lays down the tablets, and walks about. Harlequin peeps*
> *from under the table, takes the book, writes in it, and lays it*
> *up before she can turn.* [*She*] *reads*

Aye, aye, so it shall be.—
'Tell me, said he, my Bellemante,
Will you be kind to your Charmante?'

> [*She*] *reads those two lines, and is amazed*

—Ha! Heavens! what's this? I am amazed! And yet I'll venture
once more.   35

> [*She*] *writes and studies,* [*and*] *writes* [*again*]

'I blushed, and veiled my wishing eyes.'

> [*She*] *lays down the book, and walks as before*

'Wishing eyes'—

> *Harlequin writes as before. She turns and takes the tablet°*

'And answered only with my sighs.'—Ha, what is this?
Witchcraft, or some divinity of love? Some cupid sure invisible.
Once more I'll try the charm.   40

> *Bellemante writes*

'Could I a better way my love impart—'

> [*She*] *studies and walks*

'Impart—'

> *He writes as before.* [*She reads*]°

'And, without speaking, tell him all my heart?'
—'Tis here again, but where's the hand that writ it?

> [*She*] *looks about*

The little deity that will be seen   45
But only in his miracles. It cannot be a devil,

For here's no sin nor mischief in all this.

> *Enter Charmante. [Bellemante] hides the tablet; he steps to
> her and snatches it from her, and reads*

CHARMANTE (*reads*) 'Out of a great curiosity,
A shepherd this implored of me:
Tell me, said he, my Bellemante,   50
Will you be kind to your Charmante?
I blushed, and veiled my wishing eyes,
And answered only with my sighs:
Could I a better way my love impart,
And, without speaking, tell him all my heart?'   55
—Whose is this different character?° (*Looks angry*)

BELLEMANTE 'Tis yours, for aught I know.

CHARMANTE Away, my name was put here for a blind. What
rhyming fop have you been clubbing wit withal?

BELLEMANTE Ah, *mon Dieu*! Charmante jealous!   60

CHARMANTE Have I not cause? Who writ these boremes?

BELLEMANTE Some kind assisting deity, for aught I know.

CHARMANTE Some kind assisting coxcomb, that I know.
The ink's yet wet, the spark is near I find.

BELLEMANTE Ah, *malheureuse*!° How was I mistaken in this   65
man!

CHARMANTE Mistaken! What, did you take me for an easy fool to be
imposed upon? One that would be cuckolded by every feathered
fool that you should call a *beau, un gallant homme*? 'Sdeath! Who
would dote upon a fond she-fop? A vain conceited amorous   70
coquette!

> *[Charmante] goes out, [Bellemante] pulls him back. Enter
> Scaramouch, running*

SCARAMOUCH Oh, madam! hide your lover, or we are all undone.

CHARMANTE I will not hide, till I know the thing that made the
verses.

DOCTOR (*calling, as on the stairs*) Bellemante, niece! Bellemante!   75

SCARAMOUCH She's coming, sir.—Where, where shall I hide him?
Oh, the closet's open!

> *[Scaramouch] thrusts [Charmante] into the closet° by force.
> [Enter Doctor]*

DOCTOR Oh, niece! Ill luck, ill luck, I must leave you tonight; my
brother the advocate is sick, and has sent for me; 'tis three long
leagues, and dark as 'tis, I must go. They say he's dying.   80

> *[Doctor] pulls out his keys; one falls down*

Here, take my keys, and go into my study, and look over all my
papers, and bring me all those marked with a cross and figure of
three: they concern my brother and me.

> [*Bellemante*] *looks on Scaramouch, and makes pitiful signs,*
> *and goes out*

—Come, Scaramouch, and get me ready for my journey, and on
your life let not a door be opened till my return.   85

> *Exeunt* [*Doctor and Scaramouch*]. *Enter Mopsophil.*
> *Harlequin peeps from under the table*

HARLEQUIN [*aside*] Ha! Mopsophil, and alone!

MOPSOPHIL Well, 'tis a delicious thing to be rich; what a world of
lovers it invites: I have one for every hand, and the favourite for
my lips.

HARLEQUIN ([*aside*], *peeping*) Aye, him would I be glad to know.   90

MOPSOPHIL But of all my lovers, I am for the farmer's son, because
he keeps a calash; and I'll swear a coach is the most agreeable thing
about a man.

HARLEQUIN Ho, ho!

MOPSOPHIL Ah me! What's that?   95

HARLEQUIN (*answers in a shrill voice*) The ghost of a poor lover,
dwindled into a hey-ho.

> [*Harlequin*] *rises from under the table and falls at*
> [*Mopsophil's*] *feet. Scaramouch enters.* [*Mopsophil*] *runs off*
> *squeaking*

SCARAMOUCH Ha, my rival and my mistress!—Is this done like a
man of honour, Monsieur Harlequin, to take advantages to injure
me?   100

> [*Scaramouch*] *draws*

HARLEQUIN All advantages are lawful in love and war.

SCARAMOUCH 'Twas contrary to our league and covenant;° therefore
I defy thee as a traitor.

HARLEQUIN I scorn to fight with thee, because I once called thee
brother.   105

SCARAMOUCH Then thou art a poltroon, that's to say, a coward.

HARLEQUIN Coward? Nay, then I am provoked: come on.

SCARAMOUCH Pardon me, sir, I gave the coward, and you ought to
strike.

> *They go to fight ridiculously, and ever as Scaramouch passes,*
> *Harlequin leaps aside, and skips so nimbly about, he cannot*
> *touch him for his life; which after a while endeavouring in*
> *vain,* [*Scaramouch*] *lays down his sword*

If you be for dancing, sir, I have my weapons for all occasions.   110
> *Scaramouch pulls out a flute doux,° and falls to playing.*
> *Harlequin throws down his [sword], and falls a-dancing.*
> *After the dance, they shake hands*

HARLEQUIN Hey, my *bon ami*,° is not this better than duelling?

SCARAMOUCH But not altogether so heroic, sir. Well, for the future, let us have fair play; no tricks to undermine each other, but which of us is chosen to be the happy man, the other shall be content.

ELARIA (*within*) Cousin Bellemante, cousin.   115

SCARAMOUCH 'Slife, let's be gone, lest we be seen in the ladies' apartment.
> *Scaramouch slips Harlequin behind the door.° Enter Elaria*

ELARIA [*to Scaramouch*] How now, how came you here?
> [*Scaramouch*] *signs to Harlequin to go out.* [*Exit Harlequin*]

SCARAMOUCH I came to tell you, madam, my master's just taking mule to go his journey tonight, and that Don Cinthio is in the   120
street, for a lucky moment to enter in.

ELARIA But what if anyone by my father's order, or he himself, should by some chance surprise us?

SCARAMOUCH If we be, I have taken order against a discovery. I'll go see if the old gentleman be gone, and return with your   125
lover.
> [*Scaramouch*] *goes out*

ELARIA I tremble, but know not whether 'tis with fear or joy.
> *Enter Cinthio*

CINTHIO My dear Elaria!
> [*Cinthio*] *runs to embrace* [*Elaria*]; *she starts from him*
Ha; shun my arms, Elaria?

ELARIA Heavens! Why did you come so soon?   130

CINTHIO Is it too soon, whene'er 'tis safe, Elaria?

ELARIA I die with fear. Met you not Scaramouch? He went to bid you wait awhile; what shall I do?

CINTHIO Why this concern? None of the house has seen me. I saw your father taking mule.   135

ELARIA Sure you mistake; methinks I hear his voice.

DOCTOR (*below*) My key, the key of my laboratory. Why, knave, Scaramouch, where are you?

ELARIA Do you hear that, sir? Oh, I'm undone! Where shall I hide you? He approaches!   140
> [*Elaria*] *searches where to hide* [*Cinthio*]
Ha, my cousin's closet's open:° step in a little.

[Cinthio] goes in; [Elaria] puts out the candle. Enter Doctor.
She gets round the chamber to the door,° and as he advances
in, she steals out

DOCTOR Here I must have dropped it; a light, a light, there!

Enter Cinthio from the closet, pull[ing] Charmante out, they
not knowing each other

CINTHIO *[aside]* Oh, this perfidious woman! No marvel she was so
surprised and angry at my approach tonight.

CHARMANTE *[aside]* Who can this be? But I'll be prepared.   145

[Charmante] lays his hand on his sword. [Doctor] turns to the
door to call

DOCTOR Why, Scaramouch, knave, a light!

Enter Scaramouch with a light,° and seeing the two lovers
there, runs against his master, puts out the candle, and flings
him down, and falls over him. At the entrance of the candle,
Charmante slipped from Cinthio into the closet. Cinthio gropes
to find him; when Mopsophil and Elaria, hearing a great
noise, enter with a light. Cinthio, finding he was discovered,
falls to acting a madman. Scaramouch helps up the doctor,
and bows

Ha, a man, and in my house! Oh dire misfortune!—Who are you, sir?

CINTHIO Men call me Gog Magog, the spirit of power;
My right hand riches holds, my left hand honour.
Is there a city wife would be a lady?   150
Bring her to me,
Her easy cuckold shall be dubbed a knight.°

ELARIA Oh heavens! a madman, sir.

CINTHIO Is there a tawdry fop would have a title?
A rich mechanic that would be an alderman?   155
Bring 'em to me,
And I'll convert that coxcomb, and that blockhead,
Into your honour, and right worshipful.

DOCTOR Mad, stark mad!—Why, sirrah, rogue, Scaramouch: how
got this madman in?   160

While the doctor turns to Scaramouch, Cinthio speaks softly
to Elaria

CINTHIO *(aside to [Elaria])* Oh, thou perfidious maid! Who hast thou
hid in yonder conscious closet?

SCARAMOUCH Why, sir, he was brought in a chair for your advice,
but how he rambled from the parlour to this chamber, I know not.

CINTHIO Upon a wingèd horse, ycleped Pegasus,   165

Swift as the fiery racers of the sun,
I fly, I fly;
See how I mount, and cut the liquid sky.
  [*Cinthio*] *runs out*

DOCTOR Alas, poor gentleman, he's past all cure—but, sirrah, for the
  future, take you care that no young mad patients be brought into 170
  my house.

SCARAMOUCH I shall, sir; and see: [*shows the key*] here's your key you
  looked for.

DOCTOR That's well; I must be gone. Bar up the doors, and upon
  life or death let no man enter. 175
    Ex[*eunt*] *Doctor, and all* [*Elaria, Mopsophil, and*
    Scaramouch] *with him, with the light. Charmante peeps out*
    [*from the closet*], *and by degrees comes all out, listening every*
    step

CHARMANTE Who the devil could that be that pulled me from the
  closet? But at last I'm free, and the doctor's gone. I'll to Cinthio,
  and bring him to pass this night with our mistresses.
    Exit [*Charmante*]. *As he is gone off, enter Cinthio groping*

CINTHIO Now for this lucky rival, if his stars will make this last part
  of his adventure such. I hid myself in the next chamber, till I heard 180
  the doctor go, only to return to be revenged.
    [*Cinthio*] *gropes his way into the closet, with his sword drawn.*
    Enter Elaria with a light

ELARIA Scaramouch tells me Charmante is concealed in the closet,
  whom Cinthio surely has mistaken for some lover of mine, and is
  jealous; but I'll send Charmante after him, to make my peace and
  undeceive him. 185
    [*Elaria*] *goes to the door*
—Sir, sir, where are you? they are all gone, you may adventure out.
    Cinthio comes out
—Ha, Cinthio here!

CINTHIO Yes, madam, to your shame.
Now your perfidiousness is plain: false woman!
'Tis well your lover had the dexterity of escaping, I'd spoiled his 190
  making love else.
    [*Cinthio*] *gets from* [*Elaria*]; *she holds him*

ELARIA Prithee, hear me.

CINTHIO But since my ignorance of his person saves his life, live and
  possess him, till I can discover him.
    [*Cinthio*] *goes out*

ELARIA   Go, peevish fool,
         Whose jealousy believes me given to change,
         Let thy own torments be my just revenge.
         Exit

2.1

[*A room in the doctor's house*]°

An antic dance.° After the music has played, enter Elaria;
[*enter*] *to her Bellemante*

ELARIA Heavens, Bellemante! Where have you been?

BELLEMANTE Fatigued with the most disagreeable affair, for a
person of my humour, in the world. Oh, how I hate business,
which I do no more mind, than a spark does the sermon, who is
ogling his mistress at church all the while: I have been ruffling over   5
twenty reams of paper for my uncle's writings.

Enter Scaramouch

SCARAMOUCH So, so, the old gentleman is departed this wicked
world, and the house is our own for this night. Where are the
sparks? Where are the sparks?

ELARIA Nay, heaven knows.   10

BELLEMANTE How! I hope not so; I left Charmante confined to my
closet, when my uncle had like to have surprised us together. Is he
not here?

ELARIA No, he's escaped, but he has made sweet doings.

BELLEMANTE Heavens, cousin! What?   15

ELARIA My father was coming into the chamber, and had like to have
taken Cinthio with me, when, to conceal him, I put him into your
closet, not knowing of Charmante's being there, and which, in the
dark, he took for a gallant of mine. Had not my father's presence
hindered, I believe there had been murder committed; however,   20
they both escaped unknown.

SCARAMOUCH Pshaw, is this all? Lovers' quarrels are soon adjusted:
I'll to 'em, unfold the riddle, and bring 'em back. Take no care,
but go in and dress you for the ball; Mopsophil has habits which
your lovers sent to put on: the fiddles,° treat,° and all are prepared.   25

Exit Scaramouch. Enter Mopsophil

MOPSOPHIL Madam, your cousin Florinda, with a lady, is come to
visit you.

BELLEMANTE I'm glad on't; 'tis a good wench, and we'll trust her
with our mirth and secret.

They go out

[2.2]

The street

*Enter page with a flambeau,° followed by Cinthio; [Cinthio]
passes over the stage. Scaramouch follows Cinthio in a
campaign coat*

SCARAMOUCH 'Tis Cinthio.—Don Cinthio!

Scaramouch calls: [Cinthio] turns

Well, what's the quarrel? How fell ye out?

CINTHIO You may inform yourself, I believe, for these close intrigues cannot be carried out without your knowledge.

SCARAMOUCH What intrigues, sir? Be quick, for I'm in haste.   5

CINTHIO Who was the lover I surprised i'th' closet?

SCARAMOUCH *Deceptio visus,°* sir: the error of the eyes.

CINTHIO Thou dog, I felt him, too; but since the rascal escaped me,
I'll be revenged on thee.

*[Cinthio] goes to beat [Scaramouch]; he, running away, runs
against Harlequin, who is entering with Charmante, and is
like to throw them both down*

CHARMANTE Ha, what's the matter here?   10

SCARAMOUCH Signor Don Charmante.

*Then [Scaramouch] struts courageously in with [Charmante
and Harlequin]*

CHARMANTE What, Cinthio in a rage? Who's the unlucky object?

CINTHIO All man and womankind: Elaria's false.

CHARMANTE Elaria false! take heed, sure her nice virtue
Is proof against the vices of her sex.   15
Say rather Bellemante;
She who by nature's light and wavering.
The town contains not such a false impertinent.
This evening I surprised her in her chamber
Writing of verses, and between her lines,   20
Some spark had newly penned his proper stuff.°
Curse of the jilt, I'll be her fool no more.

HARLEQUIN I doubt you are mistaken in that, sir, for 'twas I was the
spark that writ the proper stuff—to do you service.

CHARMANTE Thou!   25

SCARAMOUCH Aye, we that spend our lives and fortunes here to
serve you—to be used like pimps and scoundrels. [*To Cinthio*]

298

Come, sir, satisfy him who 'twas was hid i'th' closet when he came in and found you.

CINTHIO Ha, is't possible? Was it Charmante?

CHARMANTE Was it you, Cinthio? Pox on't, what fools are we, we could not know one another by instinct?

SCARAMOUCH Well, well, dispute no more this clear case, but let's hasten to your mistresses.

CINTHIO I'm ashamed to appear before Elaria.

CHARMANTE And I to Bellemante.

SCARAMOUCH Come, come, take heart of grace; pull your hats down over your eyes; put your arms across;° sigh and look scurvily;° your simple looks are ever a token of repentance. Come, come along.

Exeunt

[2.3]

The inside of the house. The front of the scene is only a curtain or hangings to be drawn up at pleasure°

Enter Elaria, Bellemante, Mopsophil, [Florinda], and ladies, dressed in masking habits

ELARIA I am extremely pleased with these habits, cousin.

BELLEMANTE They are *à la* gothic° and *uncommune*.°

FLORINDA Your lovers have a very good fancy, cousin, I long to see 'em.

ELARIA And so do I. I wonder Scaramouch stays so, and what success he has.

BELLEMANTE You have no cause to doubt, you can so easily acquit yourself; but I, what shall I do, who can no more imagine who should write those boremes, than who I shall love next, if I break off with Charmante?

FLORINDA If he be a man of honour, cousin, when a maid protests her innocence—

BELLEMANTE Aye, but he's a man of wit too, cousin, and knows when women protest most, they likely lie most.

ELARIA Most commonly, for truth needs no asseveration.

BELLEMANTE That's according to the disposition of your lover, for some believe you most, when you most abuse and cheat 'em; some are so obstinate, they would damn a woman with protesting, before she can convince 'em.

ELARIA Such a one is not worth convincing; I would not make the world wise at the expense of a virtue.   20

BELLEMANTE Nay, he shall e'en remain as heaven made him for me, since there are men enough for all uses.

> *Enter Charmante and Cinthio, dressed in their gothic habits,*
> *Scaramouch, Harlequin, and music.° Charmante and Cinthio*
> *kneel*

CINTHIO Can you forgive us?

> *Elaria takes him up*

BELLEMANTE That, Cinthio, you're convinced, I do not wonder; but how Charmante's goodness is inspired, I know not.   25

> *[Bellemante] takes [Charmante] up*

CHARMANTE Let it suffice I'm satisfied, my Bellemante.

ELARIA Pray know my cousin Florinda.

> *[Cinthio and Charmante] salute [Florinda]*

BELLEMANTE Come, let's not lose time, since we are all friends.

CHARMANTE The best use we can make of it, is to talk of love.

BELLEMANTE Oh, we shall have time enough for that hereafter.   30
Besides, you may make love in dancing as well as in sitting; you may gaze, sigh, and press the hand, and now and then receive a kiss; what would you more?

CHARMANTE Yes, wish a little more.

BELLEMANTE We were unreasonable to forbid you that cold joy; nor   35
shall you wish long in vain, if you bring matters so about, to get us with my uncle's consent.

ELARIA Our fortunes depending solely on his pleasure, which is too considerable to lose.

CINTHIO All things are ordered as I have written you at large; our   40
scenes and all our properties are ready; we have no more to do but to banter the old gentleman into a little more faith, which the next visit of our new cabalist, Charmante, will complete.

> *The music plays. Enter some antics,° and dance. [Elaria,*
> *Bellemante, Cinthio, and Charmante] all sit still the while*

ELARIA Your dancers have performed well, but 'twere fit we knew whom we trusted with this evening's intrigue.   45

CINTHIO Those, madam, who are to assist us in carrying on a greater intrigue, the gaining of you. They are our kinsmen.

ELARIA Then they are doubly welcome.

> *Here is a song in dialogue, with flute doux and harpsicals,°*
> *[between a] shepherd and shepherdess; which ended, they all*
> *dance a figure dance°*

CINTHIO Hark, what noise is that? sure 'tis in the next room.

DOCTOR (*within*) Scaramouch, Scaramouch!   50

Scaramouch runs to the door, and holds it fast

SCARAMOUCH Ha! The devil in the likeness of my old master's voice, for 'tis impossible it should be he himself.

CHARMANTE If it be he, how got he in? Did you not secure the doors?

ELARIA He always has a key to open 'em. Oh! what shall we do? There's no escaping him; he's in the next room, through which 55 you are to pass.

DOCTOR Scaramouch, knave, where are you?

SCARAMOUCH 'Tis he, 'tis he: follow me, all!

[Scaramouch] goes with all the company behind the front curtain

DOCTOR (*without*) I tell you, sirrah, I heard the noise of fiddles.

PETER (*without*) No, surely, sir, 'twas a mistake.   60

Knocking [is heard] at the door. Scaramouch, having placed them all in the hanging,° in which they make the figures, where they stand without motion in postures, comes out. He opens the door with a candle in his hand. Enter the doctor and Peter with a light

SCARAMOUCH Bless me, sir! Is it you or your ghost?

DOCTOR 'Twere good for you, sir, if I were a thing of air; but as I am a substantial mortal, I will lay it on as substantially!

[The doctor] canes [Scaramouch, who] cries

SCARAMOUCH What d'ye mean, sir? What d'ye mean?

DOCTOR Sirrah, must I stand waiting your leisure, while you are 65 roguing here? I will reward ye.

[The doctor] beats [Scaramouch]

SCARAMOUCH Aye, and I shall deserve it richly, sir, when you know all.

DOCTOR I guess all, sirrah, and I heard all, and you shall be rewarded for all. Where have you hid the fiddles, you rogue?   70

SCARAMOUCH Fiddles, sir!

DOCTOR Aye, fiddles, knave.

SCARAMOUCH Fiddles, sir! Where?

DOCTOR Here; here I heard 'em, thou false steward of thy master's treasure.   75

SCARAMOUCH Fiddles, sir! Sure 'twas wind got into your head, and whistled in your ears, riding so late, sir.

DOCTOR Aye, thou false varlet, there's another debt I owe thee, for bringing me so damnable a lie: my brother's well; I met his valet but a league from town, and found thy roguery out.   80

[The doctor] beats [Scaramouch, who] cries

SCARAMOUCH Is this the reward I have for being so diligent since you went?

DOCTOR In what, thou villain? In what?

The curtain is drawn up, and discovers the hangings where all of them stand

SCARAMOUCH Why, look you, sir, I have, to surprise you with pleasure, against° you came home, been putting up this piece of tapestry;° the best in Italy, for the rareness of the figures, sir. 85

DOCTOR Ha! Hum, it is indeed a stately piece of work; how came I by 'em?

SCARAMOUCH 'Twas sent your reverence from the virtuoso,° or some of the cabalists. 90

DOCTOR I must confess, the workmanship is excellent; but still I do insist I heard the music.

SCARAMOUCH 'Twas then the tuning of the spheres;° some serenade, sir, from the inhabitants of the moon.

DOCTOR Hum, from the moon; and that may be. 95

SCARAMOUCH Lord, d'ye think I would deceive your reverence?

DOCTOR (*aside*) From the moon, a serenade. I see no signs on't here, indeed it must be so. I'll think on't more at leisure.

[Doctor] looks on the hangings

—Prithee, what story's this?°

SCARAMOUCH Why, sir,—'tis— 100

DOCTOR Hold up the candles higher, and nearer.

Peter and Scaramouch hold candles near. [Doctor] takes a perspective° and looks through it; and coming nearer, Harlequin, who is placed on a tree° in the hangings, hits him on the head with his truncheon. [Doctor] starts, and looks about. [Harlequin] sits still

SCARAMOUCH Sir—

DOCTOR What was that struck me?

SCARAMOUCH Struck you, sir? Imagination.

DOCTOR Can my imagination feel, sirrah? 105

SCARAMOUCH Oh, the most tenderly of any part about one, sir!

DOCTOR Hum, that may be.

SCARAMOUCH Are you a great philosopher, and know not that, sir?

DOCTOR (*aside*) This fellow has a glimpse of profundity.

[Doctor] looks [at the hangings] again

—I like the figures well. 110

SCARAMOUCH You will, when you see 'em by daylight, sir.

Harlequin hits [doctor] again. The doctor sees him

DOCTOR Ha; is that imagination, too? Betrayed, betrayed, undone!
Run for my pistols, call up my servants, Peter; a plot upon my
daughter and my niece!

> *[Doctor] runs out with Peter. Scaramouch puts out the candle.*
> *[The company] come[s] out of the hanging, which is drawn*
> *away. [Scaramouch] places [everyone] in a row just at the*
> *entrance°*

SCARAMOUCH Here, here, fear nothing; hold by each other, that   115
when I go out, all may go; that is, slip out when you hear the
doctor is come in again, which he will certainly do, and all depart
to your respective lodgings.

CINTHIO And leave thee to bear the brunt?

SCARAMOUCH Take you no care for that; I'll put it into my bill of   120
charges, and be paid all together.

> *Enter the doctor with pistols, and Peter*

DOCTOR What, by dark? That shall not save you, villains, traitors to
my glory and repose.—Peter, hold fast the door, let none escape.°

> *They all slip out [except Mopsophil,° who remains hiding]*

PETER I'll warrant you, sir.

> *Doctor gropes about, then stamps and calls*

DOCTOR Lights there, lights! I'm sure they could not 'scape.   125

PETER Impossible, sir.

> *Enter Scaramouch undressed in his shirt, with a light, [and]*
> *starts*

SCARAMOUCH Bless me! What's here?

DOCTOR (*amazed to see him enter so*) Ha! Who art thou?

SCARAMOUCH I? Who the devil are you, an you go to that?

> *[Scaramouch] rubs his eyes, and brings the candle nearer.*
> *Looks on [the doctor]*

—Mercy upon us! Why, what, is't you, sir, returned so soon?   130

DOCTOR (*looking sometimes on [Scaramouch], sometimes about*) Returned!

SCARAMOUCH Aye, sir, did you not go out of town last night, to your
brother the advocate?

DOCTOR Thou villain, thou question'st me, as if thou knew'st not
that I was returned.   135

SCARAMOUCH I know, sir? how should I know? I'm sure I am but
just waked from the sweetest dream—

DOCTOR You dream still, sirrah, but I shall wake your rogueship. Were
you not here but now, showing me a piece of tapestry, you villain?

SCARAMOUCH Tapestry?   140

Mopsophil [is] listening all the while

DOCTOR (*offering a pistol*) Yes, rogue, yes, for which I'll have thy life!

SCARAMOUCH Are you stark mad, sir, or do I dream still?

DOCTOR Tell me, and tell me quickly, rogue, who were those traitors that were hid but now in the disguise of a piece of hangings?

[Doctor] holds the pistol to [Scaramouch's] breast

SCARAMOUCH Bless me! You amaze me, sir. What conformity has   145
every word you say, to my rare dream! Pray let me feel you, sir;
are you human?

DOCTOR You shall feel I am, sirrah, if thou confess not.

SCARAMOUCH Confess, sir! What should I confess? I understand not
your cabalistical language, but in mine, I confess that you have   150
waked me from the rarest dream: where methought the emperor
of the moon world was in our house, dancing and revelling; and
methoughts his grace was fallen desperately in love with Mistress
Elaria, and that his brother, the prince, sir, of Thunderland, was
also in love with Mistress Bellemante; and methoughts they   155
descended to court 'em in your absence. And that at last you
surprised 'em, and that they transformed themselves into a suit of
hangings to deceive you. But at last, methought you grew angry at
something, and they all fled to heaven again; and after a deal of
thunder and lightning, I waked, sir, and hearing human voices   160
here, came to see what the matter was.

*This while the doctor lessens his signs of rage by degrees, and
at last stands in deep contemplation*

DOCTOR May I credit this?

SCARAMOUCH Credit it! By all the honour of your house, by my
unseparable veneration for the mathematics, 'tis true, sir.

DOCTOR [*aside*] That famous Rosicrucian, who yesterday visited me,   165
told me the emperor of the moon was in love with a fair mortal.
This dream is inspiration in this fellow; he must have wondrous
virtue in him, to be worthy of these divine intelligences. But if that
mortal should be Elaria! but no more, I dare not yet suppose it.
Perhaps the thing was real and no dream, for oftentimes the   170
grosser part is hurried away in sleep, by the force of imagination,
and is wonderfully agitated. This fellow might be present in his
sleep; of this we've frequent instances. I'll to my daughter and my
niece, and hear what knowledge they may have of this.

MOPSOPHIL [*aside*] Will you so? I'll secure you, the frolic shall go   175
round.°

[Exit Mopsophil]°

DOCTOR Scaramouch, if you have not deceived me in this matter, time will convince me farther; if it rest here, I shall believe you false.

SCARAMOUCH Good sir, suspend your judgement and your anger, then.   180

DOCTOR I'll do't. Go back to bed.

SCARAMOUCH No, sir; 'tis morning now, and I'm up for all day.

    Exeunt Doctor and Peter

This madness is a pretty sort of a pleasant disease, when it tickles but in one vein. Why, here's my master now: as great a scholar, as grave and wise a man, in all argument and discourse, as can be met   185
with; yet name but the moon, and he runs into ridicule, and grows as mad as the wind.

    Well doctor, if thou canst be madder yet,
    We'll find a medicine that shall cure your fit—
    Better than all Galenists.°   190

    Exit

[2.4]

    Scene draws off [to show Bellemante's chamber,° and]
    discovers Elaria, Bellemante, and Mopsophil in night-gowns

MOPSOPHIL You have your lessons; stand to it bravely, and the town's our own, madam.

    [Elaria and Bellemante] put themselves in postures of sleeping,
    leaning on the table, Mopsophil lying at their feet. Enter
    Doctor, softly

DOCTOR Ha, not in bed! This gives me mortal fears.

BELLEMANTE (*speak[ing] as in her sleep*) Ah, prince—

DOCTOR Ha, prince!   5

    [Doctor] goes nearer and listens

BELLEMANTE (*in a feigned voice*) How little faith I give to all your courtship, who leaves our orb so soon.

DOCTOR Ha, said she orb?

    [Doctor] goes nearer

BELLEMANTE But since you are of a celestial race,
And easily can penetrate   10
Into the utmost limits of the thought,
Why should I fear to tell you of your conquest?
—And thus implore your aid.

*[Bellemante] rises and runs to the doctor. [She] kneels, and
holds him fast. He shows signs of joy*

DOCTOR I am ravished!

BELLEMANTE Ah, prince divine, take pity on a mortal—   15

DOCTOR I am rapt!

BELLEMANTE And take me with you to the world above.

DOCTOR (*leaping, and jumping from her hands*) The moon, the moon
she means; I am transported, overjoyed, and ecstasied!

[Bellemante] seems to wake

BELLEMANTE Ha, my uncle come again to interrupt us!   20

DOCTOR Hide nothing from me, my dear Bellemante, since all
already is discovered to me, and more.

[Elaria seems to wake]

ELARIA Oh, why have you waked me from the softest dream that
ever maid was blessed with?

DOCTOR (*with over-joy*) What—what, my best Elaria?   25

ELARIA Methought I entertained a demi-god, one of the gay inhabitants of the moon.

BELLEMANTE I'm sure mine was no dream: I waked, I heard, I saw,
I spoke; and danced to the music of the spheres; and methought
my glorious lover tied a diamond chain about my arm—(*shows her*   30
arm) and see, 'tis all substantial.

ELARIA And mine a ring, of more than mortal lustre.

DOCTOR ([*aside*], *stifling his joy*) Heaven keep me moderate, lest
excess of joy should make my virtue less!

[*To Elaria and Bellemante*] There is a wondrous mystery in this.   35
A mighty blessing does attend your fates.
Go in, and pray to the chaste powers above
To give you virtue fit for such rewards.

[Elaria, Bellemante, and Mopsophil] go in

—How this agrees with what the learned cabalist informed me of
last night! He said that great Iredonozar, the emperor of the moon,   40
was enamoured on a fair mortal. It must be so; and either he
descended to court my daughter personally, which, for the rareness
of the novelty, she takes to be a dream, or else what they and I
beheld was visionary, by way of a sublime intelligence.° And,
possibly, 'tis only thus the people of that world converse with   45
mortals. I must be satisfied in this main point of deep philosophy.

I'll to my study, for I cannot rest,
Till I this weighty mystery have discussed.

Exit very gravely

[2.5]

The garden

Enter Scaramouch with a ladder

SCARAMOUCH Though I am come off *en cavalier*° with my master, I
am not with my mistress, whom I promised to console this night,
and 'tis° but just I should make good this morning; 'twill be rude
to surprise her sleeping, and more gallant to wake her with a
serenade at her window.   5

> *[Scaramouch] sets the ladder to [Mopsophil's] window,° fetches*
> *his lute, and goes up the ladder. He plays and sings this song*

When maidens are young and in their spring
Of pleasure, of pleasure, let 'em take their full swing,
    Full swing, full swing,
      And love, and dance, and play, and sing.
      For Silvia, believe it, when youth is done,   10
There's nought but hum drum, hum drum, hum drum;
There's nought but hum drum, hum drum, hum drum.

Then Silvia be wise, be wise, be wise,
Though painting and dressing, for a while, are supplies,
    And may surprise;   15
      But when the fire's going out in your eyes,
      It twinkles, it twinkles, it twinkles, and dies.
And then to hear love, to hear love from you,
I'd as lief hear an owl cry, wit to woo,
    Wit to woo, wit to woo.   20

Enter Mopsophil above

MOPSOPHIL What woeful ditty-making mortal's this,
That ere the lark her early note has sung,
Does doleful love beneath my casement thrum?
—Ah, Signor Scaramouch, is it you?

SCARAMOUCH Who should it be, that takes such pains to sue?   25

MOPSOPHIL Ah, lover most true blue!°

Enter Harlequin in women's clothes

HARLEQUIN *[aside]* If I can now but get admittance, I shall not only
deliver the young ladies their letters from their lovers, but get
some opportunity, in this disguise, to slip this billet doux into
Mopsophil's hand, and bob my comrade Scaramouch. Ha, what do   30
I see? My mistress at the window, courting my rival! Ah, gipsy*!*

SCARAMOUCH But we lose precious time, since you design me a kind
hour in your chamber.

HARLEQUIN [*aside*] Ah, traitor!

MOPSOPHIL You'll be sure to keep it from Harlequin.   35

HARLEQUIN [*aside*] Ah yes; he, (hang him, fool), he takes you for a
saint.

SCARAMOUCH Harlequin! Hang him, shotten herring.°

HARLEQUIN [*aside*] Aye, a cully, a noddy.

MOPSOPHIL A mere zany.°   40

HARLEQUIN [*aside*] Ah, hard-hearted Turk!

MOPSOPHIL Fit for nothing but a cuckold.

HARLEQUIN Monster of ingratitude! How shall I be revenged?
      [*As*] *Scaramouch* [*is*] *going over the balcony,* [*Harlequin*]
      cries out in a woman's voice
—Hold, hold, thou perjured traitor!

MOPSOPHIL Ha, discovered! A woman in the garden!   45

HARLEQUIN Come down, come down, thou false perfidious
wretch!

SCARAMOUCH Who, in the devil's name, art thou? And to whom
dost thou speak?

HARLEQUIN (*bawling out*) To thee, thou false deceiver, that hast   50
broke thy vows, thy lawful vows of wedlock; (*crying*) oh, oh, that
I should live to see the day!

SCARAMOUCH Who mean you, woman?

HARLEQUIN Whom should I mean, but thou—my lawful spouse?

MOPSOPHIL Oh, villain! Lawful spouse! Let me come to her.   55
      Scaramouch comes down [*the ladder*]*, as Mopsophil flings out*
      of the balcony°

SCARAMOUCH The woman's mad! [*To Harlequin*] Hark'ee, jade, how
long have you been thus distracted?

HARLEQUIN E'er since I loved and trusted thee, false varlet. See
here: the witness of my love and shame.
      [*Harlequin*] *bawls, and points to 'her' belly. Just then*
      Mopsophil enters

MOPSOPHIL How! with child! [*To Scaramouch*] Out, villain, was I   60
made a property?°

SCARAMOUCH Hear me.

HARLEQUIN Oh, thou heathen Christian! Was not one woman
enough?

MOPSOPHIL Aye, sirrah, answer to that!   65

SCARAMOUCH [*aside*] I shall be sacrificed.

MOPSOPHIL I am resolved to marry tomorrow, either to the apothecary or the farmer, men I never saw, to be revenged on thee, thou
termagant° infidel.°

Enter the doctor

DOCTOR What noise, what out-cry, what tumult's this? 70

HARLEQUIN Ha, the doctor! What shall I do?

[Harlequin] gets to the door. Scaramouch pulls 'her' in

DOCTOR *[aside]* A woman! Some bawd, I am sure. *[To Harlequin]*
Woman, what's your business here, ha?

HARLEQUIN I came, an't like your signorship, to madam the governante here, to serve her in the quality of a *fille de chambre*,° to the 75
young ladies.

DOCTOR A *fille de chambre*! *[Aside]* 'Tis so, a she-pimp.

HARLEQUIN Ah, signor!

[Harlequin] makes his little dapper leg° instead of a curtsey

DOCTOR How now, what, do you mock me?

HARLEQUIN Oh, signor! 80

[Harlequin] gets nearer the door

MOPSOPHIL Stay, stay, mistress; and what service are you able to do
the signor's daughters?

HARLEQUIN Is this signor Doctor Baliardo, Madam?

MOPSOPHIL Yes.

HARLEQUIN Oh! He's a very handsome gentleman, indeed. 85

DOCTOR Aye, aye; what service can you do, mistress?

HARLEQUIN Why, signor, I can tie a cravat the best of any person in
Naples, and I can comb a periwig—and I can—

DOCTOR Very proper service for young ladies; you, I believe, have
been *fille de chambre* to some young cavaliers. 90

HARLEQUIN Most true, signor; why should not the cavaliers keep
filles de chambre, as well as great ladies *valets de chambre*?

DOCTOR Indeed, 'tis equally reasonable. *(Aside)* 'Tis a bawd. *[To
Harlequin]* But have you never served ladies?

HARLEQUIN Oh yes! I served a parson's wife. 95

DOCTOR Is that a great lady?

HARLEQUIN Aye, surely, sir, what is she else? for she wore her
mantuas of *brocade d'or*, petticoats laced up to the gathers,° her
points, her patches, paints and perfumes, and sat in the uppermost
place in the church too. 100

MOPSOPHIL But have you never served countesses and duchesses?

HARLEQUIN Oh, yes, madam! The last I served, was an alderman's
wife in the city.

MOPSOPHIL Was that a countess or a duchess?

HARLEQUIN Aye, certainly, for they have all the money; and then for   105
clothes, jewels, and rich furniture, and eating, they outdo the very
vice-reine° herself.

DOCTOR This is a very ignorant running bawd; therefore first search
her for billets doux, and then have her pumped.

HARLEQUIN Ah, signor, signor!   110

Scaramouch searches [Harlequin, and] finds letters

SCARAMOUCH [*aside*] Ha, to Elaria—and Bellemante?

[*Scaramouch*] *reads the outside* [*of the letters, which he*] *pops
into his bosom*

These are from their lovers. Ha, a note to Mopsophil! [*Aside to
Harlequin*] Oh, rogue! have I found you?

HARLEQUIN [*aside to Scaramouch*] If you have, 'tis but trick for your
trick, signor Scaramouch, and you may spare the pumping.   115

SCARAMOUCH [*aside to Harlequin*] For once, sirrah, I'll bring you off,
and deliver your letters. [*To Doctor*] Sir, do you not know who this
is? Why, 'tis a rival of mine, who put on this disguise to cheat me
of mistress Mopsophil. See, here's a billet to her.

DOCTOR What is he?   120

SCARAMOUCH A mongrel° dancing-master; therefore, sir, since all
the injury's mine, I'll pardon him for a dance, and let the agility
of his heels save his bones, with your permission, sir.

DOCTOR With all my heart, and am glad he comes off so comically.

*Harlequin dances. A knocking at the gate. Scaramouch goes
and returns*

SCARAMOUCH Sir, sir, here's the rare philosopher who was here   125
yesterday.

DOCTOR Give him entrance, and all depart.

*Enter Charmante. [Exeunt Scaramouch, Harlequin, and
Mopsophil]*

CHARMANTE Blessed be those stars, that first conducted me to so
much worth and virtue; you are their darling, sir, for whom they
wear their brightest lustre. Your fortune is established; you are   130
made, sir.

DOCTOR [*aside*] Let me contain my joy! ([*To Charmante*], *keeping in
an impatient joy*) May I be worthy, sir, to apprehend you?

CHARMANTE After long searching, watching, fasting, praying, and
using all the virtuous means in nature, whereby we solely do attain   135
the highest knowledge in philosophy; it was resolved, by strong
intelligence, you were the happy sire of that bright nymph, that

had effascinated, charmed and conquered the mighty emperor
Iredonozar, the monarch of the moon.

DOCTOR (*aside*) I am undone with joy! Ruined with transport!   140
    [*To Charmante,*] *stifling his joy, which breaks out*
Can it—can it, sir—be possible—

CHARMANTE Receive the blessing, sir, with moderation.

DOCTOR I do, sir, I do.

CHARMANTE This very night, by their great art they find,
He will descend, and show himself in glory.   145
An honour, sir, no mortal has received
This sixty hundred years.

DOCTOR (*look[ing] sad*) Hum, say you so, sir? No emperor ever
descend this sixty hundred years? (*Aside*) Was I deceived last
night?   150

CHARMANTE Oh! yes, sir, often in disguise, in several shapes and
forms, which did of old occasion so many fabulous tales of all the
shapes of Jupiter;° but never in their proper glory, sir, as emperors.
This is an honour only designed to you.

DOCTOR (*joyful*) And will his grace be here in person, sir?   155

CHARMANTE In person; and with him, a man of mighty quality, sir:
'tis thought—the prince of Thunderland; but that's but whispered,
sir, in the cabal, and that he loves your niece.

DOCTOR [*aside*] Miraculous! How this agrees with all I've seen and
heard.—Tonight, say you, sir?   160

CHARMANTE So 'tis conjectured, sir. Some of the cabalists are of
opinion that last night there was some sally from the moon.

DOCTOR About what hour, sir?

CHARMANTE The meridian of the night, sir, about the hours of
twelve or one; but who descended, or in what shape, is yet   165
uncertain.

DOCTOR This I believe, sir.

CHARMANTE Why, sir?

DOCTOR May I communicate a secret of that nature?

CHARMANTE To any of the cabalists,° but none else.   170

DOCTOR Then know: last night, my daughter and my niece were
entertained by those illustrious heroes.

CHARMANTE Who, sir? The emperor, and prince his cousin?

DOCTOR Most certain, sir. But whether they appeared in solid
bodies, or fantomical, is yet a question, for at my unlucky   175
approach, they all transformed themselves into a piece of hangings.

CHARMANTE 'Tis frequent, sir; their shapes are numerous, and 'tis
also in their power to transform all they touch, by virtue of a
certain stone they call the Ebula.°   180

DOCTOR That wondrous Ebula, which Gonsales had?

CHARMANTE The same; by virtue of which, all weight was taken
from him, and then with ease the lofty traveller flew from
Parnassus° Hill, and from Hymettus° Mount, and high Gerania,°
and Acrocorinthus,° thence to Taygetus,° so to Olympus' top,°   185
from whence he had but one step to the moon. Dizzy he grants he
was.

DOCTOR No wonder, sir; oh, happy great Gonsales!

CHARMANTE Your virtue, sir, will render you as happy; but I must
haste. This night prepare your daughter and your niece, and let   190
your house be dressed, perfumed, and clean.

DOCTOR It shall be all performed, sir.

CHARMANTE Be modest, sir, and humble in your elevation, for
nothing shows the wit so poor, as wonder, nor birth so mean, as
pride.   195

DOCTOR I humbly thank your admonition, sir, and shall, in all I can,
struggle with human frailty.

> [*The doctor*], *bare, brings Charmante to the door. Exeunt*
> [*Doctor and Charmante*]. *Enter Scaramouch, peeping, at the*
> *other door*

SCARAMOUCH So, so, all things go gloriously forward but my own
amour, and there is no convincing this obstinate woman that 'twas
that rogue Harlequin in disguise that claimed me; so that I cannot   200
so much as come to deliver the young ladies their letters from their
lovers. I must get in with this damned mistress of mine, or all our
plot will be spoiled for want of intelligence. Hum; the devil does
not use to fail me at a dead lift.° I must deliver these letters, and
I must have this wench, though but to be revenged on her for   205
abusing me. Let me see: she is resolved for the apothecary or the
farmer. Well, say no more, honest Scaramouch, thou shalt find a
friend at need of me: and if I do not fit you with a spouse, say that
a woman has out-witted me.

> *Exit*

3.1

*The street, with the town gate, where an officer stands with a
staff like a London constable*

*Enter Harlequin riding in a calash. [He] comes through the
gate towards the stage,° dressed like a gentleman sitting in
[the calash]. The officer lays hold of his horse°*

OFFICER Hold, hold, sir; you, I suppose, know the customs that are
due to this city of Naples, from all persons that pass the gates in
coach, chariot, calash, or *siège volant?°*

HARLEQUIN I am not ignorant of the custom, sir, but what's that to
me?   5

OFFICER Not to you, sir! Why, what privilege have you above the rest?

HARLEQUIN Privilege, for what, sir?

OFFICER Why, for passing, sir, with any of the before-named
carriages.

HARLEQUIN Art mad? Dost not see I am a plain baker, and this   10
my cart, that comes to carry bread for the viceroy's, and the city's
use? Ha!

OFFICER Are you mad, sir, to think I cannot see a gentleman farmer
and a calash, from a baker and a cart?

HARLEQUIN Drunk, by this day; and so early, too? Oh, you're a   15
special officer! Unhand my horse, sirrah, or you shall pay for all
the damage you do me.

OFFICER Hey day! Here's a fine cheat upon the viceroy. Sir, pay me,
or I'll seize your horse.

Harlequin strikes [the officer]. They scuffle a little

Nay, an you be so brisk, I'll call the clerk from his office.—(*Calls*) 20
Mr Clerk, Mr Clerk!

*[The officer] goes to the entrance to call the clerk; [in] the
meantime Harlequin whips a frock over himself, and puts
down the hind part of the chariot, and then 'tis a cart.° Enter
clerk*

CLERK What's the matter here?

OFFICER Here's a fellow, sir, will persuade me his calash is a cart,
and refuses the customs for passing the gate.

CLERK A calash—where? I see only a carter and his cart.   25

The officer looks on [Harlequin]

OFFICER Ha! What a devil, was I blind?

HARLEQUIN Mr Clerk, I am a baker, that come with bread to sell, and this fellow here has stopped me this hour, and made me lose the sale of my ware; and being drunk, will out-face me I am a farmer, and this cart a calash.   30

CLERK He's in an error, friend, pass on.

HARLEQUIN No, sir, I'll have satisfaction first, or the viceroy shall know how he's served by drunken officers, that nuisance to a civil government.

CLERK What do you demand, friend?   35

HARLEQUIN Demand? I demand a crown, sir.

OFFICER This is very hard, Mr Clerk: if ever I saw in my life, I thought I saw a gentleman and a calash.

CLERK Come, come, gratify him, and see better hereafter.

OFFICER Here, sir; if I must, I must.   40
          [*The officer*] *gives* [*Harlequin*] *a crown*

CLERK Pass on, friend.
          Exit clerk. Harlequin, unseen [*by the officer*], *puts up the*
          back of his calash, and whips off his frock, and goes to drive
          on. The officer looks on him, and stops him again

OFFICER Hum, I'll swear it is a calash.—Mr Clerk, Mr Clerk, come back, come back!
          [*The officer*] *runs out to call* [*the clerk*]. [*Harlequin*] *changes*
          as before. Enter officer and clerk

OFFICER Come, sir, let your own eyes convince you, sir.

CLERK Convince me, of what, you sot?   45

OFFICER That this is a gentleman, and that a—ha!
          [*The officer*] *looks about on Harlequin*

CLERK Stark drunk, sirrah! If you trouble me at every mistake of yours thus, you shall quit your office.

OFFICER I beg your pardon, sir; I am a little in drink, I confess, a little blind and mad, sir. [*Aside*] This must be the devil, that's   50
certain.
          The clerk goes out. Harlequin puts up his calash again, and
          pulls off his frock and drives out
Well, now to my thinking, 'tis as plain a calash again, as ever I saw in my life, and yet I'm satisfied 'tis nothing but a cart.
          Exit

[3.2]

Scene changes to the doctor's house. The hall

Enter Scaramouch in a chair, which, set down and opened on all sides and on the top, represents an apothecary's shop,° the inside being painted with shelves and rows of pots and bottles; Scaramouch sitting in it dressed in black, with a short black cloak, a ruff, and little hat

SCARAMOUCH The devil's in't, if either the doctor, my master, or Mopsophil, know me in this disguise; and thus, I may not only gain my mistress, and out-wit Harlequin, but deliver the ladies those letters from their lovers, which I took out of his pocket this morning; and who would suspect an apothecary for a pimp? Nor can the jade Mopsophil, in honour, refuse a person of my gravity, and (*pointing to his shop*) so well set up. Hum, the doctor here first; this is not so well, but I'm prepared with impudence for all encounters.

Enter the doctor. Scaramouch salutes him gravely

—Most reverend Doctor Baliardo. (*Bows*)

DOCTOR Signor. (*Bows*)

SCARAMOUCH I might, through great pusillanimity,° blush to give you this anxiety, did I not opine you were as gracious as communitive° and eminent; and though you have no cognizance of me, your humble servant, yet I have of you, you being so greatly famed for your admirable skill, both in Galenical and Paracelsian phenomenas,° and other approved felicities in vulnerary emetics, and purgative experiences.

DOCTOR Signor, your opinion honours me. [*Aside*] A rare man this.

SCARAMOUCH And though I am at present busied in writing (those few observations I have accumulated in my peregrinations, sir), yet the ambition I aspired to, of being an ocular and aurial° witness of your singularity, made me trespass on your sublimer affairs.

DOCTOR Signor—

SCARAMOUCH Besides a violent inclination, sir, of being initiated into the denomination of your learned family, by the conjugal circumference of a matrimonial tie, with that singularly accomplished person, madam the governante of your hostel.°

DOCTOR (*aside*) Hum, a sweetheart for Mopsophil!

SCARAMOUCH And, if I may obtain your condescension to my hymenaeal propositions, I doubt not my operation with the fair one.

DOCTOR Signor, she is much honoured in the overture, and my abilities shall not be wanting to fix the concord. But have you been a traveller, sir?

SCARAMOUCH Without circumlocution, sir, I have seen all the   35
regions beneath the sun and moon.

DOCTOR Moon, sir! You never travelled thither, sir?

SCARAMOUCH Not *in propria persona*,° signor, but by speculation° I have, and made most considerable remarks on that incomparable *terra firma*,° of which I have the completest map in Christendom;   40
and which Gonsales himself omitted in his *Cosmographia of the Lunar Mundus*.°

DOCTOR A map of the *Lunar Mundus*, sir! May I crave the honour of seeing it?

SCARAMOUCH You shall, sir, together with the map of *Terra Incog-*   45
nita:° a great rarity, indeed, sir.
    Enter Bellemante

DOCTOR Jewels, sir, worth a king's ransom!

BELLEMANTE [*aside*] Ha, what figure of a thing have we here, bantering my credulous uncle? This must be some scout sent from our forlorn hope,° to discover the enemy, and bring in fresh   50
intelligence.
    [*Scaramouch winks at Bellemante*]
Hum, that wink tipped me some tidings, and she deserves not a good look, who understands not the language of the eyes. [*To the doctor*] Sir, dinner's on the table.

DOCTOR Let it wait, I am employed.   55
    [*Bellemante*] *creeps to the other side of Scaramouch, who makes signs with his hand to her*

BELLEMANTE [*aside*] Ha, 'tis so: this fellow has some novel° for us, some letters or instructions, but how to get it?
    As Scaramouch talks to the doctor, he takes the letters by degrees out of his pocket, and unseen [by the doctor], gives them to Bellemante, behind him

DOCTOR But this map, signor; I protest you have filled me with curiosity. Has it signified all things so exactly, say you?

SCARAMOUCH Omitted nothing, signor: no city, town, village or   60
villa; no castle, river, bridge, lake, spring or mineral.

DOCTOR Are any, sir, of those admirable mineral waters there, so frequent in our world?

SCARAMOUCH In abundance, sir: the famous Garamanteen,° a young Italian, sir, lately come from thence, gives us an account of an   65

excellent scaturrigo,° that has lately made an ebullition° there, in
great reputation with the lunary ladies.

DOCTOR Indeed, sir! Be pleased, signor, to solve me some queries
that may enode° some appearances° of the virtue of the water you
speak of.   70

SCARAMOUCH [aside] Pox upon him, what questions he asks; but I
must on.—Why, sir, you must know—the tincture° of this water,
upon stagnation, ceruleates,° and the crocus upon the stones
flaveces; this he observes—to be, sir, the indication of a generous°
water.°   75

DOCTOR (gravely nodding) Hum.

SCARAMOUCH Now, sir, be pleased to observe the three regions: if
they be bright, without doubt Mars is powerful; if the middle
region or camera be pallid, Filia Solis is breeding.

DOCTOR Hum.   80

SCARAMOUCH And then the third region: if the faeces be volatile, the
birth will soon come in Balneo.° This I observed also in the
laboratory of that ingenious chemist Lysidono,° and with much
pleasure animadverted that mineral of the same zenith and
nadir,° of that now so famous water in England, near that famous   85
metropolis, called Islington.°

DOCTOR Signor.

SCARAMOUCH For, sir, upon the infusion, the crow's head immediately procures the seal of Hermes; and had not Lac Virginis been
too soon sucked up, I believe we might have seen the consumma-   90
tion of Amalgama.°

> Bellemante, having got her letters, goes off. She makes signs
> to [Scaramouch] to stay° a little. He nods

DOCTOR Most likely, sir.

SCARAMOUCH But, sir, this Garamanteen relates the strangest operation of a mineral in the lunar world, that ever I heard of.

DOCTOR As how, I pray, sir?   95

SCARAMOUCH Why, sir, a water impregnated to a circulation with
prima materia;° upon my honour, sir, the strongest I ever drank of.

DOCTOR How, sir! Did you drink of it?

SCARAMOUCH I only speak the words of Garamanteen, sir. (Aside)
Pox on him, I shall be trapped.   100

DOCTOR Cry mercy, sir. (Bows)

SCARAMOUCH The lunary physicians, sir, call it urinam vulcani,° it
calybeates everyone's excrements more or less according to the
gradus of the natural calor.° To my knowledge, sir, a smith of a

very fiery constitution is grown very opulent by drinking these   105
waters.

DOCTOR How, sir, grown rich by drinking the waters, and to your
knowledge?

SCARAMOUCH [*aside*] The devil's in my tongue. [*To the doctor*] To my
knowledge, sir: for what a man of honour relates, I may safely affirm.   110

DOCTOR Excuse me, signor.

> [*The doctor*] *puts off his hat again, gravely*

SCARAMOUCH For, sir, conceive me how he grew rich: since he
drank those waters he never buys any iron, but hammers it out of
stercus proprius.°

> *Enter Bellemante with a billet*

BELLEMANTE Sir, 'tis three o'clock, and dinner will be cold.   115

> [*Bellemante*] *goes behind Scaramouch, and gives him the note,
> and goes out*

DOCTOR [*to Bellemante as she goes out*] I come, sweetheart. [*To
Scaramouch*] But this is wonderful.

SCARAMOUCH Aye, sir, and if at any time nature be too infirm, and
he prove costive,° he has no more to do, but to apply a loadstone
ad anum.°   120

DOCTOR Is't possible?

SCARAMOUCH Most true, sir, and that facilitates the journey *per
viscera.*° But I detain you, sir; another time, sir; I will now only
beg the honour of a word or two with the governante, before I go.

DOCTOR Sir, she shall wait on you, and I shall be proud of the   125
honour of your conversation.

> [*Scaramouch and doctor*] *bow. Exit doctor. Enter to*
> [*Scaramouch*] *Harlequin, dressed like a farmer, as before*

HARLEQUIN [*aside*] Hum, what have we here, a tailor, or a tumbler?

SCARAMOUCH [*aside*] Ha, who's this? Hum, what if it should be the
farmer that the doctor has promised Mopsophil to? My heart
misgives me.   130

> [*Harlequin and Scaramouch*] *look at each other a while*

—Who would you speak with, friend?

HARLEQUIN [*aside*] This is, perhaps, my rival, the apothecary. [*To
Scaramouch*] Speak with, sir, why, what's that to you?

SCARAMOUCH Have you affairs with Signor Doctor, sir?

HARLEQUIN It may be I have, it may be I have not. What then, sir?   135

> *While they seem in angry dispute, enter Mopsophil*

MOPSOPHIL [*aside*] Signor Doctor tells me I have a lover waits me;
sure it must be the farmer or the apothecary. No matter which, so

a lover, that welcomest man alive. I am resolved to take the first
good offer, though but in revenge of Harlequin and Scaramouch,
for putting tricks upon me. [*Mopsophil looks at Harlequin and*   140
Scaramouch] Ha, two of 'em!

SCARAMOUCH [*aside*] My mistress here!

> [*Harlequin and Scaramouch*] *bow and advance, both putting*
> *the other by*

MOPSOPHIL Hold, gentlemen; do not worry me. Which of you
would speak with me?

[HARLEQUIN AND SCARAMOUCH] I, I, I, madam—   145

MOSOPHIL Both of you?

[HARLEQUIN AND SCARAMOUCH] No, madam, I, I.

MOPSOPHIL If both lovers, you are both welcome; but let's have fair
play, and take your turns to speak.

HARLEQUIN [*to Scaramouch*] Aye, signor, 'tis most uncivil to inter-   150
rupt me.

SCARAMOUCH [*to Harlequin*] And disingenuous, sir, to intrude on
me.

> [*Harlequin and Scaramouch continue*] *putting one another by*

MOPSOPHIL Let me then speak first.

HARLEQUIN I'm dumb.   155

SCARAMOUCH I acquiesce.

MOPSOPHIL I was informed there was a person here had propositions of marriage to make me.

HARLEQUIN That's I, that's I.

> [*Harlequin*] *shoves Scaramouch away*

SCARAMOUCH And I attend to that consequential *finis*.   160

> [*Scaramouch*] *shoves Harlequin away*

HARLEQUIN I know not what you mean by your *finis*, signor, but I
am come to offer myself this gentlewoman's servant, her lover, her
husband, her dog in a halter,° or anything.

SCARAMOUCH (*in rage*) Him I pronounce a poltroon, and an ignomi-
nious utensil, that dares lay claim to the renowned lady of my   165
primum mobile;° that is, my best affections.

HARLEQUIN I fear not your hard words, sir; but dare aloud pronounce, if Donna Mopsophil like me, the farmer, as well as I like
her, 'tis a match, and my chariot is ready at the gate to bear her
off, d'ye see.   170

MOPSOPHIL (*aside*) Ah, how that chariot pleads.

SCARAMOUCH And I pronounce, that being intoxicated with the
sweet eyes of this refulgent lady, I come to tender her my noblest

particulars, being already most advantageously set up with the circumstantial implements of my occupation.   175

    [Scaramouch] points to the shop

MOPSOPHIL *[aside]* A city apothecary: a most genteel calling. Which shall I choose? *[To Scaramouch]* Signor Apothecary, I'll not expostulate the circumstantial reasons that have occasioned me this honour.

SCARAMOUCH Incomparable lady, the elegancy of your repartees   180 most excellently denote the profundity of your capacity.

HARLEQUIN What the devil's all this? Good Mr Conjurer, stand by, and don't fright the gentlewoman with your elegant profundities.

    [Harlequin] puts [Scaramouch] by

SCARAMOUCH *(in rage)* How, a conjurer! I will chastise thy vulgar ignorance, that yclepes a philosopher a conjurer.   185

HARLEQUIN 'Losophers! Prithee, if thou be'st a man, speak like a man, then.

SCARAMOUCH Why, what do I speak like? What do I speak like?

HARLEQUIN What do you speak like? Why, you speak like a wheel-barrow.   190

SCARAMOUCH How!

HARLEQUIN And how!

    [Harlequin and Scaramouch] come up close together at half
    sword.° [They] parry;° stare on each other for a while; then
    put up [their swords] and bow to each other civilly

MOPSOPHIL That's well, gentlemen; let's have all peace, while I survey you both, and see which likes me best.

    She goes between them, and surveys them both, they making
    ridiculous bows on both sides, and grimaces, the while

[Aside] Ha: now, on my conscience, my two foolish lovers,   195 Harlequin and Scaramouch; how, are my hopes defeated? But faith, I'll fit you° both.

    She views 'em both

SCARAMOUCH *(aside)* So, she's considering still; I shall be the happy dog.

HARLEQUIN *(aside)* She's taking aim; she cannot choose but like me   200 best.

SCARAMOUCH *(bowing and smiling)* Well, madam, how does my person propagate?

MOPSOPHIL Faith, signor, now I look better on you, I do not like your phisnomy° so well as your intellects; you discovering some   205 circumstantial symptoms that ever denote a villainous inconstancy.

SCARAMOUCH Ah, you are pleased, madam.

MOPSOPHIL You are mistaken, signor: I am displeased at your grey
eyes, and black eye-brows and beard; I never knew a man with
those signs, true to his mistress or his friend. And I would sooner   210
wed that scoundrel Scaramouch, that very civil pimp, that mere
pair of chemical bellows° that blow the doctor's projecting fires,°
that deputy urinal-shaker,° that very Guzman of Salamanca,° than
a fellow of your infallible *signum mallis.*°

HARLEQUIN Ha, ha, ha. [*To Scaramouch*] You have your answer,   215
Signor Friskin,° and may shut up your shop and be gone.—Ha,
ha, ha.

SCARAMOUCH (*aside*) Hum, sure the jade knows me.

MOPSOPHIL And as for you, signor—

HARLEQUIN (*bowing and smiling*) Ha, madam—   220

MOPSOPHIL Those lantern-jaws° of yours, with that most villainous
sneer and grin, and a certain fierce air of your eyes, looks altogether
most fanatically, which, with your notorious whey beard, are
certain signs of knavery and cowardice; therefore I'd rather wed
that spider Harlequin, that skeleton buffoon,° that ape of man, that   225
Jack of Lent,° that very top that's of no use but when 'tis whipped
and lashed, that piteous property I'd rather wed than thee.

HARLEQUIN A very fair declaration.

MOPSOPHIL You understand me; and so, adieu, sweet glister-pipe,
and Signor dirty-boots,° ha, ha, ha.   230

> [*Mopsophil*] *runs out.* [*Harlequin and Scaramouch*] *stand*
> *looking simply on each other, without speaking awhile*

SCARAMOUCH (*aside*) That I should not know that rogue Harlequin!

HARLEQUIN (*aside*) That I should take this fool for a physician!—
How long have you commenced apothecary, signor?

SCARAMOUCH Ever since you turned farmer. Are not you a damned
rogue to put these tricks upon me, and most dishonourably break   235
all articles between us?

HARLEQUIN Are not you a damned son of a—something—to break
articles with me?

SCARAMOUCH No more words, sir, no more words, I find it must
come to action: draw. (*Draws* [*his sword*])   240

HARLEQUIN Draw, so I can draw, sir.

> [*Harlequin*] *draws* [*his sword*]. *They make a ridiculous*
> *cowardly fight. Enter the doctor, which they seeing, come on*
> *with more courage. He runs between 'em and with his cane*
> *beats the swords down*

DOCTOR Hold, hold! What mean you, gentlemen?

SCARAMOUCH Let me go, sir; I am provoked beyond measure, sir.

DOCTOR You must excuse me, signor.

> [*The doctor*] *parleys with Harlequin*

SCARAMOUCH (*aside*) I dare not discover the fool for his master's   245
sake, and it may spoil our intrigue anon; besides, he'll then
discover me, and I shall be discarded for bantering the doctor. [*To
the doctor*] A man of honour to be so basely affronted here!

> *The doctor comes to appease Scaramouch*

HARLEQUIN [*aside*] Should I discover this rascal, he would tell the
old gentleman I was the same that attempted his house today in   250
women's clothes, and I should be kicked and beaten most insatiably.°

SCARAMOUCH What, signor, for a man of parts to be imposed upon,
and [*holding his chest, as if wounded*] whipped through the lungs
here, like a mountebank's zany for sham cures! Mr Doctor, I must   255
tell you 'tis not civil.

DOCTOR I am extremely sorry for it, sir, and you shall see how I will
have this fellow handled for the affront to a person of your gravity,
and in my house.—[*Calls*] Here, Pedro!

> *Enter Pedro*

Take this intruder, or bring some of your fellows hither, and toss   260
him in a blanket.

> *Exit Pedro. Harlequin going to creep away, Scaramouch*
> *holds him*

HARLEQUIN (*aside to* [*Scaramouch*]) Hark'ee, bring me off, or I'll
discover all your intrigue.

SCARAMOUCH Let me alone.°

DOCTOR I'll warrant you, some rogue that has some plot on my niece   265
and daughter.

SCARAMOUCH No, no, sir, he comes to impose the grossest lie upon
you that ever was heard of.

> *Enter Pedro with others, with a blanket. They put Harlequin*
> *in it, and toss him*

HARLEQUIN Hold, hold; I'll confess all, rather than endure it.

DOCTOR [*to Pedro*] Hold. [*To Harlequin*] What will you confess, sir?   270

> [*Harlequin*] *comes out* [*of the blanket*]. [*He*] *makes sick faces*

SCARAMOUCH That he's the greatest impostor in nature. Would you
think it, sir? He pretends to be no less than an ambassador from
the emperor of the moon, sir.

DOCTOR Ha! Ambassador from the emperor of the moon!

[The doctor] pulls off his hat

SCARAMOUCH Aye, sir; thereupon I laughed, thereupon he grew   275
angry; I laughed at his resentment, and thereupon we drew; and
this was the high quarrel, sir.

DOCTOR Hum, ambassador from the moon. (*Pauses*)

SCARAMOUCH [*to Harlequin*] I have brought you off; manage him as
well as you can.   280

HARLEQUIN (*aside*) Brought me off, yes, out of the frying-pan into
the fire. Why, how the devil shall I act an ambassador?

DOCTOR [*aside*] It must be so, for how should either of these know
I expected that honour?

He addresses him with profound civility to Harlequin

Sir, if the figure you make, approaching so near ours of this world,   285
have made us commit any indecent indignity to your high
character, you ought to pardon the frailty of our mortal education
and ignorance, having never before been blessed with the descen-
sion of any from your world.

HARLEQUIN (*aside*) What the devil shall I say now? [*To the doctor*] I   290
confess, I am as you see by my garb, sir, a little incognito, because
the public message I bring, is very private: which is, that the
mighty Iredonozar, emperor of the moon, with his most worthy
brother, the prince of Thunderland, intend to sup with you
tonight. Therefore be sure you get good wine—though, by the   295
way, let me tell you, 'tis for the sake of your fair daughter.

SCARAMOUCH [*aside*] I'll leave the rogue to his own management.—
I presume by your whispering, sir, you would be private, and
humbly begging pardon, take my leave.

HARLEQUIN You have it, friend.   300

Exit Scaramouch

—Does your niece and daughter drink,° sir?

DOCTOR Drink, sir?

HARLEQUIN Aye, sir, drink hard.

DOCTOR Do the women of your world drink hard, sir?

HARLEQUIN According to their quality, sir, more or less; the greater   305
the quality, the more profuse the quantity.

DOCTOR Why, that's just as 'tis here;° but your men of quality, your
statesmen, sir, I presume they are sober, learned and wise.

HARLEQUIN Faith, no, sir, but they are, for the most part, what's as
good, very proud, and promising, sir, most liberal of their word to   310
every fawning suitor, to purchase the state of long attendance, and
cringing as they pass; but the devil of a performance, without you

get the knack of bribing in the right place and time; but yet they
all defy it, sir.

DOCTOR Just, just as 'tis here. But pray, sir, how do these great men   315
live with their wives?

HARLEQUIN Most nobly, sir: my lord keeps his coach, my lady hers;
my lord his bed, my lady hers; and very rarely see one another,
unless they chance to meet in a visit, in the park, the Mall,° the
tour,° or at the basset-table, where they civilly salute and part, he   320
to his mistress, she to play—°

DOCTOR Good lack! Just as 'tis here.

HARLEQUIN —Where, if she chance to lose her money, rather than
give out, she borrows of the next amorous coxcomb, who, from
that minute, hopes, and is sure to be paid again one way or other,   325
the next kind opportunity.

DOCTOR Just as 'tis here.

HARLEQUIN As for the young fellows that have money, they have no
mercy upon their own persons, but wearing nature off as fast as
they can, swear, and whore, and drink, and borrow as long as any   330
rooking citizen will lend; till having dearly purchased the heroic
title of a bully or a sharper, they live pitied of their friends, and
despised by their whores, and depart this transitory world diverse
and sundry ways.

DOCTOR Just, just as 'tis here.   335

HARLEQUIN As for the citizen, sir, the courtier lies with his wife; he,
in revenge, cheats him of his estate, till rich enough to marry his
daughter to a courtier, again give him all—unless his wife's
over-gallantry break him;° and thus the world runs round.

DOCTOR The very same 'tis here. Is there no preferment, sir, for men   340
of parts and merit?

HARLEQUIN Parts and merit! What's that? A livery, or the handsome
tying a cravat; for the great men prefer none but their footmen and
valets.

DOCTOR By my troth, just as 'tis here. Sir, I find you are a person   345
of most profound intelligence: under favour, sir, are you a native
of the moon or this world?

HARLEQUIN [aside] The devil's in him for hard questions.—I am a
Neapolitan, sir.

DOCTOR Sir, I honour you. [Aside] Good luck, my countryman!—   350
How got you to the region of the moon, sir?

HARLEQUIN [aside] A plaguy inquisitive old fool.—Why, sir, [aside]
pox on't, what shall I say?—I being—one day in a musing

melancholy, walking by the seaside—there arose, sir, a great mist,
by the sun's exhaling° of the vapours of the earth, sir.   355

DOCTOR Right, sir.

HARLEQUIN In this fog or mist, sir, I was exhaled.

DOCTOR The exhalations of the sun, draw you to the moon, sir?

HARLEQUIN [*aside*] I am condemned to the blanket again.—I say, sir,
I was exhaled up, but in my way, being too heavy, was dropped   360
into the sea.°

DOCTOR How, sir, into the sea?

HARLEQUIN The sea, sir, where the emperor's fisherman casting his
nets, drew me up, and took me for a strange and monstrous fish,
sir, and as such, presented me to his mightiness, who, going to   365
have me spitchcocked for his own eating—

DOCTOR How, sir, eating?

HARLEQUIN What did me I, sir (life being sweet), but fell on my
knees, and besought his gloriousness not to eat me, for I was no
fish but a man; he asked me of what country, I told him of Naples;   370
whereupon the emperor, overjoyed, asked me if I knew that most
reverend and most learned Doctor Baliardo, and his fair daughter.
I told him I did; whereupon he made me his bed-fellow, and the
confidant to his amour to Signora Elaria.

DOCTOR Bless me, sir! how came the emperor to know my daughter?   375

HARLEQUIN [*aside*] There he is again with his damned hard questions.—Know her, sir? Why, you were walking abroad one day—

DOCTOR My daughter never goes abroad, sir, farther than our garden.

HARLEQUIN Aye, there it was indeed, sir; and as his highness was
taking a survey of this lower world—through a long perspective,   380
sir—he saw you and your daughter and niece, and from that very
moment, fell most desperately in love. But hark: the sound of
timbrels, kettle-drums and trumpets! The emperor, sir, is on his
way: prepare for his reception.

A strange noise is heard of brass kettles, and pans, and bells,
and many tinkling things

DOCTOR I'm in a rapture. How shall I pay my gratitude for this great   385
negotiation? But as I may, I humbly offer, sir.

[The doctor] presents [Harlequin] with a rich ring and a purse
of gold

HARLEQUIN Sir, as an honour done the emperor, I take your ring
and gold. I must go meet his highness.

[Harlequin] takes leave. Enter to [the doctor] Scaramouch, as
himself

SCARAMOUCH Oh, sir! we are astonished with the dreadful sound of the sweetest music that ever mortal heard, but know not whence it comes. Have you not heard it, sir?   390

DOCTOR Heard it, yes, fool! 'Tis the music of the spheres: the emperor of the moon world is descending.

SCARAMOUCH How, sir? No marvel then, that looking towards the south, I saw such splendid glories in the air.   395

DOCTOR Ha, saw'st thou aught descending in the air?

SCARAMOUCH Oh, yes, sir, wonders! Haste to the old gallery, whence, with the help of your telescope, you may discover all.

DOCTOR I would not lose a moment for the lower universe.

Enter Elaria, Bellemante, [and] Mopsophil, dressed in rich, antic habits

ELARIA Sir, we are dressed as you commanded us; what is your farther pleasure?   400

DOCTOR It well becomes the honour you're designed for, this night, to wed two princes. Come with me and know your happy fates.

Exeunt doctor and Scaramouch

ELARIA Bless me! My father, in all the rest of his discourse, shows so much sense and reason, I cannot think him mad, but feigns all   405
this to try us.

BELLEMANTE Not mad! Marry, heaven forbid, thou art always creating fears to startle one; why, if he be not mad, his want of sleep this eight-and-forty hours, the noise of strange unheard-of instruments, with the fantastic splendour of the unusual sight, will   410
so turn his brain and dazzle him, that in grace of goodness, he may be mad. If he be not—come, let's after him to the gallery, for I long to see in what showing equipage our princely lovers will address to us.

Exeunt

[3.3]

The gallery,° richly adorned, with scenes and lights°

Enter doctor, Elaria, Bellemante, and Mopsophil. Soft music is heard

BELLEMANTE Ha; heavens! What's here? What palace is this? No part of our house, I'm sure.

ELARIA 'Tis rather the apartment of some monarch.

DOCTOR [*aside*] I'm all amazement too, but must not show my
    ignorance.—Yes, Elaria, this is prepared to entertain two princes.   5
BELLEMANTE Are you sure on't, sir? Are we not, think you, in that
    world above I often heard you speak of? In the moon, sir?
DOCTOR (*aside*) How shall I resolve her? For aught I know, we are.
ELARIA Sure, sir, 'tis some enchantment.
DOCTOR Let not thy female ignorance profane the highest mysteries of   10
    natural philosophy. To fools it seems enchantment, but I've a sense
    can reach it: sit, and expect the event. Hark! [*Aside*] I am amazed, but
    must conceal my wonder, that joy of fools, and appear wise in gravity.
BELLEMANTE Whence comes this charming sound, sir?
DOCTOR From the spheres: it is familiar to me.   15
> *The scene in the front draws off, and shows the hill of Parnassus;*
> *a noble large walk of trees leading to it, with eight or ten negroes*
> *upon pedestals, ranged on each side of the walks.° Next Kepler*
> *and Galileus descend on each side, opposite to each other, in*
> *chariots, with perspectives in their hands, as viewing the machine*
> *of the zodiac.° Soft music plays still*
DOCTOR Methought I saw the figure of two men descend from
    yonder cloud, on yonder hill.
ELARIA I thought so too, but they are disappeared,° and the winged
    chariots fled.
> *Enter Kepler and Galileus*
BELLEMANTE See, sir, they approach.   20
> *The doctor rises, and bows*
KEPLER Most reverend sir, we from the upper world thus low salute
    you. Kepler and Galileus we are called, sent as interpreters to great
    Iredonozar, the emperor of the moon, who is descending.
DOCTOR [*bowing*] Most reverend bards, profound philosophers, thus
    low I bow to pay my humble gratitude.   25
KEPLER The emperor, sir, salutes you, and your fair daughter.
GALILEUS And, sir, the prince of Thunderland salutes you and your
    fair niece.
DOCTOR Thus low I fall to thank their royal goodness.
> [*The doctor*] *kneels. They take him up*
BELLEMANTE Came you, most reverend bards, from the moon world?   30
KEPLER Most lovely maid, we did.
DOCTOR May I presume to ask the manner how?
KEPLER By cloud, sir, through the regions of the air, down to the
    famed Parnassus; thence by water, along the river Helicon;° the
    rest by post,° upon two winged eagles.°   35

DOCTOR Sir, are there store of our world° inhabiting the moon?
KEPLER Oh, of all nations, sir, that lie beneath it; in the emperor's
train, sir, you will behold abundance. Look up and see the orbal
world descending; observe the zodiac, sir, with her twelve signs.

Next the zodiac descends, a symphony playing all the while;
when it is landed, it delivers the twelve signs.° Then the song,
the persons of the zodiac being the singers; after which the
negroes dance and mingle in the chorus

A SONG FOR THE ZODIAC

Let murmuring lovers no longer repine,   40
    But their hearts and their voices advance;
Let the nymphs and the swains in the kind chorus join,
    And the satyrs and fauns in a dance.
Let nature put on her beauty of May,
    And the fields and the meadows adorn;   45
Let the woods and the mountains resound with the joy,
    And the echoes their triumph return.

CHORUS

    For since Love wore his darts,
        And virgins grew coy;
    Since these wounded hearts,   50
        And those could destroy,
There ne'er was more cause for your triumphs and joy.

Hark, hark, the music of the spheres,
    Some wonder approaching declares;
Such, such as has not blessed your eyes and ears   55
    This thousand, thousand, thousand years.
See, see what the force of Love can make,
    Who rules in heaven, in earth and sea;
Behold how he commands the zodiac,
    While the fixed signs unhinging all obey.°   60
        Not one of which, but represents
            The attributes of Love,
        Who governs all the elements
            In harmony above.

CHORUS

    For since Love wore his darts,   65

And virgins grew coy;
Since these wounded hearts,
And those could destroy,
There ne'er was more cause for your triumphs and joy.

The wanton Aries first descends,   70
*   To show the vigour and the play*
Beginning Love, beginning Love attends—°
When the young passion is all over joy;
He bleats his soft pain to the fair curlèd throng,
And he leaps, and he bounds, and loves all the day long.   75

At once Love's courage and his slavery
*   In Taurus is expressed,*
Though o'er the plains he conqueror be,
*   The generous beast*
Does to the yoke submit his noble breast;   80
While Gemini, smiling and twining of arms,
*   Shows Love's soft endearments and charms.*
And Cancer's slow motion the degrees do express,
*   Respectful Love arrives to happiness.°*
*   Leo his strength and majesty,*   85
*   Virgo his blushing modesty,*
*   And Libra all his equity.*
His subtlety does Scorpio show,
And Sagittarius all his loose desire,
By Capricorn his forward humour know,   90
And Aqua, lovers' tears that raise his fire,
While Pisces, which intwined do move,
Show the soft play, and wanton arts of Love.

CHORUS

For since Love wore his darts,
*   And virgins grew coy;*   95
Since these wounded hearts,
*   And those could destroy,*
There ne'er was more cause for your triumphs and joy.

[KEPLER] See how she turns, and sends her signs to earth.° Behold
the ram, Aries; see, Taurus next descends; then Gemini: see how   100
the boys embrace. Next Cancer, then Leo, then the virgin; next to
her Libra; Scorpio, Sagittary, Capricorn, Aquarius, Pisces. This
eight thousand years no emperor has descended but incognito; but

when he does, to make his journey more magnificent, the zodiac,
sir, attends him.   105
DOCTOR 'Tis all amazing, sir.
KEPLER Now, sir, behold, the globic world descends two thousand
leagues below its wonted station, to show obedience to its proper
monarch.

> *After which, the globe of the moon° appears, first, like a new*
> *moon; as it moves forward it increases, till it comes to the*
> *full. When it is descended, it opens, and shows the emperor*
> *and the prince. They come forth with all their train, the flutes*
> *playing a symphony before [the emperor], which prepares the*
> *song; which ended, the dancers mingle as before*

SONG

> *All joy to mortals, joy and mirth,*   110
> * Eternal IOs sing;°*
> *The gods of love descend to earth,*
> * Their darts have lost the sting.*
> *The youth shall now complain no more*
> * On Silvia's needless scorn,*   115
> *But she shall love, if he adore,*
> * And melt when he shall burn.*
>
> *The nymph no longer shall be shy,*
> * But leave the jilting road;*
> *And Daphne now no more shall fly*   120
> * The wounded panting god;*
> *But all shall be serene and fair;*
> * No sad complaints of love*
> *Shall fill the gentle whispering air,*
> * No echoing sighs the grove.*   125
>
> *Beneath the shades young Strephon lies,*
> * Of all his wish possessed;*
> *Gazing on Silvia's charming eyes,*
> * Whose soul is there confessed.*
> *All soft and sweet the maid appears,*   130
> * With looks that know no art,*
> *And though she yields with trembling fears,*
> * She yields with all her heart.*

[KEPLER] See, sir, the cloud of foreigners appears: French, English, Spaniards, Danes, Turks, Russians, Indians, and the nearer climes   135
of Christendom; and lastly, sir, behold the mighty emperor.

> *A chariot appears, made like a half moon, in which is Cinthio*
> *for the emperor, richly dressed, and Charmante for the prince,*
> *rich, with a good many heroes attending. Cinthio's train [is]*
> *borne by four cupids. The song continues while they descend*
> *and land.° They address themselves to Elaria and Bellemante.*
> *Doctor falls on his face, the rest bow very low as they pass.*
> *They make signs to Kepler*

KEPLER The emperor would have you rise, sir; he will expect no
ceremony from the father of his mistress.

> *[Kepler] takes [the doctor] up*

DOCTOR I cannot, sir, behold his mightiness; the splendour of his
majesty confounds me.   140

KEPLER You must be moderate, sir, it is expected.

> *The two lovers make all the signs of love in dumb show to the*
> *ladies, while the soft music plays again from the end of the*
> *song*

DOCTOR Shall I not have the joy to hear their heavenly voices, sir?

KEPLER They never speak to any subject, sir, when they appear in
royalty, but by interpreters, and that by way of stentraphon,° in
manner of the Delphic oracles.°   145

DOCTOR Any way, so I may hear the sense of what they would say.

KEPLER No doubt you will. But see, the emperor commands, by
signs, his foreigners to dance.

> *Soft music changes. A very antic dance. The dance ended, the*
> *front scene draws off, and shows a temple,° with an altar, one*
> *speaking through a stentraphon from behind it. Soft music*
> *plays the while*

KEPLER Most learned sir, the emperor now is going to declare
himself, according to his custom, to his subjects. Listen.   150

STENTRAPHON Most reverend sir, whose virtue did incite us,
Whose daughter's charms did more invite us;
We come to grace her with that honour,
That never mortal yet had done her.
Once only, Jove was known in story   155
To visit Semele in glory.°
But fatal 'twas; he so enjoyed her,
Her own ambitious flame destroyed her.
His charms too fierce for flesh and blood,

She died embracing of her god.   160
We gentler marks of passion give;
The maid we love, shall love and live,
Whom visibly we thus will grace,
Above the rest of human race.
Say, is't your will that we should wed her,   165
And nightly in disguises bed her?

DOCTOR The glory is too great for mortal wife.

    [The doctor] kneels in transport

STENTRAPHON What then remains, but that we consummate
This happy marriage in our splendid state?

DOCTOR Thus low I kneel, in thanks for this great blessing.   170

    Cinthio takes Elaria by the hand; Charmante [takes]
    Bellemante; two of the singers in white being priests, they lead
    'em to the altar, the whole company dividing on either side.
    Where, while a hymeneal song is sung, the priest joins their
    hands. The song ended, and they married, they come forth;
    but before they come forward, two chariots descend,° one on
    one side above, and the other on the other side; in which is
    Harlequin dressed like a mock hero, with others, and
    Scaramouch in the other, dressed so in helmets

SCARAMOUCH Stay, mighty emperor, and vouchsafe to be the um-
pire of our difference.

    Cinthio makes signs to Kepler

KEPLER What are you?

SCARAMOUCH Two neighbouring princes to your vast dominion.

HARLEQUIN Knights of the sun,° our honourable titles,   175
And fight for that fair mortal, Mopsophil.

MOPSOPHIL *[aside]* Bless us! My two precious lovers, I'll warrant;
well, I had better take up with one of them, than lie alone tonight.

SCARAMOUCH Long as two rivals have we loved and hoped,
Both equally endeavoured, and both failed;   180
At last by joint consent, we both agreed
To try our titles by the dint of lance,
And chose your mightiness for arbitrator.

KEPLER The emperor gives consent.

    They both [are] all armed with gilded lances and shields of
    black, with golden suns painted. The music plays a fighting
    tune. They fight at barriers,° to the tune. Harlequin is often
    foiled, but advances still; at last Scaramouch throws him, and
    is conqueror; all give judgement for him

KEPLER (*to Scaramouch*) The emperor pronounces you are victor.   185

DOCTOR Receive your mistress, sir, as the reward of your undoubted
valour.

   [*The doctor*] *presents Mopsophil* [*to Scaramouch*]

SCARAMOUCH Your humble servant, sir, and Scaramouch, returns
you humble thanks.

   [*Scaramouch*] *puts off his helmet*

DOCTOR Ha, Scaramouch!   190

   [*The doctor*] *bawls out, and falls in a chair. They all go to
   him*

My heart misgives me. (*Bawling out*) Oh, I am undone and cheated
every way!

KEPLER Be patient, sir, and call up all your virtue;
 You're only cured, sir, of a disease
 That long has reigned over your nobler faculties.   195
 Sir, I am your physician, friend and counsellor;
 It was not in the power of herbs or minerals,
 Of reason, common sense, and right religion,
 To draw you from an error that unmanned you.

DOCTOR I will be patient, gentlemen, and hear you.   200
 —Are not you Ferdinand?

KEPLER I am; and these are gentlemen of quality,
 That long have loved your daughter and your niece.
 Don Cinthio this, and this, Don Charmante,
 The viceroy's nephews, both;   205
 Who found, as men, 'twas impossible to enjoy 'em,
 And therefore tried this stratagem.

CINTHIO Sir, I beseech you, mitigate your grief;
 Although indeed we are but mortal men,
 Yet we shall love you, serve you, and obey you.   210

DOCTOR Are not you then the emperor of the moon?
 And you the prince of Thunderland?

CINTHIO There's no such person, sir.
 These stories are the phantoms of mad brains,
 To puzzle fools withal; the wise laugh at 'em.   215
 Come sir, you shall no longer be imposed upon.

DOCTOR No emperor of the moon; and no moon world!

CHARMANTE Ridiculous inventions.
 If we'd not loved you, you'd been still imposed on;
 We had brought a scandal on your learned name,   220
 And all succeeding ages had despised it.

DOCTOR (*leap[ing] up*) Burn all my books, and let my study blaze;°
Burn all to ashes, and be sure the wind
Scatter the vile contagious monstrous lies.
—Most noble youths, you've honoured me with your alliance, and   225
you, and all your friends, assistances° in this glorious miracle, I
invite tonight to revel with me.—Come, all, and see my happy
recantation of all the follies fables have inspired till now. Be
pleasant to repeat your story, to tell me by what kind degrees you
cozened me. (*Gravely to himself*) I see there's nothing in philo-   230
sophy.—Of all that writ, he was the wisest bard, who spoke this
mighty truth:

> He that knew all that ever learning writ,
> Knew only this: that he knew nothing yet.°

Epilogue

To be spoken by Mrs Cooke

With our old plays, as with dull wife it fares,
To whom you have been married tedious years.
You cry, 'she's wondrous good, it is confessed,
But still 'tis *chapon böuillé* at the best;°
That constant dish can never make a feast.'   5
Yet the palled pleasure you must still pursue,
You give so small encouragement for new;
And who would drudge for such a wretched age,
Who want the bravery to support one stage?°
The wiser wits have now new measures set,   10
And taken up new trades, that they may eat;
No more your nice fantastic pleasures serve;
Your pimps you pay, but let your poets starve.
They long in vain for better usage hoped,
Till quite undone and tired, they dropped and dropped;   15
Not one is left will write for thin third day—
Like desperate picaroons, no-prize no-pay,
And when they've done their best, the recompense
Is, 'damn the sot, his play wants common sense.'
Ill-natured wits, who can so ill requite   20
The drudging slaves who for your pleasure write!
   Look back on flourishing Rome, ye proud ingrates,

And see how she her thriving poets treats:
Wisely she prized 'em at the noblest rate,
As necessary ministers of state,   25
And contributions raised to make 'em great.
They from the public bank she did maintain,
And freed from want, they only writ for fame;
And were as useful in a city held,
As formidable armies in the field.   30
They but a conquest over men pursued,
While these, by gentler force, the soul subdued.
Not Rome in all her happiest pomp could show
A greater Caesar than we boast of now;
Augustus reigns—but poets still are low.   35
   May Caesar live; and while his mighty hand°
Is scattering plenty over all the land,
With god-like bounty recompensing all,
Some fruitful drops may on the muses fall—
Since honest pens do his just cause afford   40
Equal advantage with the useful sword.

EXPLANATORY NOTES

The abbreviations used in the notes for editions of the plays are given in the Note on the Texts, pp. xxv–xxvi.

The Rover

Cast *Mrs Quin*: Anne Quin (*fl.* 1660–83); because her name is spelt 'Gwin' in Q and some other early sources, she has sometimes been confused with Nell Gwyn, who had left the stage by this date.

Prologue 2 *of a different society*: belonging to different factions within a professional or social group.

3 *Rabel's drops*: a patent medicine.

9 *cabal*: faction, clique. In Behn's time often applied as an acronym to Charles II's group of ministers in 1667–73: Clifford, Arlington, Buckingham, Ashley-Cooper, and Lauderdale.

10 *hit your humour*: accurately portray your characteristics.

15 *take*: succeed on the stage.

16 *censure*: judge, criticize.

31 *but to mimic good extempore*: i.e. they take great pains, only to produce an imitation of the kind of verse others can recite as they make it up.

38 *I asked him*: the play is presented as by a man; Behn's name does not appear on the title-page till the third issue of the first edition.

43 *cits*: citizens, city-dwellers; a term often applied contemptuously to middle-class tradespeople.

May-day coaches: a mocking reference to the social pretensions of cits, who parade in coaches on the May Day holiday, imitating the behaviour of their social superiors.

1.1.27 *Inglese*: *Anglese* Q1–3, C1–2, S, L, J, T; Englishman.

35 *Carnival*: this setting, often used in comedies of the 1660s and 1670s, establishes the holiday atmosphere appropriate to comedy and provides a good excuse for the many disguises called for by the plot. As a short feast before the Lent fast, the carnival is also a fitting emblem for Hellena's brief encounter with the world before she is to be sent to a nunnery.

36 *proper*: (1) excellent, fine; (2) handsome, well made.

45 *devotee*: C2, S; *devote* Q1–3, C1, L.

48 *siege of Pamplona*: Pamplona is a town in Northern Spain, 25 miles from the French border and once the capital of Navarre. Of strategic

336

importance because it guarded the pass through the Pyrenees, it was heavily fortified, and for many years France and Spain fought over it. During the 1650s France and Spain were at war. Belvile, who apparently joined the French army as a mercenary after his exile from England, has evidently been part of the invading force in a recent action, in which the Spaniards Don Pedro and Florinda have been among the besieged. His gallantry towards defeated enemies is a typical motif of heroic drama. He has now left the French army and is visiting Spanish-owned Naples on friendly terms—a change of loyalties appropriate in a romantic lover who puts his mistress first, but also in tune with the sentiments of his prince, the exiled Charles II, who, when French support for him was withdrawn, negotiated a treaty with Spain in 1656. In *Thomaso*, it is Thomaso who saved Serulina when Pamplona was sacked: see *Thomaso*, Part I, 3.1.

53 S.D. *masking habit*: masquerade costume. As he puts it on onstage, Don Pedro's probably consists of a cloak and a mask.

62–4 *I would not . . . sister*: cf. *Thomaso*, Part I, 3.4, Serulina to Pedro: 'I would not see you presume upon the ill customs of our Countrey so far as to make a slave of your sister.'

73 *criminal for my sake*: Belvile's protection of Florinda involved acting against the side he was officially fighting on.

80–1 *what jewels . . . eyes and heart*: here, and in the following exchanges, Behn adapts dialogue from *Thomaso*, Part II, 2.1, to her different dramatic situation. Hellena is given words which Harrigo uses to mock Serulina's suitor Don Alphonso, and to persuade Serulina to favour Thomaso, while Pedro is given speeches of Serulina's.

83 *from the Indies*: traders to the Indies were proverbial for immense wealth. Spain had a great deal of trade with the West Indies during the seventeenth century.

87 *increase . . . family*: he may bring riches to make her money bags bigger but he won't make her pregnant.

101 *Indian breeding*: the time he has spent in the Indies.

102 dog days: during July and August, when the dog-star is in the sky; proverbial for oppressive heat.

104 *King Sancho the First*: there were kings called Sancho in Navarre and in Castile in the Middle Ages.

107 *furbished*: J; *furbrusht* Q1–3, C1; *furbisht* C2, S. Cleaned up, given a new look.

114–16 *That honour . . . sheets*: cf. *Thomaso*, Part II, 2.1, Harrigo to Serulina: 'that honour being pass'd, the Gyant stretches himself, yawns and sighs a belch or two, stales in your pot, farts as loud as a Musket . . . expects you in his foul sheets.'

126 *worse than adultery*: closely follows *Thomaso*, Part II, 2.1, where the servant Calis voices these sentiments. Hellena's expression of such an attitude is unusually free for a heroine even in Restoration comedy. In the 1986 Stratford production, Imogen Stubbs emphasized Hellena's consciousness of the limits she is transgressing by stopping in confusion when she realized she had voiced these sentiments in front of her brother. Hellena's outspokenness throughout this scene had to be toned down during the eighteenth century: this entire speech, and several of her phrases elsewhere, were cut in some performances.

127 *Hôtel de Dieu*: a hospital founded by a religious order.

133 *Don Vincentio!* . . .: Closely follows a speech of Harrigo's in *Thomaso*, Part II, 2.1.

134 *Gambo*: the Gambia, in West Africa. The Portuguese, Dutch, French, and English had all traded there. The reference is topical for England in the 1670s rather than for the play's setting, since the Royal African Company had been established to trade with the Gambia in 1672.

bell and baudle: bauble: mere trinkets, with a play on bauble = penis. Don Vincentio's supposed impotence has been Hellena's subject for her last few speeches, but this is her most bawdy reference to it, and may be what prompts Don Pedro to lose his temper and order for her to be locked up (l. 136).

141–4 *Shall I . . . me*: closely follows a speech of Serulina's in *Thomaso*, Part II, 2.1.

160 *I ne'er . . . near*: blank verse is frequently employed in the play to express heightened feeling or indicate formality. Florinda's use of it here shows how seriously she takes her predicament, in contrast to Hellena, who expects to solve difficulties by means of comic trickery.

178 *let's ramble*: in the Restoration period, 'to ramble' often means to go out looking for sex, and derivatives of 'range' and 'rove' are associated with ramble in this sense. Hellena's suggestion appropriates for the women an activity supposedly reserved for men, and suggests that she would like to be a 'rover' like Willmore.

188 *want*: lack.

1.2 S.D. *A long street*: painted wings carry the street scene, while the back-shutters are opened, showing the depth of the stage and allowing plenty of room for action in the scenic area.

2 *like mere Lent*: Belvile's melancholy looks are more appropriate to the fasting days of Lent than to the Carnival that precedes them.

46 *parliaments and protectors*: in the 1650s England was ruled by a series of parliaments and by Cromwell as Protector. The government confiscated the estates of many royalists, so the poverty of Willmore and his friends indicates their loyalty to the royalist cause.

47–8 *more grace . . . cavaliering*: Blunt's relationship to the exiled cavaliers is ambiguous. He has money because he has not, like them, had his estates sequestered, and his use of the word 'grace' here may pun on the spiritual grace claimed by the Puritan sects who dominated the Parliamentary party. In the New Cross Theatre production of *The Rover* in 1991, Blunt was played as a Puritan parliamentarian, set off from the cavaliers by dress and manners. This worked effectively to give added point to Blunt's gulling and humiliation later on, and the idea fits well with the anti-Puritan satire common in Behn's plays. However, Belvile does call Blunt 'one of us' a few lines further on, and the later mockery of him is based on his stock country-squire foolishness rather than on ideological differences. Blunt's claim to 'follow [the court] to do it no good' (l. 51) probably means that he is an idle traveller not actively helping the royalist cause, not that he has any malicious intent.

52 *pick a hole in my coat*: idiomatic expression, similar to 'pick a bone with me'.

54 *the Commonwealth*: the republican government of England from 1649 to 1653, replaced by Cromwell's Protectorate.

62 *the prince*: the exiled Charles II.

67 *honest*: i.e. a royalist. 'Honest' is often used to mean 'royalist' in Restoration plays dealing with this period. See Sir Robert Howard's *The Committee* (1665), which also has a character called Blunt, who (unlike Behn's Blunt) does risk losing his estates for his royalist principles.

68 S.D. (*embrace Blunt*): S.D. placed at Willmore's speech, J; placed after Belvile's speech, Q1–3, C1–2, L. Stage-directions in the early texts are often ambiguously placed; here, it makes more sense for Willmore to embrace Blunt in greeting (perhaps pulling Blunt to his heart as he says 'an interest here') than for Belvile to embrace him on introducing him.

89 *thy proper still*: par o th extende metapho wome = roses. Roses were distilled by being placed in a still (a kind of boiler) which was heated, and the vapour formed was then condensed into a liquid. Willmore thinks that the best 'still' for this 'rose' is within a pair of sheets with him, so they can be heated together.

99 *kiss the bed the bush grew in*: continuing, and slightly altering, the women = roses metaphor, Willmore here (and at l. 91 above) makes a play on bush = pubic hair. He is unusually explicit in his references to sexual activities.

103 S.D. *from the farther end of the scenes*: from right upstage
S.D. *dressed all over with horns*: horns were the emblem of the cuckold.

111 *gardener . . . breeding*: referring to the man bearing the paper with its advertisement: descended from Adam, the first gardener, and inheriting his skill in growing flowers = producing sexually available women).

112–13 *a wake in Essex*: the first of many references to Essex, Blunt's home, as a joke-place, where the people act contrarily, or are especially stupid. Essex was traditionally the butt of Londoners' jokes. Wakes (memorials to the dead) ought to be sad occasions, so a wake in Essex is carnivalesque. The point of the comparison is that fornication 'ought' to be a matter of carnivalesque rule-breaking, but here in Naples it is officially, and even gravely and ceremoniously, on offer.

116–17 *even the monsieurs . . . good manners*: even the French, the epitome of good manners, do not authorize fornication (here ironically treated as a polite activity), in the way the Neapolitans do.

119 *baffled by bravos*: ruined by hired soldiers, whose presence means that group-fighting, rather than honourable single combat, is the norm.

119–22 *an age . . . New Bridge*: I have not traced the reference to the French-man and the hangman. The general sense is that the hangman beat the Frenchman in their contest, just as the French beat the Dutch in theirs: a reference to an incident in 1672, when Nieuwerbrug (New Bridge), a Dutch garrison post on a branch of the Rhine, fell to the French.

127 *cross their hands*: give them money.

137 *I hope*: I suppose.

143 *parlous*: keen, shrewd.

151 *Venus . . . element*: the sea is Venus' (Aphrodite's) element, as she was born out of the foam; but the sea-goddess and goddess of love did not help Willmore when he was at sea, since there were no women there.

173 *Jephtha's daughter*: Jephtha sacrificed his daughter to God in thanks for a military victory: before she was killed she was allowed two months to 'lament her virginity'. See Judges 11: 37–40.

179 *I have an implicit faith*: I'll believe without demonstration; from a theological term for acceptance through trust in spiritual authority.

201–4 *This is . . . people*: cf. *Thomaso*, Part I, 1.3: 'They are strangers, I know by their staring, and English, by Don Harrigo; If he has metal he follows me, and if I have wit he's mine; for they say 'tis a kind hearted Nation.'

226 *sibyl*: prophetess in classical legend. The best-known is the Cumaean sibyl visited by Aeneas. The word is loosely applied to a female fortune-teller.

258 *Ho*: *Who* Q1–3, C1–2, S, L, J.

269 *Let her alone for that*: don't worry, you can rely on her for that.

271 *contrive . . . chains*: Jesuits were outlawed in England. Here they are credited with the capacity to go on plotting against the lawful authorities even when captured and imprisoned.

274 *a lost English boy . . .*: cf. *Thomaso*, Part I, 1.5, Thomaso: 'to cry a lost English boy of thirty, 'twould be welcome news to his friends if he had

any . . . I hope she'll find him a young Traveller, and dress him fit for our mirth.'

276 *sell him for Peru*: slave-labour was used for the Spaniards' mining operations in Peru, a part of their extensive colonies.

the rogue's sturdy: a rogue was an itinerant of the lowest class, and there was legislation against sturdy (healthy) rogues.

282–90 *Why . . . broke*: parts of this speech are taken from *Thomaso*, Part I, 1.5.

311 *Paduana*: a woman from Padua, a city of Northern Italy which was part of the Venetian republic, and so independent of the Spaniards who ran Naples at this time. Angellica's background is emblematic of her position in the plot, as an independent outsider. The discussion of Angellica in this and the following speeches is taken in part from *Thomaso*, Part I, 1.1.

316–17 *gay as on a monarch's birthday*: the monarch's birthday was a festival marked in the court by the wearing of new clothes.

2.1.10–11 *not . . . hopes*: not of low enough rank to be likely to be seduced.

48–53 *Give her . . . not everybody*: adapted from a speech of Edwardo's in *Thomaso*, Part I, 2.1.

59 *hazard in one bottom*: risk as a cargo in a single ship.

69 *Why yes . . .*: adapted from an exchange in *Thomaso*, Part I, 2.1, where Thomaso denounces the whores and Edwardo asks where they live.

77 *calf*: fool.

107 *What's this? . . . credit*: adapted from a discussion between minor characters in *Thomaso*, Part I, 2.1.

110 *a portion for the Infanta*: enough to make a dowry for the king of Spain's daughter. Frederick is exaggerating: Hellena's fortune, for instance, is many times the thousand crowns demanded by Angellica.

111 *won't she trust?*: won't she let me have it on tick?

112 *credit*: (1) deferred payment; (2) reputation for virtue.

164 s.d. *Song (to a lute above)*: the player and singer are in Angellica's balcony, hidden behind the curtain that she throws open at the end of the song. Angellica and Moretta might play and sing themselves, or professional musicians might be used.

191 *prove*: (1) experience; (2) demonstrate.

195 *Tilting*: (1) duelling; (2) thrusting (with sexual connotation).

199 *Molo*: mole; a large stone pier.

249–50 *Spaniards . . . affront*: Spaniards were famous for a strict code of masculine honour involving great sensitivity to insult.

253 *ne'er recover Flanders*: Flanders was part of the Spanish Netherlands for much of the seventeenth century. During the century Spain lost some of its territory in wars with other European powers. Parts of Flanders

341

were ceded to France in 1659, and there were further French incursions into the Spanish Netherlands in the 1660s and 1670s.

273 *Frederick*: Q3, C1–2, S, J, L, T; *Pedro* Q1–2.

276 *saluting*: kissing in greeting or departing.

2.2 S.D. *Willmore, Angellica, and Moretta*: this scene is adapted from *Thomaso*, Part I, 2.4. Killigrew's Angellica voices more explicit feminist protest, decrying the double standard of honour, and defending a whore's actions while calling her trade a slavery. She is also humbler, wishing she could be a virgin who could beg Willmore to marry her.

11–14 *You . . . sin*: prose Q1–3, C1–2, L, S.

22 *Worcester*: Charles II was beaten by Cromwell's forces in the battle of Worcester, 3 September 1651.

24 *corporal*: Moretta's disrespect for Willmore shows in her giving him a lower rank than the 'captain' attributed to him by Angellica (and earlier by Hellena).

27 *high i'th' mouth*: elevated.

30 *serve me*: Willmore addresses Moretta as the shopkeeper who will sell him the goods, i.e. Angellica.

31–2 *stinks of the gun room*: is smelly and dirty from Willmore's life on board a fighting ship.

52 *Yes . . . gentleman*: Willmore moves into the loose blank verse that dominates the rest of the scene, giving his exchanges with Angellica an elevated tone that contrasts sharply with the comic banter he has indulged in with Hellena.

88–9 *Withdraw*: presumably Moretta moves away a little distance from the lovers here; but her presence on stage during the following exchanges (perhaps silently expressing her disapproval) sounds a sceptical note in the midst of Willmore's most romantic scene.

99–102 *Thou shouldst . . . joys*: Q places line-breaks after 'love' and 'vanity'. I take Angellica's meaning to be 'you wouldn't have to buy my love if you were capable of forgetting that I have been a courtesan, and treating me like a lover'. An alternative possibility is 'You could never buy my love. Could you forget that I have been a courtesan?' The New Cross production interpreted it in this way, with Angellica pausing, and Willmore looking disappointed, after 'thou shouldst not buy my love'.

140–1 *hopes . . . pretends*: Willmore's false concord of verb and subject is common in this period.

163 *loyally lousy*: lice-infested because of the rough, beggarly life he leads in his prince's service.

3.1 S.D. *A street*: perhaps a new street scene, since the 'long street' is not specified here as it is in 1.2 and 2.1.

7 *the road to Loretto*: Loretto, a town on the Adriatic, near Ancona, was a noted pilgrimage resort; the road to it would have been crowded with pilgrims, and with beggars and gipsies wanting the pilgrims' money.

34 *the pip*: vague term for an illness, especially depression; usually used jokingly.

45 *venture a cast*: (1) risk a dice-throw; (2) be willing to be thrown to the ground.

46 *observed*: L, T; *observe* Q1–2, J; *observ'd* Q3, C1–2, S.

62 *not a word*: Q3, C1–2, S, J; *not word* Q1–2, T.

67–82 *conjures . . . nest*: Pedro's supposed speech is likened to a magician's invocation of spirits; this will either lay (exorcise) the god of love, or else break the women's hearts, figured here as the nest occupied by Cupid as 'bird' (so called because the god is 'soft-winged').

87–90 *Does not . . . lovers*: cf. *Thomaso*, Part I, 3.2. Thomaso: 'Do's not the little god appear upon my Brow to distinguish me from the Common Crow'd of Lovers.'

107 *charming*: working like a magical spell.

108 *'tis he and she gold*: *she* Q3, C1–2, S, L, J, T; *the* Q1–2. Cf. *Thomaso*, Part I, 3.2: ''tis He and She Gold while 'tis here, and begets young pleasures.'

111 *All . . . sting*: cf. *Thomaso*, Part I, 3.2: 'All the hony of Marriage, but none of the sting, Ned.'

138 *capuchin*: member of an austere monastic order dating from the sixteenth century.

146–7 *staying that swingeing stomach*: allaying that furious appetite.

211 *bills of exchange*: orders directing payment of money, often used by travellers.

285 *beating the bush*: a term from game-shooting: scaring the birds for someone else to shoot them.

3.2 S.D. *Lucetta's house*: Lucetta's trick on Blunt in scenes 3.2–3.4 is based on an episode in *Thomaso*, Part I. Killigrew's Lucetta is more serious than Behn's, lamenting her life as a whore and complaining of being Philippo's slave. Edwardo is not dropped into a sewer like Blunt, but by mistake kisses a man he finds in Lucetta's bed, and afterwards fights him.

3.3 S.D. *The scene . . . bed*: a discovery scene. The shutters representing Lucetta's house are drawn back to reveal her bedchamber, a scene set at the second shutter position. The alcove is possibly painted on the shutter behind the bed.

5 *to quit scores*: to make things even between us.

6 S.D. *undresses himself*: Blunt's undressing to shirt and drawers onstage provoked criticisms of indecency during the eighteenth century, and in some performances the actor went offstage to undress.

18 S.D. *puts out the candle*: the action is now understood to be taking place in the dark, though the stage-lighting has not changed. The audience can see the bed, and watch it disappear, but Blunt cannot.

S.D. *the bed descends*: the bed is placed on a large trapdoor and is lowered into the trap.

27 S.D. *lights . . . let down*: Blunt uses a second, smaller trapdoor.

38 *a medal of his king*: a medallion bearing the king's head. The king is presumably Charles I, though an audience in the 1670s would think more immediately of Charles II.

40–2 *old Queen Bess's . . . justify the theft*: Philippo uses the fact that Blunt's gold was minted in the reign of Elizabeth I as a mock-justification for stealing it, on the basis that this helps the Spanish avenge her defeat of their Armada in 1588.

43 *bowed gold*: curved gold.

3.4 S.D. *the scene changes . . . commo-shore*: the shutters representing Lucetta's chamber are drawn back, either to reveal fresh ones (presumably representing a street scene) in the groove immediately behind, still at the same shutter position, or to reveal the dark backcloth of the theatre. Blunt climbs up using the same trapdoor as before, which now represents the entrance to the sewer. In *Thomaso*, Edwardo leaves Lucetta's house in his drawers, vowing revenge: unlike Blunt he succeeds in this, and Lucetta enters a later scene '*with her face bound up, cut by Edwardo's Bravos*'.

2 *without a clue*: without any thread to guide him through the underground passages he is supposed to have travelled.

13 *fop*: a general term for a fool or idiot, with no specific reference to fancy clothes or affected manners.

15 *a ballad*: Blunt imagines his mishap publicized in a ballad. In *Thomaso*, Part I, 5.12, Matthias comments on Edwardo's mishap: 'Now do I smell a ballad . . . of the two Bearded Lovers, kissing like the Divel and the Collier.'

the Prado: the Neapolitan setting is momentarily forgotten here: following *Thomaso*, which is set in Madrid, Behn names the public park of Madrid.

16 *annihilated*: blotted out of existence (as Lucetta was, from Blunt's point of view, when she disappeared).

18–19 *at home, would*: at home, that would.

3.5 S.D. *The garden in the night*: this scene is based on *Thomaso*, Part I, 4.1, where Edwardo accosts Serulina.

S.D. *in an undress*: in loose, informal clothing.

15 *wench*: whore.

27 *disguised*: drunk.

36 *vow you*: *you vow* Q1–3, C1–2, S, L, J, T. This seems to be an error in Q: Willmore is talking of his own possible vows to Florinda, not hers to him, and 'you vow' does not work well as an inversion in this context.

3.6.23 *distinguish her woman*: recognize her as a woman.

26 *mere*: complete, absolute.

43 S.D. *offers to go in*: Willmore starts to go in at Angellica's door, but is stopped by the arrival of Antonio and his page.

64 *St Jago*: Santiago, Spanish form of St James.

4.1 S.D. *Discovers Belvile*: the shutters with the street scene for 3.6 are drawn back to reveal Belvile.

17–19 *In vain . . . Angellica*: verse Q1–3, C1–2, S, T; prose L, J.

29–32 *You shall . . . punished*: verse Q1–3, C1–2, S, T; prose L, J.

33 *generosity*: the proper behaviour of a generous, i.e. high-ranking, person.

34–6 *It had . . . wounded*: verse Q1–3, C1–2, S, T; prose L, J.

68–70 *That opinion . . . imitate*: verse Q1–3, C1, S, T; prose C2, L, J.

71–2 *You say . . . the habit*: verse Q1–3, C1–2, S, T; prose L, J.

4.2.1–4 *I'm dying . . . fights*: verse Q1–3, C1–2, S, T; prose L, J.

14 *I escaped*: C1–2, S, L, J, T; *escaped* Q1–3.

31 *Or . . . or*: either . . . or.

32–3 *Can he . . . prize*: verse Q1–3, C1–2, S, T; prose L, J.

41 *you . . . that dares*: Florinda's false concord of verb and subject is common at the time.

108 *punctual in my word*: punctilious in performing what I have promised.

131–2 *For . . . quality*: previous editions (apart from C2, which sets prose) break the line after 'no'.

145–6 *Oh . . . sin*: L; other editions break the line after 'all'.

165 *there are of those*: there do indeed exist some.

261 *she*: Willmore refers to the woman Hellena claims to serve as page. Some editions emend to *he*, changing the referent to Hellena in her boy disguise.

291 *inhumanly*: Q2–3, C1–2, S; *unhumanely* Q1, L, J; *inhumanely* T.

347 *German motion*: German puppet; i.e. something lifeless, combining reputed German dullness with a puppet's lack of animation.

361–2 *You cannot undeceive . . . her*: prose Q1–3, C1–2, S, L, J, T.

368 *foppery*: foolishness (a more general term than the modern one, not necessarily implying affected dress or behaviour).

394 *miss*: mistress.

For . . . kind: Willmore's rhyming couplet on exit is a device commonly used to close a scene on a comic note, but here Angellica is left to hold the stage and end the scene with a serious soliloquy. In some eighteenth-century performances Angellica's speech here was omitted, reducing her role and giving more prominence to Willmore's.

403 *name*: reputation.

4.3 S.D. *A street*: either the long street, or a street scene at the second shutter position. Some scenic depth is suggested by the S.D. 'from the farther end of the scene' (following l. 62).

48 *in this fresco*: exposed to the open air in this way.

58 *simply*: foolishly.

59–60 *an the rogue . . . ask first*: unless he learns to look like a humble borrower, and ask for a favour. Previous editions read 'and', a common variant of 'an' (if); some editions (Q2–3, C1–2, S, T) emend the subjunctive 'know' to indicative 'knows', rendering the sense something like 'and furthermore he doesn't know how to . . .'.

66 *warrant her prize*: guarantee that she's fair game (a prize ship was one that could be captured according to law).

4.4 S.D. *Another street*: the shutters close over the previous street scene, covering the change to Blunt's chamber which is to be revealed in 4.5, another discovery scene.

4.5 S.D. *Blunt's chamber*: this scene is based on *Thomaso*, Part II, 2.4, where Serulina enters Edwardo's house. Some eighteenth-century perform-ances of *The Rover* cut Blunt's speeches, reducing the violence and misogyny in the scene.

10 *faithless as a physician*: doctors were commonly supposed to be inclined to atheism.

93 *you had e'en confessed*: you might as well have confessed.

109 *cormorant at whore and bacon*: cormorants were proverbially insatiable birds. Belvile is here said to tackle both women and food with indiscriminate greed.

139 S.D. *locks the door*: Blunt, having moved from the scenic area to the forestage, locks one proscenium door, standing for the entrance to his chamber, and leaves by another door, understood to lead to another room in the house.

5.1 S.D. *at his chamber door*: the proscenium door Blunt locked before.

33 S.D. *looks simply*: looks foolish and abashed.

93 *I shall discover all*: I shall reveal everything.

93–4 *one at once*: one at a time.

96 *the propriety of her*: the ownership of her.

155 S.D. *kneels*: Willmore's position here, as one of the group begging Florinda's pardon, contrasts with Thomaso's in *Thomaso*, Part II, 3.4, where he harangues the men who have threatened Serulina.

159 *a father*: a priest (to marry Belvile to Florinda).

198 *this juggling knot*: this cheating, trick-playing (marriage) knot.

268 *fever*: Q3, C2, L, J; *favour* Q1–2, C1, S, T.

275 *charge*: expenditure.

280 *you'll find will be*: L: L notes 'emendation from M not i Luttrel cop o Q1' *you'l wil be* Q1; *he'll be* Q2, C1, T; *will be* Q3, C2.

308 S.D. *Offers . . . gold*: in *Thomaso*, Part II, 5.7, Thomaso promises Paulina that Angellica will have her money back; there is no suggestion that it will be refused.

336 *do not use to be*: am not accustomed to being.

386–7 *clap you on board for prize*: take you onto the ship like a prisoner taken in war.

427 *clawed away with broadsides*: (of a ship) beaten off course by another ship's artillery.

431 *one*: L, T; *on* Q1–3, C1–2, S, J.

431–2 *come to the lure*: of a trained bird, to come to its handler (part of Willmore's comparison of Hellena to a hawk or falcon). He means that while she is happy with him she'll remain faithful.

452–3 *left-handed bridegroom*: unofficial bridegroom.

469–70 *let me . . . sheriff's charge*: let me be hanged.

484–6 *fine name . . . call you?*: Hellena teases Willmore for dubbing himself 'the constant', suggesting that he is only likely to be constant to his faulkner (falconer) because of the pleasures of hawking, or to his butler because of his love of drinking (butlers took care of and poured wine); and that, if he is constant, he ought to come when he is whistled for.

487–8 *name without crossing himself*: perhaps a teasing reference to Hellena's supposed destiny as a nun; he hopes her name won't be so holy he'll need to genuflect when he hears it.

512 *a prince, aboard his little wooden world*: refers to Willmore's authority on his ship, and implies an analogy between the hero and Charles II, the exiled prince who is 'lord of the watery element' (1.2.63).

522 *three hundred thousand crowns*: Q1–2, C1–2, S, L, J, T; *two* Q3. Q3's emendation makes all the references to Hellena's fortune consistent, but the inconsistency may be deliberate. Angellica may have been mistaken about Hellena's money, and this late revelation of even more money for Willmore might be exploited by Hellena's slightly stressing 'three', and Willmore's silently expressing his delight.

522–3 *you cannot keep from me*: Hellena is careful to emphasize her control over her fortune; presumably, because she has inherited from her uncle, her nearer relatives have no power to disinherit her.

548 *in the Inquisition for Judaism*: imprisoned and questioned by the authorities of the Catholic Church, on suspicion of being a Jew. The tortures perpetrated by the Inquisition were legendary.

551–2 *a bag of bays*: a bag of spices for cooking.

556 *(To Hellena) . . . little rover?*: Q1 places S.D. after 'my little rover'. Given the inconsistency of placing of directions in Q1 this leaves this part of Blunt's speech ambiguous: he might address Belvile, who has just spoken, here, and only turn to Hellena at 'Lady'; but 'little' fits Hellena better, and 'my little rover', addressed to her, emphasizes Blunt's reaction to Hellena's male clothes, and offers a further hint of her wish to be like the rover Willmore.

568 *a cast of his office*: a sample of his function; i.e. to marry people.

Epilogue 5 *conventicling*: attending conventicles (Dissenting meetings). Behn claims, tongue-in-cheek, that Puritan reformation is so fashionable that her play about cavaliers in a Catholic country is bound to fail; in fact *The Rover* was very popular.

7 *That mutinous tribe*: Dissenters.

12 *the spirit moves*: a reference to the reliance of members of Puritan sects on the guidance offered by the spirit within them.

13 *maggot*: whimsical notion; refers back to 'spirit', and indicates contempt for the notion of inner spiritual guidance.

19–20 *seldom sees . . . old Blackfriars way*: hardly watches plays except for revivals of the ones that used to be put on at the Blackfriars playhouse, the pre-Civil War theatre.

21 *bamboo*: a cane.

35 *the half-crown spare*: save the half-crown he would otherwise spend at the playhouse.

39 *dammee*: damny Q1. A variant of 'damn me'. The fool is practising a bold, bullying stare which he can try out in the mirror but wouldn't dare to adopt in the street.

42 *Nokes, or Tony Leigh*: James Nokes and Anthony Leigh, well-known comic actors who often worked as a duo. They played together in some of Behn's plays, including *The Feigned Courtesans* and *The Lucky Chance*.

Postscript 3 *'Thomaso' altered*: Behn's play is, in fact, considerably indebted to Sir Thomas Killigrew's *Thomaso, or the Wanderer*, written in 1654 but not published till after the Restoration.

4 *the proprietor*: presumably Killigrew, who is *Thomaso*'s author and so its owner; he was also proprietor of the rival theatre company, the King's Company. Borrowings like Behn's were very common in this period; but possibly the booksellers feared that Killigrew would object to this use of his work by his competitors in the Duke's Company. There is no

evidence that he did so, however, and it is possible that Behn, who had connections with Killigrew, used his work with his permission.

9–10 *Spartan boys*: Spartan, which usually means hard, courageous, frugal, seems to be used here to mean 'cunning, clever at hiding one's wrongdoings'.

11 *hang . . . object*: an analogy between Angellica's picture, hung out within the action of the play, and Behn's choice to advertise her debt to Killigrew's play by using the name Angellica Bianca from it. Angellica is by no means the only 'object' taken from Killigrew, but Behn does change the names, and often considerably alters the roles, of other major characters.

12–13 *the play of 'The Novella'*: *The Novella* (1632), a comedy of intrigue by Richard Brome, from which Behn takes a few hints.

20 *especially of our sex*: a phrase inserted at a late stage: the first issue and some copies of the second issue of Q1 do not have it. The third issue of Q1 has it, and in addition, has Behn's name on the title-page for the first time. Possibly Behn decided to add this reference to her gender once her authorship was known. (See Link, pp. ix–x, and O'Donnell, pp. 34–5.)

22–3 *Virgil . . . fame*: Behn provides an English version of a complaint made by Virgil when another writer took credit for something he had written anonymously.

The Feigned Courtesans

Cast *Morosini*: C2, S, Lud, LM; *Morisini* Q, C1. C2's emendation makes the name conform with Italian usage.

Octavio . . . deformed, revengeful: Octavio seems intended as a particular type, a deformed and (therefore) spiteful man, capable of taking a mean revenge. The text rarely mentions his deformity (Cornelia call hi 'il-favoured a 2.1.57), but it may have been emphasized by make-up and acting, thus making Marcella's determination not to marry him readily sympathetic to the audience.

Silvio: not mentioned in the original cast-list, but named in the stage-directions, which sometimes confuse him with Sabina, Laura Lucretia's female attendant.

The Epistle Dedicatory *To Mrs Ellen Gwynn*: Eleanor (Nell) Gwyn (1642?–1687) was a famous comedy actress in the 1660s, creating 'gay couple' roles with the actor Charles Hart. She became a mistress of Charles II in the late 1660s and left the stage in 1671.

21–2 *give 'em*: S, LM; *give give 'em* Q.

38 *bear*: LM; *bears* Q, C1–2, S, Lud.

51 *you*: S, Lud, LM; *your* Q.

56 *two noble branches*: Nell Gwyn's children by Charles II, Charles Beauclerk, Duke of St Albans, b. 1670, and James Beauclerk, b. 1671.

61 *those glorious titles*: Nell Gwyn's children were given titles, but she was not.

66 *overbusy*: i.e. my being overbusy.

Prologue *Mrs Currer*: Dublin-born actress Elizabeth Currer (*fl.* 1673–1743) played Marcella in the original production of the play.

1 *this cursèd plotting age*: *The Feigned Courtesans* was produced during the unrest caused by the Popish Plot. Titus Oates's supposed revelation of a plot to kill Charles II to make way for his Catholic brother had stirred up panic and strong anti-Catholic feeling in England. The prologue complains that concern about the plot is ruining the theatre by reducing audiences, and mocks anti-Catholic prejudice.

13 *Jesuitical*: the Jesuits (members of the Roman Catholic Society of Jesus) were particularly hated by Protestants, and were supposed to have fomented the Popish Plot.

16 *the plot is laid in Rome*: Behn slyly compares her comedy's plot, set in Rome, with the Popish Plot, implying that any opposition to her comedy must come from the hysterical anti-Papist prejudice then current in London.

39 *tattered ensigns*: the actress points out some parts of her clothing to the audience, identifying them as clothes given her by her last lover, which served as her 'badge of office' as his mistress; their tattered state reveals how long ago the affair was, and how poor she therefore is now.

44 *the whore of Babylon*: 'Babylon the great, mother of harlots and of earth's abominations', Revelation 17: 5. Frequently used figuratively by Protestants to refer to the Church of Rome.

1.1.2 *St Peter's church*: St Peter's Basilica, an immense and splendid church famous for its art treasures. Behn underlines her Catholic setting by the mention of this Vatican church, a centre of the Counter-Reformation.

37 *wilt*: *wo't* Q, C1–2, S, Lud; *ought* LM.

49 *roll with six*: i.e. easily get six women to have sex with him.

63 *Viterboan*: native of Viterbo, a town about 40 miles from Rome.

66–7 *Who . . . best*: prose Q, C1–2, S, LM, Lud. Q and C1 introduce line-break after *whore*; I have introduced the line-break after *beauties*.

73–4 *to be . . . impossibilities*: it is as impossible to be a hermit (secluded from the opposite sex), in the supposedly aphrodisiac warmth of a southern European city like Rome, as it is to live a life of luxury (and sexual indulgence) in the cold and hostile climate of Greenland.

80 *with him*: C2, S, Lud, LM; *with* Q, C1.

89 *intelligence*: information.

98 *character*: description. Julio has not met his intended bride, so does not realize that she is the woman he has seen in St Peter's church.

133 *i'th'*: C1–2, S, Lud; *in the i'th* Q.

155 *painful*: diligent.

167 *lie at*: importune.

179 *recipe*: *receipt* Q, C1–2, S, Lud, LM.

181–2 *Medici's Villa*: LM; *Medices Villa* Q, C1–2, S. The Villa Medici, a famous Roman villa built in the sixteenth century.

189 *fops*: fools.

209 *Allons*: let's go.

1.2 s.d. *Draws off . . . discovers*: the street scene for 1.1 is drawn back to reveal Tickletext and Petro.

s.d. *a-trimming*: having his hair cut.

1 *che bella*: how lovely.

5 *Teze*: Venetian dialect form for 'be quiet'.
Barberacho: phonetic rendering of Italian 'Barberaccio', incompetent barber.

13 *'A*: she.

33 *frizz*: tightly curled hair.

42 s.d. *sets himself*: takes up a pose.

s.d. *making horns*: holding up two fingers in insulting gesture.

46 *hypocondriac*: abdominal pains. Hypochondriac was the name for diseases of the hypochondria, the parts of the abdomen just below the ribs.

58 *Piazza di Spagna*: a well-known square in Rome, called 'Spanish' because it was close to the Spanish ambassador's palace.

66 *portion*: dowry; hence, large sum of money.

77 *Illustrissimo*: most illustrious.

78 *Miphistophiloucho*: a partially Italianized form of 'Mephistopheles', with 'oucho' rendering the Italian diminutive ending *-uccio*. A little, devilish spirit, with an allusion to the character in Marlowe's *Dr Faustus*.

79 *Rabbi Manaseth-Ben-Nebiton*: a made-up name for a Jew; may allude to Manaseh-ben-Israel, who during the Interregnum negotiated with Cromwell for Jews to be allowed to live in England.

82 *the old law*: the law of the Scriptures, 'old' from a Christian point of view because superseded by the New Testament.

85 s.d. *A fart*: presumably a sound effect to give the impression of a fart from Sir Signal, whose backside is towards the audience.

101 *Corpo di me*: my body.

113 *Servitore*: your servant.

Hulichimo: Sir Signal's meaning is unclear. He is not using an Italian word here.

144 *vossignoria*: *vos signora* Q. Your ladyship.

scusa mi: *scusa mia* Q. Pardon me.

114–15 *Signora . . . Bacco*: in garbled Italian, with some French forms: most beautiful lady, I kiss your ladyship's hands; pardon me, my most illustrious sir; by Bacchus.

118 *staffiere*: *staffiera* Q. Italian for 'footman'. Q erroneously uses a feminine form.

incontanente: *incontinente* Q. Obsolete Italian, 'at once'.

119 *cazzo*: *cazo* Q. An oath from the vulgar Italian for penis.

127 *an -acho, or an -oucho*: phonetic renderings of Italian suffixes *-accio* and *-uccio*.

137 *Molto volentieri*: *multo vollentiero* Q. Most willingly.

140 *cursen name*: Christian name.

142 *bestia*: idiot.

144 *padrone mio*: *patrona mea* Q. My master.

152 *back-sword*: a sword with a single cutting edge.

157 *guards*: defensive sword-positions.

158–9 *eder . . . de . . . dey . . . den*: Petro's mock-French pronunciation of 'either', 'the', 'they', 'then'.

158–60 *quarte . . . tierce . . . parades, degagements . . . advancements . . . elongements . . . retierments*: fencing terms: 'quarte' and 'tierce' are the fourth and third sword-positions; 'parades' are parries, 'degagements' disengage the blade ready for a thrust, 'advancements' are advances, an 'elongement' is the way to stretch to make a thrust, and to make a 'retierment' is to give ground.

162–3 *St George's guard*: a guard made with a broadsword, to ward off blows to the head. Named after England's patron saint, it suits Tickletext better than Petro's fencing positions with foreign names.

164 *mettez-vous en garde*: put yourself on guard.

166 *rubbers*: bout.

178 *A tande, a tande um pew*: a phonetic rendering of either Italian 'Attendi, attendi un po'' or (more likely, as Petro is still pretending to be French) French 'Attendez, attendez un peu'; in either case meaning 'wait, wait a little'.

trust: Petro's mock-French pronunciation of *thrust*.

189 *single-rapier*: a small sword used for thrusting, in contrast to the larger back-sword, used for cutting.

206 *Ajax . . . armour*: in Ovid's *Metamorphoses*, Book 13, Ajax and Ulysses both claim the armour of the dead Achilles. It is awarded to Ulysses for his eloquence.

209 *so tall a man of hands*: so valiant a fighter.

    corpo di me: *corpo de me* Q.

212 *sophister*: university student in second or third year.

218 *Yo baco les manos*: I kiss the hands; a phrase in garbled Italian, perhaps with Spanish influence on the last two words. Correct Italian would be 'Io bacio le mani'. Behn is probably deliberately creating Sir Signal's errors here.

220 *multo bien venito*: most welcome. Again, the words may be influenced by Spanish. Modern Italian would be 'molto ben venuto'.

236 *hedging-gloves*: heavy gloves worn when repairing hedges.

251 *pew, pulpit, desk, steeple . . . ring of bells*: features of English churches, connoting Protestantism with its emphasis on gathering congregations for prayers and sermon, as opposed to the rituals and icons of Catholicism evoked in the discussion of St Peter's.

263 *close changes*: peals of bells in varying orders, rung very close together.

274–5 *fustian-fume*: ranting, bombastic display of anger.

284 *bell' ingratos*: lovely ungrateful ones. Sir Signal adds an English plural to the Italian phrase.

2.1 S.D. *The garden of Medici's villa*: a garden scene with trees painted on the side-shutters.

10–11 *that general intelligence*: such widespread information.

13 *ragion di stato*: *region de stato* Q. Reason of state.

14 *of*: from.

24 S.D. *dressed like courtesans*: they wear the courtesan's vizor (see below, l. 71); apart from this it is not clear how far actresses wore distinctive 'courtesan' costumes. Possibly loose and brightly coloured robes were used.

    attendance: one or more person(s) in attendance.

36 *Echo's love*: Echo was a nymph who pined away for love of Narcissus; only her voice remained.

37 *Ovid*: famous as an authority on love; author of *Metamorphoses* (in which the story of Echo is found), and of *Ars Amatoria* (*Art of Love*), of which Cornelia makes 'better use' in this scene.

66 *keeping courtesan*: a woman who buys a man's sexual services.

71 *the vizor*: vizard-mask, often worn by courtesans.

96 *dark-lantern men*: men carrying lanterns that can be shut to obscure the light; hence, lovers visiting secretly at night.

99 *begin*: C2, S, Lud, LM; *begins* Q, C1.

114 *St Teresa's*: Carmelite convent founded by St Teresa.

117 S.D. *walk down the garden*: i.e. they move upstage, in the scenic area behind the proscenium arch. This and other directions (see below, l. 129 S.D.) indicate that the garden scene is a 'long scene', with plenty of scope for acting in the upstage area.

129 S.D. [*Exeunt*] . . . *down the scene*: i.e. they move upstage in the scenic area and exit through the wings.

136 *Sans Cœur*: heartless.

145 *Inglese*: *Englese* Q. Englishman.

147 *That very he*: I have introduced the line-break after 'he'; otherwise lineation in this speech follows Q.

200 S.D. *walks about in the scene*: behind the proscenium arch, perhaps weaving in and out of the side-shutters which represent the groves.

222 *a little bank*: a store (of prayers, hoarded like money for future use).

259 *wants no customers*: has no shortage of customers.

275 *upon the square*: fairly, without cheating.

284 S.D. *climbs a tree*: using a standard stage tree, probably with a ladder at the back.

runs his head in a bush: presumably the bush is a free-standing cut-out shape; Tickletext's lower half remains sticking out from behind it.

290 *vot servitor, vossignoria*: *vot servitor vos signoria* Q. Your servant, your lordship. Sir Signal seems to be mixing French and Italian here: 'vot' is closer to French *votre* than to Italian *vostro*.

316 *keep it*: C1–2, S, LM; *kept* Q.

336 *che diavolo*: *che deavilo* Q; the devil. I have used the standard Italian *diavolo* throughout, where Q has variously 'deavilo' and 'diavillo'.

340 *Imbriaco*: drunk (standard Italian form would be *imbriachi*).

341 *ah, che diavolo*: *ach deavilo* Q.

343 *cinquat par cent*: dialectal form of *cinquanta per cento*, 50 per cent.

344 *andiamo a casa*: Sir Signal's translation, 'let's amble home', is correct.

350 *with a bonne grâce*: *with a bon-grace* Q; gracefully.

353 *your address*: your way of greeting a person.

358 *inviveates the pericranium*: enlivens the head.

358–9 *sapientiates*: gives knowledge to.

360 *conceive*: understand.

377 *Caccamerda orangate*: *cackamarda orangate* Q. I have adopted this spelling throughout. Petro makes up what sounds to Sir Signal like the name of a pleasant perfume; 'orangate' is not an Italian word, but to English ears sounds like a foreign word for 'orange'. 'Caccamerda',

though, reveals the evil-smelling truth to members of the audience with more Italian than Sir Signal; it is made up from juvenile and adult colloquialisms for faeces, 'poo–poo shit'.

380   S.D. *bonprovache*: a phonetic rendering of Italian 'buon pro vi faccia', bless you.

385   *dulce piquante*: sweetly spicy (perfume). A mixture of forms is used here, 'dulce' from Latin and 'piquante' from French; the correct Italian would be 'dolce piccante'.

388   *me*: C1–2, S, Lud, LM; *we* Q.

396   *flourish*: 'to flourish' means 'to gesture with arm and hand, conveying extravagant courtesy'.

416–17   *tropes and figures*: figures of speech.

431   *Perdio, Bacchus*: *pardio! Bacchus* Q; by the god, Bacchus.

443   *ecclesiastico . . .* : the Italian in this speech is mixed with some Spanish and French elements, and some obscure elements which may be meant as Petro's imitation of beggars' dialect. An English version of the speech would be: 'a certain priest, plump and rich . . . meets a poor cripple. "A poor cripple, poor cripple; cripple, cripple, cripple! . . . Charity for a poor cripple, for the love of God!" At last he begs a julio. "Nothing!" Then the poor cripple begs half a julio . . . "Nothing!" . . . "A kiss." . . . "Nothing!" . . . Pardon, pardon, my masters.'

  ecclesiastico: *eclejastio* Q; priest. I have adopted this spelling throughout; Q has variously 'eclejastio' 'eclesiastico', and 'ecclesiastico'.

444   *povero*: adopted here and subsequently where Q has variously 'paver', 'pavero', 'paure'; poor.

445   *strapiao*: cripple. The correct Italian form would be 'storpiato', but Q's reading may possibly be an imitation of beggars' dialect rather than an error.

447   *Elemosina*: *Elemosuna* Q.

  amour: *a moure* Q. French influence creeps in here; the Italian would be 'amore'.

  dievos: this shows Spanish influence; the Italian would be 'dio'.

449   *mezzo*: *mezo* Q.

452   *Scusa*: possibly meant as beggars' dialect; correct Italian would be 'scusate'.

  miei padroni: *mea patrona's* Q.

462   *povero strapado*: *paureo strapado* Q. I have corrected Sir Signal's 'paureo', which, like Petro's various versions of the word, seems to be Behn's or the compositor's error; but 'strapado' seems to be intended as Sir Signal's mangling of Petro's word for 'cripple'. The mistake is comical because it suggests the English word 'strappado', a well-known form of torture.

466 *mezzo*: *meze* Q.

 bacio: *bacoi* Q.

468 *Adds me*: a mild oath.

3.1 S.D. [*A street*]: side-shutters are changed to produce another 'long scene', with room for walking up and down the street. Because the feigned courtesans' lodgings are said to be on the Corso, Summers provides 'The Corso' as setting for 3.1 and other scenes in which the doors to their houses feature; but locations in this play are more fluid than that suggests. In 5.3, where Q gives the location 'Piazza di Spagna', the doors to the courtesans' houses also appear.

 9 *the Corso*: Via del Corso, a main thoroughfare in central Rome.

62–4 *This fine . . . him*: verse S, LM; prose Q, C1–2.

 99 S.D. *as down the street*: i.e. upstage.

115 S.D. *up the scene*: i.e. downstage.

117 *berger*: shepherd. Evening is traditionally the shepherd's hour; Galliard's speech indicates that night is meant to be approaching during this scene.

120 *fine*: fee.

121 *tenement*: (1) right of possession; (2) dwelling-place; (3) body. All three senses are invoked in Galliard's metaphor for paying for access to the courtesans.

127 *Corinna*: mentioned in Ovid's poetry as his beloved.

148 *And so . . . practice*: to give my kind of reverent love to an unworthy courtesan would be even more infamous than the courtesan's trade itself.

165 *conducts*: C1–2, S, LM; *conduct* Q, Lud.

 S.D. *appear above*: in the balcony of one of the proscenium doors, which represents the entrance to 'Silvianetta's' house.

166 *She comes . . . she comes*: Q, C1–2, S, have extra line-break at 'thy'.

168 *Thetis*: nereid or sea-nymph; sunset and sunrise were sometimes poetically expressed as the sun-god's sinking in or rising from her lap.

169–70 *A rapture . . . grace*: verse Q, C1; prose C2, S, LM.

 thou art old dog at a long grace: you always take far too long saying grace before the meal.

173 *my lady's eldest son*: proverbially over-petted and effeminate.

181 *let me mark the house*: one proscenium door represents 'Silvianetta's' entrance, the other, adjacent to it, Laura Lucretia's. Various characters' inability to distinguish between the two forms the basis for much of the comic business.

187 *one*: C2, S, Lud, LM; *on* Q, C1.

190 *sound*: whole, undamaged; with a play on 'free from syphilitic infection'.

204 *every*: C1–2, S, Lud, LM; *ever* Q.

251 *false-souled*: S, LM; *false-souly* Q, C1–2, Lud.

260–1 *what a rub's here in a fair cast*: a metaphor from bowls; what an impediment to an otherwise fortunate situation.

261 *Alegremente*: look lively, cheer up.

261–2 *defy . . . works*: derived from the baptismal promise, made by godparents, to help a godchild resist the devil.

all his: S, Lud, LM; *all's his* Q; *all's* C1–2.

285 *God a mercy*: an exclamation of surprise, from 'God have mercy'.

296 s.d. *dressed like an antiquary*: probably in a black gown to suggest a scholar.

305 *Knox . . . Cartwright*: John Knox (1505–72), Scots reformer and statesman who helped establish Presbyterianism in Scotland. Hatred of Papist 'idolatry' informs all his writing, so he is a very suitable author for Tickletext to read. Thomas Cartwright (1535–1603), English Puritan divine, imprisoned several times for Nonconformity and controversial writings.

309 *I transcribe . . . transactions*: Tickletext's habit of keeping a detailed diary is typically Puritan.

318 *one's*: C2, S, Lud, LM; *on's* Q, C1.

329 *perdio*: *par dios* Q.

tropo caro: too dear.

333 *St James's of the Incurables*: a fourteenth-century Roman hospital for sufferers with incurable diseases.

in case of: C2, S, Lud, LM; *in case* Q, C1.

375 *of his pitch*: of his height.

418 s.d. *with a lantern*: an indication that darkness has fallen. There is no difference in the stage-lighting, but the audience now assumes action is taking place in darkness.

430 s.d. *opens her lantern*: Marcella, like the other characters, carries a dark lantern which can be open and shut. Stage convention is that characters can see each other when they open their lanterns, but when they are shut it is dark. The rest of this scene gains comic effect from the blunders made by characters supposedly in the dark, while the audience in fact sees them clearly.

439 *habit*: (1) frequent practice; (2) costume.

441 *Covent Garden conventicle*: Nonconformists' meeting-house in Covent Garden.

450 s.d. *straight*: immediately.

460 s.d. *pass*: make passes at each other with their swords.

470 *cospetto di diavolo*: *caspeto de deavilo* Q; by the devil.

494 *of a hero*: C2, S, LM; *of hero* Q, C1, Lud.

496–7 *Gulf of Lions*: arm of the Mediterranean Sea, from the south coast of France to the coast of Spain.

498–9 *Vivat . . . fatto*: 'Hope lives in spite of fate', in a mangled Italian that shows the influence of French forms. Correct Italian would be 'Viva speranza in dispetto del fato'. The phrase appears in Marston's *Antonio and Mellida* (1601), 3.2.231.

501 *Che è questo?*: *Que equesto?* Q; what is this?

503 *Un maledetto spirito incarnato*: *una malladette spirito incarnate* Q; an evil spirit incarnate.

507 *spiritello*: *spiritalo* Q.

immortale: *imortallo* Q.

incorporale: *incorporalla* Q.

immateriale: *imaterialle* Q.

507–8 *uno spiritello . . . diavolo*: in a mixture of Italian and Latinate English: a little spiritual, immortal, incorporeal, inanimate, immaterial, philosophical, invisible, unintelligible devil. Sir Signal seems to be confusing Italian and English here; I have emended to the correct Italian form where he appears to be using Italian, but left the English forms where they are used in Q.

philosophical: *philosophicale* Q.

512–13 *una . . . diavolo-ship*: Tickletext mocks Sir Signal's devilish rant and promises to get rid of the 'spirit' with the 'magic spell' of his sword. The spelling seems to indicate a mock-Italian speech, adding Italian-sounding endings to English words.

512 *immateriale*: *imaterialle* Q.

conjuratione: conjuration, a spell or calling up of spirits.

516 *mio*: *mia* Q; mine.

cospetto di Bacchus: *caspeto de Baccus* Q; by Bacchus.

518 s.d. *stand*: *stands* Q, C1–2, S, LM.

523 *The Song*: the song contains some archaic and some dialectal forms, and some that are hard to interpret and are probably mistakes. I have largely kept to the readings in Q: all departures from copytext, apart from the adding of accents, are noted below. The translation offered here is partly based on Ludwig.

526 *Suffrir*: a dialect form; standard Italian would be 'soffrir'.

527 *mercè*: *mar ce* Q.

528 *Beltà*: *Bolta* Q.

530 *Del mio*: *dell meo* Q.

affetto: Lud; *offeto* Q; *offerto* C2.

531 *s'inganna*: *singunna* Q.

534 *avvolgere*: *auolgere* Q.

535 *sì*: *see* Q.

538 *Più*: *pui* Q.

alla: *alta* Q.

540 *vivo non è*: *viuo none* Q.

541 *luoco*: *luoce* Q.

543 *sbande*: *s'bande* Q.

544 *fo lo*: *fo'lo* Lud; *sato* Q.

gioco: *gioce* Q.

547 *Vergognoso fuggito*: *vergoroso faggito* Q.

Cruel love, cruel love, | My heart is not for you. | I don't want to suffer torments | Without ever hoping for mercy. | Beauty which is a tyrant, | Beauty which is a tyrant, | Is not worthy of my affections. | Your severity is mistaken, | If pains | And chains It tries to wrap round my feet. Yes, yes, cruel love, |My heart is not for you. ‖ Flatterer, flatterer, | I believe in your faith no more. | The burning of your fire | No longer lives in my heart. | Beauty gave it a place, | Beauty gave it a place, | But severity sends passion away. | I'm not playing your game any more; | For the poison | Has fled | From my shameful breast. | Yes, yes, cruel love, | My heart is not for you.

551 S.D. *music*: band of musicians.

S.D. *bass viol . . . hangs about his neck*: presumably a mock viol, perhaps of paper stretched on a wooden frame, was included with the real instruments carried by the musicians.

553 *Ananias*: the name suggests Puritanism and hypocrisy. It is the name of one of the Anabaptists in Jonson's *Alchemist*, and derives from Acts 5: 1–6, where Ananias is struck dead for lying to Peter.

555 *cuts so*: probably a variant of 'catso', an oath from Italian *cazzo* = 'penis'.

pillory: i.e. the viol round Tickletext's neck, which makes him look as if his head is in the pillory.

559 *the back way*: Petro is taking Tickletext into 'Silvianetta's' house, by an alternative route to the proscenium door which represents its front entrance. Either the wings or an opposite side proscenium door must be used, as the adjacent proscenium door is being used in this scene as Laura Lucretia's entrance.

570–1 *entrance through the garden*: Marcella, like Petro, is going to the house of 'Euphemia and Silvianetta'. She probably uses a different exit from Petro, to indicate that the two groups do not meet on their way to the house. Meanwhile Philippa is still waiting, behind the proscenium door which represents the house's front entrance, for Marcella to ring. She will later answer to Sir Signal's ring (see l. 429, l. 595 S.D.).

575 *lamentivolo fato*: lamentable fate.

582 S.D. *from the house*: from the proscenium door adjacent to the one representing Silvianetta's entrance. Laura Lucretia makes use of the darkness and the proximity of the two doors to get Silvianetta's lover to mix up the two houses and mistake her for the courtesan; the joke is on her, of course, since she assumes Silvianetta's lover must be Galliard, and so invites Julio in by mistake.

595 *con licenzia*: con licentia Q; by your leave.

602–3 *say . . . danger*: not traced.

604 *at rack and manger*: proverbial for living in luxury.

4.1 S.D. *Silvianetta's apartment*: at the opening of Act 4, the audience knows that Cornelia, Marcella, Fillamour, Galliard, Petro, Tickletext, Philippa, and Sir Signal are all in 'Silvianetta's' house, or making their way to it by one route or another. Everything is set for some comic revelations.

17 *What . . . resistance*: lineation follows LM; Q sets verse, two lines only, line-break after 'danger'.

44–6 *Ambition . . . off*: Q sets verse, two lines only, line-break after 'nothing'.

49–50 *Hast . . . repentance*: lineation follows LM; Q sets this as one verse line.

114–16 *Oh stay . . . reputation*: Q sets as two verse lines, line-break after 'fall'.

120 *what pity 'tis she is—a whore*: an echo of the title of John Ford's play, *'Tis Pity She's a Whore* (1633).

125–6 *Nay . . . pardon*: prose C1–2; verse Q.

137 *of none effect*: null and void.

144 *a small harlot of my own*: this suggests either that Petro is pimp to another, genuine whore, as well as to the feigned courtesans, or that he is himself contemplating the harlot's role; Galliard earlier credited him with being able to play the pathic (rent-boy).

my levite: i.e. Tickletext, so called because he is a minister of religion.

145–6 *Susanna . . . eldership*: refers to the story of Susanna in the Apocrypha, accused of adultery by two elders whose sexual advances she had rejected.

149 *take advantage by the forelock*: grab the opportunity; based on the traditional image of occasion or time as a man who, being bald behind, can only be seized by his forelock.

162 *scandalum infiniti*: in mangled Latin, infinite outrage.

188 S.D. *pulls [Sir Signal] by*: pulls him out of the way, so as to take his place in answering Cornelia.

191 *potentissimo*: *potentisimo* Q. Sir Signal's rendering of 'most powerful'; he ought to use the feminine form, *potentissima*, to address a lady.

214 *bell' ingrato*: *bell ingrate* Q; beautiful, ungrateful one.

215 *slights*: LM; *slight* Q, C1–2, S.

216–17 *traditor cruella*: cruel traitor. 'Cruella' is a corruption from English; the correct Italian would be 'crudele'.

230 *beside his text*: straying from what he ought to say.

267 *vagary*: *figary* Q, C1–2, S, LM, Lud; whim.

296 *Beelzebub*: name for a devil, found in the Bible and in Milton's *Paradise Lost*.

302 *vaulter*: (1) athlete; (2) sexual performer.

305 *to the scantling of a mousehole*: i.e. so small he could get into a mousehole.

4.2 S.D. *bed-chamber alcove*: the scene represents a bed-chamber, but there is no necessity for a bed on stage. There is a curtain, with a space behind, representing the chimney in which Sir Signal hides.

19 *Mi alma, mea core, mea vita*: my soul, my heart, my life; in a jumble of Italian and Spanish.

25 *what . . . have I caught, a tartar*: to 'catch a tartar' is proverbial for taking on someone who proves too difficult.

226 *serenissimo*: most serene.

5.1 S.D. [*A courtyard*]: no location in Q. Summers provides 'The Corso', and Ludwig 'A street', but a courtyard would be more appropriate for the well. However, the doors to the women's houses are still available.

from the garden: Ludwig suggests that Tickletext enters at the balcony (presumably representing the garden wall) and descends to the stage. Alternatively, 'from the garden' may indicate that they are on their way out, but still enclosed by the garden walls, which Tickletext intends to climb by the ladder Petro mentions.

5 *So the ladder's fast*: so long as the ladder's secure. See l. 12 S.D. below.

12 *à bon voyage*: *a bon viage* Q; good journey.

S.D. *Tickletext descends*: the staging here is unclear. Ludwig suggests that Tickletext descends from the balcony at this point. Alternatively, 'descends' may be an early direction referring to Tickletext's imminent descent into the well rather than to a separate descent. In this case Tickletext enters at stage level, never finds the ladder, and falls into the well in his search for it.

15 S.D. *stumbles . . . bucket*: a forestage trapdoor is used for the well into which Tickletext falls.

30 *cleanly pickle*: a 'pickle' is a predicament; 'cleanly' is of course ironical, as Sir Signal is anything but clean.

32 *like . . . collier*: proverb referring to the blackness shared by both.

35 *the man has his mare again*: proverbial expression, meaning everything is put right.

36 *Che è questo*: *que questo?* Q; what is this?

41 *like . . . labour-in-vain*: Sir Signal, thinking it will be hard to get the soot off, imagines himself as an inn-sign or shop-sign illustrating fruitless activity.

45 S.D. *appears . . . well*: the bucket, with Tickletext in it, could be raised and lowered by ropes from the flies.

70 *popped i'th' mouth*: slapped; Galliard means that the word 'quality' is like a slap in the face.

78 *êtes-vous là*: *este vous la?*: Q; are you there?

80 *professor*: one who professes religion or virtue; applied especially to Puritans.

95 S.D. *Sabina [and Silvio]*: Silvio needs to be onstage later in the scene.

97 *this ruffian*: Octavio, who, as Sabina guesses, followed Julio into Laura Lucretia's house (at the end of Act 3). We learn from this that he has interrupted Laura Lucretia's night with Julio (whom she still supposes to have been Galliard).

112 *Preventing*: anticipating.

155–7 *our coxcomb knight . . . he knew him*: multiple misunderstandings: Galliard mistook Tickletext for Sir Signal, while Laura Lucretia thinks he recognized Octavio.

232 *prove*: line break S; after *to* Q, C1–2.

240–3 *But . . . with*: prose C2; verse Q, C1, S, LM, Lud.

265 *loved . . . wise*: an echo of *Othello*, 5.2.347: 'one that lov'd not wisely, but too well'.

267 *Silvio*: this and Silvio's subsequent speeches in the scene are given to Sabina in Q. S corrects to Silvio.

5.2.5 S.D. *Silvio*: S; *Sabina* Q.

12 *Silvio*: S; *Sabina* Q.

23 S.D. *The song as by Laura Lucretia*: the song is sung by a singer offstage, giving the impression that it is Laura Lucretia who sings.

24 *Farewell . . . cares*: the first verse of this song appears, without music or attribution, in *Choyce Ayres and Songs . . . The Second Book* (London: John Playford, 1679), 31.

57 S.D. *[Exit Silvio]*: Silvio needs to leave in order to re-enter when Laura Lucretia calls her bravos at l. 204; here, where Laura Lucretia stops holding onto him and moves towards Galliard, seems a convenient point.

59–60 *How . . . her*: prose C1, LM; verse Q, C2, S.

70 *and*: *an* Q, C1–2, S, LM, Lud.

130 *owns*: openly acknowledges.

5.3.12 *ruffled me to man*: knocked off my edges, made me grow up.

55–6 *Oh . . . Octavio*: verse Q.

57–8 *To . . . her*: verse Q; prose C2.

62 *she is*: C1–2, S, Lud, LM; *she's* Q.

74 *Victoria*: victory. A Latin form is used here; Italian would be 'Vittoria'.
   the: C2, S, Lud, LM; *and* Q, C1.

82 *point me out*: identify me as.

100 *in their toil*: in the trap.

5.4.5 *king of Tropicipopican's daughter*: Tropicipopican is a fanciful name befitting the fairy-tale scene Sir Signal is imagining.

16 S.D. *a window curtain*: the chamber's window might be painted on the shutter, with a curtain hung in front of it, leaving just enough room for Tickletext and Sir Signal to hide behind; another possibility is that a curtain representing the window-curtain was hung inside one of the proscenium doors.

51 *La ye*: an exclamation conveying something like 'there, listen to that'.

89–92 *And . . . heir*: verse S, LM; prose Q, C1–2, Lud.

98 *truths should*: truths which should.

187 *none of those*: i.e. not attracted to boys; Cornelia is still in her masculine disguise.

The Epilogue *Mr Smith*: William Smith (d. 1698), actor in the Duke's Company and later co-manager of the United Company, played Filla-mour in the original production of the play.

2 *Though but one playhouse*: Drury Lane, home of the rival King's Company, was closed for a time during 1679.

21 *Nokes or Leigh*: famous comic actors, also coupled in the epilogue to *The Rover*. James Nokes played Sir Signal Buffoon, and Anthony Leigh (d. 1692) played Petro in the original production of *The Feigned Courtesans*.

25 *winter-quarters on the stage*: the theatrical season ran from autumn through to spring.

The Lucky Chance

Cast 4 *passes*: C1–2, S, J, M; *presses* Q, Co.

Epistle Dedicatory *Laurence, Lord Hyde*: (1641/2–1711) the second son of Edward Hyde, first Earl of Clarendon, Laurence Hyde became fourth Earl of Rochester in 1682, President of the Privy Council in 1684, and High Treasurer of the Exchequer in 1685. He was forced to leave the Court in 1687 because of his resistance to Roman Catholicism.

9 *Cardinal Richelieu*: (1585–1642) Richelieu, chief minister of state to Louis XIII, was an important patron of the theatre.

17–18 *known a man*: the man has not been convincingly identified; the incident may, of course, be invented by Behn for rhetorical effect. The party supposedly quitted is the Whig party, and the modern politician probably Shaftesbury, satirized in many anti-Whig plays including Behn's own *City Heiress*, Crowne's *City Politics*, and Otway's *Venice Preserved*.

22 *abbot of Aubignac*: François Hedelin (1604–76), critic, playwright, and author of *La Pratique du théâtre* (1657), the source for Behn's remarks here.

Preface 3 *censures*: the attacks on *The Lucky Chance* are known only through Behn's spirited defence in this preface. Evidently they focused on charges of indecency, provoking Behn's demand to be allowed, as a woman, the same freedom as male writers.

9 *through-stitched*: thoroughgoing; from sewing, a stitch going right through the cloth.

9–10 *a full third day*: playwrights' payments came from the profits of each third day of a play's run. Runs were often very short and a full house on the third day meant success; Behn is taunting her critics with her play's popularity despite their complaints.

19 *a natural colour*: a blush of embarrassment, instead of their usual artificial, painted colour.

22–3 *not wilfully bent on ill nature, and will*: not someone wilfully bent on ill nature, who will.

24 *lying . . . quibble*: lying in wait for a joke or play on words (so as to make accusations of indecency).

39 *Dr Davenant*: Charles Davenant (1656–1714), co-proprietor of the United Company, which staged *The Lucky Chance*.

42 *Sir Roger L'Estrange*: (1616–1704) licenser of publications from 1663 to 1688.

43–4 *Mr Killigrew*: Charles Killigrew (1655–1725), co-proprietor of the United Company. As Master of the Revels, he had the responsibility of censoring plays.

53–4 *Mr Leigh opens his night gown*: Anthony Leigh, d. 1692, a major comic actor who played Sir Feeble. Sir Feeble's throwing open his gown is specified in the stage-directions, so either it was not the improvisation Behn claims it is, or she later decided to adopt it.

57 *Oedipus*: Lee and Dryden's *Oedipus* (1678) includes an incident in which Oedipus enters 'walking asleep in his shirt'.

62 *The City Politics*: an anti-Whig play by John Crowne, first performed in 1682/3. The 'Lady Mayoress, and the old lawyer's wife' are two characters who make their husbands cuckolds during the action.

66–7 *The London Cuckolds*: Edward Ravenscroft's popular and bawdy play, first performed in 1681.

68 *Sir Courtly Nice*: John Crowne's popular comedy of 1685, in which 'the tailor to the young lady' indulges in *double entendre* in his conversations with the young lady and her aunt.

68–9 *Sir Fopling*: Etherege's *The Man of Mode, or Sir Fopling Flutter* (1676), in which Dorimant, after going to bed with Bellinda, talks about the 'joys' he has had with her.

69 *Valentinian*: Rochester's revision of Fletcher's play of the same name. Behn wrote the prologue for the first performance, in 1684.

72 *The Moor of Venice*: Shakespeare's *Othello*, played at Court in 1685.

72–3 *The Maid's Tragedy*: Beaumont and Fletcher's play, revived during the Restoration. The king makes his mistress, Evadne, marry Amintor, and the scenes mentioned here include lewd comments about the wedding night and the non-consummation of the marriage.

106–7 *by my receipts*: another reference to the play's popularity, hard to substantiate from the incomplete stage records of the time. *The London Stage* records a performance in mid-April 1686, but suggests the play had been performed before this.

112 *a wit of the town*: not identified.

113 *Will's coffee-house*: a coffee-house in Covent Garden, frequented by Dryden and his friends.

126 *insensible*: insensible person

Prologue *Mr Jevon*: Thomas Jevon (1652–88), who played Bearjest.

1 *old plays*: here and throughout the prologue reference is made to the difficult situation of the theatre. Only one company, the United, was playing at this time, and few new plays (which were more expensive to put on) were performed in the 1685–6 season.

20 *quit cost*: give a return on the expense; i.e. the theatres have already employed all the fools worth paying for.

29 *the Mall*: Pall Mall, a place for fashionable recreation.

the Ring: a circular drive in Hyde Park.

the pit: in the theatre.

1.1.1 *the day that gleams in yonder east*: an echo of *Romeo and Juliet*, 2.2.3. The time of day is indicated through dialogue; contemporary staging practices probably did not include lighting effects to indicate that it is 'break of day' (S.D. above) here.

5 *rigid laws*: killing in a duel was punishable by death; see note on l. 241 below.

16 S.D. *Jingle*: Gingle Q, C1–2, S, J, Co, M.

52 S.D. *closing*: coming closer to each other in the course of the fight.

58–9 *Why . . . dream*: verse Q, C1–2, S, Co; prose J, M.

72 *starter*: someone who easily abandons a settled habit of life.

74 *the city . . . charter*: controversy over the city of London's charter (allowing for the government of city affairs and the election of sheriffs to Parliament) was raging at the time *The Lucky Chance* was written and performed. The charter was revoked in 1683 after clashes between the aldermen, who voted in Whig sheriffs, and Charles II, who wanted Tory sheriffs. Elections, limited to groups loyal to the crown, were allowed again in 1685, and four Tory aldermen were elected. The city charter was restored by James II in 1688.

81 *a fair one*: i.e. a fair mark: (1) target, (2) vagina.

82 *he's*: M, Co; *he* Q, C1–2, S, J.

83 *Finsbury hero*: archery was practised in Finsbury Fields. Continuing the sex = archery metaphor, Gayman claims that whatever past prowess Sir Feeble may have shown as a marksman, he won't be able to keep his new target (Leticia) to himself.

94–5 *You . . . authority*: verse Q, C1–2, S, Co; prose J, M.

106–8 *I saw . . . Belmour*: prose Q, C1–2, S, Co, J, M.

112–13 *Now . . . friendship*: verse Q, C1–2, S, Co; prose J, M.

115–16 *I see . . . Julia*: verse Q, C1, Co; prose C2, S, J, M.

119 *wilt*: *wo't* Q, C1–2, S, J; *wot* Co; *would* M.

123 *presented*: pun on the military presenting of arms and the lover's presenting of gifts. Through giving Julia expensive presents, Gayman has run up debts that have led him to mortgage his estate to her husband, thus transferring its annual income to him.

129 *so many broke i'th' city*: the men are (1) sexually worn out and (2) financially bankrupt, as a consequence of what women give (sex) as well as what they take (money).

in tribulation: (1) in great trouble, (2) held in pawn. Gayman's fine clothes have been pawned.

143 *confident even to prostitution*: so brazen as even to have become a prostitute. Verse Q, C1–2, S, Co; prose J, M.

151 *Gorgon's head*: the mythological gorgons turned those who looked on them to stone.

152–3 *to graft upon*: to graft the cuckold's traditional horns upon.

157–8 *the press yard*: the area in Newgate prison from where convicted criminals were taken to be executed.

158–9 *Mr Barnardine in the play*: Barnardine in Shakespeare's *Measure for Measure*, whom Pompey tries to rouse from sleep for his execution: 'You must rise and be hanged, Master Barnardine' (4.2.20–1).

184–5 *Hold . . . taken*: verse Q, C1–2, S, Co; prose J, M.

192 *mistress*: lady-love. The term does not indicate a consummated sexual relationship between Belmour and Leticia.

200 *Holland's a commonwealth*: Holland had a republican government under the stadholder, William of Orange. After the Restoration it was a refuge for regicides and Puritans, and it became a focus of political opposition to Charles II and later James II. Monmouth was there from 1683 to 1685. Its reputation in England was as an egalitarian country without the usual respect for rank.

202 *snicker snee*: a fight with knives.

208 *spittle sermon*: the Easter sermons preached at St Bride's church, Fleet Street, originating in an endowment of the priory of St Mary Spittle (hospital). The spittle sermons were attended by the Lord Mayor and Corporation of London in their regalia, so the 'gold chain' that has supposedly attracted Leticia is the chain of office worn by her alderman husband.

224 *St Omer's*: a French city known for its Jesuit seminary, the residence of Sir Feeble's nephew has very different ideological connotations from those of The Hague, the capital of commonwealth Holland, where Sir Feeble's brother lives. St Omer's is probably introduced because Titus Oates, who 'revealed' the Popish Plot, had studied there, and the audience watching Belmour's impersonation would thus be reminded of another impostor from St Omer's. For further discussion of references to the Popish Plot here, see Coakley, 241–2.

241 *your pardon*: offenders liable to be condemned to death sometimes petitioned for pardon from the king. Belmour has been bribing influential people in the hope of getting a pardon himself, but he is in a weak position as 'the first transgressor since the act against duelling' (ll. 244–5). This probably refers to a 'Proclamation against Duelling' issued in London in 1680, declaring that there would be no more royal pardons for those who broke the laws against duelling.

248–9 *But . . . church*: verse Q, C1, Co; prose C2, S, J, M.

1.2.7 *I am*: C1–2, S, M; *am I* Q, J, Co.

43 *Mr Crap*: a fitting name for the man dunning Gayman, since *crap* was contemporary slang for money.

51 *Alsatia*: a cant name for Whitefriars, an area notorious for thieves' dens, and, as one of the 'liberties', where debtors were immune from arrest, a convenient residence for Gayman.

65 *to open*: to speak out.

66 *Billingsgate*: rough and abusive talk, like that of the women who sold their fish near Billingsgate dock.

73–80 *He . . . condition*: verse Q, C1–2, S, Co; prose J, M.

87 *cabin*: tiny 'room' made by the bed's being built into the deep wall. Gayman's is too small even to merit this description.

92–3 *as many . . . Henry VIII*: Shakespeare's play contains several crowded scenes: 1.4, a ball where the king enters accompanied by masquers; 4.1, Anne Boleyn's coronation; and 5.5, Elizabeth's christening. The porter and chamberlain in 5.4 complain about huge crowds gathering for the christening.

107–8 *That . . . keep*: verse Q, C1, Co; prose C2, S, M.

1.3.1 *Joan Sanderson*: the name of a round-dance in which successive dancers are brought into the ring with the words 'welcome Joan (or John) Sanderson' and a kiss from all dancers of the opposite sex.

2 S.D. *The rest . . . Leticia*: adapted from the S.D. *So do the rest* J, M. Q, C1–2, and S read *So to the rest*.

7–8 *bright . . . bed*: a sexualized image for sunset: Phoebus is Apollo the sun-god and Thetis the chief of the nereids or sea-nymphs.

11 *Then, then*: S, J, M; *then thou* Q, C1–2, Co.

18 *haunce in kelder*: 'Hans in the cellar', i.e. pregnancy.

19 *God so*: J; *Gots so* Q, S, Co; *Got so* C1–2; *go to* M.

24 *ye little ting*: Sir Feeble's attempts to endear himself to Leticia by using a kind of baby-talk make him ridiculous here and in other scenes with her.

27 *nown* [i.e. 'own']: *none* Q, C1–2, S, J, M, Co. More baby-talk: 'did it beat its own silly baby', either referring to his patting Leticia during this speech, or to her pushing him away from her.

31 *Dere's* [i.e. baby-talk for 'there's']: *Dear's* Q, C1–2, S, J, Co; *Dears*, M.
Fubs: term of endearment for small chubby person.

38 *touse 'em, and blowze 'em*: fondle them and disorder their clothes.

39 *apple-John*: a kind of apple that was kept for up to two years; hence the word suggests wrinkling rather than red ripeness.
affacks: an expletive perhaps derived from 'in faith'.

44 *puskin*: little puss.

46 *Saint Martin's trumpery*: sham jewellery. The name comes from the church of St Martin le Grand in Holborn, where goldsmiths, in hiding from their creditors, produced their goods illegally.

76 *none of the witnesses*: a dig at the 'witnesses' of the Popish Plot. Titus Oates, a 'Saint Omer's scholar' himself, had claimed to reveal a plot by English Jesuits at St Omers to murder Charles II.

80 *the devil to the collier*: proverbial for extreme similarity, based on the blackness of both.

111–14 *a harbour . . . men*: i.e. even a tiny Irish harbour was credited by scaremongers with being able to host a French fleet, ready to invade

England: a reference to absurd rumours of plots circulating in London during the Popish Plot, when anti-Catholic feeling ran high. From 1679 to 1681 there were rumours of a 'new and hellish . . . Irish popish plot, for the betraying that kingdom into the hands of the French, massacring all English protestants there, and utter subversion of the government and all protestant religion' (Jonathan Scott, 'England's Troubles', 123). Because most of the Irish were Catholic, and there had been an Irish uprising in 1641, Ireland was an obvious focus for English Protestant fears.

120–1 *Salamanca doctor*: Titus Oates falsely claimed to have a doctorate of divinity from Salamanca.

127–8 *three . . . death*: Bearjest is being promised Diana's dowry of three thousand pounds immediately on marriage, with the prospect of further money when Sir Feeble dies.

134–7 *Will you . . . woman*: this brief exchange gives a hint of the connection between Bearjest and Pert, revealed in 5.6 to have been secretly married.

145 *wouldst*: wo't Q, C1–2, S, J, Co; *would* M.

145–6 *free o'th' city*: a pun on different senses of 'free'. Sir Feeble is a freeman of the city but does not wish the city to make free use of his wife.

160–1 *I . . . because*: previous editions (apart from J which sets prose) break line after *eyes*.

2.1 S.D. *campaign coat*: a soldier's coat. Gayman is so poor he is wearing an old coat from his military days.

25 *laid in lavender*: pawned.

28 *the black art*: black magic. Gayman's supposed association with devils and magic is a recurring motif.

51 *laundresses' scores*: laundresses' bills.

55–6 *care not this—for my husband*: presumably the landlady snaps her fingers at 'this'.

57 *shifting*: contriving; perhaps also with a reference to changing clothes, since the landlady goes on to say that she has pawned her best clothes for Gayman's sake.

60 *Norwich mantua*: a loose silk coat. Norwich was a silk-weaving centre.

60–3 *'postle spoons . . . only Judas left*: as the landlady has been pawning her apostle spoons (small spoons with figures carved on the handle) to help her attractive young lodger, it is fitting that she only has Judas, the disciple who betrayed Christ with a kiss, left to offer her deceived husband.

65 *the George Tavern*: probably the same as 'the George in Whitefriars' mentioned in 4.1.170.

70 *slabber chops*: J; *flaber chops* Q, C1; *slaber chops* Co; *flabber chops* C2, S, M. A variant of *slobber chops*.

84 *basket hilt*: a sword with a basket-shaped piece protecting the hand as it gripped the hilt; a very old-fashioned weapon by the 1680s.

Sir Guy of Warwick: nickname for a broadsword; from the name of a hero of medieval romance.

100–1 *I . . . health*: verse Q, C1–2, S, Co; prose J, M.

105–6 *I . . . landlady*: verse Q, C1–2, S, Co; prose J, M.

136 *caudle cup*: a small cup for warm cordial drinks.

143 *to't*: in comparison to it.

176 *fields of Lincoln's Inn*: Lincoln's Inn Fields was known as a place of thieves and vagabonds. The theatre there was not open at the time *The Lucky Chance* was written.

182 *ghosts*: C1–2, S, J, M; *ghost* Q.

2.2.10 S.D. *at a distance behind*: Belmour probably enters via the wings, and stands in the scenic area while Leticia stands on the forestage.

57 *vows . . . dull priests*: this is not simply an anti-clerical jibe: Belmour and Leticia's vows, exchanged before the action of the play, could be considered under canon law as a binding pre-contract, invalidating the later marriage to Sir Feeble.

67–8 *Perhaps . . . flight*: verse Q, C1–2, S, Co; prose J, M.

94–5 *Alas . . . mind*: verse Q, C1–2, S, M, Co; prose J.

110 *Goodfacks*: an obscure oath, perhaps from 'good faith'.

155 *for countenance*: to keep up appearances.

156–7 *like Janus, or a spread-eagle*: i.e. facing firmly away from one another despite being pushed so close together. Janus, the Roman deity, has two faces looking in opposite directions, while the spread-eagle device of heraldry (often used as a sign in London at this period) sometimes has two heads.

195–7 *Faith . . . bargain*: verse Q, C1–2, S, J, M, Co.

212–13 *the gad bee's in his conundrum*: he's mad. To have a gad-bee in the brains was proverbial for crazy behaviour, while a conundrum, at this time, could mean either a whim or conceit, or be used as an abusive term for a person.

222 *t'other dance*: copulation. Cf. Thomas Heywood's *A Woman Killed with Kindness*, 1.1: 'would she dance "The shaking of the sheets", | But that's a dance her husband means to lead her'.

228–9 *toss the stocking*: it was a wedding-night custom to throw the bride's stocking among the guests.

260–2 *Stay . . . gone*: prose Q, C1–2, S, J, M, Co.

3.1 S.D. *The second song*: presumably so called to distinguish it from the first song sung by the musicians in 1.1. Other places where one of the actors breaks into song without the aid of music seem not to count as songs.

before the entry: the song is sung before the actors appear on stage. It is not clear whether the singer would be visible.

Mr Cheek: Thomas Cheek, who also wrote lyrics for two of Southerne's plays, *The Wives' Excuse* and *Oroonoko*.

12 *prefer*: C2, S, J, M, Co; *prefers* Q, C1.

23 *A pise of those bandstrings*: Sir Feeble is cursing the strings that tie his bands, or collar, for being difficult to unfasten.

45 *undone, with presenting*: financially ruined by the cost of presents.

64 *livery and seisin of her body*: 'livery of seisin' is a legal term for the delivery of property. Sir Feeble's use of it in this context underlines the treatment of wives as property in the play.

3.2 S.D. *The bedchamber*: a discovery scene, with the shutters representing Sir Feeble's house drawn back to reveal the bedchamber. There is a table, and possibly a bed, in place.

in an undress: *in an undressing* Q, C1, S, J, Co; *undressing* C2, M.

13 S.D. *throws open his gown*: this lewd gesture was criticized when the play was first performed: see Behn's comments in the preface.

16 *Daphne*: to escape being ravished by Apollo, Daphne ran from him and was turned into a laurel tree: see Ovid, *Metamorphoses*, Book 1.

36 *the city's up in arms*: riots were common in London in the late 1670s and early 1680s, because of scares associated with the Popish Plot, and opposition to the king's control of the city government. Events after the play was written, in the year of its first performance, sharpened its topicality: there were serious anti-Catholic riots in 1686.

37 *Guildhall*: the city of London's administrative headquarters.

some damnable plot: in the wake of the Popish Plot there were numerous wild rumours of Catholic plots, causing panic and civil unrest in London. Plots were suspected in Scotland, Ireland, Staffordshire, Yorkshire, and the Marches; Catholics were believed to be planning to take over England and wipe out Protestantism.

50 *give my voice*: cast my vote.

54 *his majesty's . . . safety*: the king had supposedly been threatened by the Popish Plot, and the Rye House Plot of 1683 (a Whig conspiracy) had involved planning his assassination.

3.3 S.D. *a dark-lantern*: a lantern with a slide which can be moved to cover the light. It would be used in night scenes to signify darkness, without changing the stage-lighting.

3.4 S.D. *woman*: C2, S, J, M, Co; *women* Q, C1.

1 S.D. *Song*: the singer in the original production was John Boman, an actor and singer, who also played Bredwell, though he does not sing as Bredwell here. He is probably hidden in the wings, or perhaps stands in

one of the balconies. See John Playford's *Theatre of Music* (1687), 84, which prints the song and also identifies the music as by Dr John Blow, and the words as by Mr Ousley.

19 *dost*: C2, S; *does* Q, C1, J, M.

20 *'finest* [= 'refinest']: *fines* Q1, C1, Co; *fine'st* C2, S, J; *find'st* M.

31–2 *If ... fiend*: verse Q1, C1–2, S, J; prose M.

69 *affords*: C2, S, J, M; *afford* Q, C1, Co.

74 *this essential beauty*: i.e. the gold, which Gayman probably holds up for the audience to see at this point.

3.5 S.D. *The flat scene of the hall*: from the wording, a stock piece of scenery. 'Flat scene' probably suggests a set of shutters drawn across the stage, with space behind to allow further scenes to be discovered.

3 *my lady's innocent intrigue*: Bredwell's aside here affects the audience's view of Julia, since it addresses the question: does she mean to have sex with Gayman when she tricks him to her bed? Bredwell's calling her intrigue innocent suggests not, but there is room for differing interpretations in production: Bredwell may himself have been deceived by Julia, or he may speak to the audience here with knowing irony.

17–18 *five hundred guineas*: the money Julia has stolen from her husband to give to Gayman.

71 *at hot-cockles*: sexual slang derived from the game of hot-cockles, which involved one player lying down blindfolded and guessing which of the others had hit him or her, with a play on cockle = vagina.

100 *under the same premunire*: in the same predicament, liable to the same penalty (i.e. being cuckolded). A 'premunire' was a writ issued for certain offences against the sovereignty of the king's court, or the offence itself, so this use of the word implicitly confesses that the old men's marriages are a kind of offence, for which they can expect a writ to be issued against them in the form of their wives' infidelity.

113–14 *sue you ... city jury*: Sir Cautious is indulging delusions of grandeur: *scandalum magnatum* was a statute protecting persons of high rank or office from slander. Sir Cautious thinks a city jury would uphold his complaint, partly because of the well-known tendency of juries, chosen by city sheriffs, to support their point of view, and partly as a hint that members of a city jury, being cuckolds themselves, would sympathize with his plight.

124 *Gargantua*: a giant in French folklore, and the hero of Rabelais's satire *The History of Gargantua and Pantagruel*.

125 *a tale of a tub*: a story without any truth in it.

135 *'ad, an*: 'gad, if'; *ad and* Q1, C1, S, J; *and and* C2; *ay and* Co.

138 S.D. *tells . . . seemingly*: Sir Feeble goes close to Sir Cautious and speaks quietly, to give the impression he is delivering the message.

S.D. *to the door . . . stands within*: Bredwell enters at one of the proscenium doors and turns back to speak to Gayman, who remains offstage behind the door.

156 S.D. *in an undress . . . undressed*: Lady Fulbank and Pert have changed from formal, public wear to looser informal clothes suitable for nightwear.

162 *as tall as the monument*: the monument to the Great Fire of London, a column over 200 feet high.

163–4 *a mouth . . . tide*: a mouth pouring out noise at a great rate. The river under London Bridge was very full and dangerous at high tide.

3.6.27 *prolonging*: postponing.

66 *Embraces, in a fiddlestick*: i.e. what a silly fuss about (and fancy name for) going to bed together.

4.1.75 *old Proserpine*: Proserpine was the queen of the infernal regions and the wife of Pluto, so a suitable name for the female devil Gayman says he met.

78–9 *gilded . . . geometry*: to hang by geometry was to hang in a stiff, angular way, usually referring to clothes. Gayman's clouds were perhaps made up of curtains hung in this way.

80 *laid in bed with her*: the audience, of course, now wants to know exactly what happened next: the text leaves more than one possibility open. Gayman confesses only to embracing the woman, and Lady Fulbank is angry that he didn't recognize her at that point: but possibly he did recognize the 'old Proserpine' for a lovely young woman, and doesn't want to admit that? At other points Lady Fulbank and Bredwell both claim that this encounter was quickly interrupted and remained essentially 'innocent', but if so it is odd that Gayman doesn't excuse himself to Lady Fulbank in these terms.

with much ado: C2, S, M; *much ado* Q, C1, J, Co.

115–16 *a sir-reverence under your girdle*: Sir Cautious is complaining that Gayman calls him simply 'Fulbank', without giving him his title; but 'sir-reverence' was also a slang term for a turd.

138–9 *Racking . . . me*: verse Q1, C1–2, S, Co; prose J, M.

143–5 *the mortgage . . . hour*: the term of Wasteall/Gayman's loan from Sir Cautious is ended and Sir Cautious now has the right to seize the land mortgaged to him; he is determined not to delay, or abate, this process.

170 *the George in Whitefriars*: a real contemporary tavern; there was a 'George Tavern in Whitefriars' in the years 1648–99. See Bryant Lillywhite, *London Coffee-Houses*.

181–2 *cullies . . . play*: makes cullies (dupes) of apprentices and young men in counting-houses by drawing them into gambling.

185–6 *Amsterdam and Leiden libels*: Amsterdam and Leiden, Holland's publishing centres, would have published works from English opponents of the Stuarts.

187–8 *dangerous fellow*: Sir Cautious's judgement on Wasteall's supposed anti-government writing, together with Sir Feeble's concern for his majesty's safety at 3.2.56, suggests that the two aldermen are not to be thought of as part of the city opposition to the king.

189 *for a lame soldier*: i.e. acting as a lame soldier.

190–1 *sells . . . road*: sells riding-whips on the road to Newmarket, where the horse races were held. In the context of smearing Wasteall as a government opponent, the reference might recall the foiled Rye House Plot, in which Charles II and James were to have been killed as they returned from Newmarket races.

193 *robs . . . linen*: takes linen clothes from hedges (where they were spread out to dry).

202 *he pads*: he is a highway robber or footpad.

230 *sport a die*: throw a dice.

235 *to top upon him*: to cheat or put a trick on him.

239 *not half in kelter*: out of sorts.

253–4 *as Trincalo . . . husband*: actually Stephano's remark, in Dryden and Davenant's adaptation of *The Tempest* (1667), 2.1.34–5: 'Would you were both hanged, for putting me in thought of [my wife].'

283 *looks so simply*: looks so foolishly.

286 *as pretty . . . inches*: 'tall of his inches' meant a tall fellow, while 'pretty' (sometimes used of a man at this period) implied both attractive and small: hence a joke about Bredwell's height, perhaps exploiting a height difference between the original Bredwell, John Boman, and Bearjest, played by the thin, and probably tall, Thomas Jevon (see the references to him in *Emperor* 3.2.225).

287–8 *ladies . . . gallery*: a joke, as prostitutes were known to sit in the middle gallery at the theatre.

288–9 *any foreman within the walls*: the foreman of any jury in the city.

290 *point cravat*: a cravat made from needle-point lace.

335 *not that I care this*: Bearjest probably snaps his fingers or makes some other dismissive gesture here.

341 *Amadis de Gaul*: a chivalric romance. Bearjest is fancying himself as an adventurous hero.

346 *Mum*: Co *mun* Q, C1–2, S, M.

363 *he has got a fly*: he has a supernatural spirit as his familiar, who gives him an unfair advantage.

381 *nothing*: the sexual meaning of 'nothing', with its reference to female genitals, adds innuendo to the two men's discussion of Lady Fulbank's

374

'worth'. Their bargaining here is one striking instance of the play's theme of the equation of sexual and monetary value.

417–18 *Cato . . . Hortensius*: in Plutarch's *Lives*, Cato the Younger hands his wife Marcia over to Quintus Hortensius, taking her back after Hortensius' death. While Sir Cautious is ridiculed for being willing to lend his wife, Cato's actions also show an uncomfortable similarity to the arrangement mooted at the end of the play, whereby Gayman would effectively 'lend' Lady Fulbank back to her husband until Sir Cautious's death.

426 *sound*: (1) whole, (2) free from syphilitic infection.

432 *the Gazette*: *The London Gazette*, an early newspaper.

442 *Cater tray*: Gayman has thrown a four and a three.

443 S.D. *sets up*: a gambling term for scoring at cards; perhaps indicates that Sir Cautious is counting his score.

467 *whether*: which.

485 *His wife's cracked credit*: C2, S, M; *wife' rack'd* Q, C1; *wife's racked* J, Co. A pun on two kinds of credit: the merchant's wife's 'cracked' or broken sexual reputation will keep her husband's financial credit 'entire', in one piece.

5.2.19 *chitty-face*: baby-face.

52 *thy*: *my* Q, C1–2, S, J, M, Co. An error in Q: it would be Leticia's image, not his own, that was in Belmour's heart tormenting him.

77–8 *it grieves me*: Leticia's compassion for Sir Feeble is appropriate for a feeling heroine and adds a 'softer' touch to the comedy, in contrast to some Restoration comedy where a much harder attitude to the victims of comic tricks is maintained.

5.3.11–12 *But . . . wish*: prose Q1, C1–2, S, J, M, Co.

33 *I can't intend*: I am unable.

59–60 *confine . . . circle*: a magician would draw a circle, inside which he was supposed to be safe from the devils he conjured up.

74 *lay 'em*: send the devils back to the spirit world.

77 *confess*: not in Q; added in C2.

79 *Cerberuses*: guard-dogs. In classical mythology, Cerberus is a three-headed dog who guards the entrance to the infernal regions.

85 *Pantamogan*: this seems to be Gayman's own coinage of name for his imaginary devil. It perhaps suggests 'all-mighty', from the Greek *pan*, all, and *mogan* from *hogan-mogan*, a popular corruption of a Dutch title, 'High Mightinesses'.

5.4 S.D. *discovered*: a discovery scene, with the garden shutters drawn back to reveal Lady Fulbank's antechamber at the second shutter position.

3 *alarm*: call to arms.

5 *will . . . called*: an echo of 1 *Henry IV*, 3.1.55, where Hotspur mocks Glendower's claim to be able to call up spirits.

90 *do you reason*: do right by you.

5.5 S.D. *A bed-chamber*: a second discovery scene behind the antechamber of 5.4, so right upstage.

5.6 S.D. *Scene draws over*: shutters, painted to represent the room, close over the bed-chamber of 5.5, changing the scene without any need for Gayman and Lady Fulbank to leave the stage: they are left in bed.

4 *husband . . . claim to*: Pert has entered into a form of marriage contract with Bearjest, which he is now ignoring: a written contract is produced at 5.7.165. Tricking Bearjest into marrying her now only serves to ratify the previous contract.

5.7.5 *put in print at Snow-hill*: lampoons and ballads were printed in this area, a steep hill in Holborn.

5–6 *with . . . haven*: with horns on his head like the cuckold in a street sign. A point on the Thames below Greenwich was known as 'Cuckold's Haven'.

29 *you* C1–2, S, J, M, Co; *yon* Q.

40–1 *brought . . . head*: cuckoldom is the 'old house', or inheritance, that Sir Cautious has 'entailed' upon himself (made himself the legal heir to).

47 *Like . . . trifles*: an echo of *Othello*, 5.2.350–1: 'Like the base Indian, threw a pearl away | Richer than all his tribe.'

63–4 *vow . . . bed*: the solemnity of Julia's vow dignifies a private separation. Unlike Leticia, who is pre-contracted to Belmour, Lady Fulbank cannot legally end her hated marriage, but the play endorses her rejection of her husband.

68–9 *With . . . reputation*: verse Q1, C1–2, S, J, Co; prose M.

87 *catastrophe*: (1) disaster, (2) theatrical dénouement.

97 S.D. *in an antic manner*: acting like a madman.

103 *who's will*: abbreviated form of 'who as will', meaning 'whoever will'.

108 *ere*: *e'er* Q, C1–2, S, J, M, Co.

137–8 *But . . . Belmour*: verse Q, C1–2, S, Co; prose J, M.

161–2 *my lady's cast petticoat*: derogatory reference to Pert as a lady's maid, derived from the custom of mistresses giving their old clothes to their servants.

184 *Do you consent*: a crucial question, not definitively answered in the text. Julia is being offered what she wanted: to maintain her honour as Sir Cautious's wife but to have Gayman waiting for her; but to make this an agreed bargain between the two men threatens the dignity and independent spirit she has tried to maintain. Is her refusal a tease to torment Gayman, or does she mean it? Would her consent imply a continuing affair behind her husband's back? The Royal Court produc-

tion of 1984 opted for consent, ending with Julia and Gayman standing together on stage. This was the actors' preference—the director, Jules Wright, had initially wanted the lovers to stand apart, indicating Julia's choice to remain independent of Gayman.

192 *I feigned a danger near*: Bredwell's claim that the first rendezvous between Gayman and Lady Fulbank was quickly interrupted helps to save the lady's honour, since this is the only one of the two assignations she can be held responsible for. Depending on how the actors choose to play this scene, Julia's innocence can be vindicated—or she, Bredwell, and Gayman can be conspiring to maintain a show of innocence for her husband (and thus the moral upper hand over him).

202 *I heard the news before*: this is the first time the audience has heard the news of Sir Thomas Gayman's death. Gayman's reaction here may affect the audience's view of him, raising such questions as: how long has he known this news, and has he only been pretending to be poverty-stricken?

Epilogue 4 *Nice and Flutter*: foppish characters from recent comedies: Sir Courtly Nice from Crowne's play of that name (1685), and Sir Fopling from Etherege's *The Man of Mode: or Sir Fopling Flutter* (1676).

6 *Craffey*: a character in Crowne's *City Politics* (1683): a fop who fancies himself as a poet.

10 *aftermath*: J; *After Math* S; *After Math* Q, C1, Co; *after Match* C2.

14 *en cavalier*: like a fine gentleman; perhaps with a sardonic reference to John Cutts's poem 'La Muse Cavalier', which defends the amateur gentleman-poet. Cutts was an associate of the Duke of Monmouth and a friend of Shaftesbury.

15 *whiffling*: Q, C1, S, J; *whistling* C2. Whiffling = trifling, insignificant.

17 *poll*: *pole* Q, C1–2, S, J, Co.

30 *'Tis . . . pain*: the poets who complain of the pangs of love are really suffering from venereal diseases, contracted from prostitutes (bulkers), and to be treated by sweating in tubs, the usual remedy.

33 *politic fetch*: prudent trick.

34 *Jack Ketch*: the hangman.

38–40 *the late satire on poetry*: perhaps John Cutts's 'La Muse Cavalier', which attacks an unspecified 'feeble Scribler', who is said to 'Disgrace the Theater with Senseless Farce, | Or Stately Nonsense in Heroick Verse, | With Plays, that thwart the meaning of the Stage, | And help not to instruct, but spoil the Age.'

43 *Nature in all her atom-fights*: perhaps a reference to the theory of Lucretius in *De Rerum Natura* that the world was formed by the combinations of atoms moving about in space. Behn knew Lucretius' work in the translation by her friend Thomas Creech.

Emperor of the Moon

Cast *Baliardo*: a name drived from *balordo*, 'stupid', and often used in *commedia dell'arte*. The character of the pedantic old doctor is a stock one.

Scaramouch: one of the most famous stock characters of *commedia dell'arte*, often seen in combat with Harlequin.

Cinthio: name often used for a young lover in *commedia dell'arte*.

Harlequin: one of the most famous *commedia dell'arte* characters, and the hero of Behn's source, *Arlequin empereur dans la lune*.

Elaria: Eularia is a name often used for a young lady in *commedia dell'arte*.

Kepler and Galileus: Johannes Kepler (1571–1630) and Galileo Galilei (1564–1642) both furthered the new science of astronomy with their use of telescopes, invented early in the seventeenth century, and described the heavenly bodies in ways that were imitated and burlesqued by writers of fantastic moon-voyages. Kepler also had associations with Rosicrucianism.

Epistle Dedicatory *To the Lord Marquess of Worcester, &c.*: Charles, Marquis of Worcester, 1661–98.

20 *Duke of Beauford*: Henry Somerset, first Duke of Beaufort, 1629–1700; a supporter of both Charles II and James II.

49–51 *barren . . . intermission*: *Arlequin empereur dans la lune*, Behn's main source, was a performance by Italian comedians incorporating French scenes, first put on in Paris in March 1684.

51–4 *altered . . . farce*: Behn's play has a narrative unity not evident in the printed French scenes of *Arlequin empereur*. As the Italian scenes were not printed it isn't known how they fitted with the French ones, but the Italian tradition was one of improvisation, and Behn is probably right to claim that her play has a coherence lacking in its source.

57 *all the words . . . new*: not strictly true: there are a few verbal echoes from *Arlequin empereur*. On the whole, though, the dialogue is Behn's own.

58 *calculated for his late majesty*: since Charles II died in 1685, Behn must have been working on the play before then; probably she wrote it in 1684 intending to have it performed in 1685.

70 *fanatical*: of or pertaining to the Nonconformist sects.

80–1 *town . . . one*: Behn compares the flourishing state of patronage and theatres in the period before 1642 with the circumstances of the Restoration. Only one theatre company, the United Company, operated from 1682 to 1695, and though it had two theatres, Drury Lane and Dorset Gardens, at its disposal, only one was used at a time, and Behn complains that audiences were too sparse properly to support even this level of theatrical activity.

Prologue *Jevon*: *Jevern* Q1–2, C1–2, S, HS. Thomas Jevon (1652–88), actor, dancer, singer, and playwright; a popular comedian who often spoke prologues and epilogues. He played Harlequin in the original production of the play.

20 *No woman without vizard*: i.e. no modest woman. Many women wore vizard masks to protect their modesty while attending comedies, but as prostitutes also attended the play masked the vizard was a very ambiguous signal. The sense here may be that no woman can risk twice attending such an obscene play without a vizard to conceal her identity, or, more likely, that no modest woman, that is a woman who does not wear the (prostitute's) vizard, dare attend a second time (when she would not have the excuse that she did not know about the obscenity).

30 *th' speaking head*: this recalls numerous legends about heads that could speak. The most famous was the Brazen Head said to have been made by Roger Bacon; Albertus Magnus, mentioned in 1.2.105 below, was said to have made an earthen head that spoke and moved. Little is known about the head used in the first performances of the farce. From the stage-directions it is clear that it was manipulated through the trapdoor from under the forestage. Its voice, which from the name 'Stentor' was presumably loud and booming, may have been provided by actors under the stage. The illusion aimed for is that it magically repeats Jevon's words. It is usually linked with the device mentioned in the *Newdigate Newsletter* of 26 March 1687: 'A Country man haveing invented a head & soe contrived it that whatever language or tune you speak in the Mouth of it it Repeated distinctly and Audibly.' This is probably the speaking head which the Prologue claims the company has bought a share in; the head actually used in the play is likely to have been one contrived by the actors in competition with this. The promise to the audience that they will save a sice (= sixpence) by watching the play (l. 31) suggests the existence of a rival speaking head which they would have to pay to see elsewhere.

35 S.D. *'Sawny'*: a popular Scots song, beginning 'Sawny was tall, and of noble race', which was printed in John Playford's *Choice Ayres and Songs* . . . (London, 1681).

37 [*Jevon*]: all previous editions give this line to Stentor, the speaking head; but the action makes more sense if Jevon completes the couplet. He is complaining that the actor speaking for the head has broken the illusion by asking him to speak louder instead of repeating his words.

S.D. [*the head*] *answers indirectly*: it answers obliquely, not properly repeating Jevon's words or sounds (which are not specified at this point).

39 *echo . . . northern strain*: the *echo* is the speaking head; *northern strain* refers to the song 'Sawny', subtitled 'A Northern Song' in printed sources.

41 *nothing . . . show*: a scornful remark on the popularity of a rival entertainment to the licensed theatre. There were numerous puppet shows in

Restoration London, at fairs, and at Charing Cross and Salisbury Change. In the rest of the prologue various sections of the audience are mocked for their supposed behaviour at puppet shows.

43 *Philander and Irene's love*: presumably a love-scene acted by the puppets. Philander was a common name for a lover.

44–7 *sisters . . . they*: perhaps draws a satirical parallel between puppet-show love-scenes and some amours current in contemporary gossip.

48 *her nown*: Q1, C1–2, S; *her noon* Q2, HS; her own.

ninny: foolish companion (i.e. 'Fribble', l. 50).

48–51 *city . . . kids*: the action described here is not clear. It could be that the city wife, watching the puppet show, is charmed by some stage-business involving a puppet getting into a model coach, which then overturns, giving rise to the cry from 'Fribble' (the city wife's husband, whose name implies foolishness and sexual impotence).

53 *Dog Hector, and the Bull*: refers to the bull-baiting and dog-fighting satirically supposed to be preferred as entertainments by rough men who fancy themselves as 'men of war'.

1.1 S.D. *[Elaria sings]*: previous editions do not specify the singer, but it is likely that Elaria both plays the lute and sings.

1 *A curse . . . maid*: this song, with music by Purcell, was printed as a song sheet by Thomas Cross in 1700, and said to be 'sung by Mrs Cross'. See *British Union-Catalogue of Early Music*, ed. Edith Schnapper (London, 1975), ii. 855. This was probably the actress, singer, and dancer Leticia Cross, who was on the stage in the 1690s.

30 *Roger*: a generic name for a servant.

53 *weapon-salve*: an ointment supposed to cure wounds when applied to the weapon that caused them.

sympathetic powder: a powder supposed to heal wounds through the power of correspondence or affinity, by being applied to the bloodstained garments or to the weapon.

84 *Don Quick-sottish*: like Don Quixote, with a pun on Quixote/Quick-sot. Like Cervantes's hero, famous for being taken in by chivalric romance, Dr Baliardo has taken fiction for truth; in his case books of fantastic travels have deceived him.

93 *Machiavel*: artful statesman; from the famous Florentine statesman Machiavelli, whose *Il principe* expounded the principles of statecraft.

96 *Dialogue of Icaromenippus*: Q2, HS; *Dialogue of the Lofty Traveller* Q1, C1–2, S. A Dialogue by Lucian in which Menippus tells of his trip to the moon. Various ideas mooted in later fantastic voyages, including the possibility of the moon being inhabited, are aired here. The name *Icaromenippus* indicates that Menippus is like Icarus in flying up into the

heavens. The Dialogue had recently been translated by Ferrand Spence in the third volume of his edition of Lucian's works (1684).

97 *The Man in the Moon*: title of a fantastic voyage by the supposed Spaniard 'Domingo Gonsales, the Speedy Messenger' (really Francis Godwin, Bishop of Llandaff), published in 1629. Gonsales describes travelling to the moon in a flying machine drawn by large geese called 'gansas'.

99 *A Discourse of the World in the Moon*: a moon-voyage written by Cyrano de Bergerac, English versions of which were published in 1659 and 1687.

102 *Sir John Mandeville*: the supposed author of a famous book mingling travel and romance, dating from the fourteenth century.

113 *cabalists*: (1) scholars of mystic arts; (2) members of a secret society or cabal; see *cabala* below, 1.2.25.

the Rosicrucian order: a legendary secret society whose members were thought to lay claim to secret and magical knowledge, and to knowledge of the spirit world. Behn's source for her treatment of them is the satirical work *The Count of Gabalis* (see below, 1.2.35).

124 *conjuring*: calling up spirits.

126 *all his scopes*: two of the doctor's scopes, the microscope and telescope, are inventions of the seventeenth century and instruments of the new science. The horoscope, by contrast, is ancient. The reference may be to a more modern, mathematical instrument, a kind of planisphere called a horoscope (*OED* 2c).

129 *ma très chère*: my very dear.

133 *plumés*: *plumees* Q2, HS; *plumeys* Q1, C1–2, S. Young gallants, named after their plumed hats.

135–6 *blonding . . . noir . . . brunette*: refers to the different colours—blond, black, brown—either of the young men's hair or of their plumes.

138 *tout autour*: all around.

153–5 *Chevalier . . . cannons*: 'Fair-haired cavalier, | No more patches, no more powder | No more ribbons and lace.' Bellemante is reciting a list of young men's ornaments. Mouches were black face-patches; powder was used for face and hair; ribbons and cannons, or pieces of lace, were used to trim the wide breeches then fashionable.

172 *moon-calfs*: idiots, so called because their birth was once thought to have been affected by the moon; in this context, also anticipates the suitors' later pretence to have been born on the moon.

173–4 *our governante, and keeper*: Elaria is referring to two people here: Mopsophil, the 'governante' (governess or chaperone), and Scaramouch, the 'keeper'.

179 *billets doux*: *billet doux* Q1-2, C1-2, S, HS. Scaramouch left two letters, one to Bellemante from Charmante, and one to Elaria, presumably from Cinthio.

1.2 S.D. *a telescope twenty (or more) foot long*: inspired by the 'Scène de la prothase' in *Arlequin empereur*, which features a large mounted telescope.

6 *moments critical*: times of decisive astrological influence.

14 *seems to wink at distance*: appears from a distance to have his eyes closed.

17 S.D. *Scaramouch goes to the door*: this suggests that one of the proscenium doors was being used to represent the garden gate.

23 S.D. *Scaramouch bare*: i.e. bare-headed, having taken off his hat to greet Charmante.

S.D. *in a strange fantastical habit*: exact details of such costumes are unclear, but the point is that they look strange and are sharply differentiated from the contemporary attire which is the basis for 'normal' dress in comedies of the period.

S.D. *with Harlequin*: Harlequin enters with Charmante as his servant, but immediately hides behind a bush (see below, l. 135 S.D.). Intermittently during the following scene he peeps out, allowing for added comic point; he might, for instance, make comic faces at some of Charmante's learned rhetoric, or attempt to see the nymph painted on the glass.

25 *cabala*: (1) a secret, esoteric doctrine; originally referring to Jewish tradition, here referring to Rosicrucian ideas; (2) *cabal*, a secret group or council (for its political connotations in this period, see note to *Rover*, Prologue l. 9). The members of the imaginary cabala of *EM* are the Emperor's ministers and guardians of the Rosicrucian doctrines.

Eutopia: place of ideal happiness, with a pun on the *utopia* (no place) of Sir Thomas More's famous work. With this one word, probably emphasized after a pause, Charmante can both play on the doctor's belief in the moon world, and share a joke with the audience about that world's non-existence.

26 S.D. *Salutes him low*: makes a low bow, expressing deep respect.

27 *fame*: rumour, reputation; with a reference to the early seventeenth-century pamphlet *Fama* which purported to announce the existence of the Rosicrucian brotherhood.

28 *the renowned society*: the Rosicrucians; perhaps with a satirical glance at the Royal Society.

35 *Count of Gabalis*: character in a work by Montfaucon de Villars, translated as *The Count of Gabalis: Or, The Extravagant Mysteries of the Cabalists, Exposed in Five Pleasant Discourses on the Secret Sciences* in 1680. Count Gabalis tries to convert a sceptical narrator to Rosicrucianism. Doctor Baliardo, unlike the work's narrator, has been taken in by the Count's arguments.

38 *that doctrine*: Charmante's following speeches detail Rosicrucian doctrines as described in *The Count of Gabalis*. The central idea, that mortals should copulate not with each other but with spirits of the opposite sex, provides the occasion in this scene to mock the doctor's misogyny and to prepare for the play's main trick, the pretence that godlike spirits are courting Elaria and Bellemante.

42 *deietical*: divine. Charmante's use of this nonce-word emphasizes his role as expounder of esoteric doctrines.

41–4 *salamanders ... nymphs ... gnomes ... sylphs*: the four kinds of spirits in Rosicrucian doctrine.

54 *appear in shapes*: take on visible bodies.

62 *abstinence from carnal thought*: purity was traditionally necessary for performing magic, and is emphasized in the Rosicrucian doctrines found in *The Count of Gabalis*. Rosicrucian ideas of sexual abstinence are easily satirized because desire is not so much banished as transferred to imaginary spirits. The joke here is that as soon as the doctor has renounced carnal thought he is to be excited by a picture of a nymph.

77 S.D. *a glass ... behind it*: the light, perhaps a candle, allows the picture to be shown to the audience before it is put into the telescope.

83 *Alikin*: possibly a diminutive corruption of Alif, title of the great father spirit in Arabic tradition.

84 S.D. *puts ... telescope*: the telescope is probably pointed towards the audience.

95 *Alexander ... salamander*: in *The Count of Gabalis* Alexander the Great (the son of Philip of Macedon, the 'King Philip' mentioned in this passage) is said to have been fathered by a sylph.

97–8 *famous philosopher, Merlin*: mentioned in *Gabalis*. The necromancer of Arthurian legend; perhaps with a reference to William Lilly, an astrologer who published as 'Merlinus Anglicus', and died in 1681.

102 *Egeria ... Numa Pompilius*: the love of Numa Pompilius for Egeria is related in *Gabalis*.

104 *Zoroaster* [or Zarathustra]: founder of a religion of ancient Persia. He is mentioned in *Gabalis* as the son of Noah's wife by a salamander.

Trismegistus: Hermes Trismegistus, mythical founder of the Hermetic art of alchemy; mentioned in *Gabalis*.

Apuleius: author of second-century satirical romance, *The Golden Ass*, and of *De Deo Socratis*, in which Socrates is said to have had a private demon. He was accused of performing magic.

Aquinas: Thomas Aquinas, referred to by Count Gabalis as an authority on the intimacy between mortals and spirits.

105 *Albertus Magnus*: a scholastic philosopher of the thirteenth century.

Zilphid: a version of *sylphid* (sylph), mentioned in *Gabalis*.

94–106 *Most possible . . . wise, sir*: in these speeches Charmante imitates *The Count of Gabalis*, in which the count tells of various classical, biblical, and historical persons who were begotten by, or had commerce with, the Rosicrucian spirits. Most of the ones Charmante lists are mentioned in *Gabalis*, and many are famous authorities in magic and alchemy.

117 *Iredonozar*: the name is taken from Irdonozur, the prince of the world in the moon in Godwin's *The Man in the Moone*.

120 S.D. *the glass with the emperor*: this second picture is perhaps collected from Scaramouch at the same time as the first, but not shown until now. Probably Charmante holds this up to the audience's view for a moment as he puts it in the telescope.

135 S.D. *in the hedges*: in the scenery behind the proscenium and in front of the painted shutters: probably wings painted with hedges for the garden scene, or perhaps separate bushes cut out in silhouette. Harlequin probably peeps out at this point, both to add interest to the business of Charmante's exit and Scaramouch's re-entrance, and to remind the audience that he is present and will overhear the following dialogue.

159 *transitories, mortal*: the doctor addresses Scaramouch as a mortal and admonishes him to think of spiritual things rather than transitory ones like Mopsophil and her wealth. Alternative readings are the tautological *transitories mortal* Q1; and *transitory Mortal* C2, S, replacing *transitories* with an adjective and making *mortal* refer to Mopsophil.

161 S.D. *comes out on the stage*: i.e. from behind the proscenium arch onto the forestage, closer to the audience for his important tickling scene.

169 *a caper on my own sword*: a humorous reference to stabbing himself. A caper is a frolicsome dance.

176 S.D. *[Harlequin] falls to tickle himself*: this action is taken from the 'Scène du désespoir' in *Arlequin empereur*, praised as one of the funniest of Harlequin's scenes. In Behn's version Harlequin's monologue is much shorter.

183 *common*: Q2; *mutual* Q1. The emendation may record a joke arising from the casting of Katherine Corey, who was well known in the part of Doll Common in *The Alchemist*, as Mopsophil.

195 *stand with you*: dispute with you.

1.3 S.D. *Enter Scaramouch, groping*: the groping action indicates that it is meant to be dark, though the stage is not darkened; the audience is able to watch the characters blundering as if they can't see.

24 *boremes*: a form of *bouts-rimés*, rhymed endings. Bouts-rimés are mentioned in the 'Scène d'Isabelle et Colombine' in *Arlequin empereur*, from which the idea for this scene comes. Behn expands into an action on

stage the trick with the tablets and the lover's jealousy, which are merely briefly reported in the French scene.

37 S.D. *She turns and takes the tablet*: following Summers, I have changed the order of the stage-directions to show Bellemante taking up the tablet before reading Harlequin's writing, 'And answered only with my sighs'. The quarto stage-directions are ambiguous here, introducing Harlequin's line with 'Harlequin writes' and placing Bellemante's taking the tablet after it.

42 S.D [*She reads*]: S.D. altered, as at l. 37 above, to give speech clearly to Bellemante.

56 *character*: handwriting.

65 *malheureuse*: miserable [me]! A verbal echo from the 'Scène d'Isabelle et Colombine'.

71 S.D. *into the closet*: this begins a series of comic actions making use of the proscenium doors. One door represents the entrance to the chamber; another, on the opposite side of the stage, is the entrance to the closet (i.e. a small, private room). Charmante disappears through one door as the doctor enters opposite. (See also l. 117 S.D. and l. 141 S.D. below.)

102 *league and covenant*: formal agreement. A satirical reference to the Solemn League and Covenant of the Scots and English Presbyterians in 1643.

110 S.D. *flute doux*: a high-pitched flute.

111 *bon ami*: good friend.

117 S.D. *behind the door*: i.e. the same proscenium door through which Elaria is entering. She does not see him and he slips out behind her back (l. 118 S.D.).

141 *my cousin's closet's open*: i.e. the same door which Charmante used earlier. The audience sees Cinthio go through the same door and knows it is only a matter of time before the two men discover they are sharing a closet.

S.D. *gets round . . . door*: Elaria has to cross the stage from the 'closet' to the 'chamber door' through which the doctor has just entered.

146 S.D. *Scaramouch with a light*: the comic business with light and darkness quickens in pace from here on, as the repeated loss and reappearance of light means that characters have to make quick changes between 'blind' and 'seeing' actions. The obvious artificiality of the convention makes the joke: at the entrance of one candle, making no real difference to the stage-lighting, Cinthio stops groping and starts acting like a madman, while the doctor can suddenly see him after being blind to his presence.

148-52 *Gog Magog . . . dubbed a knight*: Cinthio conflates Gog and Magog, legendary giants whose statues had stood at the Guildhall till the Great Fire of 1666. Cinthio is mocking the supposed venality of the City governors by personifying the famous Guildhall statues as a god they worship in return for money and title.

2.1   S.D. [*A room . . . house*]: no scenery is specified for this short scene, but from the dialogue the location is evidently somewhere in the house.

S.D. *An antic dance*: the dance marks an interval before the act proper opens. 'Antic' suggests that the dancers wear bizarre costumes.

25   *fiddles*: fiddlers.

treat: food.

2.2   S.D. *flambeau*: lit torch or candlestick.

7   *Deceptio visus*: Scaramouch translates the Latin in his next phrase, 'the error of the eyes'.

21   *his proper stuff*: (1) his own written matter; (2) his rubbish.

38   *put your arms across*: cross your arms. A traditional pose for woeful lovers in pictorial art.

look scurvily: look abashed and silly. While Scaramouch is speaking, the two lovers might adopt the different postures as he recommends them.

2.3   S.D. *The inside . . . pleasure*: the staging for this scene is quite elaborate. The scene opens with the actors in front of a curtain (perhaps the main curtain, perhaps a specially designed drop curtain) to be drawn up later; behind that is another curtain, the 'hanging' to be mentioned later (l. 60 S.D.); behind that a 'scene', i.e. a painted pair of shutters representing the inside of the house, which will be revealed later.

2   *à la gothic*: in the gothic manner. Exactly what a 'gothic habit' (see also l. 22 S.D.) consists of is not clear, but in general terms it seems to be a colourful masquerade dress very unlike the normal costume then fashionable. The connotations of *gothic* at this time are likely to be Teutonic rather than medieval.

uncommune: Bellemante's affected, pseudo-French pronunciation for *uncommon*.

22   S.D. *music*: the company of musicians.

43   S.D. *antics*: players dressed in bizarre costumes, perhaps as clowns.

48   S.D. *harpsicals*: harpsichord. An unusual instrument in plays, being very large to be carried on stage. It was probably played in the music-room or the pit.

S.D. *they all dance a figure dance*: i.e. a set-dance; more appropriate for the ladies and gentlemen than the presumably less decorous dance of antics earlier. It is possible 'all' is meant to be confined to 'all the dancers', but more likely that it indicates the dramatic characters. Their joining in this dance after sitting still for the first one reflects the greater trust Elaria feels once she knows the dancers are Cinthio's kinsmen.

60   S.D. *having placed them . . . hanging*: the short interval of empty fore-stage, while the doctor and Peter call from without, and the actors arrange themselves behind the front curtain, arouses audience anticipa-

tion of a spectacular tableau later in the scene. The 'tapestry' tableau is not in *Arlequin empereur*, but Behn probably took ideas from another play in the Italian repertoire, *Arlequin Jason ou la Toison d'or*, which has one scene where actors stand on pedestals, apparently turned to stone.

85 *against*: in preparation for when.

86 *tapestry*: i.e. the hanging. The characters standing in the hanging are pretending to be embroidered onto it.

89 *virtuoso*: i.e. Charmante, who in 1.2 posed as a virtuoso (an adept in Rosicrucian mysteries).

93 *tuning of the spheres*: the heavenly bodies were supposed to make music as they moved.

99 *what story's this*: what story is the tapestry illustrating? Wall-hangings were embroidered with scenes from well-known narratives.

101 S.D. *perspective*: magnifying glass.

S.D. *placed on a tree*: perhaps a wooden cut-out tree with a ladder at the back. Harlequin needs to be placed higher than the doctor so that the audience can watch him hitting him.

114 S.D. *the entrance*: one of the proscenium doors, now to be used again for the comically surreptitious exit.

123 *let none escape*: Peter's signal failure to prevent the escape could be played either as bumbling (in the 'dark' he cannot find the door and fails to notice the long queue of people) or as silent complicity with the escapers.

S.D. *except Mopsophil*: Mopsophil needs to be onstage listening at l. 140 below.

175–6 *I'll . . . round*: I promise you, this joke will be told to everyone.

S.D. *Exit Mopsophil*: Mopsophil needs to leave here to warn Elaria and Bellemante, and to take up her position in the scene about to be revealed.

190 *Better than all Galenists*: Q2; *Gallanicus* Q1. Better than all [the remedies of] physicians. Galenists were healers who followed the teachings of the Greek physician and author of medical treatises Galen (*c.* AD 130–*c.*200), especially by using herbal remedies.

2.4 S.D. *Scene draws off [to show Bellemante's chamber]*: the shutters representing the 'inside of the house' for 2.3 part to reveal the women behind; another set of shutters representing a chamber is in place behind them. Summers inserts 'Bellemante's Chamber'; earlier editions do not specify location.

44 *intelligence*: communication.

2.5.1 *en cavalier*: (1) neatly, gracefully; (2) like a gallant lover. Scaramouch has cleverly pacified the doctor but failed to meet Mopsophil as he promised.

3 *'tis*: S; *is* Q1–2, C1–2, HS.

5 S.D. *sets . . . window*: the balcony above one of the proscenium doors serves as the window.

26 *true blue*: steadfast; perhaps with a satirical reference to the Whigs. The Scottish Presbyterians were known as true blues.

38 *shotten herring*: term for a herring that has spawned; figuratively, thin and worn-out. Thomas Jevon, for whom Behn designed her Harlequin, was a very thin man.

40 *zany*: (1) servant character in the *commedia dell'arte*, which of course is precisely what both Harlequin and Scaramouch are; (2) contemptuous word for a hanger-on or someone who plays the fool.

55 S.D. *flings . . . balcony*: Mopsophil angrily sweeps out of the balcony, and climbs down to reappear a few moments later (l. 59 S.D.) through the door underneath the balcony.

61 *made a property*: made a mere tool. Mopsophil thinks Scaramouch's courtship of her has been just a means to get away from his real wife.

69 *termagant*: violent, bullying.

infidel: one who cannot keep faith.

75 *fille de chambre*: Harlequin's impersonation recalls the 'Scène de la fille de chambre' in *Arlequin empereur*, in which Harlequin applies to be a chambermaid and Pierrot, impersonating the doctor's wife, questions him in the way the doctor does in Behn's scene. The joke about ladies having valets de chambre (see below, ll. 91–2) is in the French source. The social satire about Harlequin's supposed previous employers is much more extensive in Behn's scene.

78 S.D. *makes his little dapper leg*: makes a neat little bow (appropriate to a man, not the woman he is pretending to be).

98 *laced up to the gathers*: decorated with lace all the way to where the material is gathered (at the waist); another example of the parson's wife's extravagance in dress.

106–7 *outdo the very vice-reine*: Russell (p. 270) suggests a reference to the luxury indulged in by the Duchess of Portsmouth, politically powerful mistress of Charles II.

121 *mongrel*: (1) of mixed breed, referring to Harlequin's acting both man and woman; (2) general term of abuse.

153 *shapes of Jupiter*: Jupiter adopted various animal bodies in order to pursue mortal women.

170 *cabalists*: C2, S; cabalist Q1–2, C1, HS.

180 *the Ebula*: in Godwin's *The Man in the Moone*, Gonsales is given various magic stones; one, the Ebula, helps him rise and descend through the air at will.

184 *from Parnassus . . .*: Charmante describes a journey over the mountains of Greece, all with classical or mythological associations, ascending to Olympus, the highest mountain, and then to the moon.

Parnassus: legendary mountain of the poets.

Hymettus: a mountain in Attica famous for honey.

Gerania: a mountain near Corinth.

185 *Acrocorinthus*: the top of the city of Corinth.

Taygetus: high mountain.

Olympus' top: home of the gods in Greek myth.

204 *at a dead lift*: in a crisis.

3.1 S.D. *through the gate towards the stage*: Harlequin probably enters from the wings and drives towards the forestage. It is not clear how the town gate would be represented; possibly the guard's post would be enough to suggest that Harlequin is coming through a gate.

S.D. *his horse*: probably a real one. Real horses were occasionally brought on stage in the Restoration; the comedian Joe Haines delivered an epilogue while riding a donkey at Drury Lane in 1697.

3 *siège volant*: S; *siege voglant* Q1–2, C1–2, HS. Light, two-wheeled carriage.

21 S.D. *Harlequin . . . 'tis a cart*: this trick is taken from the 'Scène du fermier de Donfront' in *Arlequin empereur*.

3.2 S.D. *a chair . . . apothecary's shop*: the chair is a sedan, a small carriage with poles for bearers to carry. The trick sedan which becomes an apothecary's shop comes from the 'Scène de l'apotiquaire' in *Arlequin empereur*, in which Harlequin poses as an apothecary.

11 *I might . . . pusillanimity*: Scaramouch's pretentious language, here and later in the scene, adds to the amusement of his apothecary disguise and continues the mockery of the doctor's obsessions. Some of the alchemical vocabulary is taken from Ben Jonson's *Alchemist*, 2.3.

13 *communitive*: here, 'full of good fellowship'. A very rare word, not recorded in *OED* (as 'of or belonging to a community') till the 1800s. Its use here is one of many examples of Scaramouch's outlandish Latinate speech in this scene.

15–16 *Galenical and Paracelsian phenomenas*: phenomena as described by Galen and Paracelsus, both famous for their work in medicine. Paracelsus (1493–1541) established the role of chemistry in medicine. He was the most important exponent of Renaissance alchemy and influenced Rosicrucian ideas.

21 *aurial*: probably a version of 'auricular', by the ear.

27 *hostel*: mansion, residence.

38 *in propria persona*: in person.

38 *by speculation*: by observation (through a telescope); the later sense of 'conjecture' is probably not present here.

40 *terra firma*: firm ground or earth, a designation comically applied to the moon here.

41–2 *Cosmographia of the Lunar Mundus*: map of the lunar world. Many works called *Cosmographia* were published in the seventeenth century.

45–6 *the map of Terra Incognita*: map of the unknown territory.

50 *forlorn hope*: group of soldiers sent out in front to begin an attack.

56 *novel*: news.

64 *Garamanteen*: not traced.

66 *scaturrigo*: scaturigo Q1–2, C1–2, S, HS. Latin for 'a spring of boiling water'.

    ebullition: ebulation Q1–2, C1–2, S, HS. Bubbling or fizzing up. The bubbling up of the lunar mineral waters supposedly produces a medicinal infusion or 'water'.

69 *enode*: solve, explain.

    appearances: S, C2; *apparances* Q2, C1, HS; *apparences* Q1; visible manifestations.

72 *the tincture . . .*: a rough and ready parody of the alchemical process, in which liquids went through a series of stages marked by colour-change. 'tincture' = colour; 'ceruleates' = turns blue; 'flaveces', Scaramouch's coinage from Latin, = turns yellow; 'crocus' is the alchemical term for the yellow stage in the process. Scaramouch correctly describes the yellow stage following the blue.

73 *ceruleates*: C2, S; *ceruberates* Q1–2, C1, HS.

74 *generous*: (1) richly coloured; (2) invigorating; (3) copious.

75 *water*: Scaramouch changes from using 'water' for medicinal infusion, to 'water' as urine, which was examined by doctors for indications of a patient's state of health.

77–82 *be pleased to observe . . . Balneo*: Scaramouch (in order to distract attention from his action with the letters) directs the doctor's gaze to the apothecary's shop, where a suitable large, round glass flask might be placed or painted. He then describes an alchemical experiment, using, as is customary, the language of conception and birth for the attainment of the philosopher's stone. The alchemical flask was divided into 'three regions' after the three regions of the universe. 'Pallid' probably refers to white colour in the flask. White is the penultimate stage in alchemy, and the white elixir was supposed to transform metals to silver; in symbolic terms this elixir was female, hence its activity is expressed in the 'breeding of Filia Solis', the daughter of the sun. The 'faeces' is the sediment left in the lowest 'third region' of the flask, here supposedly indicating the 'birth', or final achievement of the philosopher's stone. The 'balneo' was a bath of water in which a flask would be stood for gentle heating.

83 *Lysidono*: not traced; Scaramouch may be making the name up.

84–5 *zenith and nadir*: astronomical terms for the highest point of the sky, and its opposite, the point beneath the observer: loosely, 'height and depth'.

86 *Islington*: at this time a resort north of London, popular for its medicinal springs and pleasure gardens.

88–91 *upon the infusion . . . Amalgama*: Scaramouch is still using alchemical terms, but rather nonsensically here; this speech makes less sense than the last one, indicating that he is running out of ideas. The 'crow's head' is the black stage in alchemy, but it does not procure the 'seal of Hermes', or hermetic seal, as Scaramouch claims. 'Lac Virginis', literally virgin's milk, is an alchemical term for mercury. 'Amalgama' is an alchemical term for a mixture of mercury with other metals. These four terms occur in *The Alchemist*, 2.3.

91 *Amalgama*: C2, S; *Amalgena* Q1–2, C1, HS.

S.D. *signs to . . . stay*: Scaramouch has to wait for an answer to the letters; his following speeches show him increasingly desperate in his assumed role, improvising, talking nonsense, and almost being caught out by the doctor.

97 *prima materia*: C2, S; *fema materia* Q1–2, C1. The original matter, to which substances were supposedly reduced in alchemy.

102 *urinam vulcani*: the urine of Vulcan, the god of fire and metal-working, who is frequently mentioned in alchemy.

103–4 *calybeates . . . calor*: 'calybeates' (C2, S; *calibrates* Q1–2, C1) comes from Greek 'chalybeate', impregnated with iron; 'gradus' = degree; 'calor' = heat; hence, drinking the water known as Vulcan's urine puts iron in the faeces, to an extent governed by a person's body-heat.

114 *stercus proprius*: his own dung.

119 *costive*: constipated. See *The Alchemist*, 1.1.28.

120 *ad anum*: to the anus. Scaramouch continues the joke about Vulcan's urine turning the smith's faeces to iron: if he gets constipated he can be cured by a magnet to the anus.

122–3 *per viscera*: through the entrails.

163 *in a halter*: on a lead.

166 *primum mobile*: first mover; in Ptolemaic astronomy, the sphere that moves all the others. Figuratively applied to Mopsophil as the machine that moves Scaramouch's feelings.

192 S.D. *at half sword*: fighting with swords very close together.

192 S.D. [*They*] *parry*: they cross swords, each trying to ward off the other's blow rather than make an attack.

197 *I'll fit you*: I'll have my revenge on you.

205 *phisnomy*: Mopsophil's pronunciation of 'physiognomy'; the countenance, considered as an indication of character.

212 *chemical bellows*: bellows to blow the alchemist's fires.

projecting fires: projection was the last stage in the alchemical process. May also refer figuratively to the doctor's enthusiasm for (alchemical and scientific) projects.

213 *deputy urinal-shaker*: Mopsophil claims that as the doctor's assistant, Scaramouch has to shake the glass jars containing urine for diagnosis.

Guzman of Salamanca: rogue of Salamanca (university), where scientific experimentation flourished; perhaps with a reference to Titus Oates, who claimed to have a doctorate from Salamanca.

214 *signum mallis*: possibly a mistake for 'signum mali', sign of evil.

216 *Friskin*: lively, frisky person.

221 *lantern-jaws*: long thin jaws.

225 *spider . . . skeleton buffoon*: further references to the thin actor Jevon, Behn's original Harlequin.

226 *Jack of Lent*: a target set up to be thrown at.

229–30 *sweet glister-pipe, and Signor dirty-boots*: Scaramouch, the supposed apothecary, is named for the clyster-pipe used to administer enemas; Harlequin, dressed as a farmer, is 'dirty-boots'.

251–2 *insatiably*: C2, S; *unsatiably* Q1–2, C1, HS.

264 *Let me alone*: leave it to me.

301 *Does . . . drink*: the following exchange echoes a discussion of women's drinking habits in the 'Scène de la fille de chambre' in *Arlequin empereur*.

307 *just as 'tis here*: this echoes the 'Scène dernière' of *Arlequin empereur*, in which Arlequin impersonates the emperor of the moon and describes the moon world, while Colombine and the doctor interject the refrain, 'c'est tout comme ici'.

319 *the Mall*: a fashionable place to walk in St James's Park. Harlequin's satirical account of the 'moon world' relates to London.

320 *the tour*: the circuit of Hyde Park, a fashionable excursion.

321 *play*: gaming.

338–9 *unless . . . break him*: unless his wife's excessive finery should ruin his fortune.

355 *exhaling*: drawing up. The idea that the force of the sun acting on the earth's atmosphere could be harnessed for air travel is found in Cyrano de Bergerac's *Voyage to the Moon*, where the narrator flies by tying bottles full of dew around himself.

360-1 *dropped into the sea*: Harlequin's story echoes one told by Arlequin in the 'Scène de l'ambassade', in which he describes falling into a lake, and being fished out and served up to the emperor.

3.3 S.D. *The gallery*: this scene contains elements from the 'Scène dernière' of *Arlequin empereur*, and is named 'Scene the Last' in the quartos. Its staging is much more elaborate than anything in the French scenes, though. The flying machines, and the progressive use of discoveries until the whole depth of the stage is used and a large cast is assembled, make this a spectacular scene on a par with the most elaborate operas of the day.

scenes and lights: 'scenes' refers to representations of the paintings that hang in the gallery. The 'lights' may have been sconces of candles fixed to the wing-shutters, backed by reflector plates.

15 S.D. *The scene . . . walks*: the first pair of shutters, showing the gallery, slides away to reveal shutters painted to represent Parnassus, at the second shutter position. The trees are painted wings, interspersed with pedestals for the blacked-up actors.

Next . . . zodiac: the chariots are small decorated platforms which can be moved up and down. The actors train their 'perspectives' (telescopes) upstage, where the zodiac machine, a large platform, is hanging high up ready to appear.

18 *they are disappeared*: the chariots have probably moved down into the wings, and are invisible when the characters get out of them. Kepler and Galileus leave via the wings ready to re-enter further downstage.

34 *Helicon*: a legendary stream on Parnassus.

35 *by post*: very quickly, like messengers using post-horses.

two winged eagles: i.e. the chariots.

36 *store of our world*: many people from our world.

39 S.D. *the zodiac . . . signs*: the zodiac is a large flying platform, backed by a disc painted with the zodiac signs. It carries actors dressed as the signs of the zodiac, who climb out onto the stage when the machine descends.

60 *unhinging*: detaching themselves (from their fixed orbit).

72 *beginning Love attends*: that accompanies new love.

83-4 *the degrees . . . happiness*: show the slow degrees by which respectful love reaches happiness.

99 *she turns . . . earth*: possibly the disc is turned by a person standing behind it, and the zodiac characters move in the same direction as they descend, to give the impression that the zodiac machine is disgorging them.

109 S.D. *the globe of the moon*: this could be the same machine, which has been drawn back up to the flies and the zodiac disc changed for a disc representing the moon. New actors get in and the machine descends. It is not clear how the effect of the moon's waxing was obtained: perhaps by a shutter arrangement operated by someone standing behind the disc. A black shutter could be drawn back to reveal a white disc behind.

111 *IOs*: exultant shouts or songs.

136 S.D. *chariot . . . descend and land*: Quarto layout of stage-directions causes some difficulty with this complex sequence of effects. I have followed Q2's layout, but it is important to understand that this involves some repetition: the directions at ll. 109 and 136 describe one continuous action happening during song and dialogue, not two discrete events separated by song and dialogue. The first stage-direction describes the coming action in general terms while the second elaborates the details. The 'chariot' here is the same as the globe on the moon at l. 109 S.D. The emperor and prince do not descend twice, from two separate machines: their descent is indicated at l. 109 and elaborated at l. 136. The 'song continues' during this. The machine is then lifted up to leave the sight-lines clear for the subsequent spectacles. For a different interpretation of this scene, involving a chariot coming out of the moon machine, see Russell, p. 148.

144 *stentraphon*: a speaking trumpet.

145 *Delphic oracles*: in ancient Greece, the gods were supposed to speak through oracles; the most famous of these is the one at Delphi.

148 S.D. *front scene . . . temple*: in the second discovery of the scene, the shutters representing Parnassus are drawn off to reveal a third set of shutters, or a backcloth, further upstage. There is now a long vista leading to the altar. The altar may be a set piece rather than a painted representation, and the person with the stentraphon could stand inside it.

156 *Semele*: one of the mortal lovers of Jove or Zeus, killed by lightning when, in response to her own wish or 'ambitious flame' (l. 158), he visited her in his true shape.

170 S.D. *two chariots descend*: the solemn tableau of the lovers' marriage is suddenly invaded by the entrance of Harlequin and Scaramouch, using the chariots earlier used by Kepler and Galileus.

175 *Knights of the sun*: there is an echo here of the last scene in *Arlequin empereur*, in which 'Les Chevaliers du Soleil' overcome Arlequin.

184 S.D. *fight at barriers*: fight in the manner of knights at a tournament, tilting at each other with lances. An actual barrier onstage is not necessarily implied.

222 *Burn all my books*: like Don Quixote, the doctor rejects his books when he learns how they have deceived him.

226 *assistances*: (1) body of helpers; (2) persons present, audience.

233–4 *He . . . yet*: from a saying attributed to the Greek philosopher Socrates (469–399 BC): 'I know nothing except the fact of my ignorance.'

Epilogue 4 *chapon böuillé*: boiled capon.

9 *want . . . support one stage*: another complaint about small audiences: see above, Epistle Dedicatory, ll. 79–81.

36 *May Caesar live*: the epilogue's eulogy of James II as Caesar is mixed with strong hints that he should patronize the stage more. Royal patronage had been declining since the later part of Charles II's reign.

GLOSSARY

abroad out of doors, in public
ad expletive from 'Gad'
adds me mild oath ('adds' for 'Gad's')
ad's bobs variant of od's bobs, an oath from 'God's bobs' (wounds)
'adsheartlikins by God's little heart
alarm call to arms
allay (noun) alloy
allays (verb) alloys, mixes with inferior matter
alors French interjection: 'so, then'
amour love-affair
an if
animadverted observed
antic(ly) fantastic(ally), fanciful(ly), grotesque(ly)
angel gold coin, value about ten shillings in 17th cent.
apprehend understand
artificially skilfully
assafoetida a foul-smelling resin, used medicinally
aught anything
awful awe-inspiring

back-sword sword with one cutting edge; fencing exercise with such a sword
baffle (1) treat rudely, (2) foil
baffled (1) humiliated, (2) foiled
bagatelle mere trifle
balderdash a mix of liquors, trashy drink
band neckband, collar, ruff
bane ruin
bang (verb) (1) beat violently, (2) rape
banter trick, bamboozle
basset a fashionable card-game
bate leave out of consideration
bating except
batten graze
belle fine, beautiful
bellman town-crier

billet-doux love-letter
billets letters
billing caressing (from doves rubbing bill to bill)
bis repeat
black lead pencil
blast (verb) strike blind
bob cheat, make a fool of
bona roba courtesan
bottom (of a ship) the hold
bravo hired soldier or bodyguard
brisk lively
brocade d'or cloth of gold
broker (1) middleman in bargains, (2) secondhand dealer
brokering trafficking, bargaining
bubbies breasts
budget leather bag
buff, buffcoat leather coat worn by soldiers
bug words threatening words
bully swashbuckling young man, gallant, fine fellow
buss kiss
butt cask for wine or ale

cabal small group, clique
cabinet closet
calash light carriage with folding hood
canary wine from Canary islands
candid favourably disposed, free from malice
canting (1) using thieves' jargon, (2) whining, (3) hypocritically preaching
capacitated qualified
cap-a-pie head to foot
caudle warm drink for sick people
certo for certain, certainly
chair sedan
chandler seller of candles
chapman (1) seller, (2) purchaser
character description
chase gun ship's gun used in pursuit

cheapen bargain

civility-master teacher of deportment and etiquette

clap gonorrhoea

clapped infected with gonorrhea

claw away scold, revile

clean-limbed with attractive limbs

close intimate

clouterlest clumsiest

clown uncouth, rustic man

cock (verb) (1) swagger or strut, (2) tilt one's hat insolently

cogging cheating, wheedling

coil fuss

collation a light meal

communicate impart in confidence

complaisant obliging, compliant

conclave (1) meeting of cardinals to elect Pope, (2) private assembly

conjurationing invocation of spirits

conjure (1) call up spirits by magic, (2) beseech, solemnly implore

conjurement adjuration

conscious privy to secrets

consort company

contemn despise

conversation company, society

cordial reviving medicine

cornucopia profusion

cornuted cuckolded

cornuto cuckold

costive constipated

coxcomb vain foolish man

cozen defraud

crown coin worth five shillings

cully (1) dupe, (2) man who keeps mistress

culverins large cannons

current (of money) in circulation, in general use

dainty fastidious

debauches debauchees; people who indulge in sensual pleasures to the point of vice

devotee nun

discover reveal

disingenuous dishonest, ungenerous, unfair

distemper disease

distracted mad

distraction madness

divertisement amusement, diversion

divine conjecture

docity sense, gumption

document admonishment

dog (verb) pursue

dominie schoolmaster

don Spanish gentleman

dornex silk or woollen fabric used for curtains, named after Flemish weaving town

dotard feeble old man

doucement (Fr.) softly

doxy wench

draw cuts decide by lottery

dudgeon dagger

dunning demanding payment of debt

egad softened oath, from interjection 'A God'

en cavalier like a cavalier or fine gentleman

engross monopolize

en passant in passing

en prince like a prince

equipage (1) costume, (2) retinue

essay trial, attempt

fags an interjection, perhaps from 'faith'

fain gladly

fall to set about eating, fighting, or having sex

fame reputation; of a woman, specifically sexual

fancy inventive design

faulkner falconer

fiddle-faddling fussing, messing about

finis end, aim

fit be suitable for; punish suitably

flagged drooped

fleuret fencing foil

fond (1) affectionate, (2) foolish

foppery foolishness

frank generous, esp. with sexual favours

fresco the fresh air

frigate small warship

frippery trifling

fustian-fume display of anger

gaffer grandfather

gather part of dress where material is drawn in

generous behaving appropriately for one of high birth; gallant, magnanimous

gewgaws trinkets

god so interjection, from 'gadso' (penis)

goodfacks an oath, perhaps from 'good faith'

gossiping merrymaking gathering of women at child's birth

governante (1) governess, chaperone, (2) housekeeper

gownman university scholar

grate barring on convent window

gratis without payment

griping (1) painful, (2) avaricious

gutling greedy

habit costume

half pike pointed spike used as weapon

hamper entangle

handsel gift; token of good luck

hanging curtain

have at attack

Hogan Mogan high and mighty; corruption of a Dutch title

hogoes spicy sauces

hoiting romping, giddy

hope expect, suppose (not necessarily implying desire)

horn mad mad because of being cuckolded

horns traditionally supposed to be worn by cuckolds

Hymen god of marriage

impertinent (adj.) saucy, meddling, idle, absurd, (noun) absurd, unreasonable person

improve use to best advantage

inamorata lady-love

inamorato male lover

incle linen braid

in fine in short, to sum up

in fresco in the fresh air

ingrate ungrateful person

intelligence information

jack pudding buffoon

jade hussy, bold woman

jessamine jasmine

jiggeting shaking up and down

jilt (1) whore, strumpet, (2) woman who encourages and then rejects lover

joined stool wooden stool made by a joiner

jointure estate or money settled on a woman to provide for her widowhood

juggling deceptive

julio small coin; worth about the same as English sixpence in 17th cent.

languishing tender

lazar poor and diseased person, often a leper

leg make a leg = bow

lewd ignorant, unprincipled, bungling

lighter boat used for loading and unloading ships

loadstone magnet

lure (1) apparatus to which hawks are trained to return, (2) enticement

make it out prove it

mantua woman's loose gown

marry come up indignant, contemptuous interjection

mart market

mechanic (1) manual labourer, (2) one of low social status, a peasant

methought(s) it seemed to me

mewed up caged; esp. used of hawks and chickens

mien deportment, behaviour

moil drudge or labour hard

monsieur Frenchman, French servant

mooncalf idiot

morbleu French oath, a euphemism for 'mordieu' (God's death)

mountebank travelling quack who puts on performance to advertise his wares

moveables furniture and household goods

mum keep quiet

mumping grimacing

mun dialectal form of 'man'

music company of musicians

myrmidons followers